In this book Professor Peter Rutland analyses the role played by regional and local organs of the Soviet Communist Party in economic management from 1970 to 1990. Using a range of political and economic journals, newspapers and academic publications, he examines interventions in the construction industry, energy, transport, consumer goods and agriculture.

Rutland argues that party interventions hindered rather than assisted the search for efficiency in the Soviet economy, and repeated attempts to introduce more economically rational management methods failed to alter these traditional patterns of party intervention. He further demonstrates how as the Soviet economy matured and grew more complex over the last three decades, party interventions became increasingly out of tune with the needs of the economy. Yet even the calls for radical reform of the economy since 1985 were not accompanied by any decisive changes in this pattern of party intervention; this, argues Peter Rutland, casts serious doubts on the political feasibility of economic reform in a Soviet-type system.

The politics of economic stagnation in the Soviet Union presents a pioneering study of the economic and political background to Gorbachev's *perestroika* and the impact of his reformist policies. It makes an important contribution to existing literature and will be widely read by students and specialists of Soviet studies, political economy and comparative industrial policy.

THE POLITICS OF
ECONOMIC STAGNATION
IN THE SOVIET UNION

Soviet and East European Studies 88

Soviet and East European Studies, under the auspices of Cambridge University Press and the British Association for Soviet, Slavonic and East European Studies (BASSEES), promotes the publication of works presenting substantial and original research on the economics, politics, sociology and modern history of the Soviet Union and Eastern Europe.

Soviet and East European Studies

Series list continues on page 299

THE POLITICS OF ECONOMIC STAGNATION IN THE SOVIET UNION

The role of local party organs in economic management

PETER RUTLAND

Associate Professor, Wesleyan University

CAMBRIDGE
UNIVERSITY PRESS

Published by the Press Syndicate of the University of Cambridge
The Pitt Building, Trumpington Street, Cambridge CB2 1RP
40 West 20th Street, New York, NY 10011–4211, USA
10 Stamford Road, Oakleigh, Victoria 3166, Australia

First published 1993

Printed in Great Britain by Redwood Press Limited, Melksham, Wiltshire

A catalogue record for his book is available from the British Library

Library of Congress cataloguing in publication data

Rutland, Peter.
  The politics of economic stagnation in the Soviet Union: the role of local
party organs in economic management / Peter Rutland.
    p.   cm. – (Soviet and East European studies: 88)
    Includes bibliographical references and index.
    ISBN 0 521 39241 1
    1. Soviet Union – Economic policy – 1986- 2. Soviet Union – Politics and
government – 1985- 3. Kommunisticheskaia partiia Sovetskogo Soiza.
4. Industrial management – Soviet Union. I. Title. II. Series.
HC336.26.R85   1992
338.947 – dc20   91–48028   CIP

ISBN 0 521 39241 1 hardback

Contents

Figure

TABLES

Preface

For the past thirty years the key debate in Western Sovietology was over the scope for economic reform in the USSR. Economists discussed whether it was possible to introduce market forces into the command economy without unleashing full-blooded capitalism. Political scientists argued over whether a determined reform-minded leader such as Gorbachev would be able to overcome the political opposition to change.

The present author is convinced that the answer to both these questions is no. The command economy represented an integral system, which functioned according to its own political and economic logic. The scope for reform in such a system – particularly economic reform – was very narrow.[1]

Stalin put in place a set of party and ministerial bureaucracies which were able to ensure political stability while creating an industrial economy capable of taking on the Nazi war machine. However, by the 1950s and 1960s the limitations of the Stalinist model were plain for all to see. Reflecting on the disastrous experimentation of the Khrushchev years, the Brezhnev leadership realised how limited was its room for manoeuvre. The priority of the Soviet ruling elite in the 1960s and 1970s was stability and the preservation of the status quo, and they struggled to prevent social change from breaking out of the straight-jacket of existing political and economic institutions.

The price of political stability was social and economic stagnation. Twenty years of this approach brought the Soviet Union, a state richly endowed in human talent and natural resources, to the brink of economic collapse and civil war.

This book looks at one aspect of the Soviet political system during those years: the role played by regional party officials in managing, or mis-managing, the economy. Most studies of Soviet political economy concentrate on the upper reaches of the political system, and examine such topics as policy debates between academic specialists, or factional struggles within the Politburo. This study consciously avoided these approaches, choosing instead to adopt the methodology of Jerry Hough's pathbreaking study of twenty-five years ago, *The Soviet Prefects*.[2] The intention was to explore how the economy was managed at enterprise level, with a particular focus on the role of the Communist Party. While Hough's work was completed in the mid-1960s, this study examines the workings of the mature Brezhnevite system, from 1975 to 1990. Although there is some reference to the differences between the work of the Communist Party in different national republics (particularly in chapter 10), space considerations prevent a direct discussion of the national dimension *per se*.

The introductory chapter addresses methodological issues, and discusses the general character of the Soviet political system. Chapter 1 describes the basic organizational structure of the Communist Party, including the mechanics of the nomenklatura system. Subsequent chapters explore economic management on a sector-by-sector basis, including case studies of construction, energy, transport, consumer goods, and others. The book includes an investigation of party activities in the countryside (chapter 8), since work in agriculture was an exceptionally important part of the party's role in the Brezhnev era.

These case studies show a deeply rooted tension between economic and political approaches to problem-solving in the Soviet economy. In response to persistent, systemic economic difficulties party officials repeatedly resorted to their accustomed techniques of political intervention – issuing commands to nomenklatura officials, mobilizing thousands of volunteers, launching press campaigns, setting up new bureaucratic control systems, and so on. At best these campaigns brought a temporary alleviation of the economic situation. Unfortunately, in many cases these interventions actually made things worse, and their cumulative impact was to block managerial initiative and prevent any real progress towards economic efficiency.

The system staggered on until the late 1980s, when a combination of external and internal factors brought it crashing down. The concluding chapter examines the process of disintegration between 1985 and 1990. Gorbachev, for all his reformist rhetoric, was basically trying to preserve the structure of the command economy, and within it the role of the Communist Party. However, the political changes which his reforms unleashed rapidly spiralled beyond his control, and undermined the very foundations of the federal state and the centrally managed economic system. The events of August 1991 thus provide a suitable punctuation point for this story.

This book was aided by research assistance from the British Council, IREX and the National Council for Research in Soviet and East European Studies, which enabled the author to visit the USSR on six occasions between 1982 and 1990.

Thane Gustafson provided an extraordinarily detailed and useful reading of an early draft of the manuscript. Paul Gregory contributed some valuable feedback on the basis of interviews he was conducting with current and former ministry officials. It was reassuring to learn that his human informants broadly corroborated the picture that was emerging from the printed sources upon which this study was based.[3] The analysis of the Brezhnev regime in the Introduction draws upon the insights of Pal Tamas, and was strongly influenced by John Higley's work on elite theory.[4]

The work that went into the book benefited greatly from interactions with Ron Amman, Vladimir Andrle, Anders Aslund, Timothy Colton, David Dyker, Vladimir Gimpelson, Jerry Hough, Vladimir Kontorovich, Dawn Mann, Philip Pomper, Elizabeth Teague and Stephen White, not to mention innumerable panel discussants, friends, and people I met on trains in Russia. I am still in debt to my undergraduate teachers at Oxford: Archie Brown, Wlodzimierz Brus and Michael Kaser. The usual disclaimers apply to the persons and institutions listed above.

Glossary of Russian terms and abbreviations

AON	Academy of Social Sciences, a CC CPSU think tank and training school
Apparat	The full-time officials within the CPSU
Association	A firm uniting several subordinate enterprises
ASSR	Autonomous Soviet Socialist Republic
BAM	Baikal–Amur Mainline Railway
CC	Central Committee. There was one CC for the entire CPSU, and one in each of the non-Russian republics
CPSU	Communist Party of the Soviet Union
Gorispolkom	The executive committee of a city soviet
Gorkom	City committee of the CPSU
Gosplan	State Planning Committee
Gospriemka	A system of centralised quality control launched in 1987
Gossnab	State Committee on Supplies
GOST	State Committee on Standards
Instructor	The basic grade for full-time staff workers in the CPSU apparatus
KNK	People's Control Committee, a non-party organization
Kolkhoz	Collective farm
Komsomol	The All-Union Leninist Communist Youth League
Kontrol	Party supervision over managers and administrators
KPK	Party Control Committee
Krai	Region equivalent to *oblast*, but including some autonomous national areas within it
KSUK	Integrated Quality Management System
Obkom	Regional committee of the CPSU

Oblast	Region or province (pl. *oblasti*)
Oblispolkom	The executive committee of an *oblast* soviet
Orgotdel	Organization and party work department, within a *partkom*
Partkom	Generic term for party committee
Podmena	Ideological term used to criticize party officials who interfere excessively in the work of non-party administrators
PPO	Primary Party Organization
Pravo kontroliia	The right of PPOs to supervise managers and administrators
Raion	District (beneath the *oblasti*)
Raikom	District committee of the CPSU
RAPO	District Agro-Industrial Association, introduced in late 1970s
Republic	One of the 15 'union republics' that made up the USSR
RSFSR	Russian Soviet Federative Socialist Republic
Sovkhoz	State farm
Sovnarkhozy	Regional economic councils, which existed between 1957 and 1962
Tolkachi	Roving expeditors, sent out to secure supplies
TPK	Territorial-Production Complex, a type of regional planning agency
VPSh	Higher Party School

Introduction: the party in the post-totalitarian system

Understanding Soviet politics

The most distinctive feature of the Soviet political system was the role of the Communist Party. While other nations around the world are grouped into democracies and dictatorships, the Soviet Union belonged to the class of Leninist party regimes in which power is concentrated in the hands of a political party, and not a military elite, a ruling family, an economic class or a religious sect.

Leninist regimes came about in one of two ways. Some were simply imposed by force from outside. This was the case for most of Eastern Europe and for parts of the USSR (the Baltic, Caucasus, etc.). The remainder were the results of indigenous social revolutions, again involving military force and external assistance. Socialist revolutions took place in predominantly peasant societies at the periphery of the world system, whose traditional political elites were unable to respond to the social transformations set in motion by the arrival of capitalism. Leninist parties proved themselves willing and able to seize power in those societies, and constructed political and economic systems which outlived their founders.

Western scholars agree that socialist regimes have been able to achieve short-run stability, based largely on repression. There is deep disagreement, however, over the long-run viability of these systems. Is a Leninist regime able to achieve broad popular legitimacy, and shift the basis of its rule from coercion to consent? Can a ruling communist party create an economic system capable of meeting the needs of its population?

Some scholars, such as Z. Brzezinski, argue that the socialist states were an anachronism, the product of a failed experiment rooted in nineteenth-century utopian illusions, and therefore doomed to collapse.[1] On the other side, many Western academics have argued that

1

these regimes were able to pass through the initial revolutionary phase, and managed to consolidate themselves as stable, post-revolutionary political systems.[2]

In this mature phase, normal politics of the 'who gets what, when and how' variety supposedly takes place behind the façade of the old Leninist institutions. If only Western scholars looked more carefully, the argument went, they would be able to find evidence of interest group activity and pluralistic politics.[3] The implication was that the difference between socialist and capitalist regimes was merely one of degree, and that the character of political and economic life within the two systems was broadly comparable. This approach was more or less accepted by the majority of Western specialists writing on Soviet and East European affairs.

For this pluralism school, the crucial question of the past thirty years was the scope for *reform*. It was widely believed that the socialist countries would have no choice but to introduce economic reform to overcome the irrationalities of the command economy. And this economic decentralization would then open the door to greater personal freedom and a dispersal of political power. The experiments with 'market socialism' and 'reform communism' in Hungary and Czechoslovakia in the 1960s were seen as the first such attempts at systemic change, cut short by a Soviet Union which was not yet ready to risk reform. By the 1980s, however, both China and the USSR had themselves apparently embarked on systemic reform.

Developments since 1989 have cast doubt on this reform scenario, and provide powerful evidence for the view that a socialist regime cannot decentralize economic and political power without unleasing processes which undermine its stability.

The demise of socialist systems throughout Eastern Europe in 1989–90 suggested that there was no room for a third way. Once Gorbachev removed the threat of coercion, the East European regimes collapsed, liberal and hard-line alike. Ideas of reform communism were suddenly irrelevant. A similar logic of fragmentation played out within the Soviet Union itself. Gorbachev's initiation of glasnost and democratization set loose forces within Soviet society which eroded the established political and economic order. His efforts to reform and revive existing institutional structures failed, and from 1990 the system began to break up, as the republics struck out for independence.

Does the East European and Soviet experience prove conclusively that state socialism is not viable as a political-economic system? Is it only a matter of time before China, Vietnam and the other holdovers collapse? One must be wary about generalizing from the Soviet and East European cases. Unlike the European socialist states, the Asian regimes were able to draw upon nationalism as a basis of popular support. The socialist regimes in East Europe had been imposed by a foreign power at the end of World War II, and quickly collapsed once Gorbachev signalled that he was no longer prepared to use force in the region.

The situation in the USSR was more complex. Soviet socialism was only partly able to harness nationalism, since it was the inheritor of a vast and diverse multinational empire. It thus had an ambiguous and antagonistic relationship towards national identity, which was eventually to prove its downfall. More than anything else, it was the determination of the non-Russian republics to go their own way after 1988 which undermined Gorbachev's authority and derailed his reform programme.

Time will tell whether the socialist political systems outside Europe will survive. The purpose of this book is to explore the dynamics of the Soviet political system during the 1965–90 period: to find out how it worked, and why it was so resistant to reform.

The totalitarian model

The best starting point for understanding the dynamics of the Soviet system is the much-maligned totalitarian model, developed by American scholars during the 1950s. S. Bialer has noted that 'Most Western specialists of Soviet affairs trained after 1960 have come to reject the totalitarian model of Soviet politics.'[4] Nevertheless, it will be our argument here that the totalitarian paradigm accurately captured some key structural features of the Soviet political system, and is still a useful starting point for understanding the dynamics of Soviet politics.

Scholars turned against the totalitarian paradigm in part because it came to be used as a propaganda weapon in the Cold War. It served as a term of political abuse, implying the moral equivalence of the Nazi and Soviet regimes, and their inferiority to the 'free world'.

Irrespective of the uses and abuses of the theory, it would be inaccurate to suggest that the term was merely a tool of Cold War propagandists, without any intellectual value. Of the various writers who developed the concept into a systematic theory, only Hannah Arendt stands out as primarily interested in drawing out the moral implications of the theory.[5] Z. Brzezinski and C. Friedrich approached the subject as political scientists who wanted an empirically verifiable model which would help them understand the dynamics of the Soviet political system. The comparison with fascist regimes was less important for them: fascist regimes had (thankfully) proved to be unstable and short-lived. Brzezinski and Friedrich were more concerned to distinguish the totalitarian state from conventional authoritarian regimes (which they would also morally condemn) than from liberal democratic systems.[6] They built up their argument on the basis of perceived empirical characteristics of the Soviet system, and not by making moralistic arguments about its divergence from the classic tenets of Western liberalism.

The core of the Brzezinski/Friedrich model was their now familiar list of the six key characteristics of a totalitarian regime, of the sort found in Stalin's Russia:[7]

1 a distinctive, monolithic and mobilizing ideology;
2 a single party monopolizing the political arena, usually led by a single leader;
3 a state monopoly of the means of coercion;
4 a state monopoly of the means of communication;
5 a terroristic police force;
6 state control of the economy, through a preponderance of state ownership of the means of production.

Different writers have attached differing weights to the various components of the model. The only item that now seems clearly superfluous is number 3. Max Weber argued that a monopoly of the legitimate use of physical force was a defining characteristic of *any* state in the modern world, so it is hardly surprising to find this present in a totalitarian state.[8] Otherwise, it is plausible to argue that the Stalinist system in all of the countries where it was planted exhibited the five remaining characteristics enumerated above.

In recent years the totalitarian model has come under vigorous attack from 'revisionist' Western historians, who argue that the concept distorts our understanding of the Stalin era by exaggerating the degree of concentration of power.[9] This revisionist school followed in the wake of similar trends in the historiography of Nazi Germany, where writers began to stress the limits of Hitler's personal influence and the importance of competing sources of power within the Nazi state.[10]

However, one can argue that these scholars are attacking a false, reified image of the totalitarian paradigm. First, they suggest that the model collapses into a 'great man' theory of history, exaggerating the role played by the Führer and the Vozhd. J. Hough argued, for example, that 'The cohesion of the model stemmed from its assumptions about the motivations of the totalitarian leaders.'[11] In fact, 'motivations' do not feature on the checklist of characteristics of a totalitarian system, and one does not need to be a psycho-historian to apply the model. Rather, the model seeks to describe the structure of power within which one can understand the impact of the wilful actions of the supreme leader.

Second, the revisionists are sceptical as to the *totality* of power concentrated in the totalitarian state. Some authors in the totalitarian school, such as H. Arendt and A. Zinoviev, portrayed the totalitarian system as an all-consuming, destructive system which led to the 'atomisation' of the society and the disorientation of individuals within it.[12] In contrast, the revisionists argue that the Stalin revolution was not simply imposed from above, but was the outcome of social conflicts in which disoriented groups and individuals struggled to protect and advance their interests. They suggest that the image of a dominant state machine and a passive, helpless society fails to capture the fluidity and turbulence of Soviet politics in the Stalin era.

The revisionist argument is a plausible one. The historical record bears out the view that local politics (of a particular type) was an important feature of Stalinism. And it seems intuitively reasonable to argue that there must be practical limits to the centralization of power which can be achieved in any political system.

However, the revisionists are off the mark in suggesting that the authors in the totalitarian school assumed the power of the centre to be 'total'. Brzezinski remarked that 'Of course, since power is a tool used by human beings, it cannot be infinite, and limits to it naturally exist.'[13] Similarly, Fainsod pointed out that 'The totalitarian machine, at least in the Smolensk area, was far from perfect', and that 'The central controls which looked so all-inclusive and deeply penetrating on paper did not in fact operate with the thoroughness and dispatch it is so easy to attribute to them.'[14] K. Deutsch humorously observed that even such an accomplished dictator as Julius Caesar could only 'dictate' (in the literal sense) seven simultaneous letters to his scribbling clerks.[15] J. Gross argued that far from discrediting the totalitarian model, a historical analysis of the dynamics of local politics and social rivalries could help understand how the totalitarian system worked at the grass roots.[16]

Similarly, none of the mainstream totalitarianism authors made social atomization a central feature of their model. Note that it does *not* feature on the checklist of characteristics. It would be difficult to define the 'atomization' precisely enough to enable one to empirically test for its presence, except in such general terms that could be applied to all industrial societies.

It is important to stress that the totalitarian model is a paradigm or syndrome, and not an 'ideal type' in the Weberian sense.[17] It is not seeking for a single, metaphysical cause, a key which can explain the essence of the whole system. A syndrome is 'a group of signs or symptoms that occur together and characterise a particular abnormality'.[18] AIDs syndrome undoubtedly exists, even though the precise cause and means of transmission of the disease remain unknown.

For political scientists, as for historians, initial doubts about the utility of the concept of totalitarianism centred on differences between the Stalinist and Nazi cases. Indeed, there are important differences between these two systems. Most notably, the Nazi system was short-lived, and was built around the waging of aggressive wars against its neighbours.

Leaving aside the contrasts between the Nazi and Stalinist systems, there seems to be a growing consensus that it *is* possible to distinguish between totalitarian and authoritarian political systems.[19] (Official Soviet scholars were themselves prepared to use the term 'totalitarian' to describe Fascist Italy, and even Franco's Spain.)[20] While some of the listed characteristics of totalitarianism are present to a degree in many non-totalitarian political systems, proponents of the model argue that when taken together they amount to a political system qualitatively different from that found in other regimes.

When one gets down to specifics, there is in fact little controversy in distinguishing between authoritarian and totalitarian regimes. Few scholars would suggest that Brazil, Chile or even Franco's Spain were essentially similar to the Nazi or Stalinist regimes. There are two broad features which separate authoritarian and totalitarian regimes. First, authoritarian regimes leave large parts of civil society more or less intact, from religious groups to private business interests. Authoritarian regimes come nowhere near to establishing the degree of state control over the economy achieved in the socialist bloc. While many Third World states have public ownership over the majority of industrial activity, there are few that can match Stalin's efforts to wipe out private property in agriculture and services. Nor have authoritarian regimes sought to establish the degree of state control over labour allocation which Stalin achieved through the internal passport system.

Second, perhaps the most distinctive feature of authoritarian regimes is their *instability*. Their history is typically a cycle of dictatorship, oligarchy and democracy, repeated every few years.[21] In contrast, the trajectory of totalitarian regimes is much more stable: there is no pattern of countries cycling into and out of totalitarianism.

The post-totalitarian system

Let us assume that the reader is prepared to accept that the Stalinist system can accurately be characterized as totalitarian. Where does that leave the post-Stalin Soviet political system? Looking down the checklist of features, it is clear that several of them underwent fundamental changes after 1953.

(1) A mobilizing ideology

The credibility of Soviet ideology steadily faded during the period of 'developed socialism'. The illusion of a monolithic official ideology was preserved, thanks to the state monopoly of the means of communication, but it no longer had any normative popular appeal. One can question to what extent the mass of the population had accepted the ideology during the Stalin period, but at least some groups of party activists in those years were 'believers' who were genuinely motivated by the ideology. By the 1970s, however, cynicism and apathy were the norm, even within the party itself. This ideological erosion meant that this pillar of the totalitarian system ceased to play its former role. A 1989 survey of public attitudes towards twenty-three socialist values (social equality, planning, technical progress, etc.) found only one ('peaceful intentions') scored a positive rating from respondents.[22]

(2) A single party, with a single leader

The monolithic structure of single-party rule was preserved throughout the Brezhnev period, although some would argue that the party slowly fragmented into regional fiefdoms over which the centre was barely able to exert its authority.[23] The first major cracks in the system of one-party rule only appeared in the summer of 1988, with the emergence of Popular Fronts in the Baltic, and in the semi-contested elections to the Congress of People's Deputies in March 1989. These pluralistic trends culminated in March 1990 with the amendment of Article 6 of the Soviet Constitution (the article formally guaranteeing the 'leading role' of the CPSU). However, throughout the

1953–88 period, one would have to say that single party rule was preserved more or less intact.

There was also little deviation from the system's tendency to throw up a dominant single leader. Clearly, all the post-Stalin General Secretaries were more than mere 'first among equals'. The hierarchical political structure seemed to need a single hand at the centre, an acknowledged leader whose authoritative statements could be cited and commands obeyed. And yet, clearly, none of these men could be compared to Stalin (or Lenin) in the amount of power at their disposal. All of them had to operate through collegial decision-making organs (such as the Politburo, the Central Committee and the Council of Ministers), and were constrained by them to a greater or lesser extent.[24] As Khrushchev's rise and fall so graphically illustrated, the General Secretary's accession to power was conditional upon the support of a majority of his senior party colleagues. During their period in office the discretionary power of the General Secretary fluctuated over time, and varied from one policy area to another. (Generally speaking, their power was greater in foreign policy and narrower in domestic policy.) But at no point did their authority begin to approach Stalin's role in the political process.

This post-Stalinist pattern of leadership looks much more like an authoritarian regime than a totalitarian one, so this criterion registers a clear qualitative break from the Stalinist past.

(3) A state monopoly of the means of coercion

As explained above, almost all modern states enjoy a monopoly of the means of coercion, so this criterion is of little use in evaluating whether a given system can accurately be described as totalitarian or post-totalitarian.

(4) A state monopoly of the means of communication

The Brezhnev leadership managed to maintain tight control of the mass media in the USSR, mostly through self-censorship by editors who were well aware of what the Central Committee Culture Department would and would not tolerate.[25] The early 1960s saw the appearance of samizdat ('self-published' materials, circulated illegally). Although samizdat initially carried literary rather than political material, it started to chip away at the state's monopoly of information, and created the circles of writers and readers who would seize the chances provided by glasnost from 1988 on. Around one-quarter of the Soviet population read samizdat materials, and a similar proportion occasionally listened to foreign radio broadcasts (mostly jammed during the Brezhnev years).

However, in general one would have to conclude that the degree of control over public information enjoyed by the Soviet state before glasnost was beyond that found in most authoritarian states, and was compatible with the totalitarian model.

(5) A terroristic police force

The retreat from terror was the most important and decisive change in the post-Stalin era. The dismantling of the NKVD empire after 1953, and the shift towards 'socialist legality', meant that arbitrary mass terror was no longer an instrument of state power. To be sure, the USSR was still a police state, in the sense that citizens had no effective legal recourse against illegal acts by state officials, and there was still a massive political police force devoted to the suppression of political dissent.

However, after 1953 the average citizen had little to fear from the KGB if they stayed away from overt acts of political dissent. There were no longer mass arrests of innocents merely because they belonged to certain social categories (kulaks, intellectuals, Old Bolsheviks, families of 'enemies of the people', Koreans, Chechens, etc.) And the KGB dealt with individual dissidents not through torture, execution and life-long incarceration, but through threats and pressures and, if necessary, persecution via administrative, legal or medical channels. This was still an oppressive regime, but not a totalitarian one.

Most monitoring of political reliability came through the education system and the workplace, and people adopted conformist behaviour without having any direct contact with the KGB. Thus, for example, a survey of 4,500 émigrés who left the country in the late 1970s found that only 2 per cent of the sample had had any personal contact with the KGB (prior to their application for an exit visa).[26]

Despite this lack of direct personal contact, the survey revealed that more than 85 per cent of the respondents feared the KGB, and would not talk about political issues with people beyond their immediate circle of family and friends. Similarly, a survey on 'forbidden zones' in public debate, conducted inside the USSR in 1989 by the Academy of Social Sciences, found respondents still unwilling publicly to criticise various political institutions, as follows:[27]

KGB	8 per cent felt free to criticize
Regional party secretary	8 per cent
District party secretary	15 per cent
Central Committee	
or government	17 per cent
Their own director	27 per cent
Their primary party	
organization secretary	30 per cent

This apparent paradox – that mass terror had ceased, but the fear lived on – can be explained by the fact that though the USSR was no longer a totalitarian society, it was nevertheless a *post*-totalitarian society. The society still carried the memory of the totalitarian years, and feared that the political system could regress at any time.

(6) State control of the economy

The command economy represents a distinctive form of economic organization, which can be conceptually distinguished from a market or regulated-market economy. In a command economy the state tries to attain as high a degree of control over economic activity as is practically feasible, by taking the major factors of production (land, natural resources and capital) into state ownership, and enforcing strict controls over management and labour.

States with command economies differ between themselves and over time in terms of the degree of central control which they are able to establish. In the Stalinist phase, the Soviet state strove to squeeze independent economic activity to a minimum, eliminating the private sector in services and farming; subjecting labour allocation to police control; relying on gulag labour to force through construction projects; and distributing food and housing through administrative rationing. After 1953, many of these more extreme forms of centralized management were dismantled, but the basic structure of state ownership and central planning remained intact. Collective farms, for example, were not dissolved.

After Stalin's death there were repeated yet fruitless efforts to change the direction of economic policy. Housing and consumer goods (above all, food production) joined heavy industry as priority sectors. The Stalinist economy had been effective to a degree in promoting extensive growth, mobilizing the nation's resources for its industrialization drive. By the late 1950s, however, the planners ran out of surplus labour and capital. They had to shift to an intensive growth strategy, promoting greater efficiency in the utilization of resources. Despite a succession of reform packages designed to decentralize decision making (in 1957, 1965, 1973 and 1979), the basic operating features of the economy remained remarkably impervious to change.

Thus while the character of the Soviet economy had undergone some important changes since the Stalin years, it remained centrally controlled to a degree far beyond that of even the most tightly regulated market economies (such as India or Argentina).

The character of the Brezhnev regime

Reviewing the checklist of features, one can see that *some* elements of totalitarianism were still recognizably present throughout the Brezhnev era (the single party, censorship, the economy) but others underwent a fundamental qualitative change (ideology, terror). Given that the syndrome presupposed that all features should be present, this suggests that the USSR ceased to be a totalitarian political system after Stalin's death. However, it is not a simple, black or white issue. The Soviet system still bore certain distinctive features (such as the state-controlled economy, the role played by the CPSU, and the legacy of the terror) which served to separate it out from the common-or-garden authoritarian regime. The system spent forty years in an unsteady and halting transition away from its Stalinist past.[28] The Soviet political system of the Brezhnev years can best be regarded as a *post-totalitarian* regime.[29] For forty years after Stalin's death, the system was still living in his shadow, and struggled to find a viable set of institutions to fill the vacuum caused by his disappearance.

Stalin died, but the national and regional political elites which had been forged during his rule lived on. Their task was to survive without the dictator who had created them, and without several of the tools (such as the mobilizing ideology and the terror) which he had used to cement his regime in place. Developments since 1985 suggest that this political elite was fighting a losing battle, and that it would prove impossible for them to create a viable political system. In the light of the collapse of the Soviet system in 1991, the Brezhnev regime can be seen as a rearguard action by the old elite, through which they managed to secure a couple more decades of relative tranquillity.

What, then, were the principal features of the Brezhnevite regime (loosely understood as embracing the whole post-Stalin period)?[30] Soviet political shorthand now describes the period as the era of 'stagnation' (*zastoi*), in which the system was neither moving forward nor moving back. Some would challenge this interpretation, arguing that the 1960s and 1970s were years of steady economic growth and upward social mobility in which the seeds of a new 'civil society' were being germinated.[31] Reliable evidence on the pace of social modernization is hard to come by and even harder to evaluate. In any event, these social processes most definitely did *not* show up in the realm of politics, and *zastoi* seems as good a label as any for this era.

The contours of political life of the stagnation years were shaped by six broad core assumptions which were accepted by all participants in the political system. These shared values were closed to debate not simply because the central authorities would not tolerate their being challenged, but mainly because elite groups in the national and regional bureaucracies had long accepted these values as their own. And, in as much as 'the ideas of the ruling class are in every epoch the ruling ideas' (K. Marx),[32] these values were also largely unchallenged in Soviet society as whole. There were six core ideas.

1 Elite rule

It was universally agreed by all those politically active in the official system, and by many of the population at large, that a district hierarchy of power was the normal, acceptable way to run the society. The Communist Party had established its right to rule through revolution and war, and to challenge its role was unthinkable. Popular debate about politics usually revolved around discussion of whether the regional party boss (or factory director, or General Secretary) was strong or weak, clever or stupid, clean or corrupt. Few ever thought to question or challenge the power structure. There were two caveats to this authoritarian structure, however.

First, there were at least two different philosophies upon which members of the elite laid their claim to rule. On one side were the 'ideologists', officials who spent the bulk of their careers within the agitprop apparatus, and whose claim to authority rested on their ability to reproduce party dogma. On the other side were the 'experts': those with experience in economic management or a technical discipline, whose abilities were subject to some sort of practical test.[33] These practical, 'organization men' were concentrated in certain highly developed sectors of the economy, most notably the 'military-industrial complex', where the 'ideologists' left them to their own devices. In contrast, in agriculture the experts never established a dominant position, and management functions were often taken over by 'ideologists' – with disastrous results for the rural economy.

Despite the distinct backgrounds and orientations of these two elite factions, they coexisted more or less harmoniously, each recognizing the other's role in the system. Trying to probe into the relationship between these elite tendencies will be a major theme of this book (particularly in chapters 9 and 10).

The second caveat to be entered qualifying the authoritarian political culture is that while there was agreement on the elite's right to rule there was no consensus on the *privileges* which would come with these responsibilities. The elite itself was divided between ascetic and sybaritic elements, while the public at large seemed strongly hostile to the privileges enjoyed by the elite. As a result, policy oscillated, with elite families steadily accumulating privileges and wealth while periodically launching purges of corrupt elements to assuage public anger and maintain their façade of public service.

2 Cognitive control

Closely connected to this consensus on the role of the elite was an understanding that information flows had to be controlled if their monopoly of political power was to be preserved. The elite were convinced that debate about policy options should take place behind closed doors, and not in the public arena. It was thought that to release raw, critical information into the society would provoke confusion and disorder. The elite had to present a united front, and regulate the flow of information so as to steer society along the correct lines. Thus, for example, if the elite was divided over a particular policy issue, they would not dream of taking it into the public realm.

This system of cognitive control derived from the mobilizational ideology of the totalitarian era, but had a markedly different impact on society, contributing greatly to the 'stagnation' which became the byword for the Brezhnev regime. Apart from excluding the mass of citizens from public life, this arrangement also caused intra-elite communication to atrophy, since a rational discourse about policy goals and the means to realize them could not take place.

3 The USSR as a superpower

It went without saying for all sub-groups in the elite that the preservation of the USSR as a unified entity was an absolute priority.

Moreover, because of its sheer size and wealth of resources this nation-state would inevitably play a superpower role in world affairs. The wisdom of these two ideas went unchallenged within the political elite of the Brezhnev era. This may partly have been a product of a residual idealistic commitment to the legacy of the October Revolution, but more crudely stemmed from the realization that a break-up of the state would undermine their own authority.

This acceptance of the superpower state was what gave force to Moscow's claims on the outlying regions and republics. Only Moscow could see the whole picture, and define the needs of the state. So, if Moscow decreed that a new pipeline project had to be forced through, or resources had to be diverted from house-building to silo construction, the regional elites would go along. They may have quietly dragged their feet at the implementation stage, seeking to protect local interests, but would not directly challenge the rationale of the project.

4 The viability of the command economy

The elite did not see any alternative to the command economy. They were all too aware of the flaws of central planning but thought that the system could still be improved, or at least kept running for a few more years. None of them imagined that a market economy was an option. After sixty years in a command economy, the die was cast. Add to that a certain egalitarian undertow in Russian popular culture, and a healthy fear of their own dispensibility in a market economy, and one can understand why in all the debates about economic reform of the 1960s, 1970s and 1980s real systemic change was never really on the table.

5 Generational change

A further shared value of the nomenklatura under Brezhnev was an implicit understanding that the political elite was divided up into a succession of discrete generations. Given that other dimensions of political difference, such as diverging ethnic or religious values or rival regional interests, were denied their legitimacy, age was seen as a 'natural' way to carve up the political spectrum. Given Russia's turbulent history, certain age cohorts had lived through unique experiences which no subsequent generation could understand: the 1930s, the war, reconstruction. Like learning how to steer a ship through a storm, political skills could only be acquired through experience, and the younger generations had lived a much more sheltered life than their elders.

This sort of thinking would be unremarkable in traditional societies, with their veneration for elders, but it is worth drawing attention to its prominence in the Soviet system in view of the fact that it is much less visible in modern Western societies.

The deference shown by younger elite cohorts to their elders, who had lived through Stalinism and the war, was another major reason for the stagnation of the Brezhnev years. 'Younger' leaders – men in their forties and fifties – seemed prepared to loyally wait out the departure of their forebears. Only with the physical departure of this generation from the scene would the new ruling elite feel able to seek new solutions to the old problems. It is remarkable that for all his brutal frankness regarding the failings of Soviet society, Gorbachev refrained from direct personal criticism of his predecessors, and, on the contrary, stressed the continuities (and not the discontinuities) with the past.[34] The other problem was that the new elite, who had come of political age in the 1950s, did not have the sort of searing formative experiences that their elders had undergone. They pursued routine careers (in economic management or agitprop), and faced few threats or challenges. Their rallying cries were modernization, education, technology and consumerism: worthy aims, but goals upon which the system could not deliver.

6 The separation of the public and private spheres

How did society at large adapt to life under this politically entrenched elite? The general pattern was one of apathy and retreat into the realm of private life: an option which had not been available under Stalinism. The flavour of the era was graphically summarised by the Moldavian author I. Drutse, who wrote: 'We lived well, quietly drinking, quietly stealing.'[35] The authorities tolerated, even encouraged, this state of affairs, since it was conducive to their goal of political stability. This gave rise to a bizarre, almost schizophrenic socio-political structure.[36] On one side was a public sphere dominated by stilted political rhetoric, and couched in crude ideological categories. This 'wooden language' was totally divorced from day-to-day reality, and lacked any meaning for those who were obliged to utter it. On the other side was the rich, enveloping world of life among family and friends, in which all pretence could be dropped and relationships seemed to be *more* real and value-laden precisely because of the emptiness of the public sphere. Despite the fact that there was an unbridgeable chasm between the kitchen table and the public tribune, the two seemed to coexist quite smoothly within the boundaries of a single society, with both leaders and led implicitly accepting the situation as rather unnatural, but better than what had gone before.

The emergence of this dichotomy also imposed an important new constraint on the political authorities, who recognized that certain minimum concessions had to be made to keep life tolerable in the private sphere.[37] The terms of the 'contract' were modest – a chance of a private apartment, a regular supply of meat and milk products – but were sufficient to prod the leaders out of their lethargy and force them to embark upon repeated campaigns to raise productivity.

These six characteristics were clearly present throughout the whole post-Stalin era. While they did signify a certain political stability, particularly in as much as they were all accepted by the members of the ruling political elites, they were not static and unchanging. Each one contained dynamic elements which threatened the stability of the system:

1 The unanimity of the elite rested on an uneasy division of labour between the 'ideologists' and the 'experts'.
2 The tight cognitive controls led to a silting up of the decision-making process, and a disturbing lack of feedback about the real social and economic trends which lay behind the propaganda of success.
3 The assumption that the USSR had to remain a superpower plunged the country into ever-more-costly rounds of arms spending and Third World adventurism, until reality finally broke through and forced the elite to reconsider the pretence of global superpower status.
4 The consensus on the indispensibility of the command economy did not stretch to agreement over how to keep it working.
5 The acceptance of generational rule merely stored up unresolved political problems until the time came for the transfer of power to take place.
6 The public/private dichotomy led to a growing polarization between these two realms. Sooner or later, the private realm would burst forth, and declare that the emperor had no clothes. This happened in 1988–9.

The role of the Communist Party in the economy

This book will not seek to explore all the dimensions of the politics of the 'stagnation era' enumerated above. Rather, attention will focus on one link in the chain: the interaction between the political machinery and the economy. This is arguably the most important relationship in the whole system: it is also one in which hard evidence of what was happening in the Brezhnev era can be unearthed. Questions of the values of the political elite, the goals of the national leadership, or the extent of civil society are important and intriguing, but the evidence is not there to yield up definitive answers.

Economics was one area where Soviet academics and journalists were given *some* latitude to discuss what was actually happening in Soviet society. Economic policy was where political rhetoric had to come down to the realities of the shopfloor, and where the 'ideologists' and 'experts' had to work out a *modus vivendi*.

A discussion of party interventions in the economy presupposes an understanding of how the party works, and of how the economy works.

The nature of the Communist Party as a political organization

There is a general consensus on what was involved in the party's 'leading role' in Soviet society, and its three principal activities:[38]
1 Organizational work, devoted to maintaining the CPSU as a political institution.
2 Ideological monitoring of the population.
3 Supervision of the economy.
Analysts differ when it comes to the gloss they put on these activities. Some see the party as a thinly disguised mafia acting only out of self-interest, while others regard it as a relatively disinterested agency of modernization. These various frameworks for interpreting the role of the CPSU are crudely summarised in Table Intro. 1.[39] In fact, the sundry authors do not differ that markedly when it comes to their substantive analysis of the activities of the CPSU. What the table reveals is primarily differences between the authors in terms of style and background, and their relationship to debates in the discipline of political science as a whole.

An important point to note when discussing the nature of Communist Party rule is that the CPSU must be treated *sui generis*, and cannot be treated as roughly equivalent to political parties in other political systems. This is a point on which all the authors cited in Table Intro. 1 would concur. In a sense it is misleading to describe the CPSU as a political party, since much of its activity is designed to keep 'politics' to a minimum (if 'politics' is understood as a debate over alternative

Table Intro. 1. Cui Bono – whose interests does the party serve?

Vertical spectrum	Model	Authors
Serves self-interest	Mafia nomenklatura new class	K. Simis, I. Zemtsov M. Voslensky M. Djilas
Serves interests of the political system	institutional pluralism regional pluralism guarantor of stability	H. G. Skilling S. Huntington
Serves interests of society	rational administrator social contract modernizer	J. F. Hough P. Hauslohner, G. W. Breslauer R. Lowenthal

programmes for organizing public affairs). In this sense, Moscow democrats are correct when they argue that the USSR under Brezhnev was a 'no-party state' rather than a 'one-party state'.

The CPSU was much more an administrative apparatus or a corporate structure than it was a political party. That is why this book developed as a study of organizational structures and administrative procedures, rather than as a discussion of leadership goals or alternative policy programmes. In Brezhnev's USSR, the dead weight of bureaucratic practices was far more significant than the superficial pronouncements of political leaders, or the policy prognoses of their academic advisers.

The dynamics of the command economy

As for the Soviet economy, the classic works of A. Nove, M. Kaser and J. Berliner continue to provide an accurate picture of the functioning of the command economy.[40] What is remarkable is how *little* the pattern of institutional relationships changed in the thirty years after these authors starting writing in the mid-1950s.

If asked to conceptualize the shape of the Soviet economic system, most specialists would probably suggest a pyramid, with the Politburo at the apex, supported by Gosplan and the ministries, and with enterprise managers at the bottom. Life in a command economy is

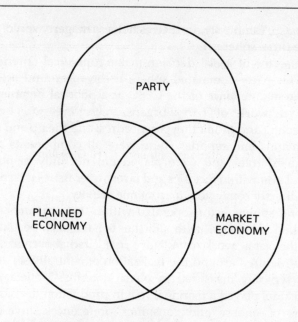

Figure Intro. 1 A schematic representation of the political economy of the Soviet Union

portrayed as an iterative game between central planners and managers, in which the latter try to do the minimum necessary to satisfy the objectives of the centre.

There is much to commend in this traditional view of the command economy, but it does not tell the whole story. The pyramid metaphor exaggerates the power of the central planners, and under-estimates the capacity of factory managers for autonomous behaviour. The planners do not have as much discretion as at first appears: they are prisoners of their own previous decisions, and prisoners of the overall pattern of economic development. A further drawback with the traditional approach is that it tends to shift analytic attention away from decision-making at factory level, which is the key locus of economic activity.

An alternative vision of the structure of the Soviet economic system can be found in Figure Intro. 1. The three competing spheres represent a pictorial abstraction of the Soviet economy, but one can argue that participants in the economy could and did make these conceptual distinctions themselves. Managers could tell when an issue should be treated as a party matter, when it was subject to the conventions of the official planning system, and when it was necessary to go outside the system (*na levo*). (Admittedly, in their actions managers would freely co-mingle the three spheres.)

In the first sector of social decision-making, political criteria predominated. This party-dominated sphere revolved around activities devoted to the maintenance of the CPSU as a political organization: running the network of party organs; recruiting and training members; selecting and promoting party cadres; and the up and down flow of commands and reports. These were all components of the party's 'vanguard role', and were played out not only in political institutions but also within factories and farms, over issues which were directly or indirectly connected to economic activity.

In the second sphere, actors operated within the structures of the official, planned economy, with all the behavioural peculiarities described in the classic works of A. Nove *et al.* cited above. Economic activity was structured around the realization of centrally set annual plan targets, typically measured in physical terms. Monetary and financial indicators played a marginal role in production decisions, as did questions of quality and consumer preferences. Investment activity and foreign trade were tightly controlled by the centre.

The third circle represents horizontal, freely conducted exchanges, loosely subject to the forces of supply and demand. The two largest types of market activity were the labour market (highly distorted, but partially free, in the sense that workers could quit) and the consumption sector (where both legal and black consumption took place under semi-market conditions).

The segment where market and plan sectors overlap is that region where market forces penetrated the planned economy. The intersection between the party and plan spheres is where party officials involved themselves in managerial decision-making, and is the main focus of this study.

The reason for presenting the crude schema in Figure Intro. 1 is to underline the deep tensions within the Soviet economic system, subject to these three powerful competing logics. Economists who construct unitary models of the 'planned economy' spend a lot of time puzzling over why it does not work as well as it 'should', and proposing reforms to correct its defects. In contrast, the model offered here emphasises that the Soviet economy was a battleground for at least three competing interests and philosophies.

Thus it is important to emphasise that the command economy did not function as an embodiment of rational social decision-making. The ministries did not constitute a homogeneous bureaucratic monolith.

On the contrary, there was fierce competition among ministries and within individual ministries, between different layers in the administrative structure. Ministry bureaucracies developed into complex, deeply entrenched structures, whose pursuit of 'departmental' self-interest was no more reflective of social welfare than was that of the most rapacious capitalist corporation.[41]

Of course, since Adam Smith's *Wealth of Nations* it has been widely acknowledged that pursuit of economic self-interest is not necessarily a bad thing for society. However, there is self-interest and self-interest. If Soviet bureaucrats had merely wanted more money, a bigger factory and so forth, there might still have been beneficial spin-offs for the economy and society as a whole. However, the problem lay in the *nature* of the self-interest being pursued. Soviet bureaucrats were above all risk-averse: they wanted a *quiet life*, and would block managerial initiatives and technological innovations which might disrupt the status quo. This sort of self-interest was not good for the economy at all.[42]

Bureaucratic culture is difficult to interpret and assess. However, one example of this departmental self-interest which can be empirically verified was the tendency of Soviet factories and ministries to pursue autarky. In conditions of excessively taut planning and generalized supply shortage, officials responded by trying to internalize as many inputs as possible. One-quarter of all workers were based in repair shops within factories, turning out spare parts and deficit machinery. Overall, roughly 20 per cent of the output of a given ministry lay outside the product range which it was supposed to specialize in.[43] These autarkic tendencies went beyond industrial goods. Ministries (through their factories) controlled 50 per cent of the nation's housing, and ran everything from livestock farms to tram systems.[44] Apart from the pursuit of autarky, the sins of 'departmentalism' included illicit stockpiling; false reporting; illegal bartering and bribery; and breaking delivery contracts by cutting corners on quality or product mix.

The scope of these activities went beyond the iterative games between managers and planners which are the focus of pyramidal models of the Soviet economy. Factory managers and ministry officials were not simply the recalcitrant executors of party policy, who could be kept in line through threats and cajoling. Ministry and enterprise bureaucracies were not some sort of aberration in the command economy: they *were* the command economy. The significance of this argument will perhaps become clearer as discussion moves on to the topic of the party interventions in the economy.

Party interventions in the economy: the prefect model revisited

The dominant model of party–economy interactions in the Brezhnev era remains J. Hough's *The Soviet Prefects*, published in 1969.[45] In opposition to the totalitarian model, which dominated the discipline in the early 1960s, Hough developed a model of the CPSU as 'system manager'.

Hough's theoretical starting point was Barrington Moore's observation that the USSR might shed its Asiatic and/or totalitarian past and develop in the direction of a 'rational-technical society'.[46] Hough argued that this hypothetical new stage had finally arrived, and augmented the Moore hypothesis by finding a role for the CPSU in the 'rational-technical' model. Drawing upon the work of the economists who had uncovered the confused, overlapping pattern of management in the Soviet economy, Hough concluded that the party could play the role of a rational coordinator, resolving bureaucratic conflicts in the interests of society at large (as interpreted by the national leadership of the CPSU). Hough also moved beyond a Weberian interpretation of efficiency, noting that the CPSU was not a bureaucratic institution in the classic Weberian mould, in that it was goal rather than rule-oriented. From the latest Western public administration studies Hough identified the important administrative role of regional coordinator, and argued that this was the function of local party organs in the Soviet economy. He described the role of regional first secretaries as 'A textbook example of the classic prefect in a modern setting.'[47]

These various elements fused together into an attractive and innovative model which has been supported and elaborated in the work of subsequent scholars.[48] The prefect analogy also provided a clear framework for the presentation of Hough's rich empirical findings on the economic tasks of local party organs in the early to mid-1960s.

Was the Communist Party as effective a system manager as Hough implied? It can be argued that the party should bear a large proportion of the blame for the economic stagnation of the 1960s and 1970s. The party could be held responsible in one of two senses. First, it was clear that the political priorities of the CPSU ruled out the possibility of a transition towards a market economy. As long as the party insisted on maintaining a command economy, one can argue that the Soviet economy was doomed to inefficiency and decay.[49] Second, one could argue that even *within* the confines of the command economy, party interventions made things worse rather than better, in that politically motivated interventions interfered with the normal functioning of the planned and market economies. The more the party sphere encroached on the economic spheres, the worse it was for the economy. This is the main hypothesis being examined in this book.

However, it is important to bear in mind the historical context. Important changes were taking place in the Soviet economy with the passage of time. The prefect system might have served the Soviet economy well in the 1930s and 1940s, when the Soviet economy was at a fairly primitive level of development. Economic policy revolved around digging coal and iron ore, building steel mills and power stations, and the forced development of certain categories of military hardware. In such an environment, it was relatively easy for the national leadership to set goals for regional party bosses and monitor their realization.

For different reasons, the party prefects can also be seen as serving a useful function in the 1950s (the period from which most of Hough's empirical materials were drawn). After Stalin's death the central ministries were in considerable disarray. Between 1957 and 1965 economic administration was radically decentralized, and local party organs played a vital role in holding the economy together. After 1965, the Soviet economy grew in complexity, with the arrival of a multitude of new products (plastics, chemicals, electronics), the accelerating pace of technical change, and increased attention to consumer demand. This all meant that party interventions in the economy were increasingly clumsy and ineffective. The Brezhnev leadership found it more and more difficult to come up with clear and simple tasks for local party organs to implement.

To a degree the CPSU was suffering from its own economic success. Stalin set in motion a juggernaut of administrative centralization which managed to produce economic expansion, albeit highly unbalanced and at huge human cost. The higher level of development thus attained brought with it new economic tasks, which proved to be beyond the capacity of the old system of political management.

1 The party and the economy: structures and principles

This chapter investigates the principles underlying party interventions in the economy, and the institutional apparatus through which such interventions took place. The CPSU saw itself, according to Article 6 of the 1977 Constitution, as 'The leading and guiding force of Soviet society and the nucleus of its political system and of all state and public organizations.'[1] This involved responsibility for the whole range of social and political activity, from child-rearing to national defence. Within this spectrum of involvement, economics played a pivotal role.

In the Brezhnev era the party pledged to put the USSR through 'accelerated socio-economic development' so that they could further perfect 'developed socialism'.[2] This involved the party in both the 'leadership' (*rukovodstvo*) and 'direction' (*napravlenie*) of Soviet society: setting the general goals for social development *and* taking concrete steps to ensure that they are brought to fruition.[3] This meant that the CPSU committed itself to active involvement in the economy. When Soviet writers talked of obeying the 'laws of social development' or a 'scientifically based economic policy' they were not suggesting a hands-off approach. Socio-economic laws, unlike the laws of physics, would not unfold by themselves, but required active human involvement.[4] The Brezhnev leadership made great play of its 'scientific' approach to social problems, using this to distinguish its own interventions from Khrushchev's 'voluntaristic' interference.[5]

Some might naively imagine that, in view of Marx and Lenin's comments on 'the withering away of the state' as socialism matured, the role of the party should diminish, and Soviet society should govern itself. While Soviet leaders paid lip service to 'socialist self-administration', in reality they saw the events of 1968 in Czechoslovakia and 1980 in Poland as showing the fragility of party control over society.[6] Rather than arguing that the CPSU should stand back from society,

Soviet ideologists continued to assert that the party's role must be preserved, even strengthened, with the passage of time.[7]

The other general theoretical point to underline is that the party insisted that its policies were the most advantageous possible for Soviet society. It saw itself as the epitome of social rationality. In the words of the Party Statutes, 'The party exists for the people and serves the people.'[8] *Kommunist* assured its readers that 'Unlike other organizations, the party expresses the interests of all workers, and not separate groups or strata of the population.'[9] This over-arching rationality means that whatever the type of activity the party is engaged in, it can be justified as an integral part of its overall mission. Authors constantly underline the principle of 'the unity. of political and economic activity', and talk in one breath of 'organizational, ideological-educational and economic activity'.[10]

Thus the CPSU would bitterly oppose the ideas advanced in the preceding chapter as to the existence of discrete logics at work in Soviet society (party, plan and market). They rightly perceived that to concede the absence of a single social rationality would have undermined their authority to rule Soviet society. The party's self-image was intrinsically hostile to ideas along the lines of a separation of powers, such as the suggestion that it could withdraw from economic activity and concentrate on political work.

How important was the economic activity of the CPSU when compared to its other functions – organizational maintenance; political socialisation of members and the general public; cultural policy; the supervision of the military, the legal system and so forth? It is impossible to answer this question definitively, in part precisely because the party itself refused to demarcate its organizational, ideological and economic functions. In an even broader sense, these functions were interdependent and inseparable, in that without its organizational cohesion the party could not have enforced its economic policies, and without a degree of ideological control the party could not have preserved its organizational base.

One way of examining this question is to look at Central Committee decrees: the chief formal means of communication between the CPSU leadership and the lower party organs. Some of them resemble what would be laws in other political systems, while others are simply evaluations of a particular party organization's performance. A content analysis of Central Committee (CC CPSU) decrees issued between 1966 and 1980 in terms of principal subject matter (aggregated by number of pages of text) showed no less than 50 per cent devoted to economic issues, leaving only 9 per cent for foreign affairs, 8 per cent for agitation work, and a variety of categories accounting for the remainder.[11] Similarly, the decrees selected for inclusion in the party workers' handbooks for 1972–83 had 35 per cent of their pages devoted to economic matters, followed by 23 per cent on foreign affairs.[12]

Our general impression from this and other types of evidence is that economic affairs were central to the routine functioning of the CPSU during the Brezhnev years. Leningrad gorkom first secretary A. Gerasimov summarized the situation thus: 'Party secretaries receive medals and gold stars not for the state or party work in their area, or for the political maturity of the party organization, but for record harvests and new factories.'[13]

In crude time terms, they accounted for something like half of all the activities of party organizations. This is apparently true even for the Politburo itself, judging by the summaries of its weekly meetings which began to be published after Andropov took over in November 1982. There is no way of quantifying the relative weight of the items on the Politburo agenda, but, despite the large number of relatively minor foreign policy issues reported, economic affairs usually took up more than half the space of these summary reports.

Thus, unlike most other political parties the world over, the CPSU spent a large proportion of its time monitoring economic activity. In the remainder of this chapter we will explore the set of structures, and their principles of operation, through which party interventions in the economy took place. The remainder of the book tries to establish how these structures were put to use in different policy areas, and evaluates the impact of party interventions on the functioning of the planned economy.

The party apparatus

The structure of the CPSU as it developed over the years was well suited to the supervision of the Soviet economy.[14] Unlike most non-communist political parties, members joined a party unit at their place of work. These party units were grouped together on a territorial basis – the so-called 'territorial-production principle'. This arrangement made it difficult to supervise life among non-working groups such as pensioners and single mothers, and in residential areas in general, although territorial party organizations could be formed at the place of residence if desired.[15]

The historical origins of the territorial-production principle are obscure. It arose in the pre-revolutionary period, out of the general Marxist belief that life in the modern world revolves around the factory, and out of the idea that the Communist Party was the party of the workers – who were to be found in factories. The production-based structure persisted long after these original ideas had lost their conviction.

Party members were grouped into Primary Party Organizations (PPOs) at the place of work, with an average of roughly 45 members per PPO. The size of the institution of employment varied considerably – 40 per cent of PPOs had less than 15 members, while 6 per cent had over 100. PPOs with more than 50 members could create subordinate *tsekh* or workshop organizations, 70 per cent of which enjoyed the rights of a full PPO as far as recruitment was concerned. Below the workshop level, in any organization where there were at least three party members a party group should be formed. There were roughly 426,000 PPOs, and beneath them 420,000 workshop organizations and another 550,000 party groups.[16]

PPOs with more than 15 members elected a bureau: otherwise they were headed by a secretary (and possibly a deputy). Party groups had their own organizer (*partgruporg*). Above the PPOs the party reverted to a territorial structure, with the following units as of 1983:

Rural district committees (raikomy)	2,886
Urban district committees (raikomy)	631
City committees (gorkomy)	873
Regional committees (obkomy)	151
Regional committees (kraikomy)	6
Republic central committees	14

The Russian Republic (RSFSR) did not have a separate Central Committee between 1966 and 1990, hence the 14 republic CCs. Kraikomy differed from obkomy in that they had ethnically based units beneath them.[17] The kraikomy had the powers of obkomy within the CPSU, so we will not distinguish between the two henceforth. The raikomy were mostly subordinate to obkomy, except that the larger gorkomy had raikomy under their own jurisdiction. Moscow had thirty-three raikomy, and Leningrad twenty-one. Some gorkomy were directly subordinate to a republican CC rather than to an obkom, while Moscow and Kiev gorkomy both enjoyed obkom status, and were directly under the CC CPSU.

With a Soviet population of 285 million and a party membership of 19 million (as of 1986), the typical obkom managed the lives of some 2 million inhabitants and 100,000 party members. Beneath the average obkom there were roughly 2,600 PPOs, 20 rural raikomy, 4 urban raikomy and 6 gorkomy. The apparatus varied in complexity from Moscow gorkom (1.1 million party members) to the Dzhizak obkom in Kazakhstan (18,000 party members). (For details on how to estimate regional party memberships, see Appendix 1.)

The obkom apparatus

The obkomy were the most powerful regional bodies of the CPSU. RSFSR, Belorussia, Uzbekistan, Kazakhstan and Ukraine were the only republics with a full layer of obkomy: elsewhere the republic CC fulfilled a similar role. The obkom was the mediating agency between the Moscow leadership and the party in the country at large: its first secretary was almost always appointed to the CC CPSU (as either a candidate or a full member).

It is clear from the CC CPSU decrees evaluating the work of obkomy which appeared two or three times a year, and from the obkom election meetings (many of which were reported in the national press), that they were held responsible for the whole gamut of social activity, from economics through to education.[18] Whether it was measures to develop the fish industry, or plans to mechanize manual labour by the year 2000, the obkom was expected to play a leading role.[19] The obkom was blamed if a significant proportion of its region's enterprises missed their output targets, or if the aggregate output level fell below the rate of growth foreseen in the annual plan.[20] It was very common for obkomy to be criticized for poor agricultural performance, for reasons which will emerge in subsequent chapters.

Obkomy were not merely held accountable for aggregate performance: they were also expected to show familiarity with the details of economic policy, whether it was the development of a particular industry (e.g. oil in Mangyshlak oblast), or a particular managerial technique (e.g. spreading the Shchekino method in Tula oblast).[21]

On top of these economic responsibilities, obkomy were also subject to criticism if they weakened their vigilance over such topics as the political education of workers; the healthy course of intra-party life; or if they failed to intervene in cases of law-breaking and suppression of criticism by senior officials.[22]

These considerable responsibilities were seen as resting on the shoulders of the individual who occupied the position of obkom first secretary, who 'is held responsible for everything'.[23] Some of the flavour of these diverse responsibilities can be gained from the following fictional account by G. Markov, in a chapter from his novel *Griadush-chemu veku* rather confidently entitled 'A typical day in the obkom.'[24] The main character, an author in a Siberian town, spends a morning in the obkom first secretary's office, and witnesses his morning's work:

> discussing changes needed in the author's book before it can pass the censor;
>
> calling in the military (with a red telephone!) to help flood victims;
>
> arranging a new flat for a woman having triplets;
>
> negotiating by phone with a Moscow ministry about the location of a new plant;
>
> sending a telegram to the Politburo to plead for help combatting air pollution;
>
> taking a call from Moscow about a forthcoming delegation from Cuba.

In meeting these wide-ranging responsibilities (even though for the most part they will be more mundane than this account suggests) the obkom had the advantage of enjoying unquestioned political authority within its region. It had the disadvantage of having a relatively small body of personnel to carry out these tasks, meaning that for the most part it had to rely upon the assiduousness of its subordinate party organs.

Only fragmentary data are available on the size of obkom staffs. The party press in the Brezhnev era only yielded two such figures – 65 in Pskov, and 55 in Khorezm, both rather small obkomy (having 70,000 and 28,000 party members respectively).[25] In 1988 *Kommunist* reported that the Belorussia CC apparatus had 240 professional staff, with 500 more employed in the 6 obkomy under its jurisdiction.[26]

The staff were grouped into functional departments, as can be seen from Table 1.1. (This was culled from the telephone book for the town of Urgench in Uzbekistan, which is where the Khorezm obkom is based.) Larger obkomy had more functional departments handling specific economic sectors – for example, Moscow gorkom had 23 departments, and Moscow obkom 18.[27]

The key department for organization and party work (*orgotdel*) monitored the general functioning of the apparatus. Its duties included the following:[28]

> passing down resolutions and instructions from above;
>
> monitoring the performance of lower organs;
>
> organizing meetings and elections at obkom level, and supervising those at lower levels;
>
> controlling cadre selection;

Table 1.1. *Staff of Khorezm obkom, 1980*

First secretary, Second secretary
Three secretaries
Two assistants
Six reception secretaries

Department	Number of staff
Organization and party work	10
Propaganda and agitation	8
Agriculture	5
Science and education	3
Industry, transport, communications	3
Construction	3
Administrative and trade institutions	3
Party commission	3
General department	6
Party finance and business affairs	5
Party records	1
Total[a]	55

[a] – Total is of 'responsible' (*otvetsvennye*) staffers. This includes the five obkom secretaries, but excludes the receptionists and assistants.
Source: Spisok abonentov Urgenchskoi gorodskoi telefonoi seti (Urgench, Izdatel'-stvo oblstnykh gazet, 1980). Made available by M. Rywkin in a seminar at Harvard University, 4 April 1985.

checking recruitment of members;
overseeing the work of public organizations such as the Komsomol
and People's Control.

This was an onerous set of duties, bearing in mind the sheer size of the CPSU in simple organizational terms – dozens of raikomy, thousands of PPOs, tens of thousands of members under each obkom.

In practice, the duties of the *orgotdel* were mostly routine in nature – keeping the paper flowing, checking that the cycle of meetings and reports was adhered to. Interspersed with this were occasional campaigns launched from above, or crises emanating from below, which called for more detailed intervention in activities lower down the chain of command. Checking on the execution of party decisions, particularly those coming down from the CC CPSU, was clearly of crucial importance. For example, control of execution was reported as taking up one-third of the agenda of the bureau of Krasnoiarsk kraikom.[29]

The propaganda and agitation (agitprop) department prepared educational materials and supervised the activities of the small army of lecturers who spread the political gospel among party members and the general public. Each obkom had a 'House of Political Education' under its control as a base for these activities, and ran a 'University of Marxism Leninism'. (More on these institutions in chapter 9.)

The functional departments supervised the work of PPOs sector by sector. Their primary duty was to monitor economic performance, although their work overlapped with that of the orgotdel when it came to cadres policy and running socialist competition drives in industry.[30]

The party commission functioned as the local branch of the Committee of Party Control (KPK), an organization based at CC CPSU level, and enjoyed a considerable degree of prestige and authority.[31] Party commissions were composed of senior, experienced party members, and acted as review bodies over the work of the party organization as a whole: handling discipline cases, appeals from party members who had been punished, and any illegalities in the conduct of party or senior administrative officials.[32] Complaints about the work of party officials were also steered through the commission.

The relationship between local party commissions and the network of party revision commissions was unclear. The latter were the local representatives of the Central Revision Commission (TsRK), a body entirely separate from the KPK.[33] The revision commissions dealt with party finances, monitoring the payment of party dues; the correct use of funds for construction of buildings and equipment; the use of party cars and apartments; and the operation of party presses. Some reports also described them as responsible for processing letters and visits from the general public, while other accounts suggest that the orgotdel carried out this work.[34]

One should not imagine that the work of these commissions was purely anodyne. Their responsibilities as troubleshooters could range fairly wide. For example, the Leningrad obkom commission reported that it carried out 1,400 investigations in 1978, including:[35]

corruption by individual cadres;
a central heating system failure;
persistent drunkenness in a raikom;
poor livestock husbandry;
implementation of shopfloor 'rationalization' suggestions;
commuter rail delays;
an illegal car pool operating out of a cooperative garage.

A considerable amount of energy must have been expended just on keeping the organization functioning smoothly. For example, in 1982 six obkomy and five republic CCs were criticized for overspending party budgets, failing to ensure full collection of party dues and illegal car use.[36]

The work of party commissions was particularly important in the disciplinary sphere, in trying to ensure that adequate and just penalties were imposed by lower organs. In Krasnodar in 1985, for example, no less than 600 party penalties levied by PPOs in the course of a discipline crackdown were increased by higher organs, on grounds of laxity.[37]

The obkom 'general department' had rather shady connotations. Rosenfeldt suggests that it was through the general department that Stalin issued his secret instructions and exercised his personal control over the party apparatus.[38] Descriptions of its work in the post-Stalin era are, however, rather difficult to find. One account suggested that it served as the clearing house for all documentation, carefully checking that the orgotdel was fulfilling its duties.[39] Particular care was taken to ensure that orders despatched from central organs were obeyed: there had to be a careful documentary record of how they were implemented. The obkom itself could put certain policy decisions in the region under its own supervision (*kontrol*), meaning that they were directly monitored by the general department.[40]

'Finance and economics' departments were responsible for the day-to-day running of the party machinery. The list in Table 1.1 shows 'responsible' (*otvetstvennye*) administrators only: 'technical' workers such as drivers and janitors are excluded. The staff could only rely on minimal additional secretarial help.[41] The two assistants and six receptionists listed at the head of the Khorezm table were probably the only secretarial staff available.

The raikom and gorkom apparatuses

The raikom apparatus was a slimmed down version of that found at obkom level. The staff was, in the words of the standard Soviet text book, 'relatively small' in size.[42] The orgotdel had five or six workers, as did the agitprop *otdel*.[43] Raikomy did not have a general department, and party commission work was usually handled by a group of non-staff party workers.[44]

Raikom functional departments were fewer in number than at obkom level: typically, one for industry and one for agriculture, each

Table 1.2. *Estimates of size of party apparatus, various regions*

	(1) Size of apparatus	(2) Total party membership	(3) Ratio of (1) to (2)
Moscow	2,000	1,100,000	1/550
Vologoda	500	91,000	1/180
Pskov	450	70,000	1/155
Orlov	400	63,000	1/158
Orenburg	650	134,000	1/205
Kaluga	600	91,000	1/152
Sverdlovsk	1,100	240,000	1/218
Krasnodar	1,300	315,000	1/240

Sources: Column (1) – A. V. Cherniak (ed.), *Tovarishch instruktor* (Moscow: Politizdat, 1984), p. 7, 8; *Partiinaia zhizn*, 18 (1984), 3; 20 (1982), 20; 16 (1978), 22; 17 (1981), 35; *Sovetskaia Kuban*, 7 July 1989, p. 2. Column (2) – estimate derived from the number of delegates the region sent to the 26th Party Congress, where there seems to have been one delegate per 3,500 party members. Delegates are listed in *26 s'ezd KPSS. Stenograficheskii otchet* (Moscow, Politizdat, 1981), vol. 3, pp. 289–529.

with around three to five workers.[45] This implies a total average raikom or gorkom staff of fifteen to thirty. Hough concluded that a gorkom in a large (several hundred thousand) city in the early 1960s had around twenty-five staff; while Voslensky estimated raikomy to have staffs of twenty to forty.[46] The very occasional figures that turn up in the literature support these estimates.[47]

We are now in a position to estimate the total number of full-time party apparatchiki relative to the total membership. Assembling all the data gathered from ten years' of *Partiinaia zhizn* and *Kommunist* produces the estimates shown in Table 1.2.

The ratios of apparatus to party membership are fairly consistent, all lying in the 1/152 to 1/218 region, with the exception of Moscow gorkom, whose apparatus seems proportionately half the size of that in other regions. One can speculate that this is because Moscow was graced with a large number of experienced, powerful PPOs in factories and educational institutions who needed less monitoring. Also, the PPOs of leading scientific and cultural institutions, and of the numerous ministries, were directly monitored by CC CPSU departments, although all such PPOs were also formally under the jurisdiction of the Moscow gorkom.

If one takes an average of all the ratios in column 3 of Table 1.2, one comes up with an estimate of 82,000 full-time party workers in the whole USSR (a ratio of 1/230, taken out of 18 million party members). Excluding Moscow from the calculation, the estimate is 100,000 (a ratio of 1/180). These estimates fall in the same range as those suggested by Hough. Our sample is confined to the RSFSR, where party density was somewhat higher than in other republics (see Appendix 1).

The mechanics of cadre selection

Given the relatively small size of the full-time staff of party organs, it is clear that the primary thrust of party supervision of the economy was channelled *indirectly*, through influence over party members who worked in economic institutions. Control over appointments was regarded as a top priority by the CPSU, ever since Stalin coined the ringing phrase 'cadres decide everything'.[48]

More recently, Gorbachev noted that 'for party committees, handling economic work means above all working with people, with cadres'.[49] Not only did accounts of party activity devote a considerable amount of attention to cadres policy, but also the information was more precise and convincing than was usually the case with other aspects of their work in industry. This seems to hold true for the whole spectrum of sources, from textbooks through to newspaper reports of party plena.

The starting point for cadre policy was the procedure for appointment and dismissal. Here we find one of the most original and well-known institutional innovations in the CPSU's box of organizational tools – the nomenklatura system. It was the party's way of keeping track of all appointments to important positions in Soviet establishments, economic and otherwise. The nomenklatura system began (of course) with Lenin, who stated that 'One must not allow the most important state positions to be filled by anyone except the ruling party.'[50]

Nomenklatury were lists of positions monitored by each level of the party hierarchy, from raikom up to CC CPSU (and presumably up to the Politburo).[51] Bureau officials at each level participated in the appointment of officials to positions within their jurisdiction. To be more precise, the nomenklatury consisted of three types of list: the list of current holders of the posts, the list of the posts themselves, and the list of the cadre 'reserve'. The reserve was the pool of candidates for nomenklatura positions, and was usually drawn up on the basis of personnel occupying deputy and second rank positions.[52] Party membership was not obligatory for inclusion in the nomenklatura – although it clearly helped one's promotion prospects.[53] Some 75 per cent of nomenklatura appointments came out of the reserve. The rest presumably came from other regions, or from persons who had not previously caught the attention of the party committee.

The nomenklatura was thus an administrative device, and not, as is sometimes implied, some sort of secret society. While members of the CC CPSU nomenklatura enjoyed special privileges (closed shops and the like), this was not true to any significant extent for people on, say, a raikom's appointment list. Bear in mind also that organizations other than the party – local soviets, ministries, etc. – also used a nomenklatura system for posts under their jurisdiction.

There was considerable regional variety in the posts covered by the system, for each party committee (partkom) itself decided the posts it would supervise.[54] The posts covered included positions within the party apparatus itself, and extended outwards into farms, factories, newspapers and educational institutions. Within the party itself, for example, raikom and gorkom instructors were not usually on the obkom list, nor were partkom secretaries of collective state farms.[55]

Outside the party, social science teachers were on raikom lists, while the heads of social science departments were monitored at obkom level.[56] An interview Hough conducted with a deputy chairman of the Belorussian sovnarkhoz in the late 1950s revealed that of 300 plant directors in Minsk, 10 were on CC CPSU lists, and 40–50 on lists maintained by the Belorussian CC.[57]

Individual partkomy were relatively free to add or delete certain posts from their lists as they saw fit.[58] This fluidity makes it difficult to estimate the total number of posts on party nomenklatury. However, culling ten years of party journals enables us to present the figures shown in Table 1.3.

The final column shows a fairly consistent ratio (8 to 12 per cent) between the size of nomenklatury of all partkomy in a given region and the number of party members. A ratio of 10 per cent applied to the total CPSU membership (say 18 million) gives us 1.8 million positions on party nomenklatury of all partkomy in the nation as a while, to which must be added the lists held by republican CCs and by the CC CPSU. Our estimate is thus higher than that of M. Voslensky, who came up with a figure of 750,000.[59]

This picture appears consistent with other evidence at our disposal. For example, CC secretary Kapitonov referred to there being 'several millions' in the reserve lists of the CPSU as a whole.[60]

Table 1.3. *Reports of size of nomenklatura, various regions*

	(1) Obkom nomenk.	(2) Obkom, raikom and gorkom nomenklatura	(3) Total party membership	(4) Ratio of (2) to (3), in %
Krasnodar	3,600	40,000[a]	325,000	12
Sverdlovsk	–	20,000	240,000	8
Bashkir	–	23,000	210,000	11
Novosibirsk	–	15,000	154,000	10
Kapakalpak	–	6,500	28,000	24
Ul'yanovsk	1,963	–	98,000	n.a.
L'vov	1,719	–	126,000	n.a.
Vinnitsa	1,400	–	105,000	n.a.
Novosibirsk	1,500	–	154,000	n.a.

[a] – The figures for Krasnodar are for 1986. Another report from 1985 claimed it only had 32,000 on its nomenklatura – *Kommunist*, 4 (1985), 34. Such discrepancies are common in Soviet data.

Sources Columns (1) and (2) – *Kommunist*, 17 (1986), 32; 11 (1983), p. 58; *Partiinaia zhizn*, 20 (1978), 42; 7 (1981), 27; 19 (1978), 42; 8 (1981), 46; *Partiinaia zhizn Uzbekistana*, 6 (1982), 51; *Voprosy istorii KPSS*, 1 (1979), 14; *Sovetskaia Sibir*, 18 August 1988, p. 1. Column (3) – see Table 1.2 for details.

Several conclusions can be drawn from this exercise. First, a large number of administrative positions were subject to party monitoring, giving the CPSU a powerful lever over economic life and over other state institutions. On the other hand, merely keeping track of the nomenklatura process must have taken up much of the time budget of party apparatchiki, leaving less opportunity for other, more direct types of intervention in the functioning of the economy.

Whatever the precise numbers involved, what did it mean for a partkom to have a particular post on its nomenklatura? This is not entirely clear. A great deal depended on the rank of the post, and the status of the organization formally responsible for the appointment. For example, an obkom may have had to deal with a factory director when appointing a chief engineer, but would negotiate with his ministry department in Moscow when the director's position itself needed to be filled. At a minimum the partkom in question presumably had the right to be consulted: it probably also enjoyed a veto power. Appointments were mostly made by collegial bodies, composed of representatives of state, party and other bodies, such as trade unions. Formally, the partkom's role was limited to the right to 'recommend'. Most accounts of appointments suggest a joint approach.[61] Party organs, particularly in more peripheral regions, may simply not have had qualified cadres in their files, and had to wait on the decisions of state bodies.[62] Only in sectors of the economy lacking a strong ministerial hierarchy were there examples of partkomy playing a solo role.[63] Party organs played an active role in personnel selection in the agricultural sector, largely because of the deficit of qualified cadres.[64]

When it came to removing faulty directors, there were more examples to be found of partkomy playing a dominant role. Sometimes they implied that sacking bad directors was entirely their own responsibility.[65] More carefully written accounts referred to them being sacked by the relevant ministry after an 'initiative' by the partkom.[66]

Thus for the most part it appears that partkomy recognized the collegiality of the process, and respected the ministry's formal rights of appointment. The only published examples of partkom recommendations being turned down were those where the local partkom was trying to protect delinquent local cadres.[67] In these cases, however, the partkom was overruled by higher party bodies, rather than by ministry officials.

The nomenklatura procedure was not the only device at the disposal of the party for influencing the placement of personnel in the economy. Partkomy had special disciplinary powers over party members: they could be forbidden to quit a certain job, or directed to another part of the economy.[68] In some cases it was fairly clear that such transfers were against the wishes of the person involved. For example, the Georgian CC moved a veterinarian from his 'cosy chair' in a Tblisi research institute to take charge of a chicken farm in a distant province.[69] Large-scale cadre mobilizations were a regular occurrence, with hundreds of party members being drafted into lagging sectors of the economy.[70]

The work of the party apparatus at raikom and obkom level

The general impression which emerges from the party literature is that of an understaffed, rushed apparatus struggling to meet the multifarious tasks imposed upon it. In these circumstances they went for short-cuts in their work which made sense from the point of view of their own interests, and perhaps the interests of their organization, but which had a less positive impact from the point of view of economic efficiency.

The instructors were the backbone of the apparatus. This was the name given to the department officials who undertook the bulk of the routine work: drafting reports, keeping records, collating information. Many reports commented that instructors were deluged with work and found it difficult to do an effective job, confining themselves to keeping the paper flowing.[71] Each instructor supervised several dozen PPOs, each of which could in turn be split into workshop groups. Thus for example one Khar'kov gorkom instructor had no less than 100 party cells to supervise.[72]

Hough noted in his 1961 dissertation that 'Instructors frequently find themselves so overburdened with the collection of information and statistics that they have little time for anything else'; and that 'Whatever may be the situation in theory, preparatory work for discussion at bureau and committee meetings has in practice been the most important function of the instructors.'[73] According to a survey in Gomel oblast, 67 per cent of instructors left their office to visit party organizations only once a week.[74] Similarly, staffers of a Moscow raikom averaged one visit to a PPO per week, while the Smolensk obkom felt obliged to institute a rule ordering everybody to go out visiting on Wednesdays.[75] The most active instructors were from the agitprop department, followed by the orgotdel – with the economic departments a poor third. This implies that most PPOs did not see their supervising instructors from one month to the next.

Similar criticisms were levelled at higher party organs in their dealings with raikomy. The first secretary of Grodno obkom was criticized for only telephoning Volkovsk raikom twice in a whole year: once concerning the sugar beet harvest, and once about a visiting delegation.[76] According to one report, 'As a rule, officials from the gorkom only attend raikom meetings when organizational questions are being discussed.'[77]

An additional factor limiting the efficacy of instructors was their relatively low status and expertise. Half the instructors in Moscow raikomy quit within three years, and in some districts of Pskov the annual turnover reached 50 per cent;[78] 62 per cent of Moscow instructors were under 35 years old, and one-third were women.[79] Part of the reason for the high turnover was the tendency to use the instructor position as a talent pool for promotion to more senior party positions.

Questions of technical competence also enter the picture. While the vast majority of party officials had some form of higher education, they were less likely to have sufficient technical knowledge to challenge the judgements of factory engineers or farmers on detailed aspects of their work. In any event, our impression was that the instructors were rarely called on to play this sort of role.

If party officials did not spend that much time out in the party organizations in the field, how did they fulfil their supervisory role? They relied on indirect, bureaucratic means: paperwork, phone calls and meetings.

A common theme in the press was to berate party organs for issuing too many instructions, often of a vague, repetitive or otherwise non-operational nature. (In Soviet parlance, non-operational means they did not mandate any specific action by lower organs.)[80] Obkomy often just rewrote CC CPSU decrees before issuing them as their own.

The obverse of issuing too many paper commands was an excessive concern with written proof that they had been carried out. Party officials at all levels had to fill out elaborate reports for their superiors, on a weekly and monthly basis.[81] Even such seemingly redundant information as the number of suggestions made at PPO meetings was dutifully recorded and forwarded up the party tree. All this paperwork was connected to what one report called the 'meeting disease'.[82] It was standard practice for raikomy and obkomy to summon dozens of groups of leaders to attend meetings in party headquarters each month.

Many Soviet citizens report that informal contacts over the telephone were what really held together the party apparatus. The more written reports were required, the more party officials would rely on informal, off-the-record contacts. Not much was said in the press about the telephone habits of party officials, so evidence is hard to come by, but our descriptions of policy interventions in subsequent chapters will confirm that telephone interventions played a key role in the political culture of the CPSU.

The position of the central party authorities on all this was somewhat ambivalent. While roundly condemning excessive paperwork (bumagotvorchestvo), the centre demanded a close accounting for all party activities.[83] After all, the obsession with the implementation of decisions started at the top. In 1983 the CC CPSU issued new instructions imposing stricter paperwork requirements with respect to the receipt and processing of critical letters and visits to party organs.[84] A general respect for the role of written records seemed to pervade the whole apparatus: recall that the key general departments in obkomy and raikomy devoted themselves to this task. Party organizers (*partgruporgy*), the lowest link in the chain, were expected to keep a diary of their activities, and even speeches at raikom meetings were often written out and entered into the record.[85]

In theory, central authorities encouraged the adoption of work methods which took the party staffer out of these bureaucratic routines. For example, it was considered good policy to send out a team (*shtab*) of party officials to supervise directly a critical harvest unit or construction site.[86] Another practice which became increasingly common in the early 1980s was hearing direct reports from economic officials (whether party members or not) in raikom or gorkom offices.[87] Hard-pressed instructors tried to ease their workload by using non-staff (*vneshtatnye*) party members to help run the party committee, mainly via permanant or temporary commissions. Moscow's 2,000 instructors were helped by 20,000 such assistants – roughly 2 per cent of the party membership.[88] There was little evidence, however, that these auxiliaries played a particularly prominent or effective role. The most successful examples would probably be the advisory councils on scientific-technical progress, drawn from local experts (see below, chapter 2).

Thus the general impression is of an extensive institutional structure which was bogged down by the amount of detailed regulation of economic life it was required to perform, but which was nevertheless well placed to oversee the domain of economic life, and to intervene selectively as conditions warranted.

The chapter now shifts its attention to the Primary Party Organizations, which were supposed to be at the cutting edge of the party's supervisory role. It was through the PPOs and their mass membership in the factories that the CPSU hoped to exert the bulk of its influence. First, however, it is worth considering the limits to party control of the economy and the problem of separating the responsibilities of party and state bodies.

The sin of *podmena*

Party leaders were consistently worried that party organizations were getting bogged down in the routine tasks of economic administration, and were losing their integrity as separate, *political* organizations. In party rhetoric, this was known as the sin of *podmena*. The literal meaning is that certain partkomy's actions lead them to 'displace' or 'supplant' the role of the state bodies that they were monitoring.

Condemnations of podmena were legion. A typical complaint was that 'Most party documents address purely production questions, whose resolution must be left primarily in the hands of economic officials.'[89] Party journals insisted that 'Party leadership has nothing in common with narrow administration,' and called for a 'clear delineation of the functions of party and state organs'.[90] Gorbachev himself criticized podmena on many occasions, seeing it as part of a general crisis of lack of responsibility for decisions in Soviet society (*adresnost*). In a speech to the CC CPSU of April 1985 he opined:[91] 'Each person must involve himself with his own business ... The party man must not replace the manager, nor the engineer replace the messenger; nor the scientist, the vegetable picker; nor the textile worker, the farmer ... Unfortunately, today this often happens.' The podmena issue became an important part of Gorbachev's campaign to transform the party's administrative style. Similarly, when B. El'tsin took over Moscow gorkom as a 'new broom', in place of the disgraced V. Grishin, he castigated the gorkom for 'shifting purely economic functions onto party organs'.[92]

Critics of podmena wanted party committees to desist from issuing detailed instructions about economic and administrative tasks.[93] For example, Frunze raikom in Moscow criticized a PPO for ordering a director to repair the safety screens around machinery.[94] It was prohibited, for example, for a PPO to 'order' (*obiazat*) a manager to do something when he was not a party member.[95] In particular, there was to be an end to the practice of proclaiming joint decrees with state bodies.[96] Local soviets were keen to issue decisions jointly with regional party bodies because without the signature of a party first secretary at the bottom of a document it would be ignored by other officials.[97]

There was something disingenuous about party leaders castigating lower officials for podmena, since it seemed to be a logical concomitant to the party's self-proclaimed leading role in the economy. Why should it have been a sin for party officials to plunge into economic management? Was it not a sign that they were taking an active role in steering the economy?

Party leaders feared podmena because it threatened to undermine the organizational integrity of the CPSU. If party officials allowed themselves to become immersed in 'operational functions' and purely 'technical-economic or administrative decisions' they would not be able to maintain 'the political character of party leadership'.[98] If they spent all their time on routine decision making (*dezhurnye voprosy*) they would not be able to exercise strategic leadership, and political considerations would take second place to 'narrowly economic' or 'technocratic' reasoning.[99]

In recognizing the dangers of podmena the party leaders came closest to the model advanced in our introduction: the idea that the party and planned economy cannot be collapsed together, but must be kept separate, marching to different tunes.

Although the concept of keeping politics separate from economics was clear, the practice was not. The party did not want to abandon its role in the economy. The trick was to pursue it through 'political methods', which meant relying on advice rather than orders, operating *through* cadres rather than in place of them. In practice, these distinctions were hard to maintain, particularly for lower-level apparatchiki who were under constant pressure from their superiors to correct economic problems.[100] Party officials frequently made contradictory statements on these subjects.[101] Despite repeated denunciation of podmena, readers were reminded that Lenin warned against those who would 'separate' (*otdelit*) the party from management.[102] A whole new section on podmena was introduced into the new Party Statutes adopted by the 27th Congress, but contained only vague generalities and did not really explain the concept – as one reader rather audaciously noted in a letter to *Kommunist*.[103]

The work of primary party organizations

The PPOs served as the point of contact between the CPSU and Soviet society at large. They enabled the party to monitor shifts and trends in public opinion, and provided a vast pool of loyal manpower which could be mobilized behind the realization of the party's policies. However, the PPOs formed the base of a vast and complex pyramid, in which power and authority was concentrated in the upper levels. Their role was to carry out routine tasks according to instructions sent down by higher authorities. Even in the Stalin period the supine position of PPOs was recognized to be a problem, which frequent reorganizations did little to solve.[104]

Aside from the full-time secretary which was allowed in PPOs with more than 150 members, PPO activities were the responsibility of rank and file party members. On top of their normal job duties, communists were expected to use whatever opportunities came their way to further the party's goals: which might mean simply excelling at their own job, or exposing corruption and mismanagement. These responsibilities applied both to rank and file party members and to those holding some sort of elective position on a bureau or commission. In theory, all members were given specific party tasks (*porucheniia*) to fulfill, at least on an annual basis, which might be either political (reading a newspaper to workmates at break time) or economic (energy conservation, for example).

Failure to carry out such duties, or any other form of moral dereliction, left the party member open to one of the array of punishments listed in Article 9 of the Party Statutes: 'comradely criticism; party censure, warning or instruction … reproof; reprimand (strict reprimand); and reprimand (strict reprimand) written in the party record card'.[105] Expulsion was the most severe punishment: 187,000 members were expelled during 1981–83.[106]

The PPO duties in the economic arena shifted in response to changes in party policy, as defined by CC CPSU decrees and pronouncements, and as elaborated in the party press. For example, after the November 1979 CC CPSU plenum PPOs were instructed to concentrate on four fields: socialist competition (organizing competitions to improve productivity); 'spreading leading experience' (introducing the latest techniques and work methods); conserving materials and energy; and promoting labour discipline (turnover, absenteeism, drunkenness).[107] Apart from exerting influence over the workers in farm and factory, PPOs were also expected to closely monitor the activities of leading enterprise officials. Many enterprise decision-making bodies were collegial in structure, with the PPO and other public organizations (Komsomol, trade unions, People's Control) able to make a direct input into factory decision making. The PPO also enjoyed some specific powers of its own. It had to be consulted in the appointment or dismissal of any technical or managerial official, and had the right (but not the obligation) to nominate candidates for any leading position.[108] PPOs did not formally have their own nomenklatura, however. Hough suggests that PPOs had a veto power over appointments.[109] A 1977 source stated the situation thus:[110]

> A manager cannot fail to take into account the opinion of the party organization. Its decisions, suggestions and recommendations, if they fully conform to party documents and Soviet laws, are binding on him. … In those circumstances where the manager is sure he is right, and considers the party organ's decision erroneous, he must turn to the higher party organ.

Formal responsibility for appointment and dismissal rested with the state institution in question, and it had the legal authority to overrule PPO appeals.

Just how much influence PPOs should exercise over cadre selection was a matter of some controversy. Even Politburo member A. Pel'she publicly hinted that it was 'an occasionally held view' that PPOs should not interfere in cadre questions.[111] In practice it seemed to be a prerogative which directors jealously preserved.

The central concept governing the economic role of PPOs was the right of supervision (*pravo kontrolia*). Article 59 of the Party Statutes empowered them to 'exercise the right of supervision over the actions of the administration' in the unit (factory, farm, hospital, shop) in which they are located'. This was a right which PPOs in economic enterprises had enjoyed since 1939, and which had been extended to PPOs in scientific and educational institutions in 1971.[112]

The right of supervision was, as Fortescue puts it, 'a difficult concept'.[113] It is hard to imagine how PPOs could effectively exercise this right without committing the sin of podmena. The right empowered PPOs to collect information on the performance of its enterprise, to hear reports (*otchety*) from its managers, and to offer suggestions and concrete help. Ideally, the supervision right should not degenerate into a search for the guilty after things went wrong, but should be conducted in a 'businesslike' fashion and oriented towards achieving specific improvements.[114] The main emphasis was on 'supervision and checking execution', i.e. carrying out party and state decisions as they apply to the enterprise.[115] Particular emphasis was placed on discouraging managers from trying to evade their plan obligations by lobbying for 'plan corrections' from their ministry.[116] PPOs were also expected to monitor performance in areas which were not directly covered by the main targets in the annual plan, such as shift coefficients, returns to capital (*fondootdacha*) and hiring limits – all often ignored by managers chasing planned output targets.[117]

In the late 1970s party leaders increasingly voiced their concern that party decrees on economic matters were not having the desired effects. More and more articles appeared stressing the centrality of decision implementation for the party apparatus.[118] These pressures bore fruit in a CC CPSU decree on the subject in 1981, which recognized that the *pravo kontrolia* was a 'bottleneck in the work of a significant number of party organizations,' and tried to persuade PPOs to take it more seriously.[119]

Since 1959 PPOs had been encouraged to set up special commissions of rank and file communists to monitor execution of decisions in specific policy areas, on either a permanant or a temporary basis.[120] (These commissions are thus a relic of Khrushchev's efforts to democratize party life.) Roughly one in six party members served on such commissions.[121] For the most part, however, PPOs merely used these commissions to shirk responsibility for monitoring problematic policy areas. Over the years the commissions proliferated, but did not have any discernable impact.[122]

The 1981 CC CPSU decree sought to persuade PPOs to take their *kontrol* duties more seriously, but did not improve the situation. One year later *Partiinaia zhizn* noted that 'Unfortunately, in a number of cases checking execution has an episodic character, leading to a mere listing of successes and failures.'[123] Chernenko (quoting Lenin) castigated those who tried to 'hide behind commissions'.[124] Nevertheless, commissions continued to receive prominent attention, and were for the first time written into the new Party Statutes (Art. 30).

PPOs which took the right of supervision seriously ran the risk of duplicating the work of the many non-party inspection agencies which looked over the shoulders of Soviet managers. There was also a problem of overlap between the duties of people as employees and as party monitors. Some cadres were given the task of supervising themselves (which was not, strictly speaking, against party rules).[125] It was particularly difficult for small PPOs to find sufficient cadres to avoid overlaps.[126]

Thus by the early 1980s there were signs of growing concern that PPOs were not fulfilling their role as the shock troops of the party on the economic front.[127] Rather than acting as a check on factory managers, they had slipped into a routine of close cooperation verging on collusion. This was reflected in CC CPSU reports on the subject, and in the debates in biennial PPO meetings which were reported in the central press.[128]

These problems were rooted in the fact that the fate of the PPO was bound up with the work of the factory or farm within which it was located. Both stood or fell by the level of plan fulfillment achieved by the enterprise, the rate of productivity increase, the avoidance of production irregularities, or whatever else was currently prioritized by the leadership.

If the performance of the enterprise was criticized, it was usual for both the management and the PPO to be reprimanded.[129] To gather some systematic evidence on this problem, the author surveyed the reports written by party officials replying to criticisms of their work which had been printed in the CC CPSU's economic weekly (*Ekonomicheskaia zhizn*) between 1976 and 1986. Of 438 printed replies, 153 were signed by PPO officers, and 62 of those were signed jointly by the enterprise director and the PPO secretary. (For more details of the survey, see Appendix 2).

Given this joint accountability, PPO secretaries saw that it was in their interest to cooperate with plant managers to achieve the best results possible. They were also aware of the danger that any criticisms they made of plant management could rebound in their direction. The relationship between PPO secretary and plant director was in any event an imbalanced one. The director held primary responsibility for the work of the plant: he had the contacts with ministry officials, suppliers and other enterprises so vital to economic success. He was more experienced and better educated (although by 1983 60 per cent of PPO secretaries had higher education – compared with only 11.4 per cent in 1956).[130] He generally enjoyed a higher social and political status: one does not find directors becoming PPO secretaries, but it was fairly common for directors to have served as PPO officials, usually a good ten to fifteen years before promotion to director.[131] This higher status was likely to translate into a loftier political position for directors in terms of membership of obkom bureaus, oblast soviets and the like. In terms of salary, PPO secretaries often received less than 250 roubles a month, while foremen in the plant earned twice as much.[132]

All this showed up in the party literature in a plethora of complaints that the PPOs rarely challenged authoritarian or capricious management. If such managers' faults were exposed, it was much more likely to be at the instigation of a journalist or People's Control investigator than as a result of a complaint from his PPO.[133] Orel obkom first secretary remarked that 'One often finds party committees who "save" communist managers to hide their own faults from investigation.'[134] The then head of the People's Control Committee, A. Pel'she, related a sorry tale of persecution of a whistleblowing accountant in an Omsk institute, asking 'Why did the raikom not reveal these developments? How could all of this go on in front of the PPO?'[135] Similarly, the PPO of Amurenergo defended the director against charges of misuse of funds, although he ended up getting an eight-year prison sentence.[136]

Some reports indicate that directors were more than willing to make full use of their leverage over the PPO. There were many reports of directors who had the PPO secretary 'in their pocket'.[137] The head of the Party Control Committee, M. Solomentsev, noted that when conflicts did occur between a PPO secretary and a director, the latter often ignored their objections, or threatened them by saying 'It's you or me!'[138] The general feeling in some collectives, he suggested, was 'Try to criticise – and you'll get it!' and when errors were exposed 'The inevitable question is: how did this happen, how come the PPO did not notice it?'

Despite these complaints of collusion between party and management officials at plant level, it was not necessarily the case that higher party bodies would back a PPO in a conflict with a director. A raikom in Orel withheld negative information about a manager from his PPO because it would be 'an undesirable infringement of the leader's authority before subordinates.'[139]

For the most part, however, the reaction of higher party bodies to this state of affairs was to bypass the PPOs, and deal directly with the individuals concerned. Disciplinary offences meted out by higher party organs were often not even discussed by the PPO.[140] There were also frequent reports of PPOs being ignored in the appointments process.[141]

It would be wrong to give the impression that the PPOs were inevitably toothless. Fortescue reads the evidence from the scientific and research establishments as suggesting a fairly high level of tension and conflict between the PPO and state officials.[142] One can find press reports of PPOs taking on factory management, although they were much less frequent than examples of collusion.[143] The only case where *Ekonomicheskaia gazeta* itself chose to back a PPO in conflict with its management was with regard to a highly polluting carbon plant in Omsk.[144] Otherwise, conflict cases only came to light as a result of appeals by individual party officials who had been persecuted by hostile managers.[145] There were relatively few such conflicts reported in the press, however, and they seemed to occur in small and isolated units (design bureaus, hospitals, etc) rather than in large industrial plants.

Thus it seems likely that PPOs did not play a strongly independent role, and cooperation and collusion with plant management was the order of the day.[146] National party leaders seemed to share this view. In an effort to increase the involvement of PPOs in disciplinary matters, a new clause was inserted into Article 9 of the revised party rules adopted in 1986, requiring for the first time that higher party organs at least inform the PPO if they were conducting a disciplinary investigation of one of its members.

Summary

   The purpose of this chapter was to describe the network of bodies through which the party exercised its supervisory role over the Soviet economy, and the organizational concepts which shaped their activity. The party's institutional structure, as it has emerged over the years, was well-suited to such a role. For example, it is difficult to think of any organizational changes or innovations which could be suggested to improve its supervisory capabilities.

However, this is not to imply that party supervision of the economy was a great success. Even based solely on the institutional analysis of this chapter, it is clear that there was a mismatch between the very wide range of responsibilities of the territorially based party organizations and the relatively small apparatus at their disposal. Goal displacement seems to have occurred, with servicing the party apparatus taking up more time than was actually spent in supervisory work. Party life revolved around a cycle of meetings, orders, reports and criticism, all derived from the principle that party organs must execute the instructions of higher party bodies.

Primary Party Organizations, being in direct contact with economic life, had more opportunity for a substantive impact on economic decision making. However, much of the time PPOs found themselves torn between the logic of party life and the logic of the planned economy. The economic laws which shaped factory life exerted a gravitational pull over the activities of the PPOs. The more they involved themselves in the minutiae of economic management, the less easy it was for them to respond to party directives. PPOs tended to collude with managers in promoting the interests of their enterprise, often in ways which went against the current priorities of the national party leadership. The national party leadership did not want PPOs to sink without trace into the planned economy: they were keen for them to preserve an independent, *political* role.

In subsequent chapters we shall explore how the practical conduct of local party organs reflected these conflicting political and economic pressures.

2 Party interventions in industry

This chapter addresses the general pattern of party interventions in industrial decision making. Chapter 3 examines three specific policy areas where the party organs played a particularly active role – supply procurement, quality control and conservation. Construction and consumer goods production are studied under the rubric of regional coordination (chapter 5), and chapter 6 is devoted to party campaigns in transport and energy.

This chapter focusses on the relationship between party organs and management officials in routine production-related decision-making. Questions of personnel selection, training and promotion are addressed in chapter 9.

The first section establishes that party officials were expected to make sure that plants under their jurisdiction met their plan targets, primarily through exhortation and criticism directed at economic managers. It is unclear, however, just how crucial satisfactory plan performance was to a party official's future career.

The chapter then looks at the role of the party in promoting innovation through integrated science policies, and in the following section examines routine party oversight of technical/production decisions, of efficiency drives, of labour policy, and of enterprise reconstruction.

The next general question addressed is the balance of power between the party and ministerial hierarchies: the autonomy of local directors, and the problems local organs had in dealing with the powerful central ministries. This was the most important factor limiting party influence over the running of Soviet industry. The final section looks at the role played by party organs in attempts to introduce changes and reforms into the Soviet economic mechanism.

Party responsibility for plan fulfilment

Soviet industrial life revolved around the plan. Success or failure in meeting annual plan targets was the primary factor determining the level of bonuses and promotion prospects of Soviet managers. Local party organs were also held accountable for poor plan performance by enterprises in their region. They were expected to monitor plan fulfilment during the course of the year, and to sound the alarm if any local plants start lagging. On top of these essentially passive duties, 'Life occasionally demands direct interference by partkomy in purely production matters, or forces them to become an abiter in a departmental dispute.'[1] So, party officials were often called upon to 'operationally resolve' problems which inhibited plan fulfilment.

In the 1940s and 1950s, monitoring plan realization was a relatively simple task. An enterprise's gross output (val), often measured in crude physical terms (tonnes, units), was decisive when it came to determining its bonus funds. Major reforms of enterprise incentives in 1965 and 1979, combined with a number of minor measures in between, considerably complicated the picture of performance measurement. The 1965 reform tried to introduce eight indicators as the basis for bonus allocation, with the main one being profits.[2] The 1979 reform tried to focus attention on labour productivity and product quality (the share of output meriting the top quality rating from the State Standards Committee).[3] However, these targets in turn had to be calculated from indicators for manning levels and gross output. The picture was complicated by additional penalties for failing to meet delivery contracts with customers (either by composition or by timing), and penalties/bonuses for economizing on materials and energy. In reality, managers still faced half-a-dozen target indicators, and not simply two. New regulations issued in July 1985, added still more bonuses for producing consumer goods or for introducing new products.[4] As of 1986, some fifty different plan indicators were in use in various wings of the central planning bureaucracy.[5] Through all these changes, factory managers had to keep on ensuring that their annual gross output plan was being met.

The multiplicity of target indicators made the Soviet manager's life very difficult. As one director put it, 'We are tangled in indicators ... we do not know which "god" to pray to ... In practice, val still reigns supreme.'[6]

The network of party organs was supposed to provide some coherence to this system. Party organs should not limit their role to checking that targets were being satisfied. They also had to help decide *which* of several competing targets should be met. Plant managers came up with their own answer to this question, but the central authorities may have had priorities which differed from those of local managers. It would have been an administrative nightmare to try to write these different priorities into plan regulations, and it was much simpler to issue general orders to party organs to the effect that 'this year focus on materials economy,' or 'don't let managers get away with ignoring contract discipline'.

Sometimes the pressure to ensure that plants in a given region were meeting their plan targets came from the very top, in the form of a reprimand from an obkom from the CC CPSU.[7] Very often it was in self-criticism by party officials (in published articles, or in reports of party election meetings) that one could find evidence of the importance attached to plan fulfilment in the work of party organs. The party press itself (in editorials, and in journalists' reports) was often active in highlighting poor plan performance, and pointing the finger of responsibility at lower party organs.[8]

Perhaps the most common measure of a region's performance was the proportion of enterprises located on its territory which failed to meet their output targets in a given year. Consider the following examples:[9]

obkom	share of enterprises missing output targets	
Kaliningrad	10 per cent	(1983)
Karaganda	20 per cent	(1975)
Novgorod	20 per cent	(1983)
Arkhangel	33 per cent	(1983)
Voroshilovgrad	15 per cent	(1975)

From this we can infer that the central party organs monitored plan fulfilment region by region, probably in terms of aggregate output and the proportion of enterprises meeting output targets. Output may have been the most important target, but was by no means the only one. Bashkir obkom judged its performance in terms of output fulfilment by product type – the plants of their region only met targets for 51 out of 117 product types.[10] Saratov obkom delivered a report (*otchet*) to the CC CPSU in 1983, and was criticized for allowing one-third of the region's enterprises to pay wage increases that exceeded the rate of productivity growth.[11] The same year, a secretary of Orel obkom confessed that 50 per cent of their enterprises infringed contract discipline.[12] Even target indicators fairly low on the list when it comes to monetary rewards, such as the thorny problems of poor capital utilization, were often the subject of party attention.[13] In principle, party organs were expected to keep their eye on all performance indicators (there were usually more than twenty in use in any given ministry), but, as a Moscow raikom secretary noted, they were satisfied if their plants were hitting five to eight of the targets.[14]

Party organs concentrated their work on trying to improve the performance of plan delinquents. Starting at PPO level, poor plan performance was often the subject of self-criticism at party election meetings. The general theory was that a successful enterprise must have a good partkom, and an enterprise performing badly must have a bad partkom. Sometimes the partkom was able to turn around an ailing plant (e.g. the assembly shop in the Briansk car works); but it was admitted that some chronic delinquents resisted the ministrations of the party (e.g. the Krasnyi Oktyabr steel mill in Volgograd, which failed its output plans for fifteen successive years).[15]

Poor plan performance was also exposed in election meetings of territorial party organs. It was invariably discussed, whether good or bad, in all PPO and local party conferences. Local party organs collected data on plan fulfilment in their district's plants on a weekly or monthly basis.[16] Party officials had to act (or appear to act), if things looked bad. For example, Iaroslavl obkom put a tractor plant under 'direct control' after its record was denounced in a press article; while the heads of departments of Brest obkom were personally censured for failing to help five lagging enterprises.[17] In Kiev, a motorcycle plant only fulfilled its 1980 plan by 75 per cent, and the raikom was blamed for failing to alert the Ministry of Automobile Production that a crisis was looming.[18] Was the ministry not responsible for knowing what was happening in its own plants, one wonders?

The latter case leads us back to the problem of podmena which we introduced in chapter 1. Holding party officials accountable for enterprise plan performance seemed to be an open invitation to interference and podmena. The first secretary of the Iakutiia obkom complained, for example, that 'Some leaders are used to turn to the obkom with any little working problem. In this way, responsibility for plan fulfilment is shifted onto the party organ.'[19] And how sensible was it anyway to have party officials responsible for all the economic activity of their region? If managers and workers were incompetent, the local party was expected to get rid of the dead wood, and use the nomenklatura system to install cadres who were up to the job. If there were not enough good cadres around, party organs were expected to set up training institutions to turn them out.

However, correcting the deficiencies of the Soviet economy was something of an abstract proposition: in reality it was unlikely that any dire consequences followed upon poor plan fulfilment by firms within a given party official's domain. Research by M. Beissinger shows that regional economic performance seemed to be unrelated to the promotion prospects of obkom first secretaries.[20] This reinforces our impression that there were very few cases where senior obkom or republic officials were dismissed for poor economic performance. Of course, this might have been happening without being reported in the sources examined for this study. One would imagine that if it were happening, the party press would have used those cases for propaganda purposes, *pour encourager les autres*. However, it was only when economic mismanagement was combined with personal corruption or favouritism that heads began to roll. Even in the purge launched by Gorbachev after 1985, leadership style rather than concrete economic results seems to have determined the allocation of punishment and rewards.[21] In any event, it strikes us as downright unrealistic to blame party officials for poor economic performance. So much depended not on the efficiency of local managers, but on the actions of planners in central ministries and suppliers in distant regions – although party officials played an important role in liaising with these external forces. Thus we may say that party leaders are held 'accountable' for regional economic performance in the sense that they had to be prepared to explain what was going on, and had to show that they had *tried* to correct the situation.

Party management of science policy

Given that we are deemed to live in the era of the 'scientific-technological revolution,' science policy was accorded a pivotal role in the CPSU's strategy to develop the Soviet economy. At a national level, the party attached considerable importance to pouring resources into the vast network of scientific establishments and higher education institutions which they assembled. This included overseeing the creation of huge new research complexes, such as the Baikonur space project and the construction of a new 250,000 person 'Academic City' in the forests outside Novosibirsk.[22]

What role did party organs play in the promotion of scientific research and in encouraging the introduction of new products and techniques? This has been the subject of detailed studies by numerous Western scholars, so this study will focus on economic enterprises, and offer only a brief summary of the role of party organs in the science sphere.

S. Fortescue suggests that the party tended to leave science in the hands of the scientists, and that party leadership was too weak to merit description as a 'vanguard' role.[23] Party organs did however help research institutes when it came to practical problems in areas such as construction, equipment or personnel, and they monitored the ideological climate in the institutes (a function which ebbed and flowed over time).

These findings concur with the results of a survey of 202 émigré scientists conducted by R. F. Miller;[24] 10–30 per cent of respondents felt that the PPO in their research institute exerted some influence over their daily life, but this was mostly to do with personal affairs (party recruitment, resolution of personal conflicts, promotion matters, etc.). Miller concludes that 'The party is evidently not accorded much of a role compared with other official bodies in research policy-making or implementation, regardless of level', and that 'from a strictly institutional standpoint, party potency does appear to be more of a myth than a reality.'[25]

While the party may have come to realise that the process of scientific discovery was better left without political interference, the introduction (vnedrenie) of new technologies into mass production was an area where party organs were expected to play a more prominent role. In 1983, when he was first secretary of Sverdlovsk obkom, B. El'tsin explained their role in these terms: 'Of course, the conduct of technology policy is the responsibility of the relevant ministry. But the obkom has no right to stand on the side as an observer if it sees errors.'[26]

Innovation proved to be the major stumbling block in Soviet efforts to reap the benefits of the scientific-technological revolution. The incentive structure of Soviet industry was inimical to the rapid assimilation of new products and processes.[27] This situation persisted despite repeated attempts to reorganize R&D and boost bonuses.[28]

One important strategy was to ask local party organs to use their political influence to push managers to accept technical change. This was done through the formation of special local scientific centres or councils, bringing scientists and plant managers together at the behest of local party officials, and encouraging the contractual agreements between institutes and factories to introduce technical change. This pattern of party intervention, according to Fortescue, went back at least to a seminal article by a secretary of Sverdlovsk obkom, published in 1954.[29]

Technical councils sprang up in many large cities in the late 1960s, and research contracts became the dominant pattern of cooperation by the middle 1970s.[30] Novosibirsk claimed that its council, which had been formed in 1969, 'fully overcame departmental barriers, thanks to support and strong supervision by party and soviet organs.'[31] These regional technology councils were most successful in the larger cities, where there was a concentration of research institutes and local factories had more funds for new investments.[32] However, even gorkomy in small towns such as Berdiansk in Ukraine tried to emulate the technique.[33] Even PPOs were exhorted to press for technical change. By 1984 884 of the larger PPOs had formed special technical progress commissions to promote innovation.[34]

A more ambitious approach adopted by some obkomy was to draw up special 'regionally integrated programmes' for technical progress. N. Ermoshenko compared the performance of several regions which had such plans with others that did not.[35] He concluded that regional programmes did accelerate innovation, while conceding that the introduction of such plans could not fully correct the weakness of territorial organs *vis-à-vis* the branch ministries when it came to innovation policy.

While the activities of the regional party officials may have produced some good results in encouraging local firms to innovate when otherwise they might not, the rate of technical progress in Soviet industry was considered unsatisfactory by both Soviet and Western observers. The regional council approach may have worked well in cities with large scientific communities, but it is difficult to see it building up a head of steam elsewhere. A. G. Osipov stressed that the scientific councils were in an awkward position: they were formed on a voluntary, consultative basis, and did not have their own budget or legal status.[36] Osipov argued that the drive to innovate had to come from *within* the factory, and could not simply be imposed or 'propagandized' from outside.

While the party's role in the strategic management of science policy was rather modest, the following section shows that it did periodically intervene in the management of technical change on the factory floor.

Party interventions in routine industrial decision-making

Apart from monitoring the realization of the major plan targets, party organs also exercised a watching brief over the whole range of economic activity in factories in their region.[37] In terms of sheer volume of activity, a large proportion of party efforts went into monitoring those secondary plan indicators which were targetted in special national campaigns. Examples of this will be discussed in the following chapters. Quality control, materials economy, energy conservation and railway wagon repair will be the primary examples. This section surveys detailed party involvement in technical policy, the promotion of efficient work organization, labour policy and enterprise reconstruction.

The first point to underline is the expectation that party officials should monitor *technical policy* in some detail, despite the fact that party organs did not really play any strategic role in technological development. Thus, for example, an article by the first deputy head of the CC CPSU engineering department consisted of nothing more than a detailed study of the advantages of the latest plasma cutting techniques (long ignored by conservative engineering research institutes).[38] Obkom first secretaries, in Moscow for a conference in 1985, were all taken on a tour of a model compressed gas filling station, to impress upon them the scope for fuel conservation which this innovation offered.[39]

Where a specific technological innovation was under way, party officials were expected to step in to ensure its successful implementation. For example, Sverdlovsk oblom and oblispolkom (regional soviet executive) intervened with the relevant ministry to get approval for a new washing machine which a local firm wanted to produce.[40] Rostov obkom set up a special team (*shtab*) to coordinate the work of the sixty-plus organizations involved in producing the new Don-1500 combine harvester.[41] In 1986 Gorbachev related the tale of a Cherkass inventor who had his new machine tool rejected, and was even thrown out of the party for his pains. 'Where was the obkom?', asked Gorbachev.[42]

The party's promotion of *economic efficiency* in general usually took second place to their concern to ensure plan fulfilment. Party organs were expected to prevent 'storming' (burst of frantic work in order to meet output targets on time), and to be on the alert for production inefficiencies. However, one doubts how much credibility can be accorded to many of these reports, or whether these functions were particularly unique to party officials.[43]

Party officials were called upon to oversee the general level of work organization, generally under the rubric of 'socialist competition'. For example, under party supervision the Gor'kii car factory ran a speed-up campaign which cut work norm overfulfilment from 130 to 107 per cent.[44]

Work with the *labour force* was clearly seen as an important party function. Given the general labour shortage, and the absence of well-developed territorial agencies to cope with this problem, party organs were often called upon to help with the recruitment and retention of labour. They were expected to prevent local managers from expanding capacity beyond the limits of the current labour force. For example, the first secretary of Sverdlovsk gorkom noted that a local firm was only able to recruit 250 workers for its new diesel plant when 1,000 were needed. He commented that 'The gorkom and gorispolkom (city executive committee) are responsible for this, as they were not sufficiently alert when discussing the plans to expand production.'[45] If managers broke labour limits which the local soviet had established they were liable to receive a party reprimand.[46]

However, local party organs had few direct controls over the movement of labour, except for the compulsory two-year placement of all college graduates, and a veto over party members who wished to change jobs.[47] What party organs could do was try to improve the local supply of skilled labour, by prevailing upon a local plant to set up a training school.[48]

Party organs often portrayed themselves as defending the interests of the workers in the face of indifference by managers or trade union officials. There was no shortage of examples on this theme, ranging from fixing transport for the night shift in a Briansk engineering works, to sacking the director of a hydro-election station in Chita because of the long queues in the canteen.[49] In 1981 in particular the party press was flooded with examples of party organ showing concern for the workers – surely a response to the challenge posed by the Solidarity movement in Poland.

One theme which was highly visible in the party's industrial policy between 1975 and 1985 was the emphasis on *reconstruction* of existing plant if new products or processes were to be introduced.[50] This was promoted as an alternative to building a new factory, because of the extreme strain under which the construction industry was operating by the end of the 1970s.

Party organs encouraged or even initiated modernization plans for individual plants.[51] It was popular in the 1970s to couch these modernization plans as part of the campaign to 'mechanize manual labour', for this was seen as a way of easing the labour shortage and of advancing the society towards communism by diminishing the number of workers engaged in manual labour.[52]

In this reconstruction campaign it was not always easy to strike a satisfactory balance between the responsibilities of local party officials on one side and managers and ministry planners on the other. The ministry was the dominant player, since it provided the funds in most cases, and drew up the revised plan targets. The main function of party officials was to petition the ministry for assistance.[53]

There was a degree of ambivalence over how much responsibility party organs themselves carried. In an article entitled 'The reconstruction of production is party business' the first secretary of Pervoural'sk obkom had to concede that 'primary responsibility for the success of reconstruction work rests with enterprise managers'.[54] Still, if it went wrong, party officials could expect admonition. A Khar'kov engineering plant partkom was castigated for a botched reconstruction plan which left them with 100 idle machines, many broken beyond repair.[55]

These cases exemplify the tension between the horizontal and vertical chains of command, i.e. the horizontal pressures which party officials exerted over local managers, and the vertical responsibilities of those managers within their own ministerial hierarchy. The next section seeks to explore these tensions.

Party interventions and the economic chain of command

Although regional party officials enjoyed political hegemony over plant managers in their territory, these managers were in charge of economic resources (cash, manpower and materials), and were administratively answerable to their superiors in the relevant ministry. Thus party officials faced two challenges: they had to use their political power to overcome the economic power of local managers, and they had to stand up to the bureaucratic power of the central ministries. These conflicting pressures were particularly important when considering the role of the party as regional coordinator (chapter 4).

When talking of the power of local managers, it is important to bear in mind the argument in chapter 1 that the factory director enjoyed a higher status than his PPO secretary. Soviet industrial management since the late 1920s was conducted on the basis of *edinonachalie*, or 'one-man management'. Neither old participatory institutions, such as trade unions and standing production conferences, nor new measures to promote shopfloor involvement, such as 1983 legislation on the rights of work collectives, had any significant impact on the autonomy of the director.[56] Even experiments with the election of managers, which began in the late 1970s and were consolidated in the June 1987

Law on the State Enterprise, were only partially successful in shifting the balance of power back towards the collective.[57] One could also argue that a director who was elected by the workforce might act with even greater authority in conflicts with party officials. In the end, worries that managers were disobeying ministry directives led to the revocation of the provision for the election of managers in June 1990.[58]

The all-powerful director is a familiar figure from Soviet literature, theatre and cinema. Historically prominent directors such as N. A. Ligachev achieved a popular status comparable to that of the Fords and the Iaccocas in the USA.[59] Directors seemed well aware of their position. The head of the Ramenskoe instrument plant stated that while education matters were left up to the 'social organizations' (i.e. the party, Komsomol and trade unions), on production questions 'I speak as the factory director, the one-man manager.'[60] Press accounts often revolved around the almost miraculous impact of the arrival of a new director.[61] One report which contained a rare reference to the impracticality of a 'one man army' approach (*odin v pole ne voin*) nevertheless finished with a glowing account of how an energetic new director turned around a lagging farm.[62] So common were such accounts that one reader of *Kommunist* was driven to ask 'Why it is that often the work of an enterprise or an organization depends almost entirely on one man – its leader?'[63]

A correct answer to this question would have to include elements of political culture (Russia's deeply ingrained authoritarian heritage) and economics. Economics played a paradoxical role, in that the tendency to focus on strong individual leaders was partly a reaction to the fact that the system dissipated responsibility among multiple officials. Against a background of officials avoiding responsibility, strong managers stood out all the more clearly.

Part of this managerial independence stemmed from the strong autarkic tendencies present in the Soviet economy, with the enterprise being seen as the core of economic life. The dominant philosophy was illustrated by the comment of the first deputy chairman of Gosplan that 'What is good for the plant is good for the state.'[64] The nature of the planning process itself was the major factor contributing to the emergence of autarkic enterprises. Planners found it easier to deal with large units, so they promoted greater vertical and horizontal integration at enterprise level than one sees in other economies. They were aided and abetted in this process by local managers, whose salaries increased with the number of personnel on their payroll.

Moreover, the less the dependence on materials or services from 'alien' (*chuzhoi*) firms, and the greater the pool of resources at their own disposal, the easier it was for local managers to insulate their operations from the devastating generalized shortages which pervaded the Soviet economy.

Any benefits in economies of scale that may have come with these massive enterprises were outweighed by the diseconomies of insufficient specialization, duplication of capacity and so forth. Autarky seemed to be a rational strategy for managers within a planned economy, but it had many negative features if judged against some external measure of social efficiency.[65] For example, to avoid dependency on municipal agencies, most firms, as noted, preferred to maintain their own truck and bus park, even though their capacity utilization and productivity were much lower than in municipal truck pools.[66]

Central policies often reinforced these autarkic tendencies. Throughout the 1970s there was an intensive campaign to mechanize manual labour. The centre put political pressure on each factory to come up with its own equipment and methods, rather than choosing to channel additional resources through specialised ministries. This policy led to what a Sumy obkom secretary described as each plant 'reinventing the wheel'.[67] The dominant mentality seemed to be that a good manager was one who behaved in an autarkic manner. Witness the case of the head of the Ul'ianovsk car factory, subsequently promoted up to be first deputy minister for the automobile industry, whose successes included the setting up of his own housing trust to build apartments for his workers.[68]

Presumably, the more autarkic the factories, the less easy it was for local party officials to exert their authority over factory directors, since the latter would have less need for party assistance in ironing out problems with supplies, excessively taut plans, etc. Moreover, party and soviet officials would have to go cap in hand to their independent local enterprises to solicit funds for regional development.

On the other hand, as was argued in chapter 1, the relationship between party officials and directors was more often symbiotic than conflictual. Having strong, autarkic industrial plants in the region meant a better chance for party officials to insulate themselves against economic failure, and the resources of these 'giants' could be called upon to help their weaker neighbours.[69]

Local party organs and the ministries

The central ministries provided the structural framework of the Soviet economy, and were the primary channels through which economic resources were allocated. Given that they were based in national and republican capitals, regional party leaders found it difficult to exercise political suasion over them, as the ministries typically juggled demands from dozens of regional officials.

The ministries were widely seen as determined pursuers of organizational self-interest, often at the expense of other organizations or local communities. Such behaviour by a ministry or its subordinate administrations (branches) was known as 'departmentalism' (*vedomstvennost*).

The main strategy at the disposal of party officials faced with a recalcitrant bureaucracy was protest and publicity. Presumably obkomy used their contacts within republican and CPSU CCs to put pressure on ministries to bow to their wishes, but such manoeuvrings were not, unfortunately, publicized in the press. There were relatively few published accounts, therefore, of party officials triumphing over departmental inertia. On the other hand, there were plenty of examples where problems were handled by the ministries on their own, without party involvement of any discernible sort, and of cases where party organs intervened but were ineffective.

This chapter will concentrate on routine industrial issues. Many of the most egregious cases of departmentalism riding roughshod over local organs came in the area of regional planning (chapter 4); while many of the more successful examples of party involvement came in areas where the party launched a special, top-priority campaign (see, for example, some of the cases in energy and transport discussed in chapter 6).

To begin with the most obvious point: the primary responsibility for dealing with economic issues rested with the ministries. It could hardly be otherwise: the party could not hope to play an active role in *all* cases where social and economic decisions were being taken. Thus, if there was a shortage of water in Penza, one went to Glavvodokanal; if there was steam heat escaping in Tiumen, to the Ministry for the Gas Industry; or if there was no machinery to de-ice roads in Novosibirsk, to Soiuzkommunmash.[70] (The first and last cases involved trusts operating under the respective ministries.) In all these cases the petitioners had to make contact with organizations located in Moscow.

Press accounts included a large number of examples where party organs were active participants, either taking steps to change the behaviour of economic officials (where local enterprises were involved), or levelling criticism and demands at higher ministerial bodies (in cases that went beyond their immediate jurisdiction). In those reported cases where party organs made representations to ministry officials, party intervention usually failed to achieve any positive results. It could be that this is a result of source bias. Perhaps *Ekonomicheskaia gazeta* preferred to publicize cases where irresponsible bureaucrats blocked honest party workers.[71] On the other hand, the Soviet press under Brezhnev was widely seen as biased towards presenting a favourable image of life in the Soviet system. If there really were cases where local party officials used their influence to alter ministerial policies to the benefit of local firms, one imagines that party officials would have been keen to publicize their triumphs.

Many of the disputes between party and ministry officials were related to enterprise plans. Ministries were frequently admonished for delays in preparing the annual plan, and for changing the plan in the course of the plan period.[72] Usually, however, party officials were expected to speak out against plan reductions (or 'corrections' as they were politely described), with ministries seen in many cases as excessively tolerant towards enterprises who failed to meet their targets.[73] In these cases party officials would be working against the interests of local directors (who presumably were happy to see plan reductions) and against the PPOs, who would often side with their directors.[74]

It is not clear that these party protests had any real impact on ministry behaviour. They may have had some deterrent value as regards future plan delays and errors, but the protests probably came too late to make any difference in the case which sparked the complaint. For example, when Donetsk obkom complained to the ferrous metals ministry about imbalances in the annual plan for a major steelmill located in their region, they had to wait more than two months for a reply.[75]

Ideally, party officials were expected to pressurise ministries to increase plans, but this did not seem to occur too often. Chernenko praised the Vladimir obkom for persuading ministries to raise the industrial growth targets for this agricultural region by 30 per cent.[76] Presumably, this involved additional resources being allocated to the region, so it was more a case of lobbying for one's own region than improving economic efficiency. Party-inspired efforts to raise plan targets without additional resource claims were usually part of a 'counter planning' campaign. Suffice it to note here that party officials often encountered indifference towards such proposals from ministry officials, for whom they meant more work.[77]

A second general type of criticism levelled at ministries was their failure to help local officials improve the performance of ailing enterprises. For example, Irkutsk obkom attacked the Ministry of Non-Ferrous Metals for allowing the Shelekov cable plant to stumble on at 60 per cent plan fulfilment for the previous 12 years.[78] Such cases were very common in the party press.[79]

Third, ministries were frequent targets for accusations of excessive paperwork and petty regulation (*bumagotvorchestvo, kantseliarshchina,* etc). This was a favourite theme for party leaders, from Brezhnev to Gorbachev.[80] B. El'tsin made much of this issue in his rise to power. He told a meeting of ideology workers in Moscow in April 1986 that 'We recently took one ministry in hand. Supplies meant for Moscow – dozens of tonnes of oranges and other food products – were being sent to Norilsk and Novosibirsk.'[81]

Complaints about bureaucratism usually came from local managers rather than party officials, as it was they who were most directly affected. The protests ranged from the serious to the mundane. A Riga perfume plant lost its permission to import vital supplies from abroad after it was put under the new unified agricultural administration (Gosagroprom) in 1986.[82] The director of an Onega tractor plant complained that regulations prevented him from giving free meals to the night shift, or double-glazing the windows if they were above head height.[83] Problems often arose from disputes between ministries themselves, much to the frustration of local managers and party officials.[84] In a 1984 survey of directors asked 'How often in the course of your work do current instructions and decrees conflict with economic common sense?' 57 per cent said 'often' and 14 per cent 'almost always'.[85]

There can be little doubt that the performance of ministries left a great deal to be desired. However, party officials often tried to shift the blame onto ministries when faced with criticism of their own vigilance.[86] These pleas and criticisms shaded over into simple lobbying for more resources for local industry. Here the boot was on the other foot, in that it might be party organs who were falling prey to the sin of 'localism' rather than ministry administrators lapsing into 'departmentalism'. Examples ranged from a Kazakh CC secretary asking the chemical ministry to expand phosphate production in the republic, to the Iakut obkom first secretary calling for a new railway link to Berkatit.[87]

There were some counter examples to be found, where party officials boasted of a good working relationship with higher ministry bodies. Presumably, party leaders wanted to show that they could get results – from potato harvesting equipment for Georgian farmers to lunch pails for Minsk construction workers.[88]

On balance, however, the criticisms seem to outweigh the tales of happy cooperation. The general impression obtained from reading the Soviet press is that the relationship between the vertical chain of economic command and the horizontal network of political direction was very strained. Only where party officials concentrated their efforts in a campaign defined as a high-priority issue by the national leadership did they find the time, energy and political muscle to override ministerial inertia. Examples of such campaigns follow in subsequent chapters. And even in these cases, the impact of party intervention was uneven.

Party supervision via the ministerial partkomy

Given the relative weakness of local party organs *vis-à-vis* the central ministries, an alternative line of attack which drew increasing attention in the late 1970s was to strengthen the role of party organizations within the ministries themselves, which all fell under the jurisdiction of the Moscow gorkom and the departments of the CC CPSU. The general problem with this approach was that ministry party organizations were too closely tied to the ministry that were supposed to be monitoring. Fortescue has shown that ministry partkom secretaries were loathe to criticize their superiors, given that they typically spent their entire career in the same ministry.[89] (A phenomenon familiar to students of organizational behaviour in the West.)

The first sign of this new strategy was a November 1974 CC CPSU decree criticizing the lack of vigilance of the partkom of the Ministry of Communications.[90] The role of ministry party organizations was the subject of a steady flow of critical articles in the press. A piece on the subject in *Partiinaia zhizn* in 1978 criticized party officials in the Ministry of Electrical Equipment for failing to respond to the fact that 80 per cent of the ministry's enterprises had their plans reduced, while a series of heated meetings took place in the partkom of the Ministry of Industrial Construction.[91]

The assault on ministry partkomy was perhaps the most important disciplinary campaign which the CPSU ran during the decade 1976–86.

It represented a determined effort to challenge the power of the ministries, and to compensate for the weakness of regional party organizations before the central authorities. It seems, however, to have failed. In 1983 another CC CPSU resolution on the communications ministry partkom repeated the same criticisms that had been made of the ministry ten years previously, in the decree which opened the campaign.[92] The year 1986 saw a flurry of critical commentary on the supine role of ministry partkomy.[93] A blistering analysis of the poor record of ministry-run research institutes in a Council of Ministers decree of July 1986 kept up the pressure.[94]

Why did the campaign fail to produce an improvement in the situation? Apart from the structural dependency of the partkomy on their ministries, referred to at the beginning of this section, one must bear in mind that 'departmentalism' was an intrinsic feature of the economic structure, rather than something produced by lazy or irresponsible officials. Just as plant managers felt powerless in the face of ministry directives, so too ministry officials often found themselves unable to influence the performance of their many subordinate plants, or were themselves hemmed in by the decisions of other ministries. It was naive to imagine that tightening discipline in ministry partkomy would resolve the problems caused by over-centralization, which were deeply rooted in the entire economic structure.

Party organs and the promotion of economic experiments

Party officials were not merely expected to exercise passive supervision, but also to promote innovatory approaches which would improve productivity and efficiency. Given that the centrally planned economy was built around a set of standard operating procedures, successful adherence to which determined managerial bonuses, there were few incentives for managers and planners to introduce organizational innovations. Managers who did try to introduce new methods faced an uphill struggle getting their initiatives accepted by the relevant ministries.

Nevertheless, as D. Slider has shown, economic experiments of one sort or another were much more common in the Soviet economy than one might imagine.[95] Most of these experiments were started 'from below', by managers seeking to cut costs and improve performance. Some innovations died out after a year or two, but others persisted for decades, sometimes spreading beyond the original plant to others in its region, or its industry. A prime example would be the introduction of work brigades in the construction industry and in the Kaluga turbine plant.[96]

A second group of experiments were encouraged or even planned by the responsible ministry. For example, the 'Shchekino method,' involving a stable wages fund and cuts in the labour force, with savings passed on to the remaining employees, was introduced at the initiative of the chemical industry ministry.[97] A third category of experiments were launched by the top party leadership, keen to try out some new techniques but not sufficiently confident (or able) to introduce the method across the whole economy.

Three general issues will be discussed in this section. First, how important a contribution did experiments make to improving the operation of the Soviet economy? Second, how significant was the role of party organs in the promotion of these experiments – and how important were these experiments to the party? Finally, we will look at the two main centrally initiated experiments that were launched after 1983.

How important were experiments to the economy? It seems clear that experiments were severely constrained by the economic conditions and bureaucratic practices which surrounded them. Thus the local labour exchanges which Slider investigated may have cut down waiting time between jobs, but could not address the structural factors which produced a general labour shortage in the Soviet economy (primarily, the soft budget constraint, which meant managers had no incentive to shed excess labour).[98] As for bureaucratic constraints, local experiments meant extra work for central planners, who had to integrate the experiment into their established procedures. For example, the formalization of the Shchekino method dragged on for years, with no less than seven major changes in the operating methodology. Sometimes, Gosplan simply refused to try to integrate regional experiments into their planning procedures.[99]

Soviet author A. Prigozhin launched a devastating critique of 'the fashion for experiments' in 1984, arguing that such experiments were usually cosmetic, were rarely based on a sound economic and technical analysis, and even where they were sensible were so constrained by the bureaucratic and economic environment that they were unable to have a meaningful impact.[100]

The second subject is the role of local party organs in the promotion of these experiments, and the reciprocal influence of successful experiments on the promotion prospects of party officials. Supporting initiatives, and spreading 'leading experience' (*peredovoi opyt*) to other

Table 2.1. *Economic initiatives approved in CC CPSU resolutions in the late 1970s*

Plant/region	Initiative/Experience[a]
1 Sverdlovsk, Rybinsk	scientific work organization (NOT)
2 Saratov	quality control
3 Shchekino combine	labour productivity in chemical plant
4 Moscow, Ivanovo	labour productivity in textiles
5 West Siberian metals plant and other Kuzabass firms	rapid completion of industrial construction
6 Moscow (Podrezkovsk) experimental wood plant	uncovering internal reserves
7 Leningrad, Donetsk, Novgorod, Vitebsk	prompt completion of construction projects in light and food industries
8 Ust-Kamenogorsk lead/zinc and Bashkir metal plants	efficient use of mined ores
9 Lyublino railway	transport efficiency
10 Moscow Ligachev car works	socialist competition to promote innovation
11 Coal industry brigades	good production performance
12 Agricultural machinery workers	high labour productivity
13 Construction firms and light industry plants	socialist competition for speeding up completion of construction projects
14 Moscow Elektrostal plant	good work in railway machinery
15 Leningrad plants	socialist competition to speed completion of Sayano–Shushensk hydro-electric plant
16 L'vov	integrated quality control system
17 Construction agencies industrial plants	socialist competition to ensure key projects were completed 1978–80
18 Leningrad collectives	cooperation of transport agencies
19 Ipatov (Stavropol region)	harvest work in 1977
20 Moscow	socialist competition for quality and efficiency in light industry
21 Yampol (Vinnitsa region)	reaching 50 centres per hectare in the sugar beet harvest
22 Moscow railways	increasing freight haulage

Notes
[a] The initiatives are variously described as *opyt* (experience), *pochin* or *initsiativa* (both of the latter meaning initiative).
Source: N. A. Petrovichev, *Vazhnyi faktor vozrastaniia rukovodiashchei roli KPSS* (Moscow, Politizdat, 1979), pp. 49–51.

Table 2.2. *Sample of organizational initiatives launched by party organs* (excluding those listed in Table 2.1)

Plant	Initiative	Number of plants copying it (where known)
1 Seversk pipe plant (Sverdlovsk)	'Labour and society: collective guarantees!'	
2 Rostov region	'Work without laggers'	
3 Moscow Ligachev car works	Plan for promoting technical change	(473)
4 Gor'kii region	'Not a single lagger amongst us'	
5 Leningrad region	'High quality work from everybody'	(1,100)
6 Minsk electrical plant	'The worker guarantees a 5 year plan of quality'	(in 15,000 brigades)
7 Minsk region	'Precise rhythm, high rate and excellent quality'	(1,400)
8 Orlov city	continuous building method	
9 Sterezhevo/Tomsk	'Outpost method' of staffing oil rigs	
10 Dnepropetrovsk combine plant	workplace attestations	
11 Poltava region	minimum tillage method	
12 L'vov region	integrated quality control system (KSUK)	
13 Zaporozhe region	mechanise manual labour by year 2000	
14 Rostov region	'Build on time – finish on time'	
15 Leningrad region	'Intensification – 90'	
16 Rybinsk motor plant	increase output with same workforce	
17 Saratov	integrated system of managing construction	

Sources:
1 – K. 14 (1985), 102; 2 – P.Z. 24 (1977), 52–6; 3–7 – P.Z. 8 (1978), 28; 8 – P.Z. 4 (1979), 38; 9 – P.Z. 14 (1980), 42; 10 – K. 1 (1985), 8; 11 – K. 13 (1985), 75; 12 – V.I. 3 (1976), 16–28; 13 – E.G. 5 (1984), 5; 14 – E.G. 25 (1982), 19; 15 – E.G. 49 (1984), 6; 16 – P.Z. 20 (1980), 21; 17 – P.Z. 18 (1981), 15.

K. – *Kommunist*; P.Z. – *Partiinaia zhizn*; E.G. – *Ekonomicheskaia gazeta*; V.I. – *Voprosy istorii KPSS*.

plants was seen as a vitally important function for local party organs. The initiative (*pochin*) had an almost mythical status for Soviet politicians.[101]

The usual pattern was for an initiative to run for a while on a local basis, then begin to receive national publicity as local party officials (and/or plant directors) began to publish articles extolling its virtues. If the initiative gained attention the campaign could snowball, leading to all-union conferences on the method, the arrival of delegations from other regions, and – the ultimate achievement – approval (*odobrenie*) in a CC CPSU resolution. Table 2.1 lists twenty-two initiatives approved by the CC CPSU in the 1970–8 period. About half of these decrees were specifically addressed to local party organizations: in the remainder the addressee was the work collective together with the party organization. Table 2.2 is the author's own sample of some of the most prominent initiatives of the 1975–85 period. How is one to balance the political and economic payoffs from these initiatives? The motives of party officials involved were fairly straightforward. Sponsorship of an initiative could improve the national political visibility of party officials, and hence their promotion prospects and ability to win resources for their region.

The benefits to society from such initiatives, however, were more opaque. In theory, the party saw itself providing the political muscle to persuade conservative economic officials to adopt new techniques. In practice, the economic advantage of the vast majority of these initiatives were unproven. At one extreme there were cases such as the Rostov 'work without laggers' campaign, whose precise administrative and economic content is obscure, no matter how closely one scrutinizes the voluminous materials published extolling its merits.[102] It seemed to amount to little more than political exhortations directed at local managers. The campaign was merely a vehicle for showcasing what party organs were already supposed to be doing. Such criticisms were voiced by the first secretary of Vologda obkom, who charged that the Rostov method was nothing but an excuse for pushing party influence into areas where it did not belong.[103]

Even where initiatives did have some economic substance, it was not always clear that their impact was entirely beneficial. There was a wave of regionally sponsored 'integrated quality control systems' in the late 1970s, most notably the L'vov method, but as will be seen in chapter 3, these did not provide a meaningful solution to the acute quality control problems facing Soviet industry. Similarly, chapter 6 discusses the 'outpost method', which involved running oil and gas exploration with temporary, flown-in workers. Despite heavy promotion by Tomsk obkom officials, its long-term disadvantages seemed to outweigh any short-run gains. Party officials themselves often criticized the penchant for false initiatives, and even Brezhnev himself warned party organs not to 'chase after quantitative measures', such as the number of people involved in the campaign, or the thousands of roubles claimed in savings.[104]

Even with regard to techniques that seemed to make good economic sense, the neutral observer finds doubts forming as to the efficacy of the political dimension. Take, for example, the Poltava minimum tillage technique, vigorously promoted by the Ukrainian CC after 1974.[105] Was it really necessary to have a massive political campaign to tell farmers how to plough? Did this not merely reinforce the stereotype of excessive party interference, which had blighted Soviet agriculture for decades?

The most celebrated agrarian initiative of the 1970s was the Ipatovo harvest team method, which involved concentrating workers and machines into large teams, with shared bonuses for collective results.[106] Ipatovo was part of Stavropol krai, and Gorbachev as kraikom first secretary personally claimed credit for the technique. The attention thus garnered in 1977–8 presumably helped him win appointment as CC CPSU secretary for agriculture in November 1978. The method later ran into criticism, on the grounds that such large teams were unwieldy and irrational.[107] Also, it should be noted that integrated harvest brigades were not a novelty, having previously been tried in many other regions.[108]

Even the most reasonable of initiatives found that political approval was not enough to overcome the environmental constraints rooted in the surrounding command economy. The Shchekino method eventually ran into the sands of bureaucratic inertia – even at the home plant which originated the scheme.[109]

Thus our conclusion would be that the party needed experiments to demonstrate its active role in promoting economic development, mainly because they carried considerable political advantages for both regional and national leaders. The problem was that the party did not necessarily need experiments that worked, or that made economic sense.

In addition to the locally grown initiatives discussed above, one can also distinguish a special category of experiments launched from the CC CPSU. Such initiatives usually made better economic sense, since there was a more systematic effort to relate them to national economic goals. They were often used as a prelude to the introduction of a wholesale economic reform, of greater permanence and scope than a mere experiment. Because of their authoritative backing they usually stood a better chance of overcoming the inertia of ministry officials wedded to their routine procedures – although they too had no guarantee of success.

Centrally sponsored experiments were a way of testing the validity of new ideas before introducing them on a universal basis. Alternatively, they could be tailored to take advantage of the attributes of a given region or sector. The two examples we will discuss nicely illustrate these two rationales. The 'big experiment' launched by Andropov in June 1983 sought to expand enterprise autonomy in five selected ministries.[110] Additional decrees in October 1984 widened the range of ministries involved, and further measures in 1985 and 1986 sought to consolidate some of its aspects in the general enterprise planning procedures.[111] The 'little experiment' began in March 1983 in five carefully selected Leningrad firms, and involved sharply increased bonuses (up to 50 per cent of base salary) for engineers who cut costs or improved productivity.[112] The idea was to reverse the decline in engineers' pay relative to that of manual workers which had taken place since the 1960s.[113]

The 'big experiment' was run by the CC CPSU itself, with strong pressure exerted on republican CCs and obkomy to clear away any bureaucratic hurdles that obstructed the experiment. For example, the Ukrainian CC had to order supply agencies to prioritize deliveries to plants participating in the experiment, since supply bottlenecks were preventing them from expanding production.[114] One can argue that these supply priorities invalidated the whole exercise, since *any* enterprise enjoying such special privileges would perform better than before, no matter what the number of additional rights they had been given.[115] Ministry partkomy were also called upon to promote the scheme, although they were severely criticized for inaction.[116] PPOs were also mobilized behind the experiment, although there were reports that many partkomy allowed themselves to become blasé about participating in yet another experiment.[117]

The 'little experiment' was more modest in scope, being confined to Leningrad. It initially seemed to be working, so the new national enterprise regulations of July 1985 included a provision to boost engineers' pay by 20 per cent as a result of productivity improvements.[118] However, by February 1986 the press was complaining that the 'little experiment' was not being adopted by firms beyond Leningrad.[119] Enterprise

wage departments had no incentive to embark upon the sort of extensive preparatory work which the Leningrad experiment required.

Even with regard to the 'big experiment' there were complaints that
the financial incentives involved were inadequate, and that complicated regulations applied by the Ministry of Finance and Gosbank
were virtually sabotaging the programme.[120] The consensus among
Western observers is that the two experiments failed to break out of
the logic of a centrally planned system and did nothing to halt Soviet
economic decline.[121] These centrally initiated experiments needed
constant political oversight from their sponsors. Once the pressure
eased, the rising tide of bureaucratic inertia, coupled with the inherent
economic pressures of a command economy, dragged them down just
as surely as they engulfed local initiatives.

Summary

The purpose of this chapter was to portray the broad responsibilities carried by local party officials for the performance of local industry. Their duties ranged from monitoring short-run plan fulfilment
through to twenty-year programmes for technological development.

However, there was no clear delineation of responsibility between
party and managerial officials, meaning that ministry planners and
local directors were by no means subservient to the regional 'prefects'.
However, this did not mean that the relationship between party and
economic officials was usually hostile. On the contrary, the two sides
normally sought to cooperate to their mutual advantage. Economic
policy is *not* after all, a zero sum game. The national party leadership
tried to strengthen the influence of the party *vis-à-vis* the branch
ministries by, for example, putting pressure on ministry partkomy to
play a more aggressive role. However, the basic pattern of relations
between the political and economic bureaucracies remained remarkably stable over the decades.

There was clearly tension between the political criteria which motivated party interventions and the economic criteria which shaped the
behaviour of planners and managers. Party organs were keen to
achieve results in terms of high-visibility plan indicators such as gross
output, while managers were more concerned to maximize enterprise
income and security. This often led to forms of managerial behaviour
which the party considered detrimental to the interests of the national
economy. These managerial strategies receive closer attention in the
case studies which follow in chapter 3.

3   Interventions in industry: case studies

This chapter examines three areas of routine industrial activity where party organs showed a high level of involvement – the problem areas of supply procurement, quality control and conservation. Taken together, these three areas accounted for the vast bulk of routine party interventions in industrial decision-making.

All three types of activity were interrelated in that they were all responses to the entrenched tendency of the planned economy to run on the basis of the maximum achievement of quantitative plan targets. The tension which planners imposed on factories meant that the slightest perturbation in performance could cause breakdowns in the chain of supplies, and the pressure to achieve output targets meant that suppliers cut corners on quality and paid scant regard to the question of conservation.

From the 1960s onwards repeated efforts were made to expand the set of plan indicators governing managerial behaviour. These attempts proved unsuccessful, and planning by volume of production remained the standard procedure for Soviet industry. Deteriorating economic performance in the late 1970s left planners with even less room for manoeuvre. Party organs were encouraged to step into these areas of supplies and quality control, to try to break through the bureaucratic inertia of planners and managers. These political interventions into the routine functioning of Soviet industry produced some positive results at the margin, but did nothing to correct the structural flaws of the Soviet economy.

Supply shortages

It was widely recognized that one of the most serious problems facing Soviet managers was the late or inadequate delivery of inputs allocated to them in the annual plan. Plans were deliberately over-optimistic, the intention being to squeeze maximum performance from managers. This left little slack to allow for crises or bottlenecks as they emerged in the course of the year. Persistent, generalized supply shortage was one of the most distinctive features of the command economy, and it defied the various half-hearted attempts planners made over the years to resolve the problem. At root, it is probably an inevitable, structural feature of a centrally planned economy. If planners abandoned the central allocation of supplies (as they did in part after 1988), they would find it more difficult to enforce final output plans, since factories would be trading with each other in transactions beyond the control of central planners.

Given the pervasiveness of the supplies problem it is not surprising that J. Hough found that party organs in the 1960s were deeply involved in trying to resolve the supply crises confronting firms in their region. He argued that there was 'large scale party participation in supplies procurement' in the 1960s, and that this represented one of the most important services the CPSU performed for Soviet industry.[1]

Our study indicates that the importance of party organs in easing supply problems diminished in the 1970s. This does not mean that the problem went away: far from it. But the industrial sector grew in scale and complexity during the Brezhnev years, while ministry officials and plant managers developed strategies which made appeal to party organs less crucial than it had been in the 1950s.

The background to the supplies problem

The institutional structure governing the allocation of supplies had a confused history in the USSR, and was clearly one of the weakest links in the system of economic administration. Narkomsnab (the People's Commissariat for Supplies) was formed out of the trade commissariat in 1930s.[2] In the 1930s the economy was growing rapidly and everything was in short supply, but the range of products was relatively small and Narkomsnab plus party officials somehow managed to steer supplies to what they deemed to be priority projects.

The psychological legacy of this period, as one Soviet author noted, was that 'lack of balance' in the economy came to be seen as 'somewhat unavoidable and even normal'.[3] Planners regarded the supply shortage as a useful weapon for them in their struggle to uncover the 'hidden reserves' which managers concealed from their watchful eyes.

After the war, the people's commissariats were renamed as ministries or state committees, and Narkomsnab became the State Committee on Supplies or Gossnab. The power of the industrial ministries increased, the economy grew more complex, and the role of Gossnab became more uncertain. Gossnab merged with Gosplan in 1953, and the centralized supply organs were dismantled in 1957 as part of Khrushchev's abortive effort to decentralize the economy and replace the central ministries with regional economic councils (sovnarkhozy). In the confusion of the sovnarkhoz period (1957–65), local party organs played a stop-gap role, chasing up inputs for local producers. Hough's model of regional party leaders as supply brokers was primarily based on evidence from the sovnarkhoz period. However, these years were atypical, representing a low point for the state supply administration in its already undistinguished history.

After 1965 considerable efforts were put into rebuilding the Gossnab network. The number of officials staffing the supply system doubled within three years, and territorial supply agencies were established in place of the ministry organs which had dominated the supply network in the pre-sovnarkhoz period.[4] This institutional growth took some of the burden of supply allocation off the shoulders of party officials.

However, Gossnab still remained organizationally weak and fragmented compared to the industrial ministries, and failed to secure control over the flow of supplies.[5] Throughout the 1970s and 1980s supply shortages remained an intrinsic feature of Soviet economic life. A 1975 survey of 1,000 Siberian directors revealed that 44 per cent named supplies as among the chief factors holding back production[6] (27 per cent said planning problems, and 14 per cent labour shortages). Similarly, a 1986 survey of 192 top managers in Cheliabinsk showed that 80 per cent of the specific problems cited related to supply issues.[7] It has been estimated that 30–50 per cent of a typical manager's time was taken up with supply-related issues.[8] The press was replete with problem stories of production held up because of supply delays. Construction materials were a notorious bottleneck, with cement in particular being in permanant shortage.[9] When construction materials did come, they arrived late – 70 per cent of building projects were *planned* to end in the last quarter of the year.[10] Spare parts for vehicles and machinery were another weak spot, coming in at 40–80 per cent of the requested level.[11] These supply shortages interacted to produce a vicious circle, what might be called a deficit multiplier. Plants producing tractor spare parts, or reinforced concrete, would in turn blame their own late deliveries on delays in the arrival of steel supplies.[12] Often the problems arose because of plan failures, where planners did not predict future demand levels, either deliberately or through omission. For example, the toothpaste deficit was due to the fact that there was only one tube producer in the nation, in Gor'kii, and its capacity was only 50 per cent of the level demanded.[13] New plants suffered more than established factories, since they lacked the established network of contacts.[14]

There was a determined effort by ministry and factory officials to gain control over their own supply problems. Ministries and factories indulged in 'self-supply' (samosnabzhenie), diversifying their activities so as to minimize their dependence on external suppliers.[15] Something like 20 per cent of the output of the average industrial ministry did not belong to the product range officially designated as its primary responsibility.[16] A ministry would always give priority in the allocation of its products to its own plants over customers in 'alien' (chuzhoi) ministries.[17]

Managers, like their ministerial superiors, also had a variety of strategies at their disposal to try to protect themselves against supply shortages.

First, they too indulged in self-supply. Factories built up well-staffed repair workshops to turn out deficit parts and equipment; 25 to 38 per cent of all workers in Soviet engineering plants were repair staff (compared to 11 per cent in the USA).[18] An estimated 20 per cent of local industry – set up to produce consumer goods – was devoted to turning out deficit industrial parts and equipment (highly profitable for the enterprise involved).[19] This activity was grossly inefficient from a macro point of view: equipment turned out in a repair shop was five to ten times more costly than the same item from a mass production line. Managers who described such practices in the press defended themselves with the argument that they simply had no alternative.[20]

Second, plant managers tried to pull the wool over the eyes of their ministerial superiors, by proposing slack plans and secretly stockpiling unused inputs and spare parts. The Ekibastuz coal trust, for example, stockpiled three years' worth of spare parts.[21] Such hoarding tied up much needed resources, and was irrational in that one factory may be stockpiling an excess of a product which was desperately needed elsewhere. Also, changes in product types could make these hoards of spares obsolete. Central planning agencies and ministries seem to have given up on this problem: little effort was made to draw up effective stock control methods.[22]

Third, managers resorted to horizontal trading of one sort or another to try to acquire deficit materials. Strictly speaking, any exchange of products should have been accompanied by a work order (nariad) from

Gossnab or one of its subordinate agencies. In practice, this was widely ignored.[23] Factories had expediters (*tolkachi*) on the payroll to 'push through' much needed supplies, using both legal and illegal methods, from persuasion, through barter, to bribery.[24] Sometimes their role was simply to steer the paperwork for officially allocated supplies through the labyrinthine Gossnab bureaucracy. For example, one steel expediter described his *via dolorosa* through eleven agencies.[25] Data on the extent of illegal transactions are of course hard to come by. A Ministry of Finance study of 700 enterprises in 1981 found that half of them broke the rules regarding paying for trips (*komandirovki*) by expediters.[26] Of all supplies obtained by plants under the Ministry of Heavy Transport Machine Building, 15 per cent were reported to be illegally traded.[27]

The ability of *tolkachi* to secure supplies depended on a wide variety of factors. One Soviet economist suggested the following:[28]

> the energy of managers and procurement officials;
> the social importance of the enterprise [i.e. its political influence, although the author is too polite to say this];
> personal contacts;
> geographical proximity to the centre;
> the size of the business trip budget.

In most cases, ministry officials did little to prevent such activities, or actively colluded in them.[29]

Only occasionally did party officials complain about such practices.[30] The first secretary of Chimkent obkom in Kazakhstan explained that 'the main reason' for the region's decline in output was inadequate supplies.[31] Regional party officials who pushed too hard in support of managers protesting supply deficiencies could find themselves accused of 'localism' (i.e. pursuing local interests at the expense of the centre). An example would be the criticisms levelled at Volgograd party officials for supporting the claims of a local refinery that its oil supplies were inadequate.[32]

Party interventions in supply procurement

In theory, the ideal form of party interventions in supply procurement was to ensure that all plans were perfectly balanced, and all production targets fully met, such that supply imbalances never arose. In the real world, party organs found themselves dragged into the resolution of supply problems. Managers facing a shortfall in supplies would petition regional party organs supervising the delinquent supplier, and/or the partkom of the supplier enterprise, to try to persuade them to meet their obligations. It was not that party organs *chose* to act as a supplies expediter: this role was forced on them by agitated plant managers. A Rostov chemical plant director described, for example, how he decided to deluge the Luga gorkom and Leningrad obkom with 200 plus telegrams to try to squeeze the ceramic parts he needed out of a Luga enterprise.[33]

Examples of such appeals are legion. The director of a Kursk electrical plant confessed that 'in the past, the obkom and gorkom received dozens of telegrams a day complaining about our lack of contract discipline'.[34] The bulk of the 7,000 telegrams Novosibirsk obkom received each year were on supply problems.[35] When the Novorossiisk cement plant started missing deliveries, the gorkom and factory together received 250 telegrams.[36] The Irkutsk gorkom sounded a 'social alarm' when deliveries of substandard coal threatened the stability of the region's power supplies.[37]

Party officials at all levels were involved in these struggles. Managers often worked in unison with their own PPO officials – witness the party organization of a Tselinograd machinery works, 'beating out' deficit supplies such as ball bearings on a partkom to partkom basis.[38] The style of intervention by higher party officials ranged from the passive (e.g. the Mari obkom first secretary talked of 'keeping ourselves informed' of the supply status of local plants) to the highly active (e.g. officials of the Uzbek CC directly distributed such deficit materials as bricks, fertilizer and seed).[39]

The party leadership was ambivalent on the advisability of direct involvement in supply issues. Gorbachev himself warned party officials not to take on 'despatcher functions'.[40] On the other hand, party officials often seemed proud of their role in solving supply bottlenecks, and were sometimes held directly accountable by higher party organs for their work in this area. For example, Vinnitsa obkom reorganized a construction trust and set up a special building supplies unit to take the pressure off local managers.[41] One party theoretician argued that party intervention was not podmena if it was limited to sorting out the economic mechanism when it 'jammed' (the examples given were supplies, railways and construction).[42]

How is one to evaluate the impact of party involvement in supplies? Two factors must be mentioned to qualify the success stories reported in the party press.

First, press accounts rarely mentioned the *real* issue which lay behind party interventions in supplies – that of priorities. The purpose of the political intervention was to get the favoured customer put at the top of the list. For every success story, there must have been other customers who got pushed further down the line. Most party interventions did not produce any more goods, they simply reorganized the queue for them. This raises in acute form the problem of *criteria*, which was broached in the introduction. Within the framework of the CPSU's goals for economic development, these supply reallocations may be seen as economically rational. However, party organs juggled a contradictory and shifting list of priorities, and one is wary about talking of a consistent rationality emerging from such party interventions. (And of course there was no guarantee that Soviet managers, or Soviet consumers, shared the priorities of the party leadership.)[43] A nice example of the centrality of the supplies problem and the importance of party priorities was the fact that when economic experiments were introduced, (for example, Andropov's cost accounting experiment in 1983, as described in the preceding chapter), firms which participated were granted supply priority – otherwise, they would have stood little chance of achieving any productivity improvements.

Second, there was no shortage of tales of failure to be found in the press. Party intercessions were often unsuccessful. Petitions from obkomy to central ministries, and even regional Gossnab agencies, were frequently ignored.[44] The first secretary of Krivorozhe gorkom complained that 'party organs often encounter problems which it is not within their powers to solve'.[45] For example, the chaos in supplies at the Mozyr oil refinery construction site, with fifty different organizations vying for scarce resources, was not alleviated by a high level meeting of party and ministerial officials.[46]

Such failures were only to be expected, given that local party organs often had to deal with plants in other regions, and had to compete for resources with other protesting party organizations of equal rank. With so many rival claims being made, it was hardly surprising that party interventions did not always produce the desired results.

Only a radical reform in economic incentives would have led to real progress on the supplies front. The fundamental problem was the lack of respect for contract discipline by supplier enterprises. The value other firms put on products was not reflected in the pricing system, and it was only the plan targets which communicated to managers what was deemed socially necessary. Attempts to build contract-fulfilment targets into the main, bonus-forming plan indicators (as in 1974 and 1977) repeatedly failed.[47] It was so common for enterprises to miss some of their contract deliveries that if financial penalties for missed deliveries had been imposed, the entire managerial class would have been impoverished overnight.[48] Thus the ministries tolerated this state of affairs, allowing plants to count some above-plan deliveries against missed contracts.[49] Gorbachev himself recognized that only a fundamental transformation in the structure of the planning system and the monetary incentives provided to managers could produce genuine improvements in the supply situation.[50]

In principle, party organs could have been mobilized to enforce contract discipline – as in a joint CC CPSU and Council of Ministers decree on the subject in 1983.[51] In reality, there were virtually no examples to be found of party organs enforcing contract discipline. It was something too abstract and complex for party organs to handle, and in any event to pursue this issue would have brought party organs into direct conflict with local managers. Raising a hue and cry about supply shortages was more to their taste. This involved simple, physical quantities rather than monetary abstractions ('Send the bricks!'), and meant party officials could work alongside managers in confronting ministry bureaucrats and managers in other regions.

The party and the struggle to improve product quality

In highlighting the supply problem as deserving their attention, party officials were focussing on a simple and highly visible problem: plants lying idle while waiting for spares, construction projects running over schedule because of cement shortages, and so on. In fact, these phenomena were just the tip of the iceberg, reflecting a deep, structural flaw in the Soviet economy: an inability to respond to consumer interests, as manifested in the chronically low quality of products. This problem proved less amenable to desk-pounding interventions by party functionaries.

The problem of poor product quality was closely related to the persistence of supply shortages. Soviet managers cut corners on quality to meet their output targets, measured in crude volume terms. In the late 1970s, as the economy was slowing down and managers were finding it harder and harder to squeeze out increased production, quality deteriorated even for such basic products as cement, milk and tea.[52] Complaints of poor quality and unusable products (*brak*) extended across the whole range of commodities, being particularly numerous in the agricultural machinery and consumer goods sectors.[53] In addition to sloppy quality control in the factories, many goods were damaged in transit due to inadequacies in the transport sector and the lack of packaging.[54]

In the Soviet economy 'producer sovereignity' ruled, and customers were powerless to arrest these trends. The generalized supply shortage meant that customer enterprises operated under the philosophy of 'take what they give you, and make what you can'.[55] Customers did not complain because they were 'scared of spoiling the relationship' (*isportit otnosheniia*) with their suppliers, which would leave them 'empty handed'.[56]

As with the supply problem, after 1964 there were some determined efforts to develop administrative structures to tackle the quality problem. In 1967 the State Committee on Standards (GOST) introduced the 'quality mark' (*znak kachestvo*).[57] After a promotion campaign under what Kosygin referred to as the 'five year plan of quality' (1976–80), 43 per cent of all the goods being produced were being awarded the quality mark.[58] There was an attempt to build up the network of quality control inspectors inside factories, and to standardise procedures. It was widely recognized, however, that incentives lay at the core of the quality problem: as long as gross output dominated, producers would pay scant regard to quality.[59]

Thus in the abortive 1979 'normed net output' reform there was an attempt to displace gross output from its commanding position in the hierarchy of plan targets. Also in that year new regulations allowed for special price supplements for high quality goods, and sharp cuts in profits for goods failing to rate the quality mark.[60] GOST had the power to fine plants with high rates of *brak*, but these sanctions were not vigorously imposed.[61]

The contribution of party organs to improving product quality

Given the problems planners had in using the plan indicators to promote quality consciousness, there were some efforts to bring the forces of the party to bear on this problem. Unfortunately, quality control was not really amenable to a dramatic, short-run campaign of the sort preferred by the CPSU.

The columns of *Ekonomicheskaia gazeta* which printed replies to criticism from party officials showed that they were often expected to answer for poor quality control in plants under their jurisdiction.[62] However, these press accounts were not terribly convincing. Most party activity seemed to involve writing quality targets into the regular socialist competition drives, such as the Moscow initiative entitled 'The workers guarantee a five year plan of quality' (1971–5), or the nation-wide competition to earn the title 'excellent quality worker'.[63] Monthly 'quality days' were also popular – although one wonders what happened to quality during the other thirty days of the month.[64] More usefully, perhaps, Kremenchug gorkom organized a regular forum where local managers could meet and exchange complaints (*pretenzii*) on quality issues.[65] Even these modest efforts sometimes brought party officials into conflict with managers or ministry officials, who saw their own interests lying elsewhere.[66]

The most prominent aspect of CPSU involvement in product quality was the launching of regional 'Integrated Systems for Quality Management' (KSUK). The best known of these systems was that begun by L'vov obkom in 1971, which received CC CPSU approval in a decree in 1975. The obkom first secretary. V. F. Dobrik, published numerous articles extolling the virtues of his scheme, and *Ekonomicheskaia gazeta* printed a special supplement on the method (a relatively rare privilege).[67] In 1976 Brezhnev personally visited the area to see the scheme in action.[68] However, accounts of the L'vov scheme were rather vague when it came to describing what it actually involved. Regional party organs simply pressed factories to create and expand their quality control departments – to do what, in a modern economy, they should have been doing anyway. Despite the publicity surrounding local party 'initiatives', most of the actual work was done by state personnel. GOST officials helped set up the L'vov scheme, and most of the 'initiators' in the factories turned out to be chief engineers.

Nevertheless, party committees in regions from Latvia to Khabarovsk sent study groups to L'vov and rushed to emulate their example.[69] The initiative continued to spread over the next five years. Some partkomy tried to go one better: Rovno, Minsk, Rostov, Latvia and Gor'kii all developed their own 'improved' versions of the L'vov method.[70] Thus what strikes the outside observer as a fairly jejune administrative improvement took off as a major political campaign.

Beneath the surface, however, all was not well. Apart from the damning evidence of continuing poor quality products flooding the market, a number of reports by quality specialists cast doubt on the utility of these integrated (KSUK) schemes, and each year GOST had to disqualify 60–70 enterprises running their own KSUKs.[71] The quality standards which they used were often 'factory standards', below GOST guidelines.[72] The proliferation of territorial KSUKs led to coordination problems, with supplier plants in one region using different criteria than their customers in a neighbouring province.[73] Also, party initiatives in quality control were typically swamped by their campaigns to promote higher gross output.[74] Even the celebrated L'vov region did not perform that well. Obkom chief Dobrik conceded that only one enterprise in six produced goods receiving the 'quality mark' in 1976.[75]

After 1982, party-run quality campaigns were quietly abandoned, and there was a return to administrative/economic methods. In 1984 a new centralized GOST system was introduced, replacing the KSUKs by then in use in half the nation's enterprises.[76] GOST also stepped up its use of special monitoring for enterprises with poor quality records.[77] New enterprise regulations issued in July 1985 allowed price supplements for high quality goods, but these were not sufficient to outweigh the bonuses tied to output plan performance.[78] A 1986 decree encouraged the formation of 'quality circles' along Japanese lines, but workers jealously guarded their guaranteed wages, and fought off efforts to penalize low-quality work with paycuts.[79]

The central weakness of the old quality control system was that quality inspectors were reluctant to challenge factory management, who decided their salaries and promotion.[80] Hence in 1987 a new independent quality control inspectorate (Gospriemka) was introduced, initially on an experimental basis in forty-two enterprises.[81] Gospriemka was modelled after the system used in defence plants, where military-appointed quality controllers (*voenpredy*) monitored output. At the beginning of 1987 it was introduced nationally in about 15 per cent of all firms.[82] In many plants, such as the massive Kama truck works, workers downed tools, fearing cuts in their bonuses. For example, a Smolensk refrigerator factory found its own 120 quality controllers joined by two externally appointed engineers, who cut the number of refrigerators they allowed to leave the factory from 800 down to 200 per day.[83] Gospriemka proved so disruptive of the established planning procedures that it was quietly abandoned. The demise of Gospriemka provides yet another illustration of the perils of partial reform.

Low quality production seemed endemic to the centrally planned economy, and there was little that sporadic party campaigns could to to alter this state of affairs.

The campaign to promote resource conservation

One of the major deficiencies of Soviet central planning was a careless attitude towards economy in the use of inputs. The domi-

nance of the gross output indicator, when measured by weight, actually encouraged designers to produce tractors, sewing machines or
whatever with as much steel in them as possible. For example, the
Azov steel mill complained that customers would not buy their lighter
'efficiency' steel, because using it would reduce their gross output, still
measured in tonnes.[84] The 'normed net output' reform of 1979 (a
confusing measure which was never fully implemented) did not alter
this state of affairs, since by using value added as the principal bonus-
forming indicator NNO sidestepped the input intensity problem.[85]
However, the new approach did allow planners to make greater use of
norms in drawing up annual plans, fixing targets for each enterprise in
terms of usage of energy or materials per rouble of final product. This
called for additional effort on the part of planners and managers, and
to force through the required change in bureaucratic behaviour the
party unleashed a conservation campaign in 1980 and 1981.

Party campaigns for the conservation of energy and materials dated
back to the 1930s. The idea of thrift in the use of materials had a
ready-made political appeal, particularly where the waste could be
seen and touched – wood rotting in the open air, metal shavings
thrown out rather than reused, etc. However, it took longer to develop
an understanding of the waste hidden in poorly designed products
and inefficient production processes.

Attention towards conservation gathered pace in the 1970s. Between
1971 and 1975 the trade unions ran a series of 'all-union public reviews'
(VOSy), resulting in a total of 25 million 'suggestions' on ways to
improve conservation in individual plants.[86] Also, in the middle of the
decade Cheliabinsk party organizations launched a self-publicity campaign to proclaim the region's role in the struggle for conservation.
There were numerous articles by Cheliabinsk obkom officials in the
national press, and the region's work won recognition in a 1977 CC
CPSU decree.[87] The Cheliabinsk campaign involved such measures as
the creation of 'technical-economic councils' of engineers and economists to advise on conservation methods, and the designation of
People's Controllers in every work brigade to monitor conservation.

Cheliabinsk was not the only regional party organization active on
this front. CC CPSU decrees between 1973 and 1980 approved the
conservation work of obkomy in Khar'kov, Kemerovo and Pavlodar.[88]
Ekonomicheskaia gazeta began running a special section entitled
'Economy and thrift', with forty-nine major articles on the theme being
published in 1980. A 1981 decree ordered party organizations to launch
'a mass movement' for energy and materials conservation.[89] Other CC

CPSU decrees followed, roughly at the rate of one every year (including another on the work of Khar'kov obkom in 1985, this time highly critical).[90]

Party organizations around the country responded with their customary vigour, mobilizing the other public organizations (Komsomol, trade unions, and People's Control) to carry the campaign to the shop floor. The usual channels of party influence were also involved. For example, 50 per cent of the party commissions in Voronezh region were dealing exclusively with conservation issues.[91] Typically, party organs would publicize the thousands of 'suggestions' collected, the number implemented, and the economic 'savings' which resulted (although the basis upon which these savings were calculated was obscure).[92]

The main framework for the 1984 campaign was the target set by Andropov in December 1983 – that each enterprise should increase output by 1 per cent above plan in 1984, and cut costs by 0.5 per cent.[93] The February 1984 CC CPSU plenum decreed that all the savings which resulted were to be transferred straight into the enterprise's social consumption fund.[94] The operating slogan for the 1985 campaign was to work two days a year on saved materials (i.e. a 1 per cent saving), but by then press attention to the issue was dropping off.[95]

Thus conservation loomed very large in the party's public campaigns on industrial management during the decade 1975–85. How successful were these drives, and what problems did they run into? On one side were the statements by party leaders, reporting that 'x million roubles were saved' in a local factory. Such claims cannot be taken seriously, given the chaotic state of Soviet accounting. On the other side, there was a wealth of anecdotal evidence pointing to the very serious managerial and technical problems which the campaign encountered.

Managers had little economic incentive to cut costs, so resisted party attempts to push them down this road. Party and soviet officials frequently complained that managers were witholding data from them on the extent of waste.[96] Ministries too were attached to their standard planning procedures, and were reluctant to complicate their work by adding another set of indicators of resource-use intensity. Energetic party conservation campaigns generally failed to overcome this ministry inertia.

Some ministries (such as auto production) did not set conservation limits at all, and in other cases the norms were very slack.[97] A Vladimir obkom secretary estimated that only 65–80 per cent of his region's enterprises had conservation limits set by their planning ministry.[98]

Gossnab conservation norms were usually stronger than those fixed by industrial ministries, but the penalties for violating them were much lower than those for failing to meet output targets.[99] This is just another example of the familiar story of too many indicators confronting factory managers, leading them to satisfy those targets (usually output and productivity related) which brought the highest rewards.

Another fundamental structural problem lying behind Soviet industry's poor conservation record was the persistent supply shortage. This meant factory managers had to seek substitute products (something designed for another purpose, or products run off in their own workshops) which were usually more input-intensive than their first choice.

Thus economically calculated self-interest remained at the core of the problem. The issue also reflected deeper problems in the Soviet system, to do with a fundamental lack of responsibility and respect for property, which seemed to come with a system where there was blanket state ownership of the means of production. For example, one account entitled 'Who is responsible for this?' focussed symbolically on a Voronezh building site where the lights were left on all day. Bouncing between Gosplan and the Ministry of Construction, the reporter could not find anybody to take the blame.[100]

It was widely recognized that conservation was largely a technological problem. It was the introduction of new products (such as plastics), or new production processes which would be the key to real, long-term improvements in conservation.[101] At the simplest level, there was an acute shortage of technical measuring devices, without which the campaign could hardly proceed in a rational manner.[102] This was a particular problem for the energy economy campaign.

Conservation campaigns were often a blunt instrument that led to technically irrational decisions. For example, measures to economize on gas in the Novolipetsk blast furnace led to greater and more wasteful use of coke and electricity.[103]

The energy conservation campaign 1978–1986

In the 1970s the USSR faced a growing energy crisis. Apart from trying to force through the development of new energy sources (the traditional, extensive, supply-side approach, discussed in chapter 6), a second line of attack was the launch of an energy conservation campaign. This drive coincided with the general materials conservation campaign, and shared many of its problems, such as the struggle to overcome bureaucratic inertia, continued reliance on planning by use of output measures of one sort or another, and shortages of measuring equipment.

The Soviet economy signally failed to show any response to the rise in world energy prices following the 1973 oil crisis. Consider the following table, constructed by E. Hewett, which shows the ratio of energy use (in thousand barrels of oil per day equivalent) to GDP (measured in billions of dollars).[104]

energy/GDP ratio	1970	1980
USSR	12.19	12.99
USA	12.72	9.83
EEC	6.04	5.15

Structural factors complicate direct comparisons between the amounts of energy used in different countries. What is interesting in the table, however, is the time trend: unlike the USA, the USSR showed no sign of shedding its energy-intensive practices during the decade.

Despite the USSR's vast energy reserves, the Soviet leadership realized in 1977 that the nation's energy demand was about to run ahead of supplies, at least in the short run. A belated conservation drive got under way in 1978.[105] The campaign tried to promote the use of more energy-efficient industrial processes by imposing limits on the amount of fuel of various types each factory could use. In addition, from 1979 crisis measures were routinely adopted to minimize the number of power cuts (black-outs or brown-outs, where the current is reduced) during winter months. Party organs were instructed to ensure that central heating systems and power stations were in good repair, to promote recycling of waste energy, and so forth.[106] The winter of 1981 was particularly bad, as were those of 1984–5 and 1985–6.

In 1980 and 1981 there was a further flurry of CC CPSU decrees on the theme.[107] To coordinate the national effort a new Energy Programme was launched in March 1983, on a scale equivalent to the 1982 Food Programme.[108] People's Control organs were active in the autumn of 1984, overseeing preparations for the forthcoming winter.[109] Power cuts nevertheless occurred, and party organizations redoubled their efforts to maintain supplies.[110]

Political pressure increased during 1985 to try to ensure that this dire situation was not repeated the following winter. In March 1985 there was a flood of public responses from senior regional party officials trying to explain their poor performance during the preceding winter.[111] Unusually, these replies included letters not only from obkom secretaries, but also some obkom first secretaries, and even officials from republican Central Committees. Presumably, this radical accountability was an innovation of the new General Secretary, M. Gorbachev. The next winter campaign began with a meeting of obkom secretaries in the CC CPSU, and Politburo urgings to exercise ceaseless vigilance.[112]

What sort of measures did local party organs adopt in the face of these strictures? At factory level, one saw party committees doing everything from selecting the optimum temperature for a furnace to ordering plants to move to night shift working so as to even the load on the power grid.[113] In Murmansk, obkom instructors even took over direct responsibility for allocating petrol supplies.[114]

Geographically isolated areas faced particular problems, since the poorly developed power grid frequently caused local overloads. This occurred in rapidly growing areas such as Tiumen, and in rural backwaters such as outlying farms in Kurgan oblast.[115] Thus, for example, to overcome power shortages in Komsomolsk-on-Amur, kraikom officials launched an all-out campaign to complete the construction of a power line from Khabarovsk.[116]

How successful were these campaigns? The word 'success' is perhaps inappropriate in this context, when one is talking about one of the world's major energy exporters suffering from power shortages. As for the aggregate impact of energy conservation measures, during the 1980s the Soviet energy/GDP ratio continued to deteriorate, rising from 12.99 in 1980 to 13.64 in 1988.[117] The USSR remained two to three times more energy intensive than other industrial countries (a crude measure, admittedly, since it does not allow for differences in economic structure).

Soviet commentators themselves were critical of the way the energy conservation campaign developed, Economist R. Leshchinev pointed out that responsibility had fallen on party organs simply because there were no state officials or bodies who could effectively be held accountable for energy use.[118] And yet, the areas of technical decision-making which could have made a decisive difference to energy use lay way beyond the scope of local party officials. Real gains in energy conservation depended on setting tight energy-use norms when designing new equipment, or locating factories close to their input sources to cut transport costs.

Why was there not a more determined effort to get the ministries themselves to impose stricter energy use targets? The central ministries were fully occupied trying to meet their output plans, and lacked the capacity to handle the quantity and complexity of information which a more differentiated approach to conservation would require. Local managers knew full well that energy norms sent down from their ministry would never be treated as as important as their out targets.[119] Also, there was a bewildering variety of norms established by different ministries. (One factory had twenty-two different energy target indicators).[120] Holding up the whole energy conservation campaign was an acute shortage of measuring devices, particularly for electricity, for which there was a two-year waiting list.[121] Radiator regulating valves, for example, were produced in ten different factories, under nine different ministries. Current production only met half the demand, and 90 per cent of those produced did not work properly.[122]

Given the poor planning of energy norms, and the lack of monitoring equipment, attempts to impose limits met with little success. In 1983 conservation targets were only being met to the tune of 50 per cent.[123] In 1985 there seemed to be a more determined effort to make the limits stick. The Azerbaidjan CC, for example, reprimanded or fined 1,000 managers.[124]

Energy conservation is at root a long-run rather than a short-run proposition. It calls for extensive investments in new types of technology, the conversion of furnaces to run on different fuels, the development of new products, etc. Some of these measures were being taken in the USSR. Hewett suggests that the central planners did fairly well in promoting energy economy in the sphere of electric power generation – this being a large-scale, fairly standardized production technology.[125] Diesel engines are 25 per cent more fuel-efficient than petrol, and the planners managed to increase the proportion of freight carried in diesel trucks from 24 per cent in 1975 to 52 per cent in 1985.[126]

However, effective energy conservation takes careful planning, time and money – none of which are available in a crash campaign. The Soviet leaders were trying to run both a long-term restructuring and a short-term conservation campaign simultaneously, and in practice the politically prominent emergency measures distracted managers and planners from their long run goals.

Summary

Investigation of the party's role in trying to improve conservation practices brings us back to the familiar dilemma facing Soviet leaders. In order to improve any single part of the economy (in this case, conservation), they first had to improve everything else (property rights, incentive structures, supplies, pricing).

Supply shortages, poor quality control and lack of thrift in the use of material inputs represented three key problem areas in Soviet industry. Over the past half century, as the economy expanded and the range of commodities and production processes grew in complexity and technical sophistication, the rough-and-ready supervisory mechanisms put in place by Stalin proved less and less viable. These problems proved remarkably resistant to administrative reform, and were deeply entrenched, structural features of the centrally planned economy.

In the 1970s, as a way out of the administrative impasse, and as an alternative to more radical, market-oriented decentralization, the Soviet leadership mobilized local party organs to press managers to pay attention to these non-out performance indicators. It is difficult to say how successful these party interventions were, since there are no agreed criteria by which their impact could be measured. Overall, however, the supply situation clearly deteriorated in the 1970s and 1980s, and party interventions at best managed to push through supplies for top priority projects, which made the situation even worse in low-priority sectors. And even this limited impact cannot be shown for party involvement in the fields of product quality and materials conservation.

The experience of the last twenty years, as planners and party leaders struggled in vain to devise solutions to these problems, suggests that it is virtually impossible to improve performance in these three problem areas while preserving intact the system of centrally allocated output targets. Only a sweeping, systemic reform of the whole economic system, including more flexible pricing at plant level, and far greater reliance on horizontal, contractual relationships (including *real* penalties for broken contracts) could bring about the required breakthrough. No Soviet leader was prepared to contemplate such a reform.

4   The party as regional coordinator

The idea of the party as regional coordinator was central to J. Hough's model of party officials as regional 'prefects'. This chapter discusses the awkward relationship between the vertical chain of command (the ministries) and the weak horizontal forces which tried to coordinate economic activity on a regional basis.

The opening section looks at the clash between 'branch' and 'territorial' elements in the planning structure, and the attempts – largely unsuccessful – to create special regional coordination agencies. The chapter moves on to examine the impact of the associations reform of 1973, which tried to promote economic coordination by merging enterprises into larger firms, but which had the unfortunate effect of making territorial coordination even more difficult. The final section analyses the role of local soviets, which had primary responsibility for regional issues (housing, environmental protection, labour supply and so forth). Chapter 5 offers two case studies of industries uniquely regional in character – construction and consumer goods production.

J. Hough argued that regional coordination was 'the responsibility by which [local party organs] make their greatest contribution to the functioning of the administrative hierarchy'.[1] While local party officials continued to devote a great deal of time to regional coordination in the 1970s and 1980s, the limitations of their prefectorial role became more and more apparent. Regional coordination was never a major priority for Soviet planners, and relying on local party organs to pick up the pieces meant that this important systemic flaw continued to fester, and repeatedly caused problems of economic coordination.

The prefect model focusses on the fact that local party organs were expected to carry a broad 'watching brief' over all the social, political and economic activities taking place in their region. The prefect role can be interpreted in various ways.

First, obkom secretaries acted as representatives of their region, presenting claims and demands to the central authorities on behalf of their locality. Second, the prefects also served as representatives of the centre in the locality. In the first aspect they primarily advance the interests of the locality: in the second, the interests of the centre. The latter role could be described as that of a 'governor', rather than a 'prefect'.[2]

In principle, the two roles are not contradictory, and in practice they blurred together. A good 'representative' would be cognizant of what the centre expected from his region; a good 'governor' would realize that ignoring local interests would threaten the interests of the centre in the long run. Also, the danger of entropy is high in any governor system, since centrally appointed officials often come to identify with the interests of the region to which they were despatched (a process known in the British Empire as 'going native').

The Soviet system was a mixture of these two tendencies. While party cadres were strongly inculcated with the political values of the centre, there was little cadre mobility between regions, and Moscow preferred to appoint locally based officials even to the most senior posts in a given oblast (see chapter 10). By combining strong socialization with local recruitment, the CPSU hoped for a synthesis of central and local interests.

What then, were the regional duties which local party organizations were expected to fulfil? Their myriad political and ideological duties can be regarded as part of their regional role, since they were directed at the population occupying a given territory. These activities ranged from running agitprop campaigns and overseeing the local press to monitoring conscription of army recruits. An important part of these regional duties was law and order: supervising the work of local legal organs; overseeing the auxiliary police (the 14 million strong *druzhinny*); and even mounting recruiting drives for the regular police.[3] A new campaign on the law and order front, such as Gorbachev's sobriety drive, would throw party officials into a frenzy of activity, closing vodka shops and arranging for distilleries to switch to making confectionery.[4]

Arguably, it was these political activities that were the core of the party organs' regional role, and *not* its tasks in the economic arena. It is relevant to point out that the economic coordinator functions of party prefects assumed that they had successfully mastered the politics and law and order functions. Their ability to act as an economic coordinator stemmed from their position as the unchallenged repository of political authority in the region. If, to offer a hypothetical example, it was known that a local procurator was not cooperating with obkom officials, local managers would be less willing to break laws on the orders of party officials trying to solve some pressing local problem.

Party officials were also expected to react as the responsible regional power if a crisis arose. For example, Rostov obkom instructed lower party organs to inform them 'In cases of interruption of supplies to the population of food and other necessities; or in the work of transport organs; or interruptions in heat, water and energy supplies; or in case of infringements of labour discipline or other negative phenomena.'[5]

Regional party officials were also called upon as 'firemen' to handle emergencies, from a hurricane in Ivanovo to an outbreak of a sugar beet disease in Poltava.[6] It is not clear how effective party officials were as firemen. In the aftermath of the accident at Chernobyl, for example, party officials were not particularly prominent – it was officials from the Ministry of Internal Affairs (the police) and the Council of Ministers that took control, with local party confined to mobilizing Komsomol volunteers to run the evacuation (48 hours later).[7] On a smaller scale, it was the Dnepropetrovsk gorispolkom (city soviet executive) chairman who was hauled from his bed at 1 am to cope with a landslide, and not the party chief.[8]

Branch versus territorial planning

Emergency interventions aside, what sort of coordination did local party organs perform in the Soviet economy? To answer this question it is important to understand that economic administration in the USSR was dominated by vertically structured administrative hierarchies.

There was a clear rift between the sixty-five or so branch ministries which ran the bulk of the USSR's enterprises, and administrative agencies based in a given territory (soviets, regional planning agencies and the local party organs). The fact that industrial management was structured along vertical branch lines, exhibiting all the features of 'departmentalism' described in previous chapters, meant that precious little room was left for territorial administrative agencies. Local organs were at the mercy of industrial enterprises taking orders direct from Moscow or the republican capital.

This rift between vertical and horizontal institutions was one of the most serious structural flaws in the Soviet economic system.[9] Some Soviet writers tried to make the best of the situation, arguing that the USSR had no need for the niceties of 'bourgeois' regional planning, but generally speaking most Soviet leaders and economists expressed great consternation at the imbalance between the branch and territorial organs.[10]

In the Soviet Union regional planning of any sort was virtually ignored in most areas until the early 1970s. It is indicative, for example, that there was no ministry for regional planning or urban affairs. *Kommunist* commented that 'The power of ministries in a region is often stronger than that of the local soviet organs. It is enough to look at how the ministries have practically "torn asunder" entire cities such as Bratsk, Togliatti, Miass, each building "their own" part of town at a respectable distance from "the others".'[11] People's Deputy A. Denisov commented, 'Is all power in this country concentrated in the hands of the party? No, it lies in the sphere of the material producers, who dictate their conditions to the party and the soviets.'[12]

How was it that the vertical agencies came to enjoy such a dominant position over regional organs? It dates back to the deliberate policy of crash industrial growth inaugurated during the first five-year plan. The social infrastructure was starved of resources so as to maximize the rate of investment in heavy industry. Housing, roads, shops and hospitals were only developed to the minimum level necessary to support industrial projects.

Because social infrastructure had such a low priority, there was no need to develop strong administrative agencies to monitor its growth. Such regional agencies, geographically dispersed around the country, would anyway be much more difficult to control than was the case with industrial plants. Industrial location policy too was not attuned to questions of labour availability and regional integration. Industries were located simply on the basis of proximity to natural resources and strategic considerations.[13]

This state of affairs could not last. As the economy grew more complex, the neglect of the social infrastructure proved counterproductive, and regional planning had to be given more attention. E. Ligachev conceded that 'Attempts to solve current production problems by cutting back on social spending were fairly common, and led to a boomerang blow to production itself.'[14]

The sovnarkhoz reform of 1957 represented a radical attempt to shift the economy from vertical to horizontal principles of management, by devolving administration from the central ministries to 105 regional councils.[15] Khrushchev wanted to shift resources into consumer goods and housing, and thought that the ministries would never do this effectively on their own. He also wanted to placate his regional party allies, whose power was considerably enhanced by the reform. Industry had been accustomed to functioning on an integrated, national basis. When the focus shifted to oblast level, they had to turn to local party officials for help with their economic problems. With the central ministries removed, the national party leadership also had to rely more on regional party leaders to ensure that national plan targets were being met.[16]

Over the 1957–62 period, however, the power of regional party officials steadily decreased, as central planning organs reasserted their authority. In 1962 the sovnarkhozy were reorganized and merged, meaning that the new units were larger than a single obkom. They took control over all local industry, which had hitherto been under the control of oblast soviets. Furthermore, a major overhaul of the CPSU in 1962, which divided the party into agricultural and industrial hierarchies, weakened the powers of the 'prefects' by splitting their domains. The role of the CC CPSU apparatus was augmented, since that was the only point where the two chains of command converged.[17] At the same time, the creation of a unified Party–State Control Committee stripped the party of important supervisory responsibilities. J. Azrael argues that the 1962 reforms 'dealt the entire party *apparat* a potentially crippling blow. And the concurrent changes in industrial organization clearly indicated that it was the state bureaucracy which had been singled out as the principal repository of the authority being wrenched from the obkomy.'[18]

Thus, Khrushchev revoked his decentralization reform of 1957 because it ended up giving too much power to the regions, and disrupted the functioning of the economy. The chaos which resulted from these hasty reforms contributed greatly to Khrushchev's ouster in 1964, after which some sort of status quo ante was restored. The sovnarkhozy and the Party–State Control Committee were abolished in 1965, and the agricultural and industrial party organs were reunited.

After 1965 there were no more radical efforts to correct the imbalance between branch and territorial planning. Policy advanced along two fronts: attempts to bolster the role of local soviets, and the creation of special territorial planning agencies to handle particular crises in regional development.

Neither of these solutions was very successful, and party organs continued to find themselves playing the role of regional coordinator of last resort.[19] Brezhnev used the party as a counterbalance to the ministerial bureaucracies, and Gorbachev continued the practice of holding local party organs responsible if things went wrong in their territory.[20]

However, regional coordination through party intervention was not very effective in resolving the branch/regional dichotomy. For example, Gorbachev criticized party organs in Astrakhan for allowing the housing situation to deteriorate to the point where it threatened the gas field's production.[21] In fact, this problem had already been discussed in the Politburo a year before, and was a response to urgent appeals from the area going back at least to 1983.[22]

The first secretary of Turgai obkom noted that 'There are a number of problems which are not within our power to solve.'[23] There were innumerable press reports where party officials criticized ministries for poor regional coordination, and demanded that they rectify the situation, but these stories only occasionally had happy endings. Given that ministry officials were not subordinate to the regional prefects, they were able to ignore their demands with impunity – unless the central party apparatus, or the national press, mobilized on the obkom's behalf.

Apart from the question of the obkom's ability to function as an effective coordinator, one must also ask whether party officials were *really* expected to take on this role. They were clearly called to account if something went badly wrong in their region, such as a breakdown in food supplies or heating, leading to public unrest. But in very few press accounts were party organs held directly responsible for regional imbalances and irrationalities, which were widely recognized to be a structural feature of the administrative system.

Bear in mind also that although party organs were regionally located, they were also locked into the industrial structure through their PPOs, and through direct contacts with factory officials. Obkomy and raikomy were not purely regional entities: they had a foot in both the regional and branch camps. Successful plan fulfilment by local factories was more important to them than a smoothly functioning regional economy.

Efforts to create new territorial coordination agencies

The utilization of specially created territorial planning agencies alongside the branch ministries went back to the very first five-year plan.[24] In the 1930s there were 244 'production complexes' where attempts were made to plan the integrated development of new industrial regions (typically based around mining). From 1971 special 'territorial-production complexes' were set up, many of which were located in natural resource basins along the new Baikal–Amur Railway (BAM).[25]

The TPKs lacked effective managerial power. They merely served to provide a framework for the exchange of information between the agencies developing the complex, and a point of reference for local politicians seeking to improve regional resource allocation. Officials called in vain for TPKs to be granted executive powers over the branch ministries.[26]

Gosplan was used to planning through the branch system, and never regarded territorial planning as a high priority. Its own industrial location plans were not mandatory, and in fact one in three of the new enterprises built in the RSFSR were left out of Gosplan projections because of information-gathering delays.[27] Suggestions by economists to beef up the TPKs, and allocate capital funds through them rather than through the ministries, fell on stony ground.[28] After 1982 there was an attempt to revive Gosplan's regional planning balances, but this meant nothing more than another set of forms for local managers to fill in.[29]

The only region where serious efforts were made to develop an integrated regional plan was the vitally important oil and gas complex of West Siberia, centred on Tiumen. This region alone provided some one-third of total Soviet gas output and one half of oil output (as of 1981), and planners saw it providing the entire increment in fuel production in the 1981–5 period.[30] In 1981 Gosplan set up a special inter-departmental commission to plan Tiumen, and the USSR Council of Ministers established a Commission for the Oil and Gas Industries of Western Siberia.[31] Only in this sort of top priority project, with strong support at the highest political level, were any serious efforts made to modify the branch planning approach.

One technique which attracted considerable academic attention was the drawing up of 'goal related programmes', whereby plan balances were calculated separately for individual projects. Some 170 were prepared for the 1981–5 period, mostly in the mining and consumer goods industries.[32] However, these programmes were largely paper exercises, and it is unclear whether they actually influenced resource allocation in the annual plans.

Other initiatives to improve local coordination included industrial estates (promuzly), of which there were variously reported to be 75 or 500 such estates in the USSR, uniting 6–7,000 enterprises.[33] Unfortunately, Gosplan did not incorporate these estates into its plans, and the State Construction Committee (Gosstroi), which abolished its own promuzel section in 1976, had no power to oblige ministries to use them, nor to contribute to the general costs if they did build there.[34]

A spontaneous development of the late 1960s, originating in Leningrad, was the emergence of local 'directors' councils'.[35] Once a month the directors of leading plants in a given region would gather for an informal meeting, to discuss such matters as housing construction, supply shortages, or the lending of scarce equipment between plants.[36] These clubs represented the branch approach's *own* solution to the problems of territorial coordination. The Elektrosila director made it clear that the original idea for the Leningrad club came from the directors themselves, and not from the party.[37]

The impact of the 1973 associations reform

The grouping of enterprises into 'production' and 'industrial' associations in 1973 was designed to promote greater industrial concentration and specialization, and improve planning by bridging the gulf between factory and ministry. It was hoped that associations would be geared towards strategic and financially oriented decision-making, in place of the production engineer mentality which dominated in individual plants. It represented an attempt to introduce by the back door the sort of cost-consciousness which the 1965 reforms had tried (and failed) to promote through partial marketization.[38]

However, like its predecessors the 1973 reform failed to change the habitual patterns of decision-making within the ministries. Unfortunately, it did have the side effect of weakening still further the already strained forces for regional coordination of industrial policy.

By 1981 roughly half of all Soviet industry (measured by manpower and by share of output) was administered through associations, of which there were 4,150, with an average of four enterprises each.[39] Member enterprises might be scattered over different raiony, oblasti or even republics, making it more difficult for Gosplan to monitor locational policy, and more difficult for local party and soviet officials to keep track of industrial policy.[40] Where the head enterprise of the trust was located within a given oblast, relations could proceed roughly as before. However, disputes arose between regional political organs and the local subsidiaries (*filialy*) of associations based elsewhere.

The merging of plants into associations was pushed through in a hasty and controversial campaign, with little attention to rationalizing the industrial structure.[41] Some directors resented losing their judicial independence, and some ministries objected to 'lose' a plant to another agency.[42] Party officials were reluctant to see local plants turned into subsidiaries, since their output would no longer count towards oblast or republic output figures, and there were complaints that party organs were not consulted before reorganizations were carried out.[43]

The problems multiplied once the associations started to do business. There were many complaints that resources were concentrated in the head enterprise of the association, while the subsidiaries lost much of their pre-association status and resources.[44] The Zakarpatiia obkom first secretary complained that the big L'vov-based associations such as Elektron set up subsidiaries in the Carpathian district with scant regard to environmental protection.[45] Obkom suggestions for house-building and environmental protection were dismissed by the association in a single telegram, as if the plant was an unwanted 'stepson'. A Sverdlovsk raikom secretary complained that their local construction materials plant was put under an association run out of Berezovsk in Tiumen province, 400 km distant, and was starved of supplies.[46] Supply requests from local party officials on behalf of the Tomsk gas trust were met with 'stubborn silence' from its new boss, the Vostok combine.[47] An excavator plant in Ivano-Frankovsk was put under an association based in Kiev (450 km distant), which used it to produce spare parts instead of manufacturing excavators – much needed in the locality.[48]

Apart from subsidiaries being snubbed by associations, there were also complaints in the opposite direction, where local party and soviet organs refused to help with housing and services if they belonged to 'alien' (*chuzhoi*) enterprises (i.e. headquartered in another district).[49]

It is difficult to judge whether the restructuring which followed the associations reform made sense from the point of view of economic efficiency. It may have promoted specialization, but sometimes led to expensive trans-shipments of semi-finished goods. The reform provided an opportunity for departmental interests to consolidate their position at the expense of local authorities, with the existing regional power centres (L'vov and Kiev in the above examples) also strengthening themselves in relation to weaker provinces.[50] In response to these problems, there was a partial dismantling of the association structure in engineering industries in 1985. The 'all-union industrial associations' (VPOs) were broken up, quadrupling the number of smaller 'production associations' (POs).[51] This should have reduced the problems of long-distance coordination, and improved the chances for local influence.

The associations reform posed a challenge for the party itself, as

Dunmore has documented.[52] The associations violated the party's territorial principle, in that it was often impossible to unite the factory PPOs under a single territorial party organ. There was no agreement on to what extent the party structure should be adapted to parallel the association structure. In the end three alternative models were approved: a fully unified PPO for each association; a hybrid model relying on periodic meetings of PPO secretaries to coordinate their work; and a system where each subsidiary plant had its own PPO, possibly under different raikomy or obkomy. Each association's party organization could decide the structure most appropriate to that firm's degree of geographical dispersion and economic autonomy. By 1977, there were 689 unified PPOs, 516 hybrids and 1,800 independent PPOs.[53]

Whatever the structure adopted, the work of party organs was more complicated than before. Initially, the party leadership seemed to favour the unified model. The Gor'kii automobile plant was used by the CC CPSU as the model example of a unified PPO, covering 12,500 communists in six different plants.[54] However, the Gor'kii plants were all located in the same city. It was much harder to make the unified PPO work where subsidiaries were dispersed over a wide geographic area.

The associations reform disrupted the traditional allocation of responsibilities between territorial and industrial agencies within the CPSU. The party organizations of subsidiaries often found their loyalties divided between their factory and geographical superiors. *Kommunist* recognised that 'There are cases where the party organization of the subsidiary stops helping local organs with auxiliary farm work, public welfare, etc.'[55] Some subsidiary PPOs 'completely lost touch' with the local raikom, and the loss of a large and active factory party organization (up to one half of a raikom's total membership, perhaps) could have a serious impact on the raikom's ability to function effectively.[56]

The role of local soviets

In general, local party organs relied on the network of soviets, and their administrative agencies, to monitor the work of local industry and services, and to supervise regional planning. Party 'leadership' (*rukovodstvo*) of the soviets was direct and intimate, and career transfers between soviet and party positions at local level were common. Local party and soviet officials usually operated as parts of a single entity, constituting the 'local powers' (*mestnye vlasti*).[57] Prior to 1990, there were no published cases of soviets clashing with party officials in an attempt to assert their independence, except in corruption cases.

The functions of local soviets fell into two categories: regulatory duties (regional planning, labour planning, environmental protection, law and order, citizen complaints and People's Control); and the provision of a wide range of goods and services (local industry, housing, public catering, consumer services, health, education, construction and transport). In both sets, responsibility was shared with local enterprises in an ill-defined manner, varying considerably from city to city.[58] An idea of the breadth of the soviets' responsibilities can be gleaned from an account of a typical open day complaints session at Zhitomir regional executive (*oblispolkom*), where the following sorts of topics were raised:[59]

waste not being recycled at a local flax plant;
lack of materials to repair private homes;
an unkempt kolkhoz kitchen garden;
poorly stacked village stores;
waiting lists for apartments.

As far as the citizens themselves were concerned, housing issues accounted for the bulk of contacts with soviet organs.[60] Work in housing, agriculture, forestry, land use, and environmental protection reportedly took up the bulk of the time of soviet officials.[61]

Repeated attempts were made to define the soviets' planning role in stronger terms, beginning in 1957 and continuing with decrees in 1971 and 1977.[62] New planning procedures were introduced in 1981 obliging enterprises to submit information to their local soviet regarding land use, labour requirements, consumer goods output and environmental impact.[63] However, as the Politburo noted in 1984: 'The powers of the soviets to secure the integrated socio-economic development of their territory have not been fully utilized.'[64] An *Ekonomicheskaia gazeta* journalist complained that not only were soviets not exercising their powers – they were not even writing to the newspaper to explain what the problem was.[65]

The reason was that the soviets lacked the economic resources and political muscle to substantiate their paper powers. *Kommunist* noted that 'The shortcoming of all these public organs lies in the fact that they do not wield real power, based on financial and material resources.'[66] Politburo member V. Kuznetsov commented that 'soviets often lie under the thumb of economic organs'.[67]

Resources – material, financial and human – were to be found in factories and farms, and local soviets were forced to play the role of 'supplicant' (prositel), trying to wheedle resources out of local enterprises.[68] The L'vov obkom first secretary described having to 'beat out' the funds for an additional 22,000 school places from local plants, complaining that it was irrational, since such resources should be allocated on the basis of demographically defined need, and not be subject to local power struggles.[69] On the other side, directors complained of being deluged with requests and demands for help with all sorts of local projects – hospitals, roads, schools, etc.[70]

Thus, local soviets failed in their role as regional coordinators, despite their impressive formal responsibilities, and party interventions to bolster their role did improve the situation. One may question whether it was wise to leave such an important role up to the local soviets, since they lacked the administrative and other resources to take up their burgeoning functions. Moreover, just as central ministries were guilty of 'departmentalism', so regional organs were accused of the sin of 'localism' – putting the interests of their area ahead of those of other regions. Party officials complained about dependence on suppliers in other regions, and boasted of their efforts to prevent the 'export' of deficit food and consumer goods outside their territory.[71] Administrative coordination across regions and republics was generally very weak. For example, one-third of the agronomist graduates sent from neighbouring oblasti to serve their compulsory two-year assignment in Kherson failed to show up; while there was reported to be massive confusion at the junction between the Southern and South Eastern railroads.[72] The unfortunate sovnarkhoz experience between 1957 and 1965, of course, represented the most powerful example of what would happen to the Soviet economy were 'localist' tendencies to be given a freer rein.

To see how this all worked in practice, the following salient policy areas will be examined: economic planning, housing and social infrastructure, labour planning and environmental protection.

1 Economic planning

Of all their sundry responsibilities, local soviets were perhaps least effective in the sphere of economic planning. Serious attempts at regional planning only began in the mid-1970s – for example, Donetsk oblispolkom began drawing up an oblast plan for the first time in 1972, and struggled to monitor local enterprises under sixty-five different ministries.[73] Enterprises were legally obliged to send information on their next year's plan to the soviet, but Ross found that only 30 per cent did so (largely because they themselves did not possess such information until well into the plan year).[74]

The worst examples of departments overwhelming local attempts to regulate the economy came from peripheral or rapidly developing areas. Chita obkom struggled to supervise sixty-eight separate forestry enterprises under eighteen different departments.[75] Recreational development around Lake Issyk Kul in Kirghizia was out of control, with more than 100 different organizations building health resorts.[76] Major cities could also be plagued by coordination problems. Erevan, for example, had forty different construction agencies, which wilfully ignored the gorkom's planning rules.[77]

Problems in the development of infrastructure were a recurrent theme, from the construction of dams to the coordination of transport networks. Another common complaint was irrational trans-shipment of industrial supplies over vast distances when local resources were available, the problem being that ministries had no incentive to cut costs, and preferred to supply themselves from their own enterprises. Thus steel was sent 4,000 km from a tractor plant in Minsk to a construction plant in Tashkent; and machine tool castings went 7,000 km from Amur to Vitebsk.[78] Ministries often refused to yield control over a local factory, or reneged on promises to build a new port or power station.[79]

There were of course some positive examples on the other side of the coin, where party organs claimed to have conquered bureaucratic intransigence. Voronezh obkom managed to persuade twelve different ministries to provide the town with a new water supply.[80] Party interventions seem to have enjoyed the most success in a few major cities. According to one author, 'Specialists agree that no city apart from Moscow, Leningrad, Sverdlovsk and certain others is carrying out anything like a comprehensive socio-economic development programme.'[81] Leningrad was famous for its integrated transport plan, while Sverdlovsk's regional planning achievements were showcased in national conferences, and it was one of the few to be incorporated into Gosplan projections.[82] Note, however, that Sverdlovsk plans were indicative, not mandatory, with obkom first secretary B. El'tsin complaining that 'By no means are we always able to achieve full cooperation with certain ministries and departments.'[83]

Problems in local coordination were typically described by the participants in terms of a clash between regional and branch interests. Party officials frequently took the opportunity in published articles to petition the central ministries for additional resources and new projects, and it seemed to be an accepted convention that deputies to the Supreme Soviet laced their speeches with demands for more resources for their region.[84]

These examples of regional demands provide reinforcing evidence for the view that local party and soviet organs sought to defend the interests of their region. However, once again local agencies were appearing in a supplicatory role, and there were few visible mechanisms to make the central ministries respond to their demands.

2 Housing and social infrastructure

While industrial location policy remained largely the prerogative of the ministries, the soviets and their party allies made a more determined effort to shape housing and the social infrastructure. After 1957 local soviets had a right to establish themselves as the sole contractor for new housing in their city, but few soviets were in practice able to take advantage of these powers.[85] The average city soviet controlled only 40 per cent of the city's housing. The remainder was run by enterprises, who usually built it themselves, using their own resources. The proportion of housing under soviet control ranged from 87 per cent in Leningrad and 77 per cent in Kiev, down to 16 per cent in Voroshilovgrad.[86] Repeated efforts to raise this percentage were unsuccessful. Directors jealously guarded their housing, as it was a major resource in attracting workers to the plant.[87] Local enterprises themselves faced a struggle to extract funds for housing construction from their ministries, and then had to scramble to acquire the requisite building materials.[88] Even when factories offered to transfer housing to local soviets, many of them were reluctant to take it on, because they lacked the resources to keep it in good repair.[89]

The situation was much the same for all the other elements of the social infrastructure. 'Off budget' funds (i.e. funds coming from the enterprises, not the soviets) accounted for 65–80 per cent of infrastructural projects.[90] For example, within the RSFSR 4,000 enterprises had their own water supply, 1,700 ran their own hotels, and 15 had their own tram services.[91]

The most severe problems occurred in areas experiencing rapid growth, particularly hitherto barren areas of Siberia. They faced the daunting task of building up their infrastructure from scratch, under harsh environmental conditions, and with no established local firms to turn to for material support. Also, in the rush to develop their natural resources industrial projects had priority over housing and other services.

The party was actually rather proud of the role it played in harnessing the wealth of Siberia.[92] H. Chung argues that the 'Siberian lobby' of local politicians and scientists was very effective in 1968–70 and 1977 in persuading the centre to increase the flow of resources to their region.[93]

In fact, the 'propaganda of success' which grew up around these Siberian districts did not reflect the true situation. The cases of Krasnoiarsk and West Siberia will be discussed in the context of energy policy (chapter 6). Suffice it to note here that outlying towns such as Tobol'sk and Norilsk faced insuperable problems in getting the industrial construction trusts to pay some attention to housing and social infrastructure.[94] Similar problems beset Iakutia, to the north-east of Krasnoiarsk; 280 new agencies moved into the area between 1976 and 1980, and 'narrow departmentalism' meant that the housing plans for Neriungri (serving the BAM railroad) were only 50 per cent fulfilled.[95] In the light of these problems, the Siberian regional leaders' plans for massive, integrated development were successfully challenged by central planners advocating a more limited, cost-conscious approach.[96]

Even among the well-established cities, only Leningrad, Moscow and Sverdlovsk drew up social plans analysing infrastructural development on a systematic basis.[97] And even Moscow gorkom found that it received only thirteen replies from the forty-two ministries it wrote to regarding their social plans.[98] The most widely touted example of integrated urban development was the Poti experiment in Georgia. But Poti too had its problems: one account described the town as remaining at the whim of thirteen different ministries, 'each doing what he wants'.[99]

3 Labour planning

Steering the flow of labour was long an important priority for the Soviet leadership, given that the economy suffered from a chronic labour shortage (albeit a shortage induced by the lack of mechanisms for the rational utilization of labour).

Local soviets were encouraged to impose limits on labour hiring if their town was experiencing a deficit of workers.[100] However, as the Chernigov obkom first secretary pointed out, local soviets had no sanctions to restrain firm hirings.[101] There were many clashes over this issue between party organs and local directors. For example, Iaroslavl obkom's attempts to levy fines on individual directors who exceeded their labour limits were simply ignored by the Ministry of Light Industry.[102] The reported successes came where soviets tried to help firms locate labour, rather than merely fixing limits.[103]

4 Environmental protection

Ecological issues had been notoriously neglected since the early decades of Soviet industrialization.[104] Under pressure from Soviet scientists, the issue crept onto the Soviet policy agenda in the late 1960s, and the soviets were the obvious agency to be tasked with monitoring environmental protection. However, Soviet policy makers proved reluctant to invest the political and economic resources necessary to effect a radical turnaround in ministry behaviour. The choice of the soviets as the monitoring agency did not help the programme. Its demise was illustrated by the fact that in 1980 *Ekonomicheskaia gazeta* wound up the special environment section which it had begun in 1976.

The production ministries accorded a low priority to anti-pollution programmes, and there was little attempt to establish common criteria.[105] A 1979 CC CPSU decree on the issue urged party organs to take a more active role, and the press yielded a fair crop of cases where party organs tried to take on ministerial agencies over this issue.[106] In Kemerovo, for example, the gorkom mounted a campaign in 1981 to combat air pollution, and managed to get the chief engineer of a guilty coke plant fired.[107] Despite this, the ministries remained lethargic. The funds allocated for anti-pollution measures in Kemerovo plants were not even fully used, because of the lack of equipment, and where air purification systems had been installed 88 per cent of them were out of order.[108] In 1984 the Politburo itself addressed the Kemerovo problem, instructing five ministries to bring their plants into line.[109] There were countless similar cases of party organs clashing with industrial ministries over the reluctance of factories to limit pollution, from a paper mill in Gor'kii to a steel plant in Volgograd.[110]

A few of these interventions claimed success – for example, the Altai kraikom said that it had halted pollution of the Alei river.[111] But in most cases of reported environmental damage, no mention was made of any action by local party organs, examples ranging from air pollution in Togliatti to the sorry condition of the River Dnestr.[112]

Local organs were too weak, and economic decision-making too centralized, for any real inroads to be made into this problem. It is interesting to note that one author found something to praise from the sovnarkhoz period, reporting that Volgograd plant stopped recycling waste from neighbouring factories in 1965 when it was shifted from local to central control.[113]

Soviet leaders also tried to tackle the problem from the top down, forming a special Commission for Environmental Conservation and the Rational Utilisation of Natural Resources under the Council of Ministers in 1981.[114] However, mounting economic stringency meant that the resources for a full-scale assault on the pollution problem were lacking.

Summary

Local party officials continued to play an important role as regional coordinators in an economic system otherwise dominated by the vertical hierarchies of the industrial ministries. However, regional coordination was clearly one of the weakest links in the Soviet economic system.

Attempts to develop administrative organs responsible for territorial coordination (either special agencies such as the TPKs, or the local soviets) were largely unsuccessful. After 1986, as the economy worsened, ministries responded by setting up even more auxiliary plants under their control to serve their own needs.[115] Over the years, the seemingly endless economic reform debates repeatedly returned to the need for radical measures to reduce the power of the branch ministries, and bolster the regional elements in the planning system, but without result.[116]

The regional role which party organs were performing must be seen as something of a stop-gap measure which few would regard as providing a lasting solution to the problem of weak territorial coordination. In only a few cases were party interventions successful in controlling pollution, in promoting a more balanced development of the social infrastructure, or in easing the strain on the local labour market. Where party officials did get involved in coordination problems, they had their own political agenda to pursue.[117]

Take the case of environmental protection. It was easy for party officials to call upon ministries to clean up polluting factories, since it was simply another case of lobbying the central authorities for more resources. If the ministries had responded with proposals to close down polluting plants, local party leaders would have been forced to go beyond political posturing, and ask serious questions about the trade-offs between economic growth and physical well-being. Under the old system, however, there was simply no mechanism for presenting such choices.

Reliance on political mechanisms of coordination trapped the Soviet planning system into a vicious circle of 'departmentalism' and 'localism', where ministerial arrogance confronted local politicians struggling by hook or by crook to keep their region afloat.

5   Regional coordination: case studies

This chapter presents two case studies of party organs intervening in territorially defined economic activity: the construction industry and consumer goods production, both of which were the subject of high profile party campaigns in the late 1970s.

Construction activity was self-evidently 'regional' in character, in that it had to take place in a particular location. It is not surprising, therefore, to find regional party organs sharing the responsibility for its development. Consumer goods production was not necessarily region-specific, but it developed that way in the USSR, largely because it was placed at the bottom of the central planners' list of priorities. In the past twenty-five years, local party organizations were activated to try to improve consumer goods production in both quantity and quality.

Party organizations saw themselves stepping in where existing state territorial coordination agencies, primarily the soviets, had failed. However, party organizations also proved unable to bring about any lasting improvement in these sectors, which became increasingly serious bottlenecks in the development of the economy. Beneath all the brouhaha surrounding party interventions in construction and consumer goods, the structural factors which held back their development remained intact.

Party coordination of the construction sector

Construction was an important but often-overlooked sector of the Soviet economy. Rapid growth of the sort the Soviet economy experienced made construction more important than in more mature economies. In 1981, there were 11.3 million employees, working in 32,000 different construction organizations – compared to 37 million industrial workers in 44,600 enterprises.[1] Thus some 10 per cent of the total labour force was engaged in construction work (and this did not include the construction materials industries).

Construction is a unique form of economic activity: it takes place in a given location, and is a one-off affair.[2] This was particularly true in the USSR, where repairs and maintenance were usually carried out by agencies other than those who erected the building, meaning that the builders' responsibility ended once the project was handed over.

This specificity in space and time leads to certain unique problems for the construction industry. In both capitalist and socialist economies quality control is difficult in the construction industry, because of its one-off nature. In a capitalist economy, the building sector is extraordinarily vulnerable to the booms and slumps of the business cycle.

The socialist economy did not face a business cycle *per se*, but generated some construction rhythms of its own. Given the nature of the plan cycle, there were many new start-ups at the beginning of a five-year plan. As problems emerged during construction, most sites inevitably ran over their schedule (a problem which also dogs large-scale projects in the West). Because of the peculiar Soviet incentive structure (the generally 'soft' nature of the budget constraint, and a tendency to overlook the value of capital as a factor of production) there were no incentives for planners and managers to finish projects on time.[3] The important thing for them was to win the fight to have their project written into the plan. How rapidly the project was completed and entered into productive use was another matter.

These problems meant that despite the considerable resources devoted to construction in Soviet economic development, it was always seen as a bottleneck sector; whether it was the massive industrial projects of the first five-year-plan, the housing boom of the 1960s, or during the stagnation of the late 1970s. In the latter period planners focused on unfinished projects as the key measure of the unused resources locked up in construction. Unfinished projects as a proportion of total investments rose from 69 to 91 per cent in 1965–79, and in 1979 one construction contract in three was broken.[4] False plan reports (*pripiski*) were widespread in construction, and even projects that were nominally completed on schedule usually required many months or even years of additional work.

The fact that construction occurs in a specific time and place calls for a high degree of local coordination. All the requisite labour and materials must be assembled in a particular location, and the project will only be in operation for a few years. This leaves no opportunity for building to become integrated into local planning procedures over a lengthy period of learning, nor to build up the network of contacts and mutual trading necessary to survive in the command economy. Delays in the arrival of supplies could be more harmful in construction than in industry, since there was less scope for stockpiling, and the opportunities for switching workers to other activities were fewer. On top of all this, there were the uncertainties of the weather.

These factors meant that construction as an economic sector had more characteristics in common with agriculture than with industry. In both agriculture and construction, local party organs felt they had to intervene to compensate for the absence of a well-developed administrative system of the sort that had been established in industry.

The geographically dispersed nature of building activity, combined with the autarkic tendencies of the branch ministries, led to a mushrooming of independent construction agencies. Given the problems that had dogged construction for half a century, ministries preferred to take things into their own hands and operate their own construction agencies. This led to a massive duplication of effort. For example, in Kalinin oblast there were 300 construction agencies at work, under 36 different ministries.[5] In Leningrad both the RSFSR and USSR Ministries of Health had their own construction enterprises.[6] Kazakhstan had 300 separate construction materials plants, under 23 different ministries.[7]

These autarkic tendencies were condoned and even encouraged by the national leadership. For example, special ministries were set up in 1972 and 1979 to oversee construction for the oil and gas industry and in the Far East/Baikal region.[8] The plethora of agencies made it difficult to plan the resources needed for construction activity in a given region, and to coordinate the work on individual projects, which often involved multiple agencies.[9] There were periodic pleas for a single construction ministry to be designated to handle all the work in a given region, but these fell on deaf ears.[10] Even the Central Statistical Administration did not bother to gather much data on construction activity. For example, they collected virtually no data on in-house reconstruction work.[11]

In response to these problems, Soviet leaders made it clear that they expected local party organs to break through the bottlenecks. A particularly vigorous campaign was launched in the years 1976–8.[12] Each year the CC CPSU issued a list of 100–150 key sites (10 per cent of the total number), and regional officials were instructed to concentrate on getting those finished.[13] The obverse of this policy was that party officials were expected to dissuade local managers from starting new projects. The Irkutsk obkom first secretary dutifully castigated the 'silent agreement' between ministries and local managers to start up new sites; but in Volgograd and Donetsk it was the obkom itself which was criticized for encouraging such expansionism.[14]

Concomitant with the stress on preventing project overruns was an emphasis on reconstruction of existing enterprises, thought to be cheaper and easier to control than green field sites. Reconstruction received extensive attention in the late 1970s, being described in 1981 as 'the watchword of the last two five-year plans'.[15] This was one of the policies that was pursued most vigorously by the new Gorbachev leadership. In 1985, new instructions imposed a 10 per cent limit on construction agencies for *new* building activity (meaning that 90 per cent had to be reconstruction).[16]

Considerable pressure was put on party organs to promote these policies. The party press and CC CPSU decrees praised effective policies and criticized delinquents, right up to obkom level.[17] The author's survey of *Ekonomicheskaia gazeta* 1976–86 found a total of 69 signed replies to criticism by party officials on construction problems (out of a total of 438 such replies) (see Appendix 2). It is interesting that in a 1980 article by the head of the Party Control Committee, A. Pel'she, just about all the specific examples of dereliction of duty were drawn from the building sector.[18]

The Soviet press abounded with examples of partkomy playing an active, direct role in construction projects, often forcing local firms to release manpower or materials for a local priority site.[19] Sometimes even republic level party officials were involved: for example, the Ukrainian CC stepped in to ensure that the Khar'kov tractor plant was finished on time.[20] 'Crisis teams' (*avral'nye komandy*, or *shtaby*) of party officials were despatched to sites to ensure that progress was being made.[21] For example, the first secretary of Lipetsk obkom himself led a team overseeing the reconstruction of the Novolipetsk metals plant.[22] Party committees also adjudicated disputes between local firms, and tried to liase with firms and ministry offices elsewhere in the USSR.

These press accounts were typically much more detailed than reports of party work in industry. In construction, party officials talked of 'the operational elimination of problems on site' with scant regard to the strictures against party organs taking on the work of non-party organizations (i.e. podmena).[23] Only very occasionally was the party's role in construction questioned. For example, a journalist reporting on a Chuvash obkom conference asked 'Is it right for party decisions to govern the erection of fences and transportation of sand?'[24] Some accounts recognised that party work did not always have the desired effects.[25]

Moving from on-site supervision to the question of coordination and dispute resolution, one finds a less positive picture. Partkomy disliked being deluged with requests for assistance with supplies.[26] They also found it difficult to liaise with the bewildering variety of construction units in a given region. The six-person Khar'kov obkom construction department had to supervise 240 agencies answering to 35 different ministries.[27] In theory, of course, all construction supplies should have been coordinated by the regional offices of Gossnab – but regulations to that effect issued in 1969 and 1979 were ignored.[28] Sheer distance was often a major problem (geographical and bureaucratic, but especially both together). Problems in the construction of a Samarkand phosphate plant had to be resolved by appeals to Moscow; while Magadan gorkom had to negotiate through the State Construction Committee (Gosstroi) in Moscow to change the specifications of its Leningrad suppliers (all at a distance of 11,000 km).[29] The Lithuanian CC was unable to overcome departmental opposition to its plan to unify the republic's cement factories; and despite 'repeated suggestions' from Vladimir obkom the construction materials ministry refused to rebuild a local plant.[30]

There were of course some coordination successes. The Novgorod obkom managed to arrange for the completion of a new fertiliser plant, and the city of Orel had a well-publicized success in forming a single trust to coordinate all housing construction in the city.[31] Tatar obkom and Naberezhnye Chelny gorkom successfully 'forced through' construction of the giant Kama truck plant, coordinating the work of sixty different building organizations.[32]

Much party activity focussed on the problem of labour shortages, which were endemic in the building sector, trying to reduce labour turnover by improving housing and social facilities.[33] Another favourite strategy was to promote the mechanization of manual labour, and the introduction of progressive work methods such as the brigade system.

One of the most visible patterns of intervention in the labour sphere was the organization of mass recruitment drives, usually via the Komsomol. Apart from their economic utility, these campaigns had important political overtones, the idea being to inculcate feelings of self-sacrifice and patriotism in youth. The first such construction brigades set off for Kazakhstan in 1959, in the wake of the mobilization of agricultural volunteers who had conquered the Virgin Lands five years earlier.[34] In the 1970s roughly 7 per cent of the construction labour force was recruited through these mobilizations.[35] About one quarter of them were deployed within their own oblast, typically on rural projects where regular workers could not be found. Great prominence was given to recruiting for high priority national projects, often in remote locations. In 1982 there were 135 designated all-union sites, including BAM and all 15 atomic reactor complexes. Some 300,000 Komsomol volunteers were sent to the crucial West Siberian front between 1978 and 1982.[36]

Mass recruitment for high-priority construction sites was well-suited to the campaign approach. It was fairly easy to organize: the central staff in Komsomol headquarters in Moscow designated the sites and allocated recruitment quotas to oblast Komsomol committees. No bureaucratic toes were trodden on, and it did not even cost very much money. Above all, it had the simple, direct political appeal of building the country's future.

Despite its political advantages, labour mobilization of this type did have its drawbacks. For one thing, its episodic nature meant that it would only work in construction, and not in other sectors. There was an attempt to launch a Komsomol recruitment (prizyv) for workers in trade and retailing in 1983, but it proved unsuccessful.[37] Even as far as construction was concerned, however, some cast doubt on the economic value of these mobilizations.[38] The sudden temporary influx of young workers often caused housing and supply problems, and the workers frequently lacked the requisite skills. For these reasons some building trusts refused to accept these volunteers. In 1984 the number of designated sites was cut by half, with a view to improving the planning of living conditions and work organization.[39] Also, it was reiterated that the volunteers should enjoy the same rates of pay as regular workers recruited through the Orgnabor network.

Apart from the labour mobilization programme, there are grounds for scepticism about the economic value of other types of party intervention in the construction industry. The heavy emphasis on 'priority projects' may have made sense as part of a national development strategy, but meant sacrificing many small projects which were regarded as necessary by the ministries or local soviets who were undertaking them. What were the criteria lying behind the ranking of projects? Could these criteria be construed as economically rational? The choices were made by the national party leadership and represented neither the logic of the market, nor the logic of the mainstream planned economy itself. The fact that construction remained a bottleneck for so long implies that the prioritization approach was sidestepping the key structural problems. One reason that the approach did not produce the desired results was that there were simply too many priority projects. Resources were distributed too thinly, and people were less and less likely to take the priority projects seriously.

What of the specific campaigns to concentrate on finishing existing projects, and encouraging reconstruction rather than green field sites? At first glance these seem reasonable from the economic point of view. The growing number of unfinished projects certainly needed pruning back. However, according to one source the dramatic 40 per cent drop in incomplete projects that was achieved in 1981–2 was not primarily due to local party interventions. Rather, it reflected the fact that the Construction Bank was finally allowed to get tough as creditor, fining 820 enterprises for allowing project overruns, and persuading others to delete 5,300 new projects from their 1982 plans.[40]

As for reconstruction, it is by no means clear that this political slogan (for such it became) was in the best interests of the construction industry, or the economy in general. Reconstructing an existing plant was often more expensive than building a brand new factory, and lower profit norms made it unattractive for construction organizations.[41] It was also disadvantageous for the host enterprise, since it disrupted current production, and unlike new construction did not bring with it any additional housing funds.[42]

Thus despite all the impressive coordinating activity by party committees in the field of construction, one must conclude that political activism was not an effective substitute for a sound economic mechanism, which would have involved real financial rewards for prompt deliveries of supplies and for timely completion of projects.

The party and the expansion of consumer goods production

Stimulating the production of consumer goods was one of the most important functions of local party and soviet organs in the 1970s and 1980s. This activity was treated as a regional coordination issue by the CPSU. The branch system was dominated by heavy industry and consumer goods industries failed to establish a successful niche within the branch structure. The central planners had to turn to territorial agencies to try to correct the situation.

Another factor contributing to the classification of consumer goods as a regional problem was that while heavy industry's output could be aggregated into abstract national income figures, consumer goods and services faced a reality test: they had to be delivered to specific consumers living in particular locations. As one Soviet commentator put it, 'People live, as it were, "horizontally", not "vertically".'[43]

This relegation of consumer products to regional organs reflected the desire of central planners in the 1930s to steer society's resources into the development of heavy industry. There was no need for a sturdy network of light industry ministries, as no resources were going to be devoted to these products. G. Malenkov perceived that this state of affairs could not last, and in 1953–5 he tried – and failed – to shift industrial structure away from heavy industry towards consumer goods. Nevertheless, over the next three decades the production of consumer goods did gather momentum, but in a very curious manner. The industrial ministries themselves began to produce various types of consumer goods, on an *ad hoc* basis. They did this because they wanted to provide goods for their own workers and officials. Each ministry had its own 'worker supplies department' to coordinate the procurement of food and consumer goods, which were distributed to workers through weekly or monthly orders (*zakazy*) in each factory.[44]

More generally, managers saw this side production as a way to boost the amount of economic activity under their control. In the beginning, it was easy to turn a profit on these items. They were produced with simple techniques, using odd stocks of spare materials and machinery, and could be run off during slack periods of the year when the main product line of the plant was faltering. The sellers' market in consumer goods meant that there was no problem in disposing of the products, and there were no powerful customers (as there sometimes were in heavy industry) to press you for quality improvements.

Thus Soviet consumer goods production developed in a fairly anarchic fashion. By the late 1970s fifty-five different firms were producing washing machines, thirty-six were making refrigerators, twenty-four making electric shavers, and so on;[45] 90 per cent of these consumer items were designed by the producing enterprise, so the number of different models circulating was almost as large as the number of producers.[46] As consumer goods production grew, so too did the share produced by heavy industry plants – 19 per cent in 1986, 28 per cent in 1975 and 50 per cent in 1982.[47] Most of the remainder were produced in enterprises directly run by the light industry ministries, and only about 7 per cent of goods and 12 per cent of services were provided by plants subordinate to local soviets.[48]

As J. Cooper has shown, even defence industry plants were producing consumer goods, since at least 1953.[49] He estimates that 42 per cent of the output of the nine defence ministries went for civilian purposes, with defence plants being the main manufacturers of certain types of consumer durable, producing 47 per cent of all refrigerators, and 100 per cent of all cameras, radios and televisions.

However, this expanding production was insufficient to satisfy Soviet consumers. Between 1968 and 1983 wages rose faster than the supply of consumer goods, and consumers became more selective in what they were willing to buy.[50]

Why was it that Soviet plants ended up producing 'anti-products', that nobody wanted?[51] The problem with relying on heavy industry to produce consumer goods was that little attention was paid to quality. Most of this manufacturing lay outside of Gosplan regulation – only after 1984 were firms required to report all consumer goods production in their plan returns.[52] There was little guidance for directors as to product range or design, and firms lacked the resources or inclination to set up market research divisions of their own. Confused directors deluged the small central consumer demand research institute (VNIIKS) with requests for advice about what to produce.[53] These flaws led for example to an acute shortage of light bulbs, shortly followed by a massive glut.[54] Most heavy industry plants were not equipped to produce a wide range of consumer goods, particularly not the more complex modern items. Only 10 per cent of these plants had a separate shop for consumer goods production, and these were usually deprived of the best workers and materials.[55]

The situation was still more serious with regard to consumer services. There was less incentive and opportunity for heavy industry to provide services, and where they did it was usually on site, exclusively for the use of their own employees. Thus for example as of 1983 twenty-four of the seventy-two RSFSR oblasti lacked a single repair facility for consumer durables.[56]

Local soviets had the daunting task of trying to bring some order to this chaos. They had the right to supervise consumer goods production in all factories in their territory. A CC CPSU decree of March 1981 gave local soviets the formal right to sell locally 50 per cent of all above-plan consumer goods production in their area, in an effort to limit the extent to which factories could ship out consumer goods to other plants under their ministry.[57] Local soviets lacked the resources and political muscle to do an effective job, and it was regional party officials who were called upon to try to improve the situation.

The role of local party organs in expanding the output of consumer goods

The party's policy was to accept that the bulk of consumer goods production would take place inside heavy industry, but to encourage them to expand their output and be more responsive to consumer preferences.

A study of central pronouncements from Brezhnev to Gorbachev reveals the seriousness with which local party organs were charged with improving the supply of consumer goods. In 1985 Gorbachev warned party organs not to try to shift all the blame for sluggish consumer goods production onto the central ministries.[58] There was a steady stream of joint decrees of the CC CPSU and Council of ministers urging the production of consumer goods, calling for factory patronage over local service enterprises, and praising the initiatives of Moscow and Sverdlovsk party organizations to increase consumer goods output.[59] The decree sketching out consumer production 1986–2000 stated that 'Full responsibility for guaranteeing the supply of consumer goods and services is laid on party and soviet organs, primarily by means of maximum use of local resources.'[60] Pressure from the centre intensified in 1983, with a special Politburo commission being set up under Geidar Aliev to coordinate the party's efforts in the consumer goods sector.[61] Particular attention was of course devoted to the sensitive subject of food supplies. E. Ligachev told a meeting of obkom secretaries in July 1985 that 'All party organs are obliged to exercise daily concern over the fullest security of food products for the population.'[62] (This is a topic addressed separately in the chapter on agriculture.)

All this central concern translated into a flurry of activity by local soviet and party organs. Mainly this took the form of stepping up the pressure on local factories to increase their consumer goods output. Many republican and oblast party organs gave enterprises a minimum target of 3 or 4 per cent of total output to be in consumer goods.[63] Heavy industry plants were encouraged to enter into cooperation agreements with local light industry plants.[64] Even such unlikely enterprises as a shipyard were expected to develop consumer goods lines.[65] Regional party organs duly reported impressive rates of growth in locally produced consumer goods.[66]

Party interventions sometimes went into extraordinary detail on the finer points of consumer demand. Party committees discussed such matters as the technological problems of producing stiff shirt collars, the suitability of pre-cooked food for student canteens, and the absence of small-size shoes.[67] The party's main theoretical journal carried a discussion of how to keep bread from going stale, and the problem of mushy macaroni (reason: not enough hard grain).[68]

Indeed, the most detailed accounts of party involvement often related to food issues, although problems such as excessively long queues or erratic bus services were also covered. Food shortages – whether of meat, vegetables or general products – demanded immediate attention.[69] The Georgian CC itself oversaw the introduction of rationing of meat, butter and sugar in 1981.[70]

After food, clothing was the next priority item. For years the authorities strove to improve quality in the textile industry. In 1977, for example, yet another experiment in 'direct links' between shops and mills got under way, under the supervision of the CC CPSU light industry department.[71] However, as the partkom secretary of the giant Moscow GUM store noted, there was little the partkom could do to influence the behaviour of distant suppliers.[72] Similarly, the Bauman raikom in Moscow reported that the local women's clothing store was criticized at every meeting for two years, without result.[73]

On the other hand there was also a steady stream of reports of successful party interventions. The biggest success story, and one which helped project its obkom first secretary into the Politburo, was Boris El'tsin's Sverdlovsk. In a series of articles in the national press El'tsin and other local officials described how 230 party commissions boosted the number of consumer goods producers from 295 to 484 between 1980 and 1982, and persuaded local directors to set up 300 service centres throughout the region using locally gathered resources.[74] In recognition of Sverdlovsk's pioneering role, a conference sponsored by *Ekonomicheskaia gazeta* on the economic role of local soviets was held there in 1980, as was a CC CPSU seminar on consumer goods production in 1982.[75]

However, it would be a mistake to give the impression that all was well with these campaigns. The idea of trying to boost the consumer goods output of heavy industry plants was the easy way out for central planners. They could hope for an immediate rise in production without having to push through any contentious shifts in investment allocation. Also, the raw figures seemed to show plenty of room for expansion: some 20–50 per cent of heavy industry plants still did not produce any consumer items at all, and this activity amounted to only 1–3 per cent of the remaining plants' output.[76] Thus it looked as if an increase in consumer goods production could be achieved rapidly and at little cost.

In practice, however, this approach reinforced the disadvantages inherent in the system of relying upon heavy industry to produce consumer items. Given the power differential between the branch factories and local organs, interventions by local politicians were not strong enough to force significant improvements in the range and quality of consumer goods. For example, the Magadan gold trust cut the output of consumer items, in violation of obkom and oblispolkom decrees, leading to local shortages of brooms, axes, barrels, etc.[77] And it was too easy, complained the first secretary of Mari obkom, for local directors to fulfil their obligations by churning out the easiest produced consumer items, even though there was no demand for them.[78]

Party penetration of local industry workshops, retail stores and service outlets was much weaker than in industry – two to three times less, as a proportion of the workforce.[79] Raikomy found it difficult to coordinate the work of the numerous small PPOs in this sector.[80] In 1979 there were 470,000 communists in the 695,000 retail and service stores: an average of less than one communist per outlet.[81] Thus party organs could not mobilize the mass membership and PPOs to carry forward their campaign to improve quality and service, and had to rely on PPOs in local factories or research institutes to exercise patronage (sheftsvo) over local retailers.

In fact, the consumer and retail sector played a very small role in intra-party life. With a few exceptions (notably Sverdlovsk), party officials did not make a great fanfare of their work in this sector. The author's study of the contents of Ekonomicheskaia gazeta 1976–85 found only 4 out of 98 regional party conferences were devoted to consumer goods, and a mere 24 out of 757 major articles authored by party officials had this as their principal theme (see Appendix 2).

The difficulties experienced by party officials monitoring consumer goods were not purely local in nature. Their problems multiplied when they had to tackle the central bureaucracies. Speakers at a Cherkass obkom plenum complained that it could take years to get approval from the relevant central authorities to start up a new line of consumer goods production.[82] Even such a powerful party organization as Sverdlovsk had problems getting approval from the relevant ministry for a new model of washing machine.[83]

Production of some consumer items fell between the stools of different ministries, and party officials were unable to find someone to shoulder the responsibility. For example, a national shortage of baby food was blamed on the lack of coordination between the Ministries of Procurements (who checked the milk quality), Non-Ferrous Metals (who made the tins), Meat and Dairy Industry, Machinery for Light and Food Industry and the Fish Industry.[84] The dearth of ball pens in Alma Ata was taken to Glavkul'tbyttorg, part of the All-Union Ministry of Foreign Trade in Moscow, who in turn blamed the local industry ministries (responsible for pencil production) and the Ministry of Instruments, Automation Equipment and Control Systems (who made pens), and praised the Moldavian Republic's Ministry of Social Security, who were the first to manufacture propelling pencils.[85]

Thus party officials had a daunting task in overcoming the entrenched bureaucratism in this sector – yet the chosen approach of using local pressure to squeeze more consumer goods out of local factories merely reinforced these tendencies.

This all looks rather dubious from the point of view of economic rationality. Recall that 'self-supply' by factories was considerably more expensive than regular mass production by specialized enterprises: this was also true for consumer items. There were some halting efforts to improve the financial incentives for plants to produce better quality consumer items. However, here as elsewhere in the Soviet economy there was the familiar pattern of a partial reform being dragged down by the habitual practices of the untouched elements of the economic bureaucracy. An experiment to increase the autonomy of service enterprises in eight regions, launched in 1983, found that these shops were still dependent upon voluntary assistance from local factories, with the Poltava obkom having to step in, for example, to help wheedle spare parts from local bosses.[86]

Summary

Construction and consumer goods were weak spots in the Soviet economy in the 1970s and 1980s, and the national leadership tried to activate local party organs to secure some improvement in the performance of these sectors.

The construction industry, given its particular rootedness in space and time, saw considerable confusion and inefficiency as it developed under the conflicting pressures of rival branch ministries. Party officials were routinely mobilized to ensure the completion of key sites, and to put pressure on managers to cut the number of new projects, preferring to see existing sites completed and existing factories reconstructed. Construction supervision was undoubtedly a major part of the party's economic duties in recent decades. An additional task, shared with the Komsomol, was the recruitment for temporary construction work of large numbers of young people.

It is difficult to evaluate the overall impact of these party efforts. Departmental confusion remained a major bar to improved efficiency. Some economists have even challenged the wisdom of the party's emphasis on reconstruction work.

The Soviet consumer goods sector was trying to make up for several decades of neglect, and was under strong pressure from party officials both local and national to improve its performance. A market-based solution would have been to allow prices to reflect consumer demand, probably leading to a large shift in social resource allocation away from many existing heavy industry plants. Prior to 1986 the CPSU shied away from such an approach, and worked within the existing economic structure, whereby a large proportion of consumer goods production took place in heavy industry plants. Rather than channel resources into new consumer goods plants, the national leadership chose instead to use local party organs to put pressure on directors to increase the volume and range of consumer goods, and improve their quality. This approach failed to raise consumer goods production from its subordinate position in the economic structure, and was a manifest failure.

Perhaps more than any of the other sectors examined, construction and consumer goods show the limits to relying on party interventions to compensate for deficiencies in the planned economy.

6   The party as fireman: party interventions in the transport and energy sectors

Transport and energy both represented important building blocks of the Soviet economy. They loomed large in the economic work of local party organs over the last ten years of the Brezhnev era, for two main reasons. First, both ran into severe (and largely unexpected) problems, such that they became bottlenecks holding back the overall development of the economy. One can argue that it was problems in these two sectors which largely caused the levelling off in economic growth which occurred after 1978.[1]

Second, both transport and energy were difficult to plan and administer from a single centre. They involved activities scattered over huge distances, and called for a high level of organizational coordination, both spatial and temporal. Both sectors developed problems by the late 1970s – an overload of the transport infrastructure, and unexpected difficulties in expanding oil production in West Siberia.

In response to these problems, the Soviet leadership adopted a two-pronged approach, throwing massive amounts of additional investments into these sectors and mobilizing party organizations for a classic 'fireman' type campaign.

Transport and energy are obviously very complex subjects in their own right: this short chapter can only scratch the surface of their problems. In the transport sector, the chapter will concentrate on the two most prominent party campaigns of the period: the drive to improve the performance of the railways, mainly by mobilizing industrial plants to build railway wagons; and the campaign to build the Baikal–Amur Mainline railway (BAM), opening up new areas of eastern Siberia. On the energy front, attention will focus on the massive effort to open up the gas reserves of Tiumen province, followed by a sampling of the other key energy generation projects of the decade (atomic power, coal and a hydro-electric station).

Transport

The party campaign on the railways, 1978–1985

For many decades the Soviet transport network was starved of new investments while industry boomed. Sooner or later the old infrastructure had to run up against the physical limits of its existing capacity. This seems to have happened in the late 1970s.

These problems struck both the road and rail networks. Road freight reportedly increased forty-four times between 1950 and 1980, while the network of paved roads only increased threefold.[2] It is six to ten times more costly in fuel and repairs to run trucks over dirt rather than paved roads, and such additional expenses pushed up the cost of food by 40 per cent.[3] An estimated 30 per cent of the harvest was lost on these perilous journeys.[4]

Still, it was the railway sector that was in danger of imminent breakdown in the late 1970s. Rail traffic rose 460 per cent during 1950–87, while capacity only rose by 100 per cent.[5] Something like saturation point was reached, with trains on the main Moscow–Leningrad line passing every six minutes.[6] Ambler *et al.* report that while freight traffic grew at 7.5 per cent per year in 1950–75, between 1975 and 1982 it only managed to creep up at 1 per cent per year.[7]

Sheer track capacity was by no means the sole issue. The stock of wagons was also inadequate. It was openly recognized that the rail sector had been starved of investment over a lengthy period. For example, a new wagon plant set in Abakan in 1970 lacked investment and was dogged by problems for the entire decade.[8] Coordination between the twenty-six railway networks was poor, particularly when it came to wagon repair. Within the Soviet railway system, it was unclear who owned what and who was responsible for repairs, meaning that defective cars were simply shuffled around from one region to another. This lack of control meant that wagons were often tied up in loading and unloading operations for long periods.[9] Poor coordination, and the reliance of 'tonne-kilometres' as the plan measure according to which railway performance was judged, meant that irrational cross-hauling over vast distances was common.[10]

The railway overload interacted with other crisis elements in the Soviet economy in the late 1970s. Exceptionally bad weather (e.g. the winter of 1978–9) made things worse, while the post-1973 energy crisis led to fuel-saving measures such as speed limits on trains, which disrupted schedules and worsened the track overload.[11] Poor harvests and consequent grain imports meant additional demands for wagons and an overload of handling capacity.[12]

The party raised a full-scale alarm in response to this crisis. The first public sign of trouble was a meeting of party and ministry officials, held in the CC CPSU on 24 March 1979, which called for urgent measures to improve the repair and turnaround of wagons.[13] Brezhnev opened his speech to the November 1979 CC plenum with a discussion of the situation on the railways, which he described as 'an acute problem'.[14] In fact, the only attention which party organs had devoted to transport over the preceding decade was the BAM project in Siberia (discussed below). A string of CC CPSU decrees followed: in March 1980, and in June and September of 1981.[15]

1982 turned out to be the worst year since 1979, and incoming General Secretary Y. Andropov took the railways as one of the testing grounds for his new tough approach. Within five days of Andropov's maiden speech to the November 1982 CC CPSU plenum, Moscow gorkom had convened a meeting to discuss ways to improve railway performance.[16]

What, then, were the ways in which party organs responded to these calls for help in 1979 and 1982? The party's task was complicated by the fact that the twenty-six railway networks were strung out over considerable distances, each covering the territory of half-a-dozen obkomy. Of the 444,000 party members in railway enterprises, roughly one-third were organized in 148 special uzkomy, following segments of the track.[17] The uzkomy had been set up in 1967 with the aim of improving party supervision of the railways. Despite the uzkomy the organizational map of party supervision was a morass of overlapping jurisdictions. For example, seventeen different party organs were involved in the transport 'conveyor' in the Magadan region alone.[18] As a result, party efforts were largely restricted to problems which could be tackled within the confines of a given region. The two leading examples of successful party work were Cheliabinsk's wagon repair campaign and Leningrad's integrated transport plan. Note that once again it was the large industrial centres, with plenty of resources at their disposal, who were leading the field. (Rather ironically, these were also probably the regions with the best efficiency record in the first place.)

The Cheliabinsk approach relied on the ability of regional party organs to persuade local enterprises to improve the turnaround on wagons, and to repair wagons themselves. The Cheliabinsk initiative began in 1974, and their work was approved in a CC CPSU decree in

1978.[19] By 1983 some 150 Cheliabinsk enterprises were involved in (unpaid) wagon repair work for the railways.[20]

The Leningrad approach involved improved transport planning by a joint obkom/oblispolkom commission, aided by a council of PPO secretaries from transport units.[21] The Leningrad method was credited with increasing the average wagon load by 40 per cent. Leningrad's integrated planning approach (unlike that of Cheliabinsk) quickly attracted emulators from places as distant as Omsk and Vladivostok.[22] By 1983 thirty-seven regions were using the Leningrad system.[23] Some idea of the primitive state of Soviet transport planning can be gleaned from the following example. In the port of Odessa no arrangements would be made over to how to handle consignments such as large diameter pipe until after they arrived on the dockside.[24]

The Cheliabinsk approach was probably less popular because it involved imposing significant uncompensated burdens on local factories. Nevertheless, under Andropov the CC CPSU threw its weight behind the Cheliabinsk method. By February 1983 60 per cent of railway customer enterprises had been persuaded to sign contracts to repair wagons, the total number of firms involved reaching 4,000.[25] The party press criticized several obkomy, particularly in Kazakhstan, for sloth in promoting wagon repairing.[26] The Ministry of Railways partkom also came under attack.[27] People's Control organs were unleashed on the railways, reprimanding and fining managers in the hundreds, and even sending some for criminal prosecution.[28] Andropov was clearly using the railways issue to demonstrate the viability of his new tough approach to the looming crisis facing the Soviet economy.

Partkomy responded with apparently impressive claims of energy and success. Moscow gorkom claimed to get 140,000 wagons repaired by 1984, while Murmansk obkom took over direct responsibility for cargo routing.[29]

A secretary of Adzhar obkom pointed out that after decades of underinvestment the Trans-Caucasus railway was incapable of improving its performance in the manner prescribed.[30] This should serve as a reminder that despite the apparent short-run success of the Andropov campaign, the problems could have been avoided by more careful forward planning of the transport sector. The Cheliabinsk method of wagon repair was irrational in its use of resources, since it is unlikely that 4,000 enterprises of diverse configurations could repair wagons as efficiently as the special Abakan wagon plant which, as mentioned above, had been starved of investment for years. Similarly, even in the middle of these campaigns the Kremenchug wagon-building plant was still reporting that production was held up by a shortage of steel.[31]

Trying to solve deep-rooted economic problems by means of short-run political campaigns could produce results, but the costs in terms of disruption of enterprises' regular production activities must have been considerable. Moreover, the approach exemplified by the Cheliabinsk method involved promoting the sort of self-sufficient behavior by enterprises which caused a misallocation of resources and contributed to the general supply shortage, low product quality of goods, and other ills of the Soviet economy. Of course, if the local party organs had not been there to straighten out the transport crisis of 1979–83, the economy would perhaps have been in even worse shape.

The Baikal–Amur Mainline Railway

Construction of BAM began in 1974, and it became a symbol of the Soviet leadership's intention to harness the vast resources of Siberia. BAM is a 4,200 km long railway running parallel to the Trans-Siberian railway. It heads north of Lake Baikal and through Komsomolsk-on-Amur, linking up with the port of Sovetskaia Gavan. Apart from the fact that BAM opens up new deposits of natural resources, it also shortens the rail route to the sea by 4,000 km, and is located well back from the strategically sensitive border with China.

The whole project was closely monitored by the CC CPSU, receiving commendations from them on ten separate occasions.[32] The project received extensive publicity, with 'BAM: the construction site of the century' being proclaimed from posters around the country. Much publicity was generated around the Komsomol volunteers, who made up 20 per cent of the 100,000 labour force.[33]

However, unlike previous major construction projects in Siberia (such as the Bratsk or Angara hydro-electric power stations), a single construction chief was not appointed. Instead, the sixteen industrial ministries involved, and the dozens of construction agencies beneath them, were left to their own devices. The official coordinating agency, the BAM Territorial-Production Complex, had virtually no operational/executive functions. In an attempt to coordinate the management of the BAM sites, a special Ministry of Far East Construction was created in 1981.[34] Gosplan and the various ministries were most frequently blamed for these problems, but local party officials from regions elsewhere in the country who sponsored various segments of the line were also criticized for poor organization.[35] The party itself was poorly coordinated. There were no raikomy along the line, so obkomy and gorkomy had to directly monitor the work of the various projects.[36]

From the beginning, local party officials and the construction agencies focused on track laying as the main measure of success, at the expense of infrastructural development. It was easier to measure the kilometres of track laid than try to calculate the amount of work done in providing the housing, roads, electricity and water supplies that railway workers would need to operate the line. The result was that tracklaying targets were 24 per cent over-fulfilled by mid-1977, but the building teams had to use expensive portable generators because they had run ahead of the crews laying the electricity mains.[37] Of the ancillary projects (the construction of stations, villages, etc.), 60 per cent were behind schedule by 1980, and 50 per cent of managers had to be replaced because of unsatisfactory work.[38] The failure to build plants that could use local phosphorous and metals resources meant that materials had to be imported over considerable distances, with transport costs amounting to 50 per cent of their total value.[39]

The problems of Tynda, the main city along the BAM line, typified the lack of an integrated approach. It did not have a formal city plan, and in consequence, 20 per cent of the 22,000 workers lived in temporary barracks, and the city had no less than 80 separately run heating stations.[40] The main construction trust (Glavbamstroi) did not set aside any funds for permanent housing, and there were 'sharp arguments' over who was to build and pay for it.[41] The housing shortage in turn caused a problem of high labour turnover.[42]

In 1983 a Buriat obkom secretary presciently warned that even though track laying was on schedule, this only represented 40 per cent of the construction work required, and he worried that funds might dry up once the most prestigious goal had been realized.[43] Despite such concerns, in 1984 a socialist competition campaign was launched to open the line one year ahead of schedule, in time for the 67th anniversary of the October Revolution.[44] Regular press reports began to appear on the progress of this special campaign. Although the Politburo did discuss the problem of delays in auxiliary projects, the bulk of their exhortations focused on the completion of the track itself (and the bridges, tunnels, etc. that made it such a daunting task).[45]

The last link in the track was completed in Kuand, Chita oblast, in October 1984, and a celebratory meeting was held in Tynda four weeks later, with CC CPSU secretarty V. I. Dolgykh in attendance.[46] In fact, 40 per cent of the work necessary to make the railway fully operational had yet to be completed, and many of these projects were abandoned by 1987.[47] By the 1980s the economic and political rationale for the project had evaporated. Military rivalry with China had receded and the hoped-for blossoming of trade with Japan failed to materialize, while more pressing problems of economic survival had come to the fore.

Thus the BAM project exemplified the strengths and weaknesses of the campaign approach. Results were achieved: the railway was built, in a short time, in the face of tremendous natural adversity. But transient political priorities, and the desire for quick success with highly visible targets, came at the expense of sound and balanced economic development.

Energy

Just as the nation's transport network became overloaded in the late 1970s, so too did the system of energy supplies. The costs of extraction unexpectedly increased in the Tiumen oil field, which had been opened in the late 1960s, and a campaign to expand the coal industry in 1976 also ran into production delays and cost overruns. In 1980 the decision was taken to pour still more resources into Tiumen, looking this time to expand gas as well as oil. This in turn called for a massive effort to create a network of pipelines to bring the gas to European Russia and to customers in East and West Europe.

The gas pipeline campaign 1979–1982

The party's crisis mobilization role is nowhere more amply illustrated than in the campaign to develop the Tiumen gas fields and build a series of pipelines to export the gas to Europe. This campaign has been the subject of excellent studies by Gustafson and Chung: this section merely highlights some of their findings.[48]

In the early 1960s a powerful coalition emerged among regional party and industrial officials in West Siberia, dedicated to persuading Moscow of the region's massive energy potential. The two key figures were B. Shcherbina, who was Tiumen obkom first secretary 1961–73, before being promoted to be Minister of the Oil and Gas Industry, and his successor as obkom chief, G. Bogomiakov. Under the influence of these local sponsors, in 1979 the Brezhnev leadership launched a huge drive to expand gas output, to compensate for stagnation in the oil and coal sectors. Gas output was to grow by 50 per cent between 1980 and 1985, and would take up almost half of all the additional investments to be made available to Soviet industry.[49] Gustafson summarizes the key characteristics of this campaign as follows: its emergency nature, the lack of forward planning, the fact that it was run from the centre, and its reliance on a massive transfusion of resources.[50]

Any major economic campaign launched so abruptly would suffer from a lack of forward planning. Add to this the consideration that a new geographical area was being exploited, and new technologies were involved, and one begins to see the scope of the challenge facing Soviet economic managers. The new technology problem was made more acute by the US embargo on pipeline equipment which followed the declaration of martial law in Poland in December 1981. The USSR had built such a pipeline before (the Orenburg pipeline to East Europe, also relying heavily on imported pipe), but this time key US-made components for the compressors would have to be made by Soviet factories.[51]

Party organs were mobilized to ensure completion of these urgent tasks, which the routine administrative apparatus was not prepared to cope with. Party activity came on two fronts: on-site coordination of pipeline construction, and work with supplier factories, to ensure that the requisite equipment was produced.

On the equipment side, party organs in major plants around the country strove to push through orders for the West Siberia project at the maximum possible speed. As of 1980, a Ministry of Oil and Gas Industry Construction official estimated that they only had 10 per cent of the equipment they needed.[52] Supplier plants, ranging over 60 ministries, were told by the November 1981 CC CPSU plenum that 'These projects must be finished on time.'[53] Compressor technology was new for most of them, and required the diversion of designers and workers from their regular production tasks. Leningrad was a key centre, with the campaign there being under the direct supervision of senior obkom officials, but plants from Sumy to Khabarovsk were also put to work rushing through compressors.[54] The Sverdlovsk obkom was praised for the 'huge organizational work' it conducted in getting its industry to meet deadlines for the pipeline, coordinating the activity of plants under six different ministries.[55]

Most of the equipment seems to have been delivered on time, although the initial specifications were not met. This meant that the compressors installed were fewer and smaller in capacity than originally envisaged, reducing the amount of gas which the pipelines could

handle.[56] Also, this crash campaign came at considerable cost to the
mainstream activities of the plants involved. For example, the Leningrad turbine plant finished its compressors on time but missed its
regular plan targets for each year 1980–82.[57] The aggregate burden of
the pipeline project amounted to some 5 per cent of all investment in
Soviet industry 1981–4, with the oil sector accounting for another 16.4
per cent and coal 4.5 per cent.[58] Steel pipe became scarce, which
disrupted the work of other users, such as irrigation projects.[59] Other
pipeline projects had to be postponed: for example, a second north–
south pipeline from the West Siberian fields, to provide gas for idle
methanol and ammonia plants in Tomsk and Kemerovo.[60]

The construction of the pipelines themselves (six lines were eventually built) was the focal point of the whole campaign. The 20,000 km of
pipe laid, at a cost of 25,000 million roubles, amounted to a construction project greater than the BAM railway, the Atommash reactor
plant, and the Kama and Volzhskii car plants all combined.[61] The
enormity of the task meant that party organs 'were obliged to take
measures like a fire-fighting team' (v pozharnom poriadke), in Gorbachev's words.[62] Construction along the line was organized in an
innovative manner, with eight autonomous regional trusts, each
responsible for all the operations of the area, and extensive use of
integrated work brigades.[63] The Ministry of Gas and Oil Industry
Construction seems to have done its job well, judging by the fact that
its leaders were promoted.[64] The ministry's partkom was still receiving
plaudits in 1986 while other ministries, as usual, were being hauled
over the coals.

Special administrative agencies were created – of the sort denied to
other developing regions, for the most part – to foster horizontal
integration. These consisted of a council within the USSR Council of
Ministers, and an inter-departmental commission of Gosplan, based in
Tiumen, charged with 'overcoming departmentalism'.[65] In practice,
their role was unclear, and most coordination work seems to have
been done through party channels. The construction ministry partkom
was highly active, sending out nine 'operational groups' to supervise
pipelaying work, and forming ten special PPOs along the line.[66]
Officials in the twenty-six obkomy through whose territory the pipelines passed were mobilized to provide housing for the workers, and
to clear bottlenecks in supplies and equipment. For example, a secretary of Zakarpatiia obkom forced through a rail shipment of steel pipe
from Zhdanov (more than 1,000 km distant).[67]

The pipeline construction activity – particularly the main Urengoi–

Uzhgorod line, which would carry gas to Western Europe – was treated as a major political test for the Soviet Union. Completion of the pipeline would mean a victory in the 'psychological war' which began with President Reagan's embargo.[68] One party theoretician described the project as 'strengthening the USSR's international position, and that of the socialist countries, and widening their possibilities in the economic competition with imperialism.[69]

The Uzhgorod–Urengoi pipeline was completed with great fanfare in September 1983 – six months ahead of schedule.[70] However, it was easier to focus energies on welding the pipe together than it was to ensure that all necessary auxiliary work was done on time. Even after the pipeline was 'completed' 16,000 workers continued to toil on the compressor stations, and the in-field pipe network and storage facilities were seriously deficient.[71] The rush to completion led to shoddy workmanship which caused severe maintenance problems. The poor quality control was most tragically revealed by the appalling pipeline explosion in Ufa in 1989. Work on the other five lines had been put back in order to ensure that the Uzhgorod pipeline – the one that would carry gas to West Europe – was completed ahead of time.

The party considered the Tiumen campaign to be a great success. Despite the embargo, the project was completed roughly on schedule and gas production from the Tiumen region rose from 35.7 billion cubic metres in 1975 to 156 billion in 1980 and 369 billion in 1985.[72] One should not get too carried away with the party's success in boosting pipelaying, however. The USSR had routinely added 5–6,000 km of gas pipeline each year since 1965: in 1982 this went up to 9,000 km, and to 10,000 in 1983.[73] Admittedly, conditions for building in West Siberia were extreme – but so were the measures taken by the party to push the project through.

The main drawback to the Tiumen campaign was a failure to develop the social and industrial infrastructure at a pace concomitant with the expansion in the region's gas and oil production. Between 1965 and 1980 the number of workers in the oil and gas industries in Tiumen grew from 43,000 to 530,000.[74] The network of housing and social amenities lagged far behind the rate of expansion of the labour force. Although the Tiumen obkom complained loudly about these problems, in practice their own efforts too were concentrated on forcing through the industrial construction on schedule.[75]

Gustafson describes the development of the infrastructure as 'barely controlled chaos', with problems in labour turnover (50 per cent per annum), housing (targets being met by only 30–50 per cent), transportation, power supplies, exploratory drilling and so forth.[76] The housing situation was officially described as 'acute' even in 1978, *before* the main influx of workers.[77]

The Soviet press was full of frank criticism of the region's infrastructure, mostly directed at ministries acting out of 'departmental' self-interest. 'Towns sprang up on the departmental principle – each built its own one'[78], and towns which were unable to get a ministry to sponsor them (such as Iamburg), were even worse off.[79]

Initially, infrastructural development was delayed and teams of workers were flown in on a temporary basis – the 'outpost method' (*vakhtovyi metod*). This was unpopular with Tiumen officials, who wanted their region developed on a more permanent basis.[80] However, the *vakhtovyi metod* was pushed hard by other Siberians, such as the first secretary of Tomsk obkom, Egor Ligachev.[81] There may have been self-interest involved: many of the mobile teams for Tiumen were based in Tomsk. Ligachev claimed to have pioneered the outpost method for the oil industry. He convened a conference on the technique in Tomsk in 1980, and got the State Committee on Labour and Social Questions to approve it in 1982.[82] After that, however, the innovation fell out of favour. While it may have worked well for the oil industry, it proved less suitable for the gas sector. Complaints about poor living conditions continued to swell, and plan targets were not met for the three years 1982–5.

The Tiumen comrades' arguments seemed to be vindicated, in that the infrastructure had to be developed if the region's reserves were to be developed successfully in the longer term. Favourable references to the *vakhtovyi metod* dropped off. Two local economists calculated that one rouble of housing construction in Tiumen was worth four roubles of industrial construction, if one calculated for the idle machinery, poor maintenance and so on which resulted from labour shortages.[83]

The tactic the party adopted to boost infrastructural development was the same as that used to promote the construction and equipping of the pipelines – the mobilization of help from party organizations around the country. The CC CPSU took over 'direct leadership' of Tiumen's development after Kosygin's visit to the area in 1968, mobilizing 100 design bureaus around the country to help with development plans.[84] Special meetings were organized by the CC CPSU to mobilise men and materials from Moscow, Leningrad and seven of the non-Russian republics.[85] The assistance was often organized in the form of socialist competition contracts, drawn up between a Tiumen construction trust and its distant collaborator. As of 1980 out-of-province sponsors (*shefy*) were building 17 per cent of the housing and 36 per cent of the roads.[86] Komsomol organizations were also involved: by 1985 they had despatched 150,000 workers to the region for temporary tours of duty.[87] Special help for the oil and gas industry was mustered from experienced crews in the Tatar and Bashkir ASSRs. The rail network proved in need of major assistance – although, typically, it turned out that lack of housing was the main factor holding back its development.[88]

Coordination of all this outside assistance was not always smooth. The Ukrainian CC, for example, felt it necessary to reintroduce the position of CC plenipotentiary.[89] These were party organizers acting in the name of the Ukrainian CC and reporting directly to them, who were sent to sites in Tiumen being built with help from Ukrainian organizations. Stalin had relied heavily on plenipotentiaries to consolidate his grip on the party machine, but the CC CPSU had abolished the institution in 1956.

One may question whether, for example, it was an optimal strategy to rush in housing panels over a 5,000 km distance from Leningrad. Surely it would have made more sense to slow the pace, and wait for a local construction materials industry to be established? Instead, the party mistakenly assumed that an all-out campaign could overcome these problems.

Party supervision of the atomic power programme

The Tiumen oil and gas complex may have been the centre of attention at national level, but it was by no means atypical of party interventions in the energy sector as a whole.

Energy posed particular challenges to the party, since it combined many of the problems discussed in chapters 4 and 5 – the problems involved in running large-scale construction projects, and the need to coordinate economic activity in a specific region, often distant, inhospitable and not of the planners' choosing.

In the atomic field, the USSR embarked on an ambitious programme of reactor construction, which aimed to raise its share of total USSR energy consumption from 11 per cent in 1985 to 20 per cent by 1990 and 30–40 per cent by the year 2000.[90] By 1985 forty-five reactors were under construction, at fifteen sites. The key project was the Atommash plant in Volgodonsk (Rostov oblast), which was to mass-produce nuclear reactors. From the outset Atommash ran into severe problems because of design flaws (the site was unstable) and deficiencies in equipment and manpower.[91] The site was designated an all-union Komsomol 'shock-work' site, and roughly one-third of the workers came from Komsomol mobilizations.[92] The central press helped to badger delinquent suppliers, and Rostov obkom set up a special unit to arrange help from outside the province.[93] Atommash and other reactor projects in the Ukraine were put under the direct supervision of the Ukrainian Komsomol CC.[94]

Despite optimistic articles published over the name of the Rostov obkom first secretary, N. A. Bondarenko, it was clear that the Atommash project was in deep trouble.[95] A CC CPSU decree published in February 1982 called upon central and local organs to take 'exceptional measures' to maintain the planned pace of growth in atomic energy.[96] In November 1982 it was still being reported that a quarter of the machinery on site was idle because of a lack of spare parts, and Gossnab had to set up a special commission to try to improve the supply situation.[97] Amid mounting criticism of the Atommash project, and widespread allegations of corruption, the Rostov first secretary was removed from office on grounds of 'ill health' in July 1984.[98]

Meanwhile, local party organs around the country were being galvanized into action to oversee the construction of atomic power stations in their regions.[99] Despite the tribulations of Atommash, by the end of the eleventh five year plan seventeen out of twenty-two atomic power stations were completed, and by 1985 output of electricity by atomic means managed to reach 170 billion kw/h, against a planned level of 220 billion kw/h.[100] While the atomic programme was less than a complete success, it also avoided being a total failure – until Chernobyl came along, in April 1986. It is unlikely that the rapid progress that was achieved would have been possible without the constant pressure that was being exerted by the national leadership, and carried down through the regional party apparatus.

Party campaigns in the coal industry

In 1976 the CPSU launched what Gustafson described as a 'big coal' policy.[101] It was thought that increased investment in this traditional energy resource, together with the expansion in oil, gas and atomic power, would be sufficient to meet Soviet energy needs over subsequent decades.

The coal programme immediately ran into difficulties, however, as attempts to open new mines in traditional coalfields such as the Donbass ran into geological problems, and the exploitation of new fields in Siberia and Kazakhstan raised new technical challenges of how best to transport coal over long distances. In fact, during the decade 1975–85 coal production only rose by 25 million tonnes, from 701 to 726 million tonnes.[102] The increase came from the newly opened fields in Kazakhstan and West Siberia, which offset the decline in the older areas. The Kansk-Achinsk Fuel and Power Complex (KATEK) in Krasnoiarsk provided 28 million tonnes in 1975, rising to 41 million tonnes in 1985, while the Ekibastuz complex in Pavlodar oblast (Kazakh SSR) saw its output rise from 46 million tonnes to 81 million tonnes over the same period.

Opening up KATEK and Ekibastuz posed extraordinary challenges to the coal industry.[103] They were brown coal, surface deposits of low quality (high moisture content, a tendency to ignite in rail wagons, etc.), located 4,000 km distant from the major industrial consumers to the West. Their exploitation posed new technical challenges, about which the experts disagreed. One solution would be to construct huge pithead power stations, and then send coal 'by wire' using new techniques of ultra-high voltage (UHV) transmission. Alternatively, coal slurry pipelines could be constructed, or new chemical treatment processes developed to convert the coal into synthetic fuel.

Large-scale construction projects in new, undeveloped regions seemed to be a situation tailor-made for party organs to play an active role. Add to that the fact that energy was a top priority area, and one would expect the party to reproduce the success of the Tiumen project. However, this did not occur, probably because new untried technologies were involved (high voltage transmission, synfuel, coal slurry), and the experts were divided over how to proceed. Successful party intervention required a clear set of technical and economic goals if it was to stand a chance of succeeding.

The Ekibastuz project

The Ekibastuz project began in 1971, and output grew 250 per cent in the first four years.[104] Construction delays arose over the machinery plant (to produce excavators and other needed equipment), the power station and housing. The project failed to meet any of its annual plan targets after 1973. A familiar pattern developed: the press would publish criticisms of construction problems, and party officials would respond by blaming the branch ministries for not pulling their weight, while assuring their superiors that 'additional measures' were being taken.[105] For example, the first secretary of

Pavlodar obkom, B. V. Isaev, complained that the Ministry of Power
broke its promise to hand over its housing to the oblast soviet.[106] Isaev
later claimed that the coal trusts had met their housing targets for 1980,
although in reality the targets were only 50 per cent fulfilled.[107] Two
years later, Isaev was conceding that 'serious problems' were dogging
the construction projects, but was still shifting the blame onto the
Ministry of Power.[108]

Party organs had little success in trying to correct these deficiencies.
In 1980, 'The warnings of the obkom were not acted upon', and
construction of the main power complex fell behind schedule.[109] The
Ministry of Coal failed to come up with telephones for a new housing
estate, despite repeated requests from Ekibastuz gorkom.[110] Very few
party-sponsored agreements with suppliers in other regions were
concluded.[111] In 1984 Ekibastuz was 'penalized' for poor organization
of work on site by being taken off the list of Komsomol 'shock work'
projects.[112] Isaev was removed from his post as first secretary in
January 1982, at the suspiciously young age of 50. (No reasons were
given for his removal.)

Despite the numerous and persistent problems with construction
delays and housing shortages, and despite the fact that the original
optimistic development plans were not realized, Ekibastuz provided a
considerable boost to Soviet coal output, and was one of the best-
performing fields.[113] The project managed to meet its annual power
generation plan in 1984, for the first time in a decade.[114]

The Kansk–Achinsk Complex

The Kansk–Achinsk complex (KATEK) was seen as even more
promising in the long run than Ekibastuz, but its growing pains were
still more acute. Work in the area began in 1971, but despite oversight
provided by Gosplan's consultative 'Council for studying productive
forces', the thirty-plus planning institutes involved in developing the
project failed to coordinate their plans.[115] The region's territorial-
production complex – one of the earliest in the country – also failed to
conquer departmentalism. The first secretary of Krasnoiarsk kraikom,
P. S. Fedirko, conceded in 1976 that housing only stood at 20–30 per
cent of what was needed, and blamed the ministries for withholding
funds.[116] Brezhnev visited the area and noted that 'Responsibility for
[construction delays] lies both with the ministries and with the
regional leadership.'[117]

Despite the fact that gorkom officials were described as being 'constantly involved' in monitoring construction projects in the complex, press reports presented a dire picture of inadequate housing and labour turnover of 100 per cent per year.[118] Even such a mundane question as the founding of a local brick factory seemed to be beyond the powers of the kraikom and regional soviet.[119] In a rarely allowed display of pique the first secretary of Sharypovo gorkom complained that his town was being starved of resources to the benefit of Ekibastuz.[120] Progress was slow on ambitious technical plans for coal liquefaction, and the scientific coordinating council lacked effective authority to enforce its suggested solutions.[121] The Kansk–Achinsk TPK seemed unable to perform an effective coordinating role, and one kraikom secretary called for the formation of a special on-site Gosplan research institute, of the sort which had been set up for Tiumen.[122]

These persistent difficulties did not prevent a certain 'propaganda of success' building up around the KATEX development. While kraikom first secretary Fedirko did occasionally discuss the region's problems in a frank manner, his articles were often simple vehicles for self-praise and regional pride.[123] Krasnoiarsk officials often came across as Siberian patriots – for example, kraikom secretary L. G. Sizov wrote an article pointing out that the krai covered 10 per cent of Soviet territory, and had special international significance because of its natural resources and location as the gateway to Asia.[124]

Why did the campaigns to promote Ekibastuz and Kansk–Achinsk prove even less successful than the more grandiose projects such as BAM and Tiumen? Partly it was a question of priorities: the effectiveness of local party organs as regional coordinators rapidly diminished as one moved down the priority list to second and third-level projects. Without the sort of direct help from Central Committee level which top priority projects such as BAM or the gas pipeline enjoyed, local party officials could not overcome the inertia and self-interest of ministerial agencies.

Second, these coal projects faced more varied and novel technological challenges than did projects involving the more familiar technologies of railways and pipelines. In the absence of a clear technological plan to focus on, policy vacillated. For example, the project plan for the Ekibastuz field changed fifty times between 1979 and 1983.[125] In such circumstances local party officials found it difficult to make an effective contribution.

The Saiano–Shushensk hydro-electric project

Another major energy project of the 1970s was the massive Saiansk hydro-electric power station (HES), on the Enisei river in the Khakass autonomous oblast, Krasnoiarsk region.

Saiansk HES proved to be more successfully managed than the coal projects discussed in the preceding section. The planning authorities already had considerable experience dealing with HES, and with the help of the party were able to assemble a coordinated attack on the matter. The project commenced in 1975 after a lengthy period of planning. Krasnoiarsk kraikom concluded an agreement with Leningrad gorkom, whereby the two party organizations formed special supervisory councils in both cities to coordinate the work of enterprises involved in supplying equipment (in Leningrad) and in construction on site. There were 43 different enterprises involved in May 1978 (of which 28 were in Leningrad), rising to 140 (with 43 in Leningrad) by the end of the year.[126] The only other project with a similar coordinating council was Atommash, although Leningrad did have special socialist competition arrangements of this sort with a number of other projects (BAM, Kama trunk plant, atomic power stations, tractor factories and the Bratsk territorial-production complex).[127] Leningrad enterprises supplied 70 per cent of the equipment for the Saiansk project, and made much political capital out of their help for this distant Siberian province.[128]

Not all was well with the project, however. A special report on the project planning for Saiansk by the chairman of the Party Control Committee, A. Pel'she, condemned the 'scandalous irresponsibility' of its planners, who had produced a succession of faulty designs over a twenty-five year period.[129] First secretary Fedirko admitted that the kraikom had been unable to persuade the ministries of ferrous metals and heavy industry construction to merge two building trusts that were jointly building a metals plant in Khakass.[130]

Summary

Energy and transport must join construction and agriculture as sectors where regional party officials adopted a high profile role. The energy and transport sectors merited this attention from the party because of their volatile nature, and because they often involved one-off, short-run projects where stable, centralized administrative apparatuses did not have time to emerge.

Energy and transport provide many examples of dynamic and vigorous interventions in the economy by regional party organs. In most cases, these were part of national campaigns directed and led by officials at CC CPSU level. Judging by accounts in the national press and party journals, it appeared that party officials played a direct, active role in resolving problems in these fields and focussing resources and efforts on the bottleneck areas.

However, in evaluating the economic impact of these party campaigns, it is important to bear in mind their limited time span. Party interventions were geared to high-profile, high-intensity, short-run campaigns, after which attention shifted elsewhere. For example, the railway overload of the late 1970s was the result of several decades of under-investment, yet the party's campaign response was measured in months, or even weeks. Also, the chosen tactic – the Cheliabinsk approach of getting industrial users to repair wagons – represented a temporary fix to make up for a shortage of wagon repair plants, and for the lack of a sound administrative system for keeping track of disabled wagons.

The BAM campaign also shows the contradictions of short-run party interventions in a long-run economic process. The party did manage to sustain a 10-year campaign to build the railway (1974–84). However, attention was fixed on the symbolic goal of track completion, while development of the infrastructure (particularly housing) which would be needed to derive benefits from the railway was relatively neglected.

On the energy front, party organs were mobilized in an impressive fashion for the couple of years required to complete the main gas pipelines out of West Siberia. This campaign was important because its political ramifications went beyond the boundaries of the USSR: it became a test of the Soviet Union's ability to manage its own economy, and stand up to US 'blackmail'. The pipeline campaign was indeed a success: both the construction itself and the efforts to secure the production of embargoed equipment such as compressors in Soviet plants were completed on time. However, the effort swallowed a large share of the finite pool of investments in the economy, and the lack of attention to infrastructural development severely hampered the effective exploitation of the fields.

Elsewhere in the energy sector there was a variety of party efforts to force through the development of new energy sources, in atomic power, coal and hydro-electricity. All these campaigns exhibited a familiar pattern: high-intensity political pressure; mobilization of help from around the country; complaints of departmentalism and lack of cooperation from the central ministries; and concern that the major targets of the project had been pursued at the expense of the supporting infrastructure. Whether the policies succeeded or failed depended on such factors as the degree of political commitment they received from the national political leadership, and the complexity of the technical problems they faced.

Gustafson has persuasively argued that in concentrating on short-run goals the Soviet leadership grievously failed to develop a coherent energy strategy for the nation, with the result that 'energy policy has been in a permanent state of emergency since the mid-1970s ... a crisis that is ultimately self-inflicted'.[131] Moreover, the Soviet leadership proved incapable of responding to the mounting evidence of policy failure. The second major systemic flaw which Gustafson identifies is a preoccupation with the expansion of supply and only superficial efforts to curb the economy's excessive demand for energy. The party's energies went into the production campaigns described in this chapter, and not into the halting energy conservation programme discussed in chapter 3.

7   The role of the party in agriculture

A single chapter cannot do more than scratch the surface of the subject of Soviet agriculture and the role of the CPSU in the rural economy. However, the party's role in industry simply cannot be understood without giving some attention to its deep involvement in agriculture.

J. Hough himself did not attempt to incorporate agriculture into his model of the obkom first secretary as prefect, but at several points he noted that 'local party officials have been greatly tempted to neglect industry in order to have more time to devote to agriculture', and that 'for many years the greatest danger for the obkom first secretary has arisen from the agricultural sector'.[1]

This chapter will briefly review the status of agriculture and its importance for the CPSU, then map the shifting pattern of institutions through which the sector was managed from the 1960s to the 1980s. After examining the role played by party organs, three brief case studies will be presented: party campaigns to promote livestock rearing and elevator construction, and industrial sponsorship of farms.

Agriculture and the Soviet economy

The party's dominant role in farming went back to the collectivization campaign of 1929–32, which undermined the traditional structures of village life and left local party officials with the task of bringing the countryside into the domain of the Soviet economy.[2] What transpired was something resembling a process of 'primitive socialist accumulation', with food and labour being pumped out of the countryside to fuel the industrialization drive.

Agriculture became the 'poor sister' of the Soviet economy. It was starved of resources until the mid-1960s, particularly for infrastructural development (roads, housing, farm buildings).[3] The farmers lacked a rational price structure, and there were few incentives to operate efficiently. All that mattered was to meet the procurement quotas, measured by volume of basic products.

Since the late 1950s, and particularly after the March 1965 CC CPSU plenum, the state undertook a determined effort to improve the situation.[4] The main strategy was a costly transfusion of resources into the sector, through the promotion of mechanization and fertilizers; plus improving the incentive structure by raising procurement prices and converting collective farms (*kolkhozy*) into state farms (*sovkhozy*). The policy resulted in rising output, albeit at considerable cost. Between 1965 and 1980 gross output rose by 50 per cent, while labour inputs fell by 15 per cent but capital rose 350 per cent and power consumption 300 per cent.[5]

Despite these signs of mounting inefficiency, more radical solutions were rejected. For example, in the late 1960s there were experiments with partial marketization, in the form of the autonomous brigade or 'link' system. As Alexander Yanov has shown, these experiments were mostly stopped in the late 1960s, under pressure from party officials and farm managers keen to preserve the status quo.[6] Towards the end of the Brezhnev era one saw a reaffirmation of the orthodox approach: the major 'Food Programme' launched in May 1982 reiterated the policy of massive additional investment as the solution to agricultural ills.[7]

The legacy of the past was not eradicated, despite the progress achieved in the 1960s and 1970s. Agriculture continued to employ 20 per cent of the total Soviet workforce, and during the tenth five-year plan it swallowed 21 per cent of all capital investments.[8] These figures were exceptionally large by the standards of industrial economies, yet the USSR continued to experience bad harvests for roughly two out of every five years, and relied on imports to cover some 10 per cent of its food needs. Even in good years the supply of meat, dairy produce and vegetables was erratic, and rationing of such items spread through most regions of the USSR after 1978.[9]

The role of the party in Soviet agriculture

Throughout the Brezhnev era the CPSU was the dominant actor in the agricultural arena. Because the sector was a continuing source of problems, and because a stable, successful structure of economic administration had not been established, party organs continued to exercise many of the direct managerial functions which they had taken on in the 1930s.

The two key political groups which emerged in the 1930s were the political cadres of the machine-tractor stations and the staff of the local party district committee (raikom). The raikomy were the only bodies in the countryside which the state could trust with the job of grain collection. The territorial structure of party organs above PPO level was well-suited to agricultural supervision, since agriculture by definition is tied to the land, and thus a *spatially* defined management structure was appropriate – more so, for example, than for industry. In fact, in the 1920s there had been a deliberate policy of drawing oblast boundaries so that some regions would be primarily industrial and others agricultural – i.e. a deliberate spatial division of administrative responsibilities.[10] This spatial distinction between industry and agriculture became less and less appropriate over time. As agricultural technology developed, farms too became highly dependent on distant suppliers.

Party penetration of the farms themselves was weak. In the late 1970s 25 per cent of individual farm units (sub-divisions of the sovkhozy and kolkhozy) lacked a single party member, and a further 40 per cent had only one or two members.[11] Thus the PPOs never played a prominent role in farm management. The key figure was the raikom first secretary, who wielded almost mythical power over his territory.

Typically, the relationship between raikom officials and farm directors was antagonistic.[12] For the former group, meeting the centrally determined procurement quotas for their region was the overwhelming priority. Farm managers were more interested in minimizing the demands on their farm, while doing the best to raise the living standards of its members. Party officials relied on crude political pressure to impose their priorities, rather than economic levers (which were mostly lacking).

Farm directors tended to enjoy lower prestige and status than their counterparts in industry. This was particularly true of kolkhoz chairmen. For example, only one in three in Ul'ianovsk had higher education in 1978, compared with 81 per cent of the raikom first secretaries supervising them.[13] Rates of turnover of farm directors were often unacceptably high.[14]

The basic power relationship between party officials and farm managers was largely unchanged over the years, despite the fact that the administrative structure above them was subject to a bewildering series of reforms.

Changes in the management structure

The Khrushchev period saw various radical reforms in agricultural administration. The machine-tractor stations were abolished in 1957, and their personnel and equipment dispersed among the farms. The Ministry of Agriculture was dismantled in 1961, and replaced by a network of territorial-production administrations. Khrushchev split the party in two in 1962, creating a separate hierarchy of party organs to supervise agriculture.[15]

The impact of these reforms on the role of rural raikomy was unclear. The party reforms were reversed after Khrushchev's downfall, and the Ministry of Agriculture was resurrected. In 1965 the raikomy even disbanded their separate agricultural departments, to underline the break with Khrushchev's reforms, and to try to reduce the direct role of raikomy in farm decision making.[16] Despite these changes, in 1967 M. Fainsod could still write that 'At the present time party and administrative controls are more closely focused in agriculture than in any other sector of the economy.'[17]

Brezhnev tried to put agricultural administration onto a more autonomous and 'scientific' basis. As investment resources poured in, there was a mushrooming of special units to administer them. Instead of simple territorially based agencies, there was a growing number of specialized businesses integrated into republic-level associations.

For example, the Sel'khoztekhnika association, formed in 1961, took on some of the functions of the old machine tractor stations, and built up a large network of repair stations.[18] By 1982 it had grown to embrace 8,000 units, employing 1.7 million workers.[19] Similarly, Roskolkhozstroi was formed in 1967 to undertake cooperative construction projects for kolkhozy in the RSFSR.[20] Ministries serving the agricultural sector, such as the Ministry of Tractor and Agricultural Machinery Construction, also emerged as dynamic and powerful organizations.

Institutional growth continued in the 1970s. Several new ministries were created to improve performance in specific sectors: Machine Building for Animal Husbandry and Fodder Industries (1973); Fruit and Vegetable Industry (1980); and Mineral Fertilizer (1980).

These developments complicated the institutional map of Soviet agricultural administration. With different types of all-union, republican and oblast agencies, plus various nationality sub-divisions, there was a minimum of three tiers of command, in places rising to six. There were also far too many ministries involved in running agriculture –

there were six in the Ukrainian republic, for example, not counting the ministries supplying equipment.[21] These various ministries ran a host of subordinate units: repair stations, supply depots, construction trusts, and even their own farms. To control these multifarious agencies yet more bureaucracies were created, such as the State Committee for Production and Technical Supplies for Agriculture (1978). This bureaucratic expansion confused the chain of command, with farms in a given locality often being split between different overseeing agencies. For example, the six sovkhozy of Pritobol raion found themselves supervised by three different trusts.[22]

There was a growing chorus of protests about 'departmentalist' behaviour (the pursuit of bureaucratic self-interest) by this plethora of agencies. Kolkhoz directors complained about the competing targets being pursued by transport, repair and procurement agencies.[23] Even party conservatives such as E. Bugaev commented that 'There is not a single master of the land ... because the central departments jealously guard their sovereignty.'[24] A raikom secretary complained that 'The special agencies do not keep in close contact with local organs and party organizations', meaning, for example, that local farms could not get anyone to do their electrical repairs.[25] The special agencies were considered to be too independent, and 'as a rule' capable of winning any dispute with a raion farm administration.[26] While all this was going on, resources were being poured into agriculture without having any visible impact on productivity.

Meanwhile, at local level there were other institutional developments taking place. Apart from the multiplication of vertical hierarchies, there were new horizontal networks forming. A wide variety of inter-farm associations and agro-industrial complexes began to emerge in the mid-1960s, the goal being to promote better local coordination and integration of different stages of agricultural production. R. F. Miller cites data showing some 826 such operations by 1978, and remarks that 'The scope of these reorganizations is enormous, on a scale unimaginable in the advanced capitalist countries';[27] 4,500 farms were united in these bodies in 1970, and 9,000 by 1980.[28] For example, one well-established complex in Groznyi dated back to 1968, and united fifteen farms, four canneries and forty local shops into a single organization.[29]

The administrative arrangements behind these associations were loose, vague and confusing. In an attempt to straighten out the situation, in 1976 the CC CPSU issued a decree favouring the introduction of 'raion agro-industrial associations' (RAPOs) to coordinate agricultural activity in a given district.[30] The introduction of a RAPO was to be a joint decision of local party and soviet organs, subject to approval by the republican agriculture ministry.

How did these administrative developments affect the role of the party? Despite the apparent rejection of Khrushchev's model of detailed intervention, the raikom preserved a decisive role, being the only administrative organ capable of coordinating the burgeoning agricultural agencies. Thus the CC CPSU noted in a 1978 decree that 'The CC was correct and farsighted to restore and strengthen the raikom as the main political organization in the countryside', and continued to describe the role of local party officials as 'direct responsibility for the fulfilment of growing production and education tasks.'[31] Party organizations took an active role in creating new RAPOs, and in handling the confusion and clashes of interest which often accompanied these reorganizations. The RAPOs became a cornerstone of the May 1982 Food Programme. *Kommunist* editorialized that 'As the May 1982 plenum underlined, it is the raikomy which, as always, carry the main burden ... The new management organs must become their reliable assistants ... It is no secret that a great deal depends on the first secetary.'[32]

Despite the rhetoric on the need to avoid podmena, raikomy continued to be deeply involved in the planning that was done in the RAPOs.[33] It was standard practice for farm managers to send telegrams about a production problem to both the RAPO and the raikom.[34] Yet the central party authorities resisted suggestions to create unified party organizations within the RAPOs, because this might have undermined the raikom's traditional role of pressing farm directors to meet procurement quotas.[35]

Concomitant with the emergence of RAPOs was yet another wave of restructuring of higher level administration. A new layer of interdepartmental councils were created at oblast level as part of the 1982 Food Programme. After 1983, planning organs were instructed to compile 'unified' control figures for all agricultural activities in their territory, and in 1985 the five agricultural ministries were merged into one notorious 'super-ministry' – Gosagroprom.[36] Gosagroprom was created out of five all-union ministries (Agriculture, Agricultural Construction, Fruit and Vegetables, Meat and Milk, and the State Committee on Production/Technical Supplies for Agriculture). However, many other agencies still remained outside the jurisdiction of Gosagroprom: the Ministries for Bread, Irrigation and Fish Industry; the State Committee for the Wood Industry; the Central Consumer

Cooperative; and five agricultural engineering ministries (Tractors and Agricultural Machinery, Livestock Machinery, Food and Light Industry, and Fertilizer).

These reorganizations did produce some success stories, such as the Talsin and Vil'iandin RAPOs in the Baltic.[37] In most regions, however, the result was organizational chaos, contributing to the increasingly frequent breakdowns in food supplies.[38] The cost accounting principles under which RAPOs were supposed to operate were opaque, and many RAPO member units continued to be under 'dual subordination', reporting to other ministerial agencies besides the RAPO.[39] Often, the urge to merge farms ran ahead of the material resources to carry the plans through, and agency self-interest continued to thwart raikom rationalization plans.[40] One kolkhoz director summed up the state of affairs in his comments at a CC CPSU plenum in 1985: 'The RAPO has not yet fulfilled the hopes placed on it. It has not become an independent object of planning and management.'[41] The whole Gosagroprom structure was a disaster for Soviet agriculture, and was abolished in March 1989, to be replaced by a Council of Ministers Commission on Food Supplies and Procurement, itself abolished two years later.[42]

The nature of party interventions in agricultural management

There is a wealth of evidence testifying to the extensive and detailed involvement of party officials in agricultural administration. This interference ranged from routine tasks, such as spring sowing and the annual harvests, to strategic choices over agricultural techniques, mechanization and crop selection.

The rhetoric of the CPSU's national leaders made it clear that agriculture was a top priority for the party. In 1981 Brezhnev stated that agriculture was 'the central problem of the whole five year plan', and occupied 'the first place' in party tasks.[43] Even the Politburo itself apparently devoted much time to detailed discussions of agrarian problems, such as the availability of spares for the new K700 tractor, or the number of potato warehouses.[44] They insisted that local party organs must exert 'maximum influence' in the 1985 sowing campaign, and 'must take operational measures to resolve' any problems that arose.[45] Brezhnev sent a letter to a Briansk raikom praising their work with potatoes; and he publicly admonished D. Kunaev, first secretary of the Kazakh party, for allowing maize yields to fall 35 per cent behind those achieved in Uzbekistan.[46] (At this point in the meeting Kunaev interjected 'We can put that right!') In a 1984 speech Gorbachev saw no contradiction in condemning podmena, then moving on to a detailed discussion of the importance of crop rotation.[47] A year later he was criticizing individual obkomy for not doing enough to promote the use of fallow land.[48] Thus Gorbachev was continuing in the tradition set by previous Soviet leaders: denouncing podmena while calling for more active intervention by local party organs.

It seems clear, then, that party organs were held accountable for the agricultural performance of their region. Press reports showed dozens of obkomy being criticized for poor agricultural work: in Politburo and CC CPSU reports, in leaders' speeches, and in press editorials.[49] Grounds for criticism included the non-fulfilment of procurement plans, poor crop and milk yields, the failure to keep machinery in good repair, or lethargy in the introduction of cost-accounting brigades. In turn, middle-level party organs levelled criticism at their subordinate units. For example, the first secretary of Smolensk obkom took different productivity levels in neighbouring farms as 'evidence above all of the level of leadership by partkomy'.[50] Judging by the evidence provided by the Soviet press, the volume and detail of party interventions in agriculture exceeded the level of party supervision of industry. In particular, obkom level officials were far more likely to be upbraided for poor performance in agriculture than in industry.

Supporting evidence comes from the author's survey of replies to critical articles in *Ekonomicheskaia gazeta* which were signed by party officials between 1976 and 1986. (See Appendix 2 for details.) Agriculture accounted for 144 of the cases, industry for only 123. (And of the 69 cases relating to construction problems, 40 were urban sites and 29 rural sites.) Apart from the surprising prominence of agriculture – which after all accounts for less than one quarter of the Soviet economy – an interesting pattern emerges if one studies the rank of official responding to the problem; 89 per cent of the agricultural replies came from obkom secretaries – but only 8 per cent of industry replies came from obkom officials (80 per cent came from factory partkom secretaries, either alone or jointly with the director). Similarly, obkom replies came in 90 per cent of rural construction problems and only 33 per cent of urban construction cases.

This disparity is probably due to two factors. First, the territory-specific nature of agricultural production, combined with the weakly developed management agencies, left party officials bearing the burden of responsibility. Second, the national leadership chose to make agriculture a 'shock front' for the CPSU in the 1970s and 1980s. Press reports and reprimands mostly focused upon a small range of top-priority policy issues: elevator construction, livestock rearing and the introduction of contract brigades.

Apart from these specific replies to criticism, press accounts offered a great deal of evidence as to the extensive, detailed involvement of party organs in the day-to-day running of Soviet farms. Party activities were in high gear during the harvest period, in 'the battle for bread'.[51] Apart from arranging help from industrial plants (of which more below), they sent special teams (shtaby) of party and soviet officials to oversee the harvest, or formed special units of party and Komsomol members to provide additional manpower. Success in the harvest could bring lavish praise, and it was an innovation in harvest technique (the 'Ipatov method', relying on integrated work teams) which, as noted, helped win Gorbachev national prominence.[52]

Socialist competition drives were run, with slogans such as '200 eggs from each hen!'[53] Sowing and harvesting decisions were closely monitored by party officials. For example, Krasnodar kraikom 'took the decision' to gather hay from 100,000 hectares of foothills; Crimea obkom set a target of 25 per cent of land to be double cropped; and Rostov obkom promised to raise more potatoes.[54] Such examples could be multiplied many times over – and have no real equivalent in the industrial arena. Party organs were actively encouraged to get involved in these technical matters by the party press. Partiinaia zhizn explicitly declared that it was the responsibility of partkomy to find ways to increase yields.[55] Articles by obkom first secretaries often discoursed on such mundane matters as the virtues of corn or other strains of grain.[56] Poltava obkom won national acclaim for promoting 'minimal tillage' techniques (using cultivators rather than ploughs).[57] Party interventions were particularly visible with regard to support services, such as setting norms for the repair of equipment, or organizing the construction and maintenance of irrigation canals.[58] Such decisions were sometimes issued by the party committee alone, sometimes jointly with the relevant state agencies.

One topic which frequently recurred in accounts of party work in the village was the issue of labour retention. M. Solomentsev, then Chair of the RSFSR Council of Ministers, stated that 'keeping cadres in the village is the number one problem' in agriculture.[59] Labour shortages could drag down even the most successful of farms.[60] Skilled labour was the most mobile, and therefore in shortest supply. Thus, for example, the nation's farms had 5 million vehicles but only 4.5 million drivers.[61] Obkomy tried to persuade young people to stay on the land by promoting house building, setting aside special student stipends, or building workshops to provide winter employment. They considered their policies a success if one half of rural youth remained in their native village.[62] The struggle to keep villages going was a politically sensitive issue, with obkomy occasionally stepping in to veto ministerial plans to close hundreds of villages.[63] This issue was subsequently to become one of the key planks in the platform of the conservative Ligachev/Polozkov faction in the CPSU.

The range and depth of these party activities would seem to fly in the face of the strictures against podmena which were discussed in chapter 1. In fact, it was fairly common to see press reports where party organs were criticized for excessive interference.. Conferences of kolkhoz chairmen often featured vigorous protests from the floor on this theme.[64] One kolkhoz chairman complained 'Planning from above still persists. They tell us how much and when to sow, how to plough, how many pigs and cattle to raise.'[65] These points were also conceded by many party officials. A Gor'kii obkom secretary recognized that it was wrong 'to interfere with the technology of agricultural production'; and the Crimean obkom chastised one of its raikomy for setting sowing areas.[66] A Kirghiz raikom was ridiculed for insisting that all farm partkom secretaries personally attend all evening and morning milkings.[67] Krasnodar kraikom was censured for a 'noisy campaign' it launched in 1980 aimed at reaching a 1 million tonne grain harvest. In the process they forgot about crop rotation, meaning that the next harvest slumped back to 700 thousand tonnes.[68] Local officials from Volgograd to Gomel were criticized for using the militia to stop people transporting potatoes over district boundaries – their goal being to ensure that all the local crop was recorded in the region's own procurement statistics.[69] In 1985 the CC CPSU reprimanded Tselinograd obkom for excessive interference in agricultural work. It was reported, for example, that their agricultural department alone had sent out 7,000 telegrams and 854 orders in the year 1984.[70]

The debate over reform

The welter of criticisms of party podmena in agriculture reveals two things. It confirms that party committees did repeatedly intervene in the details of farm management. And it suggests that this was not the best way to run a modern agricultural system. A survey conducted in Siberia showed 90 per cent of farm officials and 84 per cent of farm workers thought they could work more effectively in different economic and organizational conditions.[71]

Reform would have to mean greater reliance on monetary indicators and financial calculation. In 1980 50 per cent of sovkhozy ran at a loss, requiring on average a subsidy of 500,000 roubles a year.[72] The good farms got the lion's share of investment resources, which meant that the other farms fell further and further behind in their productivity.[73] Farms did not face a hard budget constraint. Some obkomy arbitrarily redistributed profits from successful farms to their indigent neighbours, and the bonuses under socialist competition drives were stacked to favour the 'economically weaker farms'.[74] Very few loss-making farms were closed down (if this happened, the procedure was to merge them with a neighbour).

These problems were rooted in the irrational retail pricing of agricultural products. Meat prices, for example, were kept at 1962 levels, bread at 1955 levels, and only luxury commodities like imported coffee, chocolate and citrus fruits saw significant price increases. While prices of basic foodstuffs were kept static to placate consumers, production costs continued to rise (in so far as one can estimate the true costs of production, given the idiosyncratic Soviet prices). Gorbachev estimated the costs of meat production to be 200–300 per cent in excess of the retail price.[75] As production and sales of foodstuffs rose, so too did the subsidies: the more successful Soviet agriculture was, the worse the burden on the state budget. T. Zaslavskaia estimated in 1986 that the total burden of food subsidies to the Soviet budget was 40–50 billion roubles per year.[76] These sums amounted to 10–15 per cent of the total federal budget.[77]

While some half-hearted attempts were made to rationalize the price structure and improve incentives, party diehards argued that radical reform would lead to greater income inequalities between and within farms. They suggested that a slackening of party controls would mean the abandonment of many backward villages by skilled technicians and managers, and the complete collapse of large segments of the rural economy. Higher procurement prices would be needed to elicit higher production, but these would have to be passed on to consumers, possibly triggering urban unrest. Moreover, moves towards market pricing would undercut the power and influence of innumerable party officials, and slacken political control over the flow of the society's most politically sensitive resource – food. Thus party hardliners preferred to bury their heads in the sand, and pretended that Soviet agriculture represented 'the triumph of Leninist agrarian policy'.[78]

The only reforms that were allowed in the agricultural arena came at the margin: easing the restrictions on private plots, and promoting the use of contract brigades within farms. Contract brigades were autonomous work teams, enjoying a degree of economic independence over the fields allocated to them.[79] A major drive to introduce contract brigades was launched by Gorbachev in Stavropol province in 1976. They were recommended in the May 1982 Food Programme, and were subsequently heavily promoted through party channels.[80]

However, this reform placed new demands of flexibility and economic awareness on farm officials – demands which they were not keen to satisfy. Slowness to adapt to the innovation extended all the way up the chain of command. For example, three years after the launching of the Food Programme the Ministry of Agriculture had still not issued regulations governing renumeration in contract brigades.[81] The contract brigade approach was very similar to the experiment with the autonomous 'link' system, and like its predecessor ran into thinly disguised opposition from raikom first secretaries and farm chairmen who saw them as a threat to their economic power.[82]

Another, still more modest reform which generated an equal amount of political stress was the effort to revitalize private plots.[83] Even according to official figures, in 1985 they produced 60 per cent of the nation's potatoes, 29 per cent of vegetables, 28 per cent of meat, 28 per cent of eggs and 29 per cent of milk.[84] In the tight years of 1979–80, the Brezhnev leadership turned to the private plots to bolster food supplies. Party officials were instructed to expand private plot production, and a CC CPSU decree assured the party that 'private auxiliary farming has a socialist character'.[85] There were even attempts to integrate it further into a socialized sector – for example, running socialist competitions for fodder-raising among plot holders.[86]

Some regions experimented with combining the virtues of private plots and contract brigades, in the form of 'family links'. In Belorussia such links were reported as producing crop yields 25 per cent and meat yields 50 per cent above the regional average.[87] This all seemed anathema to party conservatives, who had long intoned that private plots were a relic of the past which would have no place in the communist future. The peasants themselves seemed to fear such a reaction. The chairman of Voronezh oblispolkom hit the nail on the head when he observed that 'Many people are not hurrying to raise fruit and vegetables on their garden plots because they are scared that the next administrative crackdown (*sharakhan'e*) will lead to their being accused of illegal earnings.'[88] Memories were still fresh of the drive

Khrushchev launched against private plots in 1962. Such fears were not without foundation. The new law 'On measures to strengthen the struggle with unearned incomes' issued in June 1986 contained some ominous clauses, promising to 'strengthen control over kolkhoz markets' (where above plan produce was sold), and stipulating a penalty of up to two years corrective labour for those who bought food in state shops and fed it to their animals.[89]

Livestock campaigns

Meat was always a sensitive political issue in the USSR. Khrushchev's desire to overtake the USA in meat production had led to the tragic 'Larionov affair' of 1959–60, in which a bogus campaign to quadruple meat production in one year eventually led to the suicide of the first secretary of Riazan obkom.[90]

As the general food situation improved during the 1960s and 1970s, there was growing recognition of meat as the bottleneck sector. Meat production grew fairly steadily during 1955–75, at 3.9 per cent per annum, but growth was only 1.1 per cent per annum between 1976 and 1980, despite a programme of massive capital investments in the livestock sector.[91] In 1980 Soviet per capita meat consumption was roughly 40 per cent of that in neighbouring Poland (then entering its third round of food riots in a decade).

By the end of the 1970s the USSR had roughly the same number of cattle per head of population as did other advanced countries. The problem was low productivity due to poor husbandry and inadequate feed. The fodder issue also was one of quality rather than quantity. Fodder volume rose 28 per cent during 1976–80, but only produced a 6 per cent increase in meat deliveries.[92] There was an excessive reliance on grain, which is deficient in proteins and amino acids when compared to other crops. Grain represented 50 per cent of Soviet feed compared to 2–10 per cent in other countries.[93] The reason was that the specialist livestock farms rarely produced their own fodder, and were dependent on outside producers, who were paid by the weight of feed delivered – and grain was cheapest to produce.

Because of this distorted incentive structure, the party's chosen solution – a programme of crash investment in large, specialized livestock farms – did not solve the problem of inadequate meat supplies. In many cases it was difficult to find the additional workers to staff these new farms, and in some cases the projects were simply abandoned.[94]

As the investment plan faltered towards the end of the 1970s, livestock became an increasingly prominent political theme. Partkomy were told to treat livestock as a 'shock front' (*udarnii front*) in the nation's agrarian programme, with particular attention to improving fodder supplies. Major socialist competition drives were launched each year to stimulate efforts to prepare fodder for the winter season.[95] Party officials at obkom level were held accountable for the gathering and storage of fodder in their region, and were frequently criticized for failing to fulfil these duties. The CC CPSU itself gave direct orders to individual obkomy to take urgent measures to increase meat production.[96] E. Ligachev, CC CPSU secretary, said in a speech to an all-union conference that obkomy bore the 'primary' responsibility for improving this sector of the economy.[97]

The depth of party involvement was shown by the convincing detail which many of these accounts display, and the precision of the language involved. For example, the Cherkass obkom organized factory assistance to build 114 feed storage barns; and only after 'direct interventions' by Vitebsk obkom officials was a local construction trust persuaded not to include a new milk plant in its 1983 plan.[98] Tatar obkom sent 4,600 communists and Komsomols to work in livestock farms during the winter of 1985.[99] Among the more unusual political campaigns were the mobilization of Young Pioneers to collect 20 million birch twigs for fodder in Kalinin; and E. Shevardnadze's proud sponsorship of a scheme to convert pig excrement into fodder when he was first secretary of the Georgia CC.[100]

These accounts suggest a depth of intervention by party organs in the livestock sector which exceeded that normally found in industrial factories, and which seemed to pay scant regard to the usual strictures against the sin of podmena.

Despite these political interventions, meat supplies did not show any dramatic improvement in the period in question. The deficiencies of the livestock sector were rooted in the irrational price structure discussed in the preceding section. The divergence between production costs and retail prices was probably greater for meat than for any other type of food product. This led to the well-known phenomenon of people buying bread in stores (at subsidized prices) to use as fodder for their livestock.[101] Such activity was not confined to individual peasants on their private plots: in one case in Dnepropetrovsk a director of a state trading organization was fired for reselling food to farms for use as fodder.[102]

Some cautious steps were taken towards a rationalization of the price structure. It was recognized that procurement prices were too low to make meat and milk production profitable. Thus the price paid to farms for meat was raised by 50 per cent in 1970 (plus a 50 per cent bonus for above-plan deliveries), and the milk price was hiked by 40 per cent in 1979.[103] Planners were reluctant to raise the procurement prices higher without a corresponding increase in consumer prices, for fear of increasing the subsidy burden on the state budget.

Poultry rearing

One sector of livestock rearing where the party enjoyed more success was poultry farming. Chicken farms were easier to build and run than cattle farms, and this probably accounts for their relative success. Egg production rose 25 per cent during 1976–80 compared to 1971–5, and chicken meat deliveries rose 29 per cent in the same period.[104] However, while the popular demand for eggs was roughly satisfied by 1976, poultry meat production lagged behind demand (again, because of poor feed).[105]

Party organizations were active in developing the poultry industry. Poultry farms were encouraged by CC CPSU decrees of 1971 and 1977, and in 1979 the first secretary of Ivanovo obkom received a commendation (*odobrenie*) from the CC CPSU for personally supervising the construction of a new chicken complex.[106] Dnepropetrovsk obkom 'mobilized all resources ... to implement a plan for rapid expansion of chicken production' in 1979.[107] These cases illustrate the active and autonomous role certain partkomy played in this sector.

There were a few complaints along the way. Some chicken farms were built too hastily, and were finished off without the requisite water and energy services.[108] Some ministries were accused of holding back funds for poultry farms because of a lack of incentives for them to help develop the sector.[109] The worst problem was that capacity was added so quickly that it ran ahead of the ability of breeder stations to produce chicks.[110] According to the head of the planning division of the main chicken trust, this was because local organs were reluctant to sink resources into investment-type activity which would not have immediate, local pay-off in eggs and meat for local consumers.[111] Thus even one of the few success stories of the decade turns out on closer inspection to provide yet another illustration of the mismatch between political and economic incentive structures.

The grain silo construction campaign

The grain silo construction campaign launched at the 25th Party Congress was typical of the way the party tried to mobilize its apparatus on an emergency basis to mount an all-out assault on some pressing economic problem. The other major agricultural construction campaign of the decade was the drive to improve irrigation facilities (which will not be discussed here).

By the mid–1970s soviet farmers were suffering from their own success – output had risen, but grain handling and storage facilities were woefully inadequate; 8.5 million tonnes of silo capacity had been built between 1966 and 1970, and 16.5 million tonnes more by 1975.[112] The plan was to add 30 million tonnes of additional capacity by 1980. The plan for 1976 was 4.8 million tonnes, of which 4.3 million tonnes was actually built.

It was common for construction in rural areas to be carried out by poorly equipped local trusts. Half of the farm building in Krasnoiarsk, for example, was done by the farms themselves, from their own resources.[113] Silo construction, however, was too complicated for farms to handle themselves, and was the responsibility of six special trusts under various republican ministries.[114]

A vast campaign was launched to ensure that the necessary resources were channelled into these agencies. Given the way the Soviet economy worked, it was not enough to simply allocate them extra funds in the annual plan. The construction organizations needed powerful friends to ensure that the funds could be 'realized' – i.e. workers hired, equipment procured, designs drawn and transport laid on. Party organs were expected to prod the other agencies involved to fulfil their responsibilities.[115]

The press was activated to push the campaign forward. *Ekonomicheskaia gazeta* sent teams of journalists to conduct 'raids' on silo building sites, and published numerous critical articles which called forth humble apologies and promises of further action from party officials.[116] Many of these replies were signed by obkom secretaries themselves, testifying to the fact that the silo campaign was being run directly out of obkom offices. Apart from applying political pressure on other agencies, obkomy also took concrete measures such as despatching their own officials to the sites as plenipotentiaries, or recruiting student construction brigades.[117]

The various press reports referred to above were candid in their comments, and bluntly described the problems which the campaign ran into. Design bureaus were slow to complete project documentation, meaning that many silos went up before the design materials arrived.[118] Shortage of cement was an acute problem, compounded by lack of transport to get the cement to the sites.[119] Farm regions often had to import cement over huge distances. Belgorod, for example, was dependent on supplies from Moscow, Zhitomir and Birobizhan (6,000 miles distant!).[120] The quality and variety of cement was poor, since cement output was still planned by weight.[121] (Not to mention the fact that for the past thirty years developed countries have been building silos out of steel, not concrete.) Another problem was that in the rush to complete the silos, teams would leave without completing the infrastructure (housing, electricity and water supplies) needed to operate the silo complex.[122]

Press attention dropped off markedly after 1978. The targets for silo construction during the tenth five-year plan were not met (although detailed figures were not released).[123] The grain storage system continued to be a major bottleneck in agricultural development. In 1980, for example, Orenburg could only store 1.3 million tonnes out of its 5.5 million tonnes harvest in silos; 2.5 million tonnes was piled in assorted warehouses, and the remainder was left in the open.[124] Some 30 per cent of the crop continued to be lost each year because of inadequate storage and poor transport facilities: uncovered trucks, long distances and unpaved roads.[125]

The elevator campaign illustrates the acute need felt for decisive party interventions to aid the agricultural sector, but also shows the limitations of the campaign approach. Silo construction is not a complex technology (it was mastered on the US plains almost a century ago), and the inability of the agrarian sector to meet its own needs in this sphere is a typical illustration of the structural imbalances of the Soviet economy.

Industry assistance to agriculture

1 Factory sponsorship

It was routine practice for industry to be drafted in to the aid of agriculture at critical periods – to help with the spring sowing or with the harvest, particularly if the prognosis for the harvest was poor and every grain had to be saved.

The traditional pattern of industrial patronage (shefstvo) was the despatch of trucks and workers at harvest time. No reliable figures were available on the extent of this cooperation, but one official put the number at 1.4 million workers in 1981, the equivalent of 6 per cent of the farm labour force, rising to 20 per cent in some districts.[126] These figures seem rather low. Soviet economist E. Manevich estimated that 15.6 million workers were sent out to farms in 1979 (a bad harvest year), for an average of one month apiece.[127] The sources broadly agree, however, that the numbers involved had more than doubled since the early 1960s, as the permanent agricultural population continued to decline.

Local soviets and partkomy were responsible for organizing these annual drives. Rural raikomy coordinated the distribution of incoming workers, while party organs in the towns put pressure on factory managers to release the required personnel and resources – in most cases at their own expense.[128] Local soviets paid financial compensation if it was necessary to buy in help from other oblasti.[129]

There were attempts to try to extend the *shefstvo* beyond the tumultuous harvest period, and provide help on a more regular basis. This usually involved help with building, equipment maintenance and the supply of spare parts. Some of the more extensive assistance drives were organized not through factories *per se*, but through the Komsomol. In 1978 some 260,000 Komsomol volunteers were engaged in agricultural construction projects in the non-black earth region.[130] About half of these volunteers were students, and half were drawn from factory Komsomol units.

Just how effective was all this help for the farms? Perhaps it served some sort of useful purpose: otherwise, why was it done year after year? But the economic logic underlying these activities seems distinctly shaky.

The *shefstvo* campaigns were run in a haphazard and uncoordinated fashion. For example, one farm in Ivanovo found itself getting help from no less than thirty-three different patrons.[131] There were frequent complaints that the work was poorly organized and not carried out with any great enthusiasm. As the first secretary of L'vov obkom put it: 'It is clear. The land needs a permanent attentive master, not a temporary helper.'[132]

These campaigns were a significant burden to the factories involved, and were highly unpopular with their directors.[133] According to Manevich, their complaints were based on sound economic reasoning, since he estimated the revenue product of workers sent to the countryside to be 25 per cent of what it would have been had they stayed in their factory.[134] The whole process created many administrative headaches. For example, the State Committee on Labour and Social Problems had to issue special regulations to try to protect the salaries of professionals sent to the countryside.[135]

The party came to realize that *shefstvo* was not the ideal solution to agriculture's ills. During the crucial year of 1979, Brezhnev criticized poorly organized *shefstvo* in his speech to the November CC CPSU plenum, and his comments were interrupted with enthusiastic applause and cries of *pravil'no!* (You're right!) from the floor.[136]

Sending skilled personnel to perform agricultural duties was a particularly blatant misuse of the nation's resources, but made good copy for journalists. Each summer would bring stories of, for example, doctors from the Novosibirsk railway hospital picking carrots, or scientists from the Institute of Geology sorting potatoes.[137] Many school classes were dispatched for a month or two of 'labour experience' in the countryside.[138]

Mobilizing urban resources to aid the farms was a policy in which party organs played a prominent and active role, but they did not see this as a satisfactory way of dealing with the USSR's long-term agricultural problems. It was a temporary stop-gap solution to the disorder in Soviet farming – one which was applied for decades.

2 Auxiliary farms

One of the more curious and instructive developments of the past two decades has been the growth of auxiliary farms set up and run by factories and mines, usually on their own initiative. They illustrate the scope for self-interested behaviour outside the plan which some Soviet economic institutions enjoyed, and showed the resource-wealth of industry when compared to agriculture. Local party organs usually aided and abetted managers in these endeavours.

The reason for industrial plants diversifying into farming was simple: it was one way of trying to guarantee food supplies for their workers. Apart from the desire to 'look after their own', it also made economic sense for managers to use food as a way of attracting and retaining workers in the labour-scarce Soviet economy. Some of the factory farms dated back to the 1930s, but they mushroomed in the late 1970s, as they found favour with CPSU leaders.[139] As one director said in 1978: 'Until recently, these auxiliary farms (*podsobnye khoziaistva*) were considered an anachronism, but now there are concrete decrees approving the practice.'[140] They also managed to survive successive waves of agricultural reform. The May 1982 Food Programme expected every industrial enterprise to have its own auxiliary farm; and the president of the new 'super ministry' Gosagroprom said in 1986 that he saw factory farms (and private plots) playing a crucial role, particularly in meat production.[141]

It is difficult to calculate the aggregate output of these auxiliary farms, but accounts indicate that they made an appreciable difference to the food supplies of individual plants. For example, the farm run by the giant Azovstal steel mill provided 20 per cent of the meat for its canteen, and that of the Tbilisi aviation plant provided 30 per cent.[142] In addition to canteen meals, factories sold meat to their workers for home consumption. The farms run by Tomskneft (an oil company) provided 25 per cent of the food supply for the whole town of Strezhevoi.[143] In 1981 a special association was formed to coordinate the factory farms around Togliatti: it was hoped that they would meet 85 per cent of the city's food needs by the end of the decade.[144] Some of these farms were sizable concerns. The Inta coal mine, for example, had a farm with 3,100 head of cattle; and the Rybinsk motor plant operation was rearing 120,000 chickens a year.[145]

Auxiliary farms were developed by diverting funds allocated to the enterprise for industrial production. This usually entailed some creative accounting, leading to occasional accusations of fiscal irregu-arlity.[146] The Novolipetsk steel combine boasted that it had developed its farm (2,000 pigs and 200 cows, meeting 20 per cent of its meat needs) 'from nothing' using their own resources.[147] They even built a 14 km road to the farm at their own expense, using their own men and materials. Some firms operated across regional boundaries, such as a Moscow construction trust which set up vegetable greenhouses in the Karachaevo-Cherkess oblast, 750 miles to the south.[148]

Sometimes help was proffered by local organs. In Tashkent the gorkom helped to coordinate the work of fourteen farms run by city enterprises.[149] Tambov obkom gave political support to some local factories when their ministry bosses tried to stop them diverting resources into their farms.[150] By no means were all the central ministries hostile to factory farms. The coal ministry, for example, set aside 3 million roubles for farm development, with the result that half of the nation's coal mines were running farms by 1983.[151]

The factory farm movement testifies to the entrepreneurial energy of some managers and local officials. However, the development was not without its drawbacks. Nationalist figures such as Anatolii Salutskii argued that the reliance on auxiliary farms was yet another example of the urban bias of the CPSU leadership, since these heavily subsidised

farms benefited the factory workers, while kolkhozy were being bled
dry by manpower shortages and lack of investment.[152] Agricultural
planners were concerned, because the output of these farms was not
reported under the state agricultural plan.[153] In fact, the farms were
entirely outside of the plan. An effort to collect central statistics on
their output began in 1983, but calls to write them into the five-year
plans were not acted upon.[154]

The unplanned nature of the farms also carried disadvantages for
the firms running them. It meant that they were not eligible to receive
equipment, fertilizer and so forth through the Gossnab system. Selk-
hoztekhnika refused to repair their equipment because they were not
'on the plan' (po planu), and there was no legal way for them to be
reimbursed for such work.[155] Keeping tractors running may have been
within the capabilities of the average factory, but providing seed,
chicks and fertilizer was not so easy for them. These problems meant
that auxiliary farms suffered from low yields and high costs.[156]

In the long run, surely, farming belongs in the hands of farmers, not
political or industrial patrons. It would seem more logical to channel
the resources to attract skilled labour and mechanize production
directly to the farms, rather than hope that these resources can be
skimmed off from industry. Auxiliary farms represented a return to a
sort of subsistence agriculture in the context of a modern, urbanized
economy, and was totally at odds with modern agricultural techniques.

Summary

The material presented in this chapter indicates that a full
appreciation of the nature of the party's role in industry cannot be
attempted without recognition of the continuing importance attached
to party work in the countryside.

Agriculture was starved of resources and attention for several
decades, and failed to build up a robust administrative-managerial
structure of the sort which emerged in Soviet industry. Local party
organs stepped into the breach, shouldering major responsibilities in
the rural economy. Beginning in the mid-1960s, massive investments
were pumped into villages, and there was a concomitant burgeoning
of administrative agencies, but this did not alter the pivotal role played
by party committees in the countryside.

Press accounts of party life in the 1970s were replete with detailed
accounts of party interventions in agricultural affairs of a type not seen
in reports from industrial plants. This subjective reading of the press is

confirmed by a content analysis of *Ekonomicheskaia gazeta* articles and letters using more objective measures (see Appendix 2 for details). The most striking conclusion to emerge from this modest exercise was the prominence occupied by agricultural affairs in the life of the CPSU. Similarly, an unexpected result to emerge from an analysis of the career background of obkom first secetaries in the 1980s (chapter 10) was the high proportion of the regional party elite with a background in agriculture.

Apart from routine monitoring of sowing, harvesting, labour retention and the economic health of their region's farms, local party leaders were periodically mobilized for national campaigns, such as those to expand livestock rearing and silo construction. These sapped the energies of party officials, but with indifferent results. Finally, this chapter examined the rather curious phenomenon of industrial sponsorship of local agriculture, including the growing practice of farms run by factories 'off the plan'. These practices illustrate the scope for autonomous economic behaviour by Soviet industrial managers, and underline the complexity of the planned economy. They also reinforce our observation that in order to understand Soviet industry, it is necessary to study it jointly with the agricultural sector.

Why did agriculture prove so troublesome for the CPSU? Why did the party remain trapped in the thankless task of trying to keep this unwieldy leviathan on course? The explanation lies largely in the dead hand of historical tradition. In the 1930s a system of political control organs was established in the countryside, their mission being to pump out resources and manpower to fuel the industrialization drive.

Soviet agricultural management never really progressed beyond this 'primitive accumulation' structure – despite the fact that in the 1960s the flow of resources was reversed, and the party began to channel huge quantities of investment and machinery into the nation's farms. Agricultural activity was simply not suited to this sort of centralized, campaign-oriented approach.

Having chosen this path, however, the party seemed unable to retrace its steps and disengage itself from farm management. They feared that if the current system of political controls and industrial sponsors were dismantled, food shipments to the towns could collapse dramatically, triggering massive urban unrest. The party apparatus seemed unable to conceive of the possibility of Soviet agriculture being run on a market basis. In a market system, of course, the rationale for the power previously enjoyed by regional party bosses in the countryside would no longer be present.

8 Non-party control organs

The Communist Party was not the only outside body charged with supervising Soviet industry to ensure that it operated in a legal and efficient manner. There was a host of administrative and voluntary social (*obshchestvennye*) organizations which performed monitoring functions in the Soviet economy.

During the Brezhnev era there was an attempt to increase the role of these supplementary bodies to ease the burden of supervisory work formerly shouldered by party organs. This would leave party officials free to concentrate on their core political and ideological functions. Despite the extensive nature of these auxiliary control activities, in fact they had a minimal impact on bureaucratic and managerial behaviour. The non-party organs fell prey to all of the problems which dogged the supervisory work of party organs – lack of time and expertise; a tendency to collude with economic managers; and a lack of authority *vis-à-vis* the ministerial hierarchies.

Thus the attempt to shift responsibility for bureaucratic supervision from party to non-party organs seems to have been a dismal failure. M. Gorbachev delivered a scathing indictment of the work of Soviet control organs in his report to the January 1987 CC CPSU meeting, arguing that the morass of commissions and inspections had produced 'miserable' results.[1] This chapter will try to explain why this policy failed – and why, despite this failure, the system persisted in relying on external control agencies.

The Committee of People's Control

Opponents of socialism might think that the best way to tackle bureaucratism was to cut back on the powers of the bureaucracies. The Soviet leadership took a different view. As one author put it in 1982, the answer to bureaucratic inefficiency is not 'the removal of the socialist state from the sphere of administration of social affairs, but ensuring a more direct, wider, more competent, and therefore more effective participation by the members of society'.[2] And the way to do that was to set up additional bureaucracies.

The problem of bureaucratism dogged the Soviet state from its earliest days. Initially, the party was too busy with the consolidation of its political power to concern itself with monitoring bureaucrats, so Lenin turned to 'control from below', encouraging popular participation in supervising state organs. The Workers' and Peasants' Inspectorate (Rabkrin) was formed in 1920, with Stalin as its head. Rabkrin was abolished in 1934, and popular control went through a number of organizational permutations over the next thirty years, emerging in 1965 as the Committee of People's Control (Komitet Narodnogo Kontrolia, or KNK).[3]

Initially, the KNK was a moribund body with a low political profile. Its standing was significantly increased by a new law in 1979, as part of the campaign for increased popular participation which accompanied the passage of the new 1977 Constitution.[4] KNK was supposed to become, in G. Shakhnazarov's words, 'the antidote to bureaucratism'.[5] The organization expanded over the next five years, with 10.1 million volunteers organized in 1.3 million groups by 1984.[6] Their work was coordinated by roughly 1,000 regional KNKs, formed by local soviets at regional or city level, or within large enterprises.

Under the 1979 law the KNK enjoyed augmented powers. Its members had the right to collect information, inspect documents, call for reports, issue binding recommendations, serve reprimands, and pass materials on to other organizations (e.g. to the procurator, for criminal prosecution). KNK committees could levy fines and remove (*otstraniat*) officials from their positions, their subsequent fate (demotion or dismissal) being determined by the employing ministry.[7] In 1980 *Ekonimicheskaia gazeta* started printing a weekly People's Control page, with reports from around the country on the activities of People's Controllers. The KNK's status peaked in 1984, when Chernenko was CPSU General Secretary.[8]

The newly invigorated KNK gave the appearance of being fairly active. In the first six months of 1984 they carried out 152,000 inspections (or 'raids' as they were called), leading to 132,000 officials and workers being reprimanded, 27,400 fined, 2,400 sacked, and 3,000 reported to the procurator.[9] These figures may well be exaggerated, as there was no evidence from regional reports in the press that such a high rate of attrition was actually taking place.[10]

Controllers concentrated on running general campaigns against fuel waste, grain losses, consumer goods shortages, etc. They also took up individual cases in response to appeals from the general public. The range of activity covered was extraordinarily wide, from chasing unregistered lambs in Stavropol to making sure trucks did not spill grain when cornering too fast in Latvia.[11] Their brief ranged from simple inefficiency to downright illegality. KNK-inspired sackings usually involved illegality in the disposition of funds.[12] Only a few examples came to light of officials being fired for dereliction of duty short of outright criminality. One example was the sacking of the director of a research institute in the Ministry of Non-Ferrous Metals for failing to promote automation in that sector.[13]

Sometimes the control campaigns were launched from on high. For example, the CC CPSU instructed the KNK to monitor the construction of eleven new oil refineries (all were completed on time), while the Ukrainian CC ordered its KNK to run a republic-wide survey on the state of consumer goods supplies.[14] The tasks of the KNK closely paralleled the work of party organs. They sometimes served as a regional coordinator (for example, criticizing the L'vov oblast for being both an importer and exporter of wood products).[15] They operated as supply expediters (for example, Ivano-Frankovsk KNK secured spare parts for a local washing machine plant from their supplier in Latvia, by appealing to the Latvian KNK).[16] An example of their quality control work was the Ishimskoe KNK persuading the Moscow Zil plant to send springs to a local tractor plant in boxes, rather than allowing them to rust in open rail wagons.[17] They could be mobilized for national priority campaigns, as when Khar'kov KNK hastened the delivery of building supplies being sent out to Siberia.[18]

In a few rare cases People's Control organs actually admonished local party officials, although it was lethargy rather than anything more heinous that party officials were accused of.[19] For example, a raikom in Semipalatinsk was upbraided for standing by while a manager systematically embezzled funds from his train depot.[20]

It is difficult to know how important a role KNK raids really played in improving Soviet economic performance and combatting lawbreaking. Press reports presented a one-sided picture, emphasizing the KNK's successes. Critical reports were suspiciously few in number, although there were occasional accounts of KNK instructions being ignored by enterprise managers.[21]

Although the evidence is inadequate for a definitive assessment, it seems reasonable to argue that the KNK lacked real autonomy, and functioned as a traditional 'transmission belt' for the party. Party officials exercised their familiar 'leading role' over KNK organs. In 1980 the partkomy of 784 leading enterprises were ordered to activate the work of People's Control in their plants.[22] The first secretary of the Kurgan obkom replied to press criticism of the poor work of the KNK in his region – a reliable indicator of where accountability really lay.[23] Of People's Control volunteers 39 per cent were party members, and 50 per cent of oblast KNK chairmen sat on their party obkom bureau, while 89 per cent of district KNK heads sat on their raikom bureaus.[24] Party theorists explicitly stated that KNK campaigns had to be tied in to the current priorities of the CPSU leadership, and that the KNK should not 'degenerate' into an ombudsman-type organization preoccupied with processing individual complaints.[25]

The multiplicity of control organs in the USSR

The Committee of People's Control was only one of many organizations charged with supervising the work of state administrators. In fact, there was a plethora of agencies carrying out this role: some general in scope, others targetted on individual problems. They included the following.
1 The CPSU itself, and within it the special control organs such as the Central Auditing Commission and the network of local 'party commissions' under Committee of Party Control (KPK).
2 The Komsomol, 42 million strong, and control organs within it such as the 'Projector' movement.
3 The Committee of People's Control (KNK).
4 The legal organs (Procuracy, Ministry of Internal Affairs, KGB).
5 Inspection teams from within each of the economic ministries.
6 The Ministry of Finance, the State Bank (Gosbank) and the sectoral banks.
7 The media.
8 Other public organizations such as the trade unions, or single-issue groups such as the 'All Union Society for the Struggle for Sobriety'.
Following sections review some of the operating characteristics of these various supervisory agencies, and their relationship to party organs.

1 Control by financial organs

The practice of 'cost accounting' (*khozraschet*) was a formative principle of the Soviet command economy from its very inception, but was respected more in the breach than in the observance. 'Control by the rouble' did not play an important role in Soviet economic history: plans were calculated in physical terms, then converted into monetary and financial targets. Profitability was always subordinate to plan fulfilment. The package of reforms introduced in 1979 saw a renewed effort to introduce real cost accounting into lagging sectors such as collective farm agriculture and construction.

These measures had some effect in 'hardening' the budget constraint of Soviet managers, judging by the stories that started to appear about firms experiencing financial difficulties.[26] According to the deputy head of Goskomselkhoztekhnika, the financial squeeze was particularly acute in the farm sector.[27]

This phenomenon is noteworthy not because it presaged any real shift towards financial discipline in the Soviet economy (it did not), but because of the hostile reaction it provoked from local party organs. The Ivanovo obkom first secretary criticized the Construction Bank for its tight credit policies, while Voronezh obkom officials complained about the impact of the credit squeeze on local farms and factories.[28]

These objections to 'control by the rouble' were evidence of the party's deep-seated ideological fear of increased reliance on money and market-type forces. There was also a healthy dose of self-interest involved: party officials did not want the fate of local farms or builders to hinge on decisions by financial regulators from outside the province.

One area where financial controls were regarded as indispensable was in the struggle with corruption and embezzlement. The General Procurator reported in 1985 that inflation of plan performance reports (*pripiski*) took place in 50 per cent of all construction materials plants, and in twenty out of twenty-four firms in the oil and chemical industry.[29] The Construction Bank found irregularities in wage payments in one in five building firms in 1981. Of these 8,830 firms they fined 1,645 and sent 1,082 for criminal prosecution.[30] The effectiveness of these financial reviews was however limited by the duplication of auditing functions between the Ministry of Finance, Gosbank and the sectoral banks.[31]

2 Control by legal organs

Legal organs played an active role in the economic sphere, not as an arbiter of inter-firm disputes, but through pursuit of a variety of activities labelled as 'economic crime'.[32]

Unfortunately, as the Minister of Justice himself noted in 1986, respect for the law amongst economic managers was very weak.[33] The command economy generated so many rules and regulations that 'Nowadays a manager who adheres strictly to the law will not achieve anything.'[34]

Regional party leaders typically exercised close control over local judges, whose appointments they controlled, giving them precise instructions on how to handle all but the most routine of cases. This system of 'telephone justice' left even less room for the legal system to play an independent role.[35]

3 The role of the press

The role of the media in Soviet society, their impact on public opinion, and their role as a feedback mechanism through which public opinion had some influence on political leadership have been extensively studied by Western scholars.[36] The press in the Brezhnev era was basically a top-down instrument, used by the CPSU to consolidate its control over society. The press played an important role in reinforcing the party's leading role in the economy, but its reports often revealed the contradictions and ambiguities in the party's approach to the economy.

Even in pre-glasnost times, the Soviet press had an investigative role, exposing corruption and inefficiency. Officials were obliged to respond to press criticisms, and newspapers could even refuse to accept replies which they deemed inadequate.[37] Newspapers could censure the conduct of local party meetings (but not central ones, of course) where journalists considered them to be insufficiently self-critical. As will be discussed in the concluding chapter, Gorbachev's perestroika relied heavily on the press to spearhead its critique of the old order, including the use of hostile press reports of party meetings up to obkom level, in an effort to push through a change in their work methods.

The investigative work of the press was usually organized on a campaign basis, focussing on a particular problem (such as alcoholism in February and March 1986).[38] *Ekonomicheskaia gazeta* maintained a list of priority projects in industry and agriculture and sent their journalists to conduct 'raids' or set up 'control posts' to send in regular reports.[39]

For the most part, this economic reporting was not the product of enquiring journalists, but was orchestrated by local party organs. Newspapers made extensive use of their network of amateur stringers, officially called 'worker correspondents' (*rabkory*). There were some 5,000 in Sverdlovsk alone, and they were recruited, trained and run by local party organs.[40] Further evidence of the party's leading role came from the fact that the press was frequently criticized by the party for not being sufficiently aggressive. For example, the trade union daily *Trud* was criticized in a 1982 CC CPSU resolution for not doing enough investigative journalism.[41] *Moskovskaia pravda*, the capital's daily, was censured for not following up on stories where problems had been exposed.[42] Examples ranged from the work of transport firms to the availability of school uniforms.

According to the editor of the Kiev *Pravda*, it was the local press that was most reluctant to pursue tough stories.[43] This was not entirely their own fault: journalists who criticized the 'local powers' could find themselves in trouble. Examples ranged from the suppression of aggressive reports in the Estonian fish industry magazine, through to the celebrated Berkhin case where a journalist was arrested for exposing illegality in the local police force.[44] The latter scandal eventually led to the sacking of the first secretary of Voroshilovgrad obkom, B. Goncharenko, in February 1987.

The press did not function in an entirely top-down manner. The question of environmental protection is the best-known example of an issue finding its way onto the political agenda through the independent actions of lobbyists and journalists. The threat of pollution of Lake Baikal became a *cause célèbre* in the late 1960s, thanks largely to the actions of concerned scientists and nationalist-inclined writers.[45] Even in this case, however, the party was not simply a neutral bystander, caught off guard by a dynamic social movement. According to an article in a Leningrad journal, the party itself launched an active campaign of 'ecological propaganda'.[46] The party's efforts were mentioned in the environmental laws passed in 1960 and 1972, and the implementation of these instructions was discussed by regional and local party bureaus. A special competition to encourage the publication of ecological articles in the press was run by the All-Union Society for Nature Protection, as a result of which it was estimated that the number of published pieces increased seven-fold in 1976–80.

It could be that this party historian was just trying to claim credit for what the journalists and scientists had begun, but it seems clear that the *spread* of the campaign, and the emergence of ecology as an issue of national debate, was due to the CPSU's adoption of the subject.

One should be careful not to exaggerate the power of the press when it came to affecting policy outcomes. Using the press as a vehicle for party propaganda limited its scope as a tool for the analysis of social ills. The transformation in much of the press since 1985 showed what could be achieved when the controls were eased. In the pre-1985 period, however, the pattern was for press reports to focus on current industrial priorities, at the expense of broader social issues. 'Alerts' coming from factories facing a production problem received priority over reports of shortages of housing or kindergarden places.[47] Quite often, critical reports produced little more than promises of action from the officials responsible.[48] Even leading party journals such as *Partiinaia zhizn* could not guarantee action in response to their reports. For example, a year after the journal intervened to get phones installed in an invalids' home in Odessa, they still had not arrived.[49]

4 Auxiliary channels of party control

Apart from the supervisory functions carried out by the party apparatus itself, there were additional channels of control which party officials could call upon.

The various 'public organizations' (*obshchestvennye organizatsii*) were at the party's disposal, and could be mobilized for economic supervision purposes. For example, in 1962 the Komsomol set up the 'Projector' organization to conduct raids on inefficiency (very similar to those conducted by the KNK).[50] Some of their drives were national in scope, and they claimed to involve 10 million participants between 1971 and 1975. In 1982 they had 1.6 million volunteers working in 22,000 posts, up from 1.1 million in 1978.[51] Even Young Pioneers could be roped into these campaigns. For example, Vinnitsa party workers arranged for children to stand along the roads in summer, checking that trucks were not spilling too much of the sugar beet harvest.[52]

Party organs relied on letters and visits from the general public to alert them to emergent problems – a phenomenon studied extensively by S. White.[53] Between 1976 and 1981 the CC CPSU alone got some 3 million letters and visits, and all party organs taken together had around 15 million.[54] These representations were synthesized into general reports, which were submitted to party bureaus. Select individual cases which looked worthy of investigation were sent down to the relevant local party organ. For example, in 1980 Ivanovo-Frankovsk obkom sent 3,336 letters down to its raikomy, and itself received 905 letters passed down from higher party organs.[55]

The primary goal of this activity was to keep the party informed about social attitudes. It was unlikely that many of the complainants found a solution to their problems. It was officially conceded, for example, that only one in six representations made to the Bryansk obkom were 'resolved' (whatever that might have meant).[56] The vast majority of the appeals related to housing problems, followed by breakdowns in retail supplies, schools and hospitals, and illegal firings.[57]

Problems of coordination and control

Far from being organized into a single, clear administrative hierarchy, economic administration was characterized by a multiplicity of control agencies, with overlapping jurisdictions and competing criteria. Soviet administrative theory deliberately encouraged this proliferation of control organs. This picture stands in contrast to the pure 'prefect' model, where there is supposedly a single, authoritative control centre.

The multiplicity of agencies meant that one agency could be played off against the other, providing a check on their reliability and efficiency. Western organization theorists refer to this as the technique of 'opposed maximisers'.[58] Second, each agency could in theory be tasked with a particular problem, reducing the scope for lower officials to be in a position where they could themselves determine the trade-offs between competing goals. The central authorities preferred to keep that power to themselves. A system of 'opposed maximisers' was of course well established in the Soviet army, with its parallel structures of line officers and political workers, and seemed to work to the party's satisfaction.[59]

This approach carried certain dangers, however. Too many control agencies were formed, diluting their impact and meaning that managers felt able to ignore their recommendations with impunity. Thus, for example, there were so many different air inspectors visiting a new steel mill in Donetsk, each with a different set of regulations, that the mill managed to go into production with no air filters at all.[60]

Another danger was that it was too easy to pretend to tackle a problem by creating a new control body – 'hiding behind commissions', as Chernenko put it.[61] One Soviet author recalled the words of Colonel Koshkarev, a character in Gogol's *Dead Souls* who suggested 'forming a commission, called "the commission to monitor the construction commission"'.[62]

The multiplicity of overseers was burdensome for factory managers, even if not particularly threatening. The director of a colour television plant in Moscow complained that 'Above us stand dozens of control inspectorates. Each has the right to proscribe, ban, exclude, insist and penalize the enterprise and its managers. But none of them are interested in the actions and demands of others ... Often our rights diverge from our responsibilities.'[63] He was not alone in drawing attention to this problem. According to one source: 'Today an industrial enterprise finds itself under the supervision of roughly two dozen state and public organs, institutions and departmental groups [*instantsii*].'[64] Factory managers often complained that their workplace was a revolving door for visiting control agencies. The average Donetsk plant received 129 monitoring teams in 1980, while in 1983 the Belotserkov rubber enterprise had 90, and a Dzambul shoe factory 112.[65]

Local party organs were expected to provide some coordination over these multitudinous control agencies. A 1981 CC CPSU decree ordered party organizations 'to work out concrete measures to eliminate parallelism and duplication in the work of the organs of People's Control, the standing committees of soviets, Komsomol "projector" teams, and committees of trade union organizations'.[66] The standard technique was for the party to set up a coordinating council with representatives from the various agencies.[67] Unfortunately, the control bodies were not always willing to cooperate, jealously guarding their independence. The Leningrad council, for example, only managed to include 22 of the 140 control agencies operating in the region.[68] Similarly, the Cheliabinsk obkom managed to persuade seventeen organizations to join their council, but others refused to participate.[69] The Primorsk council, with thirty bodies represented, found that key agencies such as Gosbank and the Ministry of Finance limited their participation to the *ex post* submission of their reports.[70]

The proliferation of control bodies spread beyond the party's control, and little effort was expended to reverse the process. Azrael suggests that this system originated in the late 1920s precisely because Stalin 'had a vested interest in confusion'.[71] While such Machiavellian designs may or may not be imputed to subsequent party leaders, the best that can be said is that they adopted an *ad hoc* approach, creating a new specialized agency to tackle each emergent supervision problem. For example, in response to complaints that expensive imported machinery was lying unused, the Chamber of Trade formed a special inspectorate to monitor the installation of imported equipment.[72]

One coordination problem which received special attention after the accession of Andropov in 1982 was the old question of *Quis custodiet ipsos custodies?* (Who guards the guards?). With so many people involved in supervisory work, in so many different agencies, it was difficult to ensure their ideological vigilance and reliability. Thus in the clean-up in corrupt Krasnodar province which began in 1983, 263 People's Control posts were themselves reprimanded for inertia or complicity in illegal acts.[73] The Kazakh KNK had to fire local People's Controllers who had covered up the illegal actions of a clinic director.[74] In North Ossetia the head of the republic procuracy was himself arraigned on criminal charges; and a raikom first secretary in Azerbaijan was sacked in 1981 for arranging the dismissal of a local whistleblower.[75]

Summary

So, the CPSU was not alone in its work of supervising the functioning of the Soviet economy. On the contrary, there were numerous and varied control agencies, relying upon legal, financial and popular means to uncover inefficiencies and illegalities in the behaviour of Soviet managers. There was a determined effort to expand the role played by these non-party organizations over the years 1975 to 1985.

These bodies should be seen as supplementing rather than displacing the supervisory functions of party organs. Party officials and members played an important role in directing the work of People's Control, the Komsomol and the press. Party organs also tried to regulate the work of the ministry inspectorates, in a largely vain attempt to rein in the rampant duplication and confusion.

The interventions of non-party control organs often seemed to make better financial, economic or technical sense than those coming from party organs. However, what they gained in being relatively free of political motivation, they lost in terms of diminished influence over managers. For all their earnest activity, these auxiliary control bodies were rarely listened to. Nevertheless, the spread of the non-party control organs during the Brezhnev years probably eased to some degree the burden of supervisory duties carried by local party officials.

9 The principles underlying the party's work with cadres

As explained in chapter 1, the party attached great importance to its role in the selection, training and promotion of cadres in non-party organizations. The theory was that rather than have party officials supervise industry directly, party influence should operate indirectly, via the line managers.

Conservative party thinkers in the Brezhnev period still subscribed to Stalin's philosophy of 'cadres decide everything', arguing that the system's institutional structure was fundamentally sound, and merely needed an infusion of fresh blood to make it function to its full potential.[1]

In published descriptions of party activity in the economy, there was much more convincing detail on their role in cadre selection than for any other aspect of their economic work.[2] For example, directors writing articles in *Ekonomicheskaia gazeta* rarely referred to the activities of party officials in their factory, but when they did it was often in connection with cadre selection.[3]

Chapter 1 described the mechanics of party work with cadres: the nomenklatura system, its role in the removal of incompetent or corrupt officials and so forth. This chapter looks at some of the principles underlying this process. What was the party looking for in the cadres it promoted? Was there tension between the demands of political loyalty and technical competence?

The Soviet image of the ideal manager

There was a considerable body of sociological literature in the USSR spelling out the ideal combination of qualities which a Soviet manager should display. The general idea was that of a New Soviet Man of Renaissance proportions. Each manager was expected to display *all* the desired qualities, from political consciousness to technical competence, and there was an unwillingness to accept the possibility of trade-offs between different attributes. The party preferred generalists, being reluctant to concede that different qualities might have been more useful in some parts of society than in others.[4]

In reality, of course, such ideal, rounded individuals did not exist (at least, not in numbers large enough to run Soviet industry). Such ideal managers did, however, dominate the novels and plays of the so-called 'production genre' of the 1970s. For example, A. Misharin's play *Four times as big as France* portrays obkom first secretary Shakhmatov as a superstar whose impeccable political credentials are matched by his doctorate, fluency in three languages and ability to be 'the first to spot a mistake in a technical drawing'.[5]

The search for exemplary 'leaders of a socialist type' started with Lenin, needless to say. Books and articles on the subject typically began with his four criteria for cadre selection:[6]

1 from the point of view of honesty;
2 from his political position;
3 knowledge of the business in question;
4 administrative ability.

A similar formula, sometimes quoted, comes from G. Dimitrov's speech to the 1935 Comintern congress:[7]

1 deepest loyalty to the affairs of the working class, trust in the party;
2 closest links with the masses;
3 the ability to work independently and not be afraid of responsibility for decisions;
4 discipline and tenacity in struggles with the class enemy against deviations from the Bolshevik line.

A recurrent theme was that the essence of leadership was working with people: being able to understand their feelings, and being on good terms with them.[8] A. Yanovitch describes this as a distinctively 'collegial' managerial style, while M. Urban talks of a Soviet commitment to 'humane administration'.[9] J. Klugman emphasises the importance of the friendship and patronage networks which Soviet administrators forged as they moved up the hierarchy.[10]

This Soviet emphasis on work 'with people' was consistent with their bias against leadership as the imposition of objective criteria, such as economic calculation or administrative/legal rules. The focus on direct human contact was one reason why the Soviet managerial structure heavily favoured direct line managers (who had regular contact with their workforce subordinates), over 'staff' managers (based away from the shopfloor, in quality control and cost departments), who were responsible for the application of objective criteria.[11]

Soviet industrial sociologists utilized a typology of democratic, authoritarian and liberal (hands-off) management styles, developed by East German theorists in the 1950s.[12] They concluded that the democratic style was best, for, although the authoritarian style could produce higher output, democratic managers had a better record in terms of labour turnover, accident rates, etc. One fairly rigorous study of leadership styles conducted in Iaroslavl in the early 1970s tried to measure the presence of the three leadership types.[13]

The role of cadre attestations

A popular approach to the evaluation of leadership among both academics and party thinkers was the use of formal points systems, designed to take into account the whole range of attributes which Soviet cadres were expected to display.

Those advocating these 'cadre attestation' systems had mixed motives. Some management scientists wanted to promote the status of their discipline through the application of 'scientific' measurement techniques, emulating large Western corporations such as IBM. Others saw them as simply a means to justify much-needed salary raises for specialists (i.e. those with higher education), whose earnings relative to the average worker had slipped from 168 per cent in 1955 to 124 per cent in 1975.[14]

Attestations were carried out by panels of officials, including representatives of public organizations such as the party and trade unions. Some panels were set up specifically to fill a particular position, but it became increasingly common to conduct a periodic review of all managerial cadres in a given institution. The attestation approach was seen as more systematic and objective than previous methods, and became widespread after a CC CPSU decree on the subject in 1973.[15] However, contrary to some initial expectations, the system was rarely used to weed out ineffective managers.[16]

Attestation panels interviewed candidates and studied their work records, which contained all their *kharakteristiki* – the evaluations of their competence and political reliability filed by previous managers and party supervisors. Some panels went to extraordinary lengths – for example, asking for the employment records of the candidate's dozen nearest relatives![17] Having assembled all this information, the panel then rated the cadre on a five point scale, on each of a list of desirable qualities. There were usually 30–40 qualities 'tested', although in one case (the Rostov Gosplan office) there were no less than 120 separate measures.[18]

Taking one methodology proposed by Leningrad sociologists as an example, one finds a comprehensive list of qualities, ranging over technical and economic skills, but including ten explicitly political qualities, in a section titled 'Party-mindedness' (*partiinost*):[19]

1 Communist convictions.
2 Recognition of individual responsibility for assigned tasks.
3 Honesty, honor.
4 Ability to subordinate individual interests to those of the state.
5 Ability to educate the workers in the spirit of Marxist–Leninist ideas.
6 Sensitive and attentive attitude towards the workers.
7 Ability to support new initiatives.
8 Person of high principles.
9 Ability to accept criticism, to be self-critical.
10 Moral–political stability.

Cognizant of the fact that many candidates were not party members, the authors reassure us that even non-party members could be expected to display *partiinost*.[20] Even if in practice these qualities were often rated in a superficial and formalistic manner, this is clear evidence of the extent to which the party tried to inject purely political criteria into personnel selection. Public discussion of the tension between competence and political reliability was not allowed during the Brezhnev era, but such complaints were quick to surface under glasnost.[21]

In the 1980s, in recognition of the bureaucratic, formalistic nature of the attestation process, the party began to advocate open selection procedures, with direct workforce participation in questioning candidates, sometimes actually voting on them. In 1982 the party's theoretical journal stated that open discussions of candidates should be 'the rule'.[22] The open process was seen as an antidote to problems of corruption and favouritism in appointments.[23] Thus in corruption-ridden Krasnodar krai the new first secretary, G. Razumovskii, reported in 1985 that in the previous three years the performance of 1,000 leading managers had been discussed in open meetings, on the basis of which 150 were removed.[24] Some Georgian party organizations began to hold open discussions of candidates for the position of factory director in 1980, which in some 'relatively rare' cases led to the rejection of candidates nominated by the local raikom.[25] Some plants experimented with direct, competitive elections of leading managers by the workforce. In 1983 the Kommutator plant in Leningrad started holding elections for managers, as did a Voronezh engineering plant in 1985.[26] In the January 1987 speech which signalled Gorbachev's shift towards democratization, Gorbachev urged all plants to select managers on the basis of competitive elections.[27]

Apart from the practical utility of 'control from below' as a way of keeping managers on their toes, cadre elections also had certain ideological advantages. In part, they were a response to the challenge posed by the emergence of an organized workers' movement in neighbouring Poland.[28] Manager elections could be portrayed as 'socialist self-administration' in action, and indicative of the 'humane' character of industrial management in the USSR. Whether electing managers made good sense from the economic point of view remained in doubt: there were mounting complaints from planners and party officials that elected managers were colluding with their workers in evading plan obligations and pushing up wages. (See the concluding chapter for more discussion of this issue.)

The role of political training

This is not the place to embark upon a detailed study of the CPSU's propaganda work in Soviet society, nor within the CPSU itself. The purpose of this short section is to draw the reader's attention to the extensive programme of political socialization for economic cadres which party organs operated. They were not content to trust the selection process to promote cadres with the required political outlook. On the contrary, cadres had to be schooled in the party's world view, with regular refresher courses to ensure that the 'ideological hardening' (*ideinaia zakalka*) did not weaken with the passage of time, or in the light of new social developments.[29]

A special network of political training institutions for leading soviet and party cadres was established in the 1930s. The system went through many changes and developed in a rather disorganized fashion, such that prior to its reorganization in 1965 there were more than sixty different programmes in operation.[30] Party training was reviewed in CC decrees of 1967, 1972, 1976 and twice in 1978.[31] For most officials in party and soviet organs, attendance at a short 2–8 week course was obligatory once every two years.[32] Some party organizations, such as Bashkir obkom and Moscow gorkom, tried to make them obligatory for *all* officials on their nomenklatura (i.e.

including factory and farm managers) at some point in their careers.[33]
According to the 1976 CC CPSU decree, such courses should include:[34]

    54 hours on the leading role of the party;
    42 hours on Marxism–Leninism and 'communist construction';
    34 hours on the party's economic policy;
    20 hours on international affairs.

These courses were usually run by 'Universities of Marxism–
Leninism', operating out of a 'House of Political Enlightenment' under
the local obkom.[35]

For officials headed for a career in the party apparatus there were
2–4 year courses at one of the Higher Party Schools (*Vysshaia partiinaia
shkola* – VPSh). There were two VPSh run by the CC CPSU, in Moscow
and Leningrad, and twenty-one other regional VPSh in various
republics and obkomy.[36] In 1967 the CC CPSU ordered that all leading
officials of oblast soviet executive committees, and all chairmen of
district and city soviets, should go through courses at the CC CPSU
VPSh, and their deputies should go through regional VPSh.[37] In 1978 a
CC CPSU decree overhauled the regional party schools, adding more
part-time courses, and unifying their leadership under the Academy of
Social Sciences (Akademiia obshchestvennykh nauk – AON).[38] The
AON was a sort of CC CPSU think tank, created back in 1953. It is
unclear precisely how many cadres passed through this system of
party education. Soviet sources give figures varying from 187,000 to
248,000 for the 1946–78 period, with 16,000 people reported as passing
through all the VPSh during 1968–78.[39]

Thus the party education system functioned both as an instrument
of intra-party training, and as a vehicle for ensuring that economic
officials would understand and cooperate with their party overseers. It
is hard to judge how effective the political training system was in
socializing economic cadres into the party's way of thinking. Despite
Herculean efforts to improve the system in the 1965–78 period, official
pronouncements continued to be highly critical.[40]

This seemed to be part of a broader problem: the gradual entropy of
Soviet ideology as a whole. Despite editorial assertions that Marxism–
Leninism was 'neither ossified nor outdated', there were numerous
indications that the *content* of the ideology had lost its vitality over
time, despite the fact that the organizational machinery continued to
turn.[41] Teachers complained that students had no grasp of even the
most basic concepts of 'scientific communism', and it was openly
admitted that social science classes were 'boring and dull'.[42]
Astonishingly, a nationwide competition run by *Partiinaia zhizn*

between 1983 and 1985 failed to produce a single winning textbook for party study courses in any of the four categories (Marxism–Leninism, economic policy, social policy, methodology).[43] None of the 5,000 rouble first prizes (equal to two years' salary) were awarded. The Marxism category elicited the poorest manuscripts: even the 1,000 rouble consolation prizes were not given out.

This fragmentary evidence can be interpreted in various ways. It could be taken as indicating that the stress on political criteria was no longer important, as people stopped taking the ideology seriously. On the other hand, the party doggedly pursued the task of revitalizing the ideological training, at considerable cost in time and energy to Soviet managers.

The role of economic training

The heavy emphasis on political training must be viewed against the background of the extremely weak state of economic training in the USSR. Managerial competence was largely seen as arising from possession of technical skills in such disciplines as engineering or agronomy, as opposed to general managerial subjects such as economics or accountancy.

Economics as a scientific discipline was out of favour on grounds of political unreliability. Economic study along Western, neo-classical lines would raise questions about the criteria underlying resource allocation which could challenge the party's right to make such decisions, or at least force party officials to justify their actions. Engineers had a narrower and more task-oriented vision, and were less likely to question the objectives of their political mentors.

Evidence for the weak development of economics training comes in both quantitative and qualitative forms. In 1980 only 13 per cent of higher and 20 per cent of specialized secondary education graduates studied economics or business studies. The USSR produced 450,000 graduate engineers and 160,000 economists that year, compared to 213,000 engineers and 205,000 economics and business graduates in the USA.[44]

On the qualitative side, Soviet economics training was limited because students specialised in narrow, applied subjects such as retailing or mining, being taught undemanding, practical information about procedures and regulations instead of general principles. Economics courses devoted roughly one-third of tuition time to the study of political materials – Marxist–Leninist tracts, the latest party decrees and speeches by party leaders.[45] In 1987 the Minister of Higher Education estimated that the average student (sciences included) had to study no less than 174 works of Marxism–Leninism in the course of their education.[46]

Factory economists and accountants were low-status professionals who performed routine data gathering tasks.[47] Very few trained economists made it into top managerial positions: the overwhelming majority of the 345 directors whose short biographies were published in *Ekonomicheskaia gazeta* during 1976–85 had studied engineering and then risen through production management positions. Less than six were identifiable as economists.[48] Thus it is hardly surprising that Soviet managers paid scant attention to costs and prices.[49]

The same arguments held true for the legal profession. Less than 2 per cent of Soviet students graduated with a law degree, and the influence of lawyers on decision-making in Soviet factories was minimal.[50] As was the case with economics, so it was with law: the CPSU did not want any discipline to take hold which might constrain the arbitrary decision making of the central planners, or force them to explain their actions in the context of some externally defined set of principles and procedures.

Thus with day-to-day management in the hands of engineers and agronomists, and with economists, accountants and lawyers nowhere in sight, the field was clear for local party officials to claim to be the sole voice speaking in the interests of society as a whole.

Of 'reds' and 'experts'

Given their image of the ideal manager, Soviet sociologists tended to avoid the question of tension between the political and economic selection criteria. They adhered to the official line that, for example, 'forming a Marxist–Leninist world outlook in engineering-technical specialists is a decisive condition for raising their creative activity'.[51]

To an outsider, however, it seems rather curious to suggest that a good engineer must be somebody who has 'communist convictions' or 'the ability to educate workers in the spirit of Marxist–Leninist ideas' (taken from the list reproduced above). Was there 'an organic unity of partiinost and competence', as the first secretary of Murmansk obkom insisted?[52] Or was it not the case that some competent cadres failed to get promoted because of lack of ideological commitment, while others rose above their level of competence because of their political activism?

In the USSR of the 1920s, and in the China of the 1950s, there was a clear dichotomy drawn between 'reds' and 'experts'. The majority of technical, military and administrative specialists had received their training under the old regime, and their political views were hostile to socialism, or at best indifferent.[53] Some of them could be persuaded to work for the new state, but there was a clear rift between the old experts and the untrained political appointees who worked alongside them.

In the 1930s the regime set about transcending the red/expert dichotomy by educating a generation of 'red specialists' whose 'redness' would be guaranteed by selection according to class origin (the lower the better) and by ideological indoctrination. The synthesis was not entirely a happy one: their training tended to be hasty and rudimentary. Many of this first generation were what J. Hough calls 'political engineers', who made up in political fervour what they lacked in technical expertise.[54]

However, higher education made great strides forward in the post-Stalin period, with the proportion of the population holding higher degrees rising from 3.8 per cent in 1959 to 14.8 per cent in 1979.[55] A new generation of specialists emerged, whose technical training was at a satisfactory level, and who seemed to accept the legitimacy of the Soviet system.[56] One-third of all specialists in the 1970s were party members, rising to over 50 per cent in major industrial plants.[57]

From the other side, meanwhile, the 'reds' became increasingly 'expert'. The following table shows the percentage of party secretaries at various levels holding higher education:[58]

	1939	1956	1983
Gorkom, raikom	4.9	25.7	99.8
Obkom, republic CC	28.6	86	99
Primary party organization	4.7	11.4	60.3

Admittedly, some of these secretaries received their higher education in party schools of dubious pedagogic merit, or in non-technical subjects such as history or politics. But the upwards trend is clearly visible. Also, experience in industry also reportedly increased over time. The proportion of raikom, gorkom, and obkom secretaries in Ukraine who had economic or technical experience rose from 55 per cent in 1972 to 75 per cent in 1982.[59] In chapter 10, these trends are subjected to closer scrutiny on the basis of an examination of the career characteristics of the obkom elite of 1976–88, and it will be suggested that some of the claims for the level of professional skill and experience of party officials may be exaggerated.

However, it did seem as if the red/expert dichotomy was ameliorated over the years by these converging forces: the specialists accepting Soviet political values, and the political overseers having greater expertise in the areas they were called upon to supervise. Thus, by 1980 Hough could write that 'The old Western notion of a conflict between "red" and "expert", which had a basis in reality in the 1920s, has become irrelevant today.'[60]

J. Azrael studied this topic in the 1960s, and came up with a less sanguine picture. While it was incorrect to see the technical intelligentsia as a fifth column bent on launching some sort of liberal/technocratic revolution, Azrael argued that 'The technocrats not only fail to recognize Marxism–Leninism as a master science, they refuse to recognize it as a science at all.'[61] He concluded that the technocracts were largely shut out from key political and economic decision making and confined to their own sphere of competence.

Hard evidence to gauge the depth of the red/expert dichotomy is hard to come by. One survey of Soviet émigrés asked how competent they considered various officials to be in carrying out their duties;[62] 30 per cent said that most or almost all party officials were competent, and 50 per cent responded in this manner for industrial managers. The military and the Academy of Sciences topped the list, with 65 per cent of respondents perceiving all or most of them as competent. This hints that party officials were regarded as somewhat less competent than other officials, but the differences are not large (and respondents may have been expressing a political judgement, and not their evaluation of 'competence').

One way of looking at this problem is to investigate the degree of overlap between the careers of party officials on one hand and economic managers on the other. Clearly, at the level of the Council of Ministers the party and administrative apparatuses merged, in that a high proportion of central ministry officials (42 per cent, in a 1981 sample of 121 top ministers that the author compiled) had experience as obkom first secretaries or staffers in the CC CPSU or republican party apparatuses.

Chapter 10 examines this question from the point of view of party officials. This section will discuss the results of a study of 345 short biographies of factory directors published between 1976 and 1985 when they wrote articles for the party's economic weekly, *Ekonomicheskaia gazeta* (on the 'Director's Tribune' page); 21 per cent of these directors had spent some time in a formal party position during their career.[63] (Service in a local soviet, People's Control or Komsomol was treated as equivalent to party work.)

Of the 74 directors with party experience, 39 had been secretary of a factory partkom, over half of them in the very same factory which they went on to lead as director. 12 had served as a party secretary at district or city level, and 5 at republic or obkom level. (The remaining 22 in this group had unspecified party/soviet work.) Most had served for 3–7 years, the longest having spent 13 years in party work. Only 2 of them had passed through Higher Party School, and 2 had served as a factory trade union secretary (both women). These findings were confirmed by a look at the 42 directors elected to the Supreme Soviet in 1979, 10 of whom (24 per cent) had served in a party position.

How is this data to be interpreted? Is 21 per cent a *lot* of directors with party experience, or just a few? The data seems to suggest a relatively *low* degree of overlap between party and managerial careers, particularly if one bears in mind that this sample is biased towards the more well-known and more political directors (i.e. those invited to write for the national party press).

There were also strong hints in some Soviet sources which testified to the tensions between the red and expert wings of Soviet society in the Brezhnev era. The pro-worker recruitment policies of the CPSU since the mid-1960s made it increasingly difficult for specialists to enter the party.[64] There were even reports that engineers had to recruit three workers to the party before they themselves were allowed to join, in a vain effort to shore up the proletarian detachment inside the party.[65] Direct evidence of the endurance of the red/expert dichotomy came from the lips of senior party officials, who rhetorically railed against slack political discipline within the party's ranks, and often blamed problems on the practice of recruiting people on the basis of technical expertise rather than their class or political credentials. Thus Brezhnev told the 26th Party Congress in 1981 that 'A number of specialists coming into the party apparatus from industry ... do not have sufficient political experience, and sometimes bring administrative-economic methods into the party organs.'[66] This theme was repeatedly echoed in articles by party functionaries over the next few years, with Ukrainian first secretary V. Shcherbitskii attacking 'technocratic and bureaucratic tendencies' in the party.[67] This line of argument did not die with Brezhnev. In 1986, for example, the first

secretary of Stavropol obkom warned that when managers were transferred into party positions 'We must scrutinise more carefully than
in the past whether such comrades can adopt political methods of
influence.'[68]

Thus party involvement in cadre selection was not an entirely
harmonious process, in which the party simply stepped in to ensure
that the best men and women were chosen for the job. Party officials
brought with them a set of political criteria which were not congruent
with the distribution of technical expertise. The gap between reds and
experts narrowed between the 1930s and 1970s, but was not completely eliminated.

The counter-argument in this debate of reds versus experts would
be that in the context of the Soviet economy political skills and a
contact network may have been *more* useful than technical skills in
getting hold of scarce supplies, or persuading planners to slacken
targets. Thus within the system as it then was, the red/expert dichotomy may not in itself have contributed to economic inefficiency.
However, if one starts to consider the possibility of a radical reform of
the economic system in the direction of greater managerial autonomy,
one's evaluation of the utility of political skills would start to change.
In a more market-driven environment these political qualities would
rapidly lose whatever functionality they possessed in the old system.

Summary

Selection of cadres was a key element in the party's strategy
for supervising Soviet industry. If the party could appoint politically
loyal managers who would carry out the party's policies of their own
volition, then the need for detailed, daily supervision of their activities
by party organs would be greatly reduced.

However, what were the criteria which party organs could use in
choosing economic officials, in an epoch when genuine ideological
self-motivation had withered to vanishing point? (And was anyway
not to be trusted?) How could the party balance the often competing
demands of technical competence and political loyalty?

This chapter reviewed the somewhat unrealistic Soviet sociological
literature on the mix of qualities required in a manager, and looked at
techniques such as cadre attestation panels which were developed in
an effort to improve cadre selection. The party continued to place a
great deal of emphasis on the importance of formal political training,
but there was little sign that these programmes were producing the

sort of politically reliable managers that the party was looking for. Despite going through several reorganizations in the course of the 1970s, the political education movement grew increasingly moribund. After Andropov's succession in 1982, the party leadership turned in desperation to an orchestrated campaign of self-criticism and purges to try to revitalize managers and party officials.

However, it was clear that these policies were not working. The CPSU was desperately using its cadre policy as a substitute for a sorely needed structural reform of the nation's political and economic institutions.

10 The obkom elite in the early 1980s

This chapter presents the results of a study of the career backgrounds of obkom first secretaries in the 1976–88 period. The primary goal was to look for evidence of the conflict between political and economic ways of thinking. J. Hough pioneered the use of career biographies as a source for the study of political change in regional party elites.[1] Did the trends which Hough identified carry through to the mid-1980s? Did the qualifications of new entrants to the apparatus in the late Brezhnev era differ from those of their predecessors?

The opening section examines the pattern of career paths into the obkom first secretary position and the degree of geographical mobility they displayed. The second section looks at the evidence for generational turnover in the 1980s (an issue central to Hough's argument). The final section examines whether the technical qualifications of regional party leaders improved over time, as Hough suggested – the implication being that this made them better able to play the role as coordinator of their region's economy.

Before presenting the results, three caveats are in order with respect to the biographical approach. First, the argument in this book is based on an analysis of how *structures* worked, rather than a study of the characteristics of *agents* within those structures. This emphasis is partly because of the dearth of information about individual behaviour within the policy process. However, it is also because of a conviction that within the deeply entrenched bureaucratic culture of the USSR political institutions shaped and determined the behaviour of the individuals who staffed them.

An example of the high degree of political institutionalization in the USSR is provided by M. McAuley's study of the criteria determining which obkom first secretaries were appointed to the CC CPSU.[2] Members were chosen on the basis of the importance of the obkom they represented, and *not* because of their personal characteristics (such as time in office, or the status of previous jobs). If one looks at the decision-making process itself one finds a heavy emphasis on collegiality, with the first secretary working as part of a team, drawing upon the skills and contacts of obkom officials and the staffers of the regional soviet.[3]

Of course, one cannot rule out the possibility that a change in personnel could lead to a change in institutional behaviour – but there was no sign that such a transformation had occurred in the time period examined here. J. Hough himself recognized the limitations of approaches based on biographical data, and in 1979 acknowledged that his earlier data had led him to place too much emphasis on the personal qualities of individual party officials.[4]

The second caveat is that the researcher must constantly guard against over-interpreting the extremely sparse data available on Soviet officials. Official biographies merely gave their age, ethnicity, education, date of joining the party, a two-line career summary, and a list of major posts held. Analysts have been tempted to read too much into this data, *faut de mieux*.[5] For example, the availability of information on officials' date of birth and the year they joined the party encouraged analysts to apply a generational analysis to Soviet politics, simply because one of the few things that could be said about Soviet officials was which 'generation' they belonged to.[6] Huntington has argued that the generational analysis of political processes begs many questions about the nature of political cleavages, and cannot be assumed to apply to all societies.[7] Another example of possible over-interpretation of the available data would be the penchant for content analysis of articles published by regional party officials. G. Breslauer has subjected these materials to detailed linguistic analysis (to uncover, for example, differing levels of 'demandingness'), although he conceded that 'the secretary (with the occasional exception of ideological secretaries) rarely writes the article himself'.[8]

The third caveat follows on from the second: one must be wary as to what the data may be taken to mean. An extensive and intricate series of assumptions need to be made in identifying, coding and aggregating the information. At what precise year did the 'post-Stalin' generation begin? Gorbachev, for example, joined the party in October 1952: does this mean he belongs to the Stalin generation? Most analysts have used date of birth as the generational cut-off, with 1925 being the dividing line between the Stalinist and post-Stalin generations (chosen presumably because that was the median age of the regional elite in the early 1980s). On this measure, Gorbachev (born in 1931) was one of the new generation.

When dealing with more complex data about career and education, the problems multiply. Is attendance at a Higher Party School to be classified as higher education (as the Soviets do themselves)? Is one to assume that 'higher education' is a homogeneous process for all involved, producing a more forward-looking, 'technocratic' mentality? Such an analysis makes implicit assumptions about the nature of a universal process of societal modernization: assumptions which would probably not stand up to careful scrutiny. Similarly, how is one to interpret a record which shows some experience in a factory? Does this prove that the person was thereafter qualified to supervise industry at any point in his future career? What if the official in fact spent his factory years as a party functionary, and never went near a machine tool or a customer? And what is the period taken as bestowing 'industrial experience' – two years? five years? Gorbachev's official biography seems to consider a couple of months as sufficient, for it describes him as 'assistant on a combine harvester 1946–50' although in fact this was merely his summer work as a schoolboy.[9] These problems do not mean that one should abandon any attempt at career analysis, merely that one needs to be very modest in interpreting the significance of the findings.

The route to the top

The high degree of political institutionalization in Brezhnev's USSR is illustrated by the fact that careers within the CPSU followed very well-defined paths. The would-be leader ascended slowly through a succession of positions ranked in a clearly defined status hierarchy.

Table 10.1 shows the posts held by officials immediately prior to their promotion to the post of obkom first secretary. Note that there was a very small number of jumping-off points for promotion. Most obkom first secretaries came directly from one of two posts: obkom second secretary, or head of an oblast soviet executive (*oblispolkom*).[10] There were surprisingly few transfers from governmental positions (only 9 per cent of cases in 1981), and these were mainly in the Autonomous Republics (ASSRs) within the RSFSR, and in the non-Russian republics. Moscow-based ministry officials rarely transferred into the regional party elite. However, the author also studied the biographies of 121 leading central ministry officials in 1981, and found that there was a fairly heavy traffic the other way;[11] 42 per cent of the ministers had served either as obkom first secretary (28 per cent) or in a leading position in a republican or CC CPSU party apparatus.

Table 10.1(a). *Prior posts of RSFSR obkom first secretaries, 1981 and 1988*

Job prior to initial appointment as first secretary	promoted within the same oblast		promoted from another location		Total	
	1981	1988	1981	1988	1981	1988
Obkom second sec.	26%	16%	7%	4%	33%	20%
Oblispolkom chair	19	11	4	3	23	14
Obkom secretary	14	7	6	3	20	10
CC CPSU apparatus	0	13	8	26	8	39
Gorkom first sec.	7	3	0	0	7	3
ASSR or rep. minister	6	6	0	3	6	9
USSR minister	0	3	0	3	0	6
Other	0	0	3	0	3	0
Total	72	59	28	42	100	100

Note: Seventy-two career biographies were included in the 1981 cohort, and seventy in the 1988 cohort. In each year, four of the men had been transferred from one obkom first secretary position to another.

Table 10.1(b). *Prior posts of non-RSFSR obkom first secretaries, 1981 and 1988*

Job prior to initial appointment as first secretary	promoted within the same oblast		promoted from another location		Total	
	1981	1988	1981	1988	1981	1988
Oblispolkom chair	17%	14.5	6	14.5	23	29
Obkom second sec.	12	6.5	7.5	13	19.5	19.5
Republic CC apparatus	0	0	14	11	14	11
Obkom secretary	8	3	6	6.5	14	9.5
Republic minister	1.5	0	10.5	11	12	11
Gorkom first sec.	3	3	5	3	8	6
Raikom first sec.	5	0	0	1.5	5	1.5
CC CPSU apparatus	0	1.5	0	10	0	11.5
Other	1.5	0	4	0	5.5	0
Total	48	28.5	53	70.5	100	100

Note: Sixty-six biographies were included in the 1981 cohort, and sixty-two in the 1988 cohort. In 1981, four of the men (21 per cent) had been transferred from one obkom first secretary position to another, and in 1988 ten (16 per cent).

On the other hand, there was a great deal of mobility between the party and positions in regional soviets. In 1981 24 per cent of the obkom secretaries had transferred directly from the post of oblispolkom chair, and a further 26 per cent had been a chair or deputy chair of an oblispolkom or raiispolkom (distinct soviet executive) at some point in their career. Party and soviet careers were so closely inter-related that official Soviet data routinely lumped the two together.

The majority of appointees were local, with remarkably low inter-regional mobility (in the RSFSR, at least). Prior to 1985, few came directly from Moscow: in the 1981 sample, only 8 per cent of the RSFSR secretaries, and *none* of those outside the RSFSR. Rigby found an identical proportion in 1976, and Blackwell's study of the non-Russian republics, 1955–78, found only two cases (both in Kazakhstan).[12] This refers only to their immediately prior jobs, but even if one looks for service in Moscow at any point in their earlier career, one only finds a further 5 per cent of the RSFSR secretaries (and none of the non-RSFSR group) having had *any* work experience in the capital.

However, a large proportion of the group did have some educational experience in Moscow; 12 per cent of the 1981 sample went through a higher education institution in Moscow (and 4 per cent in Leningrad), and a further 30 per cent studied in the CC CPSU Higher Party School in Moscow later in their careers. These proportions held true in the 1988 cohort, where the corresponding figures were 16 per cent and 31 per cent. In 1981 non-RSFSR secretaries were more likely to have gone through the CC CPSU school than Russians (35 per cent against 24 per cent), but these proportions were reversed in the 1988 sample. Tashkent and Alma Ata had more graduates represented than Leningrad (6 and 5 per cent respectively), and the single most popular educational institution was the Tashkent Agricultural Institute, with five graduates among the 1981 regional elite.

The obvious implication of this pattern of local appointments in the Brezhnev era was that central control over the lower apparatus relied on *indirect* controls, and not on sending out the centre's 'own' people. Under Brezhnev, the CC CPSU Organization and Party Work Department seems to have left local party elites to generate their own leaders, and confined the role of the centre to setting the rules of the game and monitoring the results. However, Moscow did play a direct role in the appointment of the second secretaries of republic CCs. Hodnett found 34 per cent of second secretaries, 1955–68, came straight from Moscow, and a further 12 per cent from elsewhere within the RSFSR.[13] In both

1976 and 1981, 9 of the 14 second secretaries in the non-Russian republics had come straight from Moscow.[14]

The striking bias in favour of appointing local insiders merits further discussion. In addition to the data in Table 10.1, which show the job immediately preceding appointment as first secretary, cadre careers over the ten-year period prior to promotion were examined. This showed that 60 per cent of RSFSR secretaries had spent all, and 21 per cent most, of the decade within the very oblast which they subsequently led as first secretary. Among non-RSFSR secretaries, 26 per cent had spent all ten years there, and 71 per cent had spent most of them there. There were major differences between the non-Russian republics; 31 per cent of Ukrainian secretaries spent the entire decade in the same region, but only 15 per cent of Kazakhs and Uzbeks.

Data collected by other scholars show that this localism intensified in Russian provinces during the Brezhnev years, while decreasing outside the RSFSR. Looking at the prior posts of RSFSR secretaries, Rigby found locals rising from 53 per cent in 1965 to 69 per cent in 1976.[15] Blackwell came up with figures of 41 per cent for 1955–64, rising to 72 per cent for 1965–78 for Russian obkomy, but falling from 60 to 44 per cent in Ukraine.[16]

What were the factors driving these localist tendencies, and what explains the differences over time and between regions? Many party leaders explicitly stated that local cadres were preferred over transferees from other regions.[17] The rationale was that local people knew their own region, had a network of good contacts with local managers, and could therefore do a good job of supervising the local economy. However, there may also have been a political logic at work. The system of local appointments increased the power of regional party bosses, by augmenting the scope for local patronage.

How are the differences between republics to be explained? The higher rate of geographical mobility in the non-Russian republics could simply mean that Moscow did not trust them to appoint local cadres. Another plausible explanation would be the simple logic of the bureaucratic structure. The party in the Russian republic did not have its own central apparatus between 1965 and 1990 (when the Russian Communist Party was formed), so all appointments would have to be cleared with the CC CPSU. However, outside the RSFSR there were republican CC apparatuses, and they performed this monitoring function. The pronounced pattern of local appointments implies that the key political arena where appointment decisions were made was the obkom within the RSFSR, and the republican apparatus in the outlying republics.

The paucity of transfers between republics needs no lengthy explanation, since it reflects the ethnic structure of the USSR, and the CPSU's policy of preferring native cadres to run the party in the non-Russian republics. Although Gorbachev condemned 'the mechanical distribution of posts on nationality lines' as 'vulgar internationalism', the riots which greeted the appointment of Russian G. Kolbin as first secretary of the Kazakh party in December 1986 were a sharp reminder that breaking the established ethnic conventions could unleash extremely destabilizing forces.[18] This lesson was to become all too clear over the next five years, as one region after another fell prey to ethnic discord.

The pattern of local autonomy in cadre policy was maintained through the 1981–85 period. Among the new obkom first secretaries outside the RSFSR during those five years, none came from Moscow; and only 4 out of 22 new RSFSR appointees came directly from the centre. There was a dramatic change after Gorbachev's accession to power in 1985, however. Between 1985 and 1988, no less than 82 of the 138 obkom first secretary positions changed hands (59 per cent). (See Table 10.2, and the discussion in the following section.) Of the first 24 new obkom first secretaries appointed under Gorbachev, 16 came straight from jobs in the CC CPSU apparatus. As table 10.1 indicates, by 1988 39 per cent of RSFSR secretaries and 11 per cent of non-RSFSR secretaries had been rotated through jobs in the CC CPSU apparatus before being sent back to head up an obkom.

In another break with the previous pattern, most of these centrally despatched appointees were *not* sent back to their native region. (Although most were still sent to neighbouring provinces, rather than to the other side of the country.) This new cadre policy represented a major shift in the direction of closer central control. In fact, it was Andropov rather than Gorbachev who initiated the change, since these regional officials began to be appointed as CC CPSU instructors from 1983 on.[19] However, after 1988 the situation reverted back to the pre-1985 pattern. The CC CPSU apparatus disentangled itself from detailed supervision of appointments in the regions, with the result that only a handful of the obkom first secretaries promoted in 1988–90 were brought in as CC CPSU staffers prior to appointment, and the vast majority were being selected, as before, from within their home region.[20]

The generational argument

Every year death extinguishes the memory of nearly two million Americans, while about four million are born with no memories at all.

How much obstinate, hardshell opinion is lost by this process of population replacement? How much of the way of thinking of one generation is transmitted to the next, and how much is lost in the exchange? This is nature's way of changing the world.[21]

A central element in J. Hough's model of the party as regional coordinator was that a new generation of Soviet leaders emerged during the Breszhnev period who had more pragmatic values than the Stalin generation and were better trained for their role in the economy.[22]

Two factors determine the rate of generational transfer in a political elite: the speed at which positions turn over, and the average age of those moving into the vacant posts. Table 10.2 shows the rate of turnover among obkom first secretaries. Mean turnover over the whole period 1976–88 was 16.2 per cent a year (11.2 per cent for the years 1976–85). Turnover was higher under Andropov and Gorbachev: 22 per cent during Andropov's 16 months in office, and 33 per cent during Gorbachev's first 22 months. (Bear in mind that there is some double-counting here: one quarter of the turnover was due to first secretaries moving from one region to another.)

Blackwell found the turnover rate, 1964–78, to average 10 per cent pa, and 20 per cent pa for the 1955–64 period.[23] The level of turnover under Khrushchev was, in fact, on the same scale as that witnessed after 1985. While Gorbachev replaced 82 out of 138 secretaries in 3 years, Khrushchev removed 55 out of 114 between October 1960 and October 1961.[24]

So, the data indicate that the regional elite turnover which Hough predicted finally came about in the 1982–8 period. How marked was the ensuing generational change in the obkom elite? Table 10.3 details the age profile of successive cohorts of obkom first secretaries between 1976 and 1988.[25]

Throughout the 1976–85 period the secretaries arriving in office were about 8.5 years younger than the men they were replacing: to that extent, therefore, a rejuvenation of the elite was taking place. Thus, for example, those leaving office between 1981 and 1985 had joined the party on average in 1946, and their replacements had joined in 1956. By 1988, the generation who came of political age during Khrushchev's 'thaw' had finally come to power. In 1988 the median obkom first secretary had joined the party in 1956, the year of Khrushchev's 'secret speech' attacking Stalin.

Countering this trend towards generational renewal, however, was the fact that candidates were waiting longer before getting their promotion to first secretary. The age upon appointment of new arrivals

Table 10.2. *Turnover of obkom first secretaries, 1976–1988*

Year	whole USSR (n = 138)		RSFSR (n = 72)		non-RSFSR (n = 66)	
	no.	%	no.	%	no.	%
Brezhnev period						
1976	8	6	3	4	5	8
1977	8	6	1	1	7	11
1978	23	17	8	11	15	23
1979	6	4	4	6	2	3
1980	7	5	1	1	6	9
1981	5	4	1	1	4	6
1982[a]	12	8	4	6	8	13
Andropov period						
1983	20	15	10	14	10	15
1984 (Jan.–Feb.)	10	7	6	8	4	6
Chernenko period						
Mar. 84–Feb. 85	13	9	5	7	8	13
Gorbachev period						
Mar.–Dec. 1985	27	20	16	22	11	17
1986	19	14	11	15	8	13
1987	24	17	10	14	14	21
1988[b]	12	9	9	12	3	5
Total	194		89		105	
mean turnover pa	16.2	11.7	7.4	10.3	8.8	13.3

Notes: [a] – all prior to Brezhnev's death in November 1982.
[b] – up to the end of August 1988.

1981–5 was five years higher than the age at which the cadres they were replacing had first taken office. First secretaries were being replaced by their second secretaries, rather than by more junior officials, and over the years the second secretaries were aging at almost the same rate as their superiors. Thus despite the increased turnover between 1981 and 1988, the average age of first secretaries in office actually increased between 1976 and 1988, from 54.7 to 55.6 years. Those cadres who were rotated through the CC CPSU apparatus by Andropov and Gorbachev were not an exception to this trend, since in their age profile and pattern of previous jobs they were indistinguishable from other appointees.

Thus even though turnover rates increased, there was no radical

Table 10.3. *Generational change in obkom first secretaries, 1976–1988* (figures are means, in years)

Obkom first secretaries, all USSR	Age that year	Tenure in office	Age when first appointed	Date of joining CPSU
In office, 1976	54.7	12.3	42.4	1945.9
In office, 1981	56.3	10.8	45.5	1949.1
In office, 1985	57.0	10.0	47.0	1952.8
In office, 1988	55.6	5.5	50.8	1956.9

Notes: 'Age that year' refers to January 1976 for the 1976 cohort, and so on. 'Tenure' refers to the period as an obkom first secretary in any obkom, not only the post currently occupied.

change in the age composition of the regional party elite, because of the lengthy path to the top which party cadres had to follow. There was no leap-frogging of generations, and generational change in the Soviet elite was incremental rather than precipitious. As Janos Kadar is reputed to have said, political generations do not replace each other like army divisions moving in and out of the line.

Anyway, the arrival of younger cadres would have meant little, given that their career path took them through the same agencies of socialization and the same series of positions as their predecessors. The internal political culture of the ruling elite did not undergo any fundamental changes between the 1950s and 1980s, although arguing this point through would have to be the subject of another book.

The career profile of the regional party elite

A pivotal part of Hough's prefect model is the argument that party officials in the post-Stalin period became better qualified to exercise detailed supervision over local enterprises. In the 1930s, one saw young officials such as N. S. Patolichev being sent to take charge of the Cheliabinsk obkom – and thus be responsible for one-third of the country's steel production –without ever having set eyes on a steel mill before.[26] In the 1950s and 1960s the educational level of Soviet society as a whole and the party apparatus in particular steadily improved.

Hough's criteria for measuring this improved competence boil down to possession of a technical degree and a period of work experience in industry of at least five years' duration. Hough also records those with ten years' service in industry, and those with specific experience as a factory director.

In his 1969 study, Hough found that in the top twenty-five industrial oblasti the number of obkom first secretaries with five years in industry and an engineering degree rose from 12 in 1957 to 19 in 1962.[27] Seven of them had also served as factory directors. However, there was no clear 'technocratic' trend in the eight-five oblasti outside this leading group. In the remaining regions, the number of industrial engineer's fluctuated from 14 to 19 during the years 1957–66.[28]

In a 1980 work Hough looked at the thirty-three most populous areas, and came up with the following:[29]

Obkom first secretary with:				
	1950	1960	1966	1980
engineering degree (%)	38	44	55	61
five years' experience in industry (%)	14	32	42	57

In 1979 he ranked all oblasti by degree of urbanization, and found this pattern:[30]

	in oblasti with % of population living in urban areas:			
Obkom first secretary with:	70–90	50–69	40–49	16–39
	(n = 35)	(n = 49)	(n = 29)	(n = 33)
engineering degree (%)	80	31	7	6
five years' experience in industry (%)	66	16	3	6

This is impressive evidence in support of the proposition that over time the party turned to more technically competent cadres to manage the leading industrial regions.

Let us now examine the Hough model further in the light of our study of the regional elite in 1981 and 1988. Rather than look solely at the industrial engineers, officials were allocated to one of the following four categories on the basis of their first clear five years of work experience (ignoring army service, or anomalous periods such as Gorbachev's time on the farm):

1 'Komsomol/none' – signifying those youngsters who went straight into party or Komsomol work upon completion of their education and army service, and had at least five years' uninterrupted experience in the political apparatus.

2 'Industrial' – meaning those with five years' uninterrupted experience in industry, transport or construction prior to entry into fulltime party work.

3 'Agricultural' – for those with five years' work in agriculture, including agricultural mechanisation and irrigation.

4 'Mixed' – meaning those without any clear five years' work in any of the above three categories. The 'mixed' group includes teachers (who some analysts put into a separate category, but were not sufficiently numerous in our sample to merit separate treatment); and other professionals who do not fall into any of the preceding categories, such as journalists, lawyers and economists.

In addition to the dimension of career experience, educational background was tabulated, using the categories 'engineer', 'agronomist', 'other higher', and 'only secondary'. One problem is that official Soviet statistics classified a broad range of educational institutions as 'higher' education. The Soviet education system was highly stratified (like all education systems). One doubts whether a degree from the Michurin Fruit and Vegetable Institute (from which two of the 1981 first secretaries graduated) puts the holder in the same category as somebody from Moscow State University. Such distinctions are unfortunately lost in the coding process. The 'only secondary' group includes those with a *tekhnikum* (vocational school) education, but also includes those who held a part-time (*zaochnyi*) degree, or who had attended one of the higher party schools. The justification for relegating these persons to the 'only secondary' category is that the pedagogic content of part-time and party courses was dubious, particularly when they involved senior party officials trying to improve their paper qualifications in mid-career.

Table 10.4 shows the educational and background careers of the obkom first secretaries in 1981. Hough's industrial engineers were certainly present, amounting to 19 per cent of the total, but were by no means the majority. Note, for example, that the largest single group by education were those holding agricultural degrees. This is powerful testimony to the argument made in chapter 7, that agricultural duties loomed very large in the life of regional party officials. Note also that

Table 10.4. *Educational and career profile of obkom first secretaries, 1981* (n = 138)

Background in pre-party career	Type of higher education									
	Engineer		Agrono-mist		Other higher		Only secondary		Total	
	no.	%	no.	%	no.	%	no.	%	no.	%
Komsomol/none	8	(5)	9	(7)	9	(7)	17	(12)	43	(31)
Industry	26	(19)	1	(1)	-		9	(7)	36	(26)
Agriculture	-		28	(20)	-		2	(2)	30	(22)
Mixed	7	(5)	8	(5)	3	(2)	11	(8)	29	(21)
Total	41	(30)	46	(33)	12	(9)	39	(28)	138	(110)

Note: Sixteen of the group (12 per cent) had served as a factory director or farm director at some point in their careers.

Table 10.5. *Educational and career profile of obkom first secretaries in selected regions, 1981*

Background in pre-party career	Type of higher education									
	Engineer		Agrono-mist		Other higher		Only secondary		Total	
	no.	%	no.	%	no.	%	no.	%	no.	%
(i) The top 25 industrial oblasti										
Komsomol/none	3	(12)	-		1	(4)	-		4	(26)
Industry	13	(52)	-		-		3	(12)	16	(64)
Agriculture	-		1	(4)	-		-		1	(4)
Mixed	2	(8)	-		-		1	(4)	3	(12)
Total	18	(72)	1	(4)	1	(4)	4	(16)	25	(100)
(ii) The top 25 agricultural oblasti										
Komsomol/none	-		2	(8)	2	(8)	4	(16)	8	(32)
Industry	2	(8)	-		-		-		2	(8)
Agriculture	-		8	(32)	-		2	(8)	10	(40)
Mixed	1	(4)	3	(12)	1	(4)	-		5	(20)
Total	3	(12)	13	(52)	3	(12)	6	(24)	25	(100)

Notes: For details on the ranking, see Appendix 1; nineteen of the industrial, and fifteen of the agrarian *oblasti* are located within the RSFSR, the others are in non-RSFSR republics.

the largest single career category was 'Komsomol/none' – persons who were full-time politicians since leaving college. Also, there were few with higher education apart from the technically trained engineers and agronomists.

Table 10.5 shows the background of first secretaries in the top twenty-five industrial and agricultural oblasti in 1981;[31] 18 of the 25 secretaries in the top industrial areas had engineering degrees, although only 13 of them had industrial experience; 11 had been factory directors (not shown in the table). It was not impossible for cadres to rise up solely through Komsomol/party channels to head one of these centres, but the party clearly preferred men with some sort of technical background to head these flagship regions of Soviet industry (and they were all men.)

However, the table does not prove that these officials were chosen on the basis of technical competence, rather than political loyalty. Typically, cadres were transferred to the obkom from a local industrial giant (e.g. Uralmash in Sverdlovsk), and it was the network of contacts which was probably their most valuable attribute, rather than any abstract technical skills. Of course, in the topsy-turvy world of the command economy, such political contacts may have been more valuable for a factory than business expertise.

It is clear that these industrial regions were not typical of the country as a whole. A comparison of tables 10.4 and 10.5 shows that of the 26 industrial engineers in the total 1981 sample, 13 were in the top twenty-five industrial regions. No less than 11 of the 16 former factory directors in the sample were located in the industrial regions.

Turning to the agricultural regions, we see a fair matching of first secretary backgrounds to the regions' characteristics; 13 of the 25 had agricultural training, and 10 had five years' experience working in agriculture. The picture is less clear-cut than is the case in the industrial areas; 8 had risen purely through political channels, for example.

To what extent should one be looking at these top fifty regions, and not the entire sample of 138 obkomy? As the following table indicates, the top fifty regions accounted for 47 per cent of the country's population and 60 per cent its economic activity:

Share of USSR total	Population	Industry	Agriculture
Top 25 industrial oblasti (%)	33	44	29
Top 25 agricultural oblasti	14	17	31
Top 50 oblasti	47	61	60

Table 10.6. *Educational and career profile of obkom first secretaries by generation, 1981* (n = 138)

Background in pre-party career	Engineer		Agronomist		Other higher		Only secondary		Total	
	no.	%	no.	%	no.	%	no.	%	no.	%
(i) Those born 1925 and before (n = 70)										
Komsomol/none	4	(6)	4	(6)	6	(9)	13	(19)	27	(39)
Industry	10	(14)	-		-		5	(7)	15	(21)
Agriculture	-		9	(13)	-		1	(1)	10	(14)
Mixed	2	(3)	5	(7)	3	(4)	8	(11)	18	(26)
Total	16	(23)	18	(26)	9	(13)	27	(37)	70	(100)
(ii) Those born after 1925 (n = 68)										
Komsomol/none	4	(6)	5	(7)	3	(4)	4	(6)	16	(24)
Industry	16	(24)	1	(1)	-		4	(6)	21	(31)
Agriculture	-		19	(27)	-		1	(1)	20	(30)
Mixed	5	(7)	3	(4)	-		3	(4)	11	(16)
Total	25	(35)	28	(41)	3	(4)	12	(18)	68	(100)

Type of higher education is the overall column heading spanning Engineer, Agronomist, Other higher, and Only secondary.

Note that the division between agricultural and industrial regions is rather arbitrary. The top twenty-five 'industrial' regions produced almost as much food as the top twenty-five 'agricultural' regions. This meant, incidentally, that one third of the country's major food producing regions were in the hands of the 'industrial engineer' types.

There was little difference in the career patterns of Russian and non-Russian regional officials in the 1981 cohort, once one allows for the fact that the RSFSR had a disproportionate share (nineteen out of twenty-five) of the top industrial regions. In fact, RSFSR obkomy had a higher proportion of secretaries without higher education than did the non-Russian regions (33 per cent against 23 per cent). The Russian regions also had more secretaries who rose through purely political careers (23 per cent against 20 per cent). This contradicts the common impression that because of the policy of appointing native cadres in non-Russian regions political reliability was more important than technical competence.[32]

Table 10.7. *Educational and career profile of obkom first secretaries, 1988* (n = 119)

Background in pre-party career	Type of higher education									
	Engineer		Agrono-mist		Other higher		Only secondary		Total	
	no.	%	no.	%	no.	%	no.	%	no.	%
Komsomol/none	6	(5)	4	(3)	7	(6)	9	(8)	26	(22)
Industry	32	(27)	-		-		6	(5)	38	(32)
Agriculture	-		28	(24)	-		4	(3)	32	(27)
Mixed	7	(6)	6	(5)	4	(3)	6	(5)	23	(19)
Total	45	(38)	38	(32)	11	(9)	25	(21)	119	

Tables 10.6 and 10.7 show trends over time. Table 10.6 compares the pre- and post-1925 generations in the 1981 group, and shows that there were more engineers in the younger cohort (25 against 16), more agronomists (28 against 18), and fewer who rose through the Komsomol (16 against 27). These trends bear out the Hough hypothesis of increasing reliance on expertise.

However, agricultural backgrounds grew more rapidly than engineering backgrounds, which was not something the Hough model predicted. Also, the fact that 12 per cent of the younger group lacked higher education, and 40 per cent lacked any clear work experience outside the political apparatus, indicates that non-'experts' could still achieve leading positions in regional party organizations.

Similar arguments hold true for the data in Table 10.7, which analyses the background of secretaries in office in 1988. Comparing Tables 10.4 and 10.7, one can see that the number of industrial and agricultural specialists went up between 1981 and 1988; 45 per cent of the 1988 cohort held engineering degrees, and 38 per cent had at least five years experience in industry; 32 per cent held agronomy degrees, and 27 per cent had farming experience; 17 per cent had served as a factory director at some point in their careers, and 18 per cent had been farm chairmen. The proportion of people without higher education fell (from 28 to 21 per cent), as did that of cadres with purely political careers (from 31 per cent to 22 per cent).

However, the general pattern of the regional elite found in the 1981 cohort was still preserved in their 1988 successors. The three clearly delineated paths to the top remained:

1 an engineering degree followed by at least 5–10 years production line management in heavy industry;
2 an agricultural degree and then 5–10 years in farming or regional farm administration;
3 plunging straight into Komsomol work during or shortly after college, and moving straight on into positions in the party and/or soviet apparatus.

Among the 137 new faces who were promoted to obkom first secretary between 1976 and 1986, 21 per cent rose straight up through the Komsomol, and 20 per cent more lacked any clear work experience. While 39 held engineering degrees, 32 had been educated in agricultural institutes. Only 9 per cent of the 1988 cohort held degrees outside the fields of engineering or agriculture. Remarkable few economists, lawyers, journalists and teachers found their way into the regional party elite, and this pattern did not alter with the passage of time.

The comparison with other party officials

This chapter has focussed exclusively on obkom first secretaries. These were the most important regional political officials: they were also the only group for whom there was a fairly complete set of biographical data.

Other scholars have laboured long and hard to try to push career analysis down below the first secretary level. J. Moses' study of obkom bureau members, for example, found a high level of what he termed 'functional specialization';[33] 94 per cent of the obkom secretaries (not first secretaries) responsible for agriculture had a career background in agriculture, and 79 per cent of industry and ideology secretaries had career backgrounds in their respective fields. Comparing the post-1971 and pre-1953 indicated that there was a clear time trend away from 'mixed generalists' towards functional specialists.[34] These findings support the Hough model, with its stress on the increasing relevance of professional competence.

Summary

What then, is to be learned from the study of the career background of obkom first secretaries? Once cadres entered the party/soviet apparatus, their careers followed well-defined paths, with remarkably little geographic mobility outside the oblast in the RSFSR. For two-thirds of regional party bosses, their experience in Moscow was confined to a brief spell at the CC CPSU Academy of Social Sciences or the Moscow Higher Party School. Under Andropov and Gorbachev regional officials began to be promoted up to the CC apparatus for a year or two, before being returned to run a regional party organization, typically in a province adjacent to their home base.

It is hard to assess the validity of the argument that a generational shift took place in the regional elites during the 1970s and 1980s. While the new appointees were clearly younger and better educated, and may well have subjectively sensed a psychological break from the Stalin era, the biographical data do not show a dramatic and radical break from the established pattern of career advancement. Generational replacement was an incremental rather than synoptic process.

The biographical data do suggest a gradually increasing reliance on technical expertise, as the Hough model predicted; although for reasons discussed above one can challenge whether possession of a technical degree really signifies a 'technocratic', non-political mindset.

Perhaps the most surprising discovery was the large group of cadres who rose up through the agricultural wing of the party apparatus. This is powerful testimony to the prominent role party organs continued to play in agricultural management.

11   Party and economy under perestroika

After 1985, the established political and economic order began to fall apart. It is somewhat idle to speculate over whether the collapse was inevitable, or whether it could have been prevented or at least postponed if Gorbachev had acted differently. Instead, this chapter will analyse developments from the point of view of the party's role in the economy.

In general, the years 1985 to 1991 showed the CPSU to be a very brittle organization. It displayed little ability to bend with the winds of change, and instead tried to persist in its old ways, until the whole structure shattered. Interestingly, while the party jettisoned its political powers one by one (control over the press, control over local soviets, etc.), the regional party apparatus clung to its core role of economic supervision till the bitter end. Only with the suspension of the CPSU in August 1991 was the party's grip over the economy prised loose.

As glasnost and democratization took hold the traditional, routine duties of regional party organs were steadily overtaken by the accelerating pace of political change. Regional party officials found themselves fighting for their political survival in semi-free elections, and struggling to cope with a flood of additional challenges: ecological catastrophes, inter-ethnic strife, and a surge of worker unrest of unprecedented proportions.

For the first time, the privileges of the nomenklatura came under direct attack in the press. One should recall that prior to 1987 even mentioning the existence of the nomenklatura system in the press was forbidden. Even the party's own journals began carrying angry letters, complaining for example that 'A day doesn't go by without a report of some party organs defending obvious degenerates, swindlers, bribe-takers and thieves.'[1] In Georgia, Uzbekistan, Azerbaijan and Kazakhstan hundreds of special shops, guest houses and medical clinics were transferred to public use, while party secretaries in the Slavic republics gave interviews either denying that such privileges were available in their regions, or announcing that they were being shut down.[2] Regional party organizations began cutting the number of nomenklatura positions under their supervision.[3]

In addition, after January 1987 many positions within the party apparatus were opened up to competitive elections between alternative candidates (although the electors were of course party members, and not the public at large).[4] The democratization of cadre selection was meant to supplement, but not replace, party control of the nomenklatura. Conservative party officials managed to subvert the democratization process, by constructing a multi-stage hierarchy of indirect elections, and putting heavy pressure on PPOs and party meetings to vote for their nominees.[5] The result was the overwhelmingly conservative and anti-perestroika character of the delegates elected to the 19th Party Conference in June 1988 and the 28th Party Congress in July 1990. Gorbachev switched the focus of his democratization strategy to the soviets, and by 1989 it was clear that 'The democratization of the party was lagging behind the democratization of society.'[6] This was a curious position for a vanguard party to find itself in.

Glasnost and perestroika were foisted on a recalcitrant party apparatus by the Gorbachev leadership. While regional party officials paid lip service to Gorbachev's reform goals, in practice they treated perestroika as just another slogan calling for token compliance. One of the most surprising aspects of Soviet politics under Gorbachev was how *few* genuine supporters of perestroika emerged from the regional party apparatus. V. Brovkin's 1990 study found only a handful of committed Gorbachev supporters among provincial party secretaries.[7] Party officials at raikom and PPO level were equally hostile to perestroika, meaning that 'the brake from below is just as powerful as the brake from above'.[8] The high point of party reformism was the formation of the 'Democratic Platform' in January 1990, but they faded into obscurity after winning the allegiance of a mere 2 per cent of the delegates to the 28th Party Congress in July 1990.[9]

Despite these challenges, in most regions effective control over resource allocation continued to rest with the party apparatus. Consider the following results of a December 1989 public opinion poll, conducted for the Central Committee think tank, the Academy of Social Sciences. In answer to the question 'Who has real power in your town?' local newspaper readers replied as follows:[10]

	Moscow	Gor'kii	L'vov	Tashkent	Nab. Chelny
Party	51%	55	65	46	33
Managers	10	24	5	12	33
Black marketeers	29	10	10	32	22
Soviets	6	8	7	7	6

The power that the party exercised, however, was based on bureaucratic control rather than political support. A survey of party members showed that only 14 per cent considered their obkom first secretary to be a 'political leader', and 23 per cent their PPO secretary; (59 per cent granted Gorbachev this designation, however).[11]

In this concluding chapter, there is no space to discuss all aspects of the lively regional politics which emerged under perestroika. Attention will concentrate on how these developments affected party work in the economy. In order to address this question, twenty-seven regional party newspapers were examined for selected months over the period 1988–90, for signs of a shift in the pattern of party interventions in the economy. This study showed that despite the turmoil in Soviet society and the dramatic developments in national politics, there was remarkably little change in the economic role being played by party officials on the ground. The biggest change was an increasing willingness to admit the seriousness of the economic crisis, and a frank recognition of the fact that the actions of local leaders were not proving effective at warding off the impending catastrophe.

The role of party officials did not change because, despite five years of perestroika, the basic structure of the economic system remained intact. Without a significant shift towards market forces, and above all a reliance on *monetary* relations as the main medium of economic exchange, one could hardly expect to see party officials abandoning their role as economic brokers.

However, perestroika *did* have a significant impact on the ministerial bureaucracies in Moscow. In 1987–8 their staffs were slashed by one third or more, and they were subject to a series of bewildering reorganizations.[12] Paradoxically, this may have increased the pressure on local party officials to play an active economic role, since managers found it more and more difficult to get results by playing the vertical chain of command. However, the apparatus of the CC CPSU was also slashed by 700 jobs in 1988 (roughly one-third), so obkom officials were largely left to their own devices.[13] They received much less from Moscow by way of either help or instructions than they did prior to 1988.[14]

Gorbachev's vision of the party's role

What, then, were Gorbachev's plans for party activity in the Soviet economy? After 1985 interpreting Gorbachev's motives became something of a cottage industry in the West, but there was no consensus on how radical his reformist intentions really were.

Gorbachev was fully occupied with the struggle to consolidate his own political power, and in coping with immediate crises (Chernobyl, arms control, East Europe, the Baltic, etc.). He barely had the time to spell out what would be the precise political and economic arrangements in his preferred, post-perestroika future. His ambiguity and silence left plenty of scope for commentators, Soviet and Western, to project onto Gorbachev their *own* interpretation of the sort of reforms the USSR needed. Speculation aside, however, there was precious little sign of a decisive shift in the role Gorbachev expected the CPSU to play in the Soviet economy.

It was true that he roundly condemned 'petty tutelage' and 'administrative-command methods', i.e. stimulating popular involvement in decision making, rather than issuing direct orders to managers.[15] It was also true that he was exasperated with bureaucratic, formalistic party practices, and urged officials to concentrate on human needs rather than abstract production figures.[16] However, in railing against podmena Gorbachev was merely mimicking all previous General Secretaries. Gorbachev advisor F. Burlatsky claimed that his ideas of democratization and political methods of rule could be traced back to a *Pravda* editorial written by Iu. Andropov back in 1964.[17] The only major institutional innovation which Gorbachev introduced was competitive elections for managers – and, as will be discussed below, this had a limited effect, and was largely revoked in 1990.

More worrying was the way that Gorbachev, while pleading for a *new* role, continued to call upon the party to carry out its traditional functions, and adhered to a Leninist analysis of the party's historical role. The message seemed to be that the style had to change, but the tasks would stay the same.[18] In a 1987 speech he stated that 'When we raise the question of freeing the party from tasks which do not belong to it, we do not mean that the party should free itself from economic questions.'[19] In his speech to the July 1989 CC CPSU plenum Gorbachev argued that 'There is a crisis – not of the party, but of its old functions', and that while reforming the party 'we want also to strengthen it'. He reasserted that 'The party cannot leave the economy, not in the future and especially not in the present,' and that 'The party was created and continues to work as an instrument in the struggle for power.'[20] In his speech to the February 1990 CC CPSU plenum which removed the 'leading role' of the party from the Soviet Constitution (Article 6), Gorbachev rejected calls for an alteration in the party's basic structure (for example, the elimination of gorkomy and raikomy).[21]

Gorbachev still berated individual obkomy if their region fell behind in agricultural production or social development, and called upon CC CPSU departments to account for lags in the introduction of new technology.[22] Just about all the various forms of party intervention during the Brezhnev era described in this book were endorsed by Gorbachev – auxiliary farms attached to factories, forcing heavy industry plants to turn out consumer goods, and so on.[23] Gorbachev tried to be innovative in coming up with new, more aggressive central political campaigns, such as the initiative in March 1985 to make republican and regional party first secretaries personally accountable for energy supplies in their region.[24]

Even in the farm sector, where Gorbachev's return to the issue of leaseholding (repeatedly blocked by previous Soviet leaders) offered real hope for a turnaround, he did not confront the need to weaken the power of the raikomy.[25] He did not seem to see any contradiction between condemning podmena at the beginning of a speech and then going on to lecture on the virtues of specific agricultural policies, such as crop rotation.[26]

The sluggish pace of economic reform

Neither the regional nor the national press showed any sign that serious economic reforms had started to bite. What it did show was that the planning system was in serious disarray, and even routine tasks were often proving difficult to carry out.[27] Several waves of innovation were launched from on high after 1985, but each ran into the sands of bureaucratic inertia, stiffened by opposition from the political apparatus. The reformist zeal of the central authorities was expended on 'running to stay in the same place'.[28]

A new system of external quality control, Gospriemka, was the major innovation of 1987, but was soon under attack as yet another example of the old-style economic reform – trying to use administratively imposed sanctions to solve economic problems.[29] In theory, all firms were supposedly put on full economic accountability (*khozraschet*) in January 1988, and plan targets were abolished in favor of 'state orders' (*goszakazy*), which would only be issued for strategic commodities.[30] Otherwise, firms were supposed to find their own customers and suppliers.

There were some isolated signs that the new emphasis on economic self-sufficiency was starting to bite, and that some firms were for the first time facing a 'hard budget' constraint. There were cases of factories cutting wages, cancelling December bonus salaries, and refusing to hire new workers.[31] However, such reports were swamped by complaints from directors that ministries continued to dictate output targets and 'correct' plans at will.[32] It was admitted that the new *goszakazy* in fact covered 90 per cent of industrial output.[33] 'Proximity to the Moscow beltway (*sadovoe koltso*), and not work results' continued to determine enterprise profits.[34]

Cutbacks in the number of commodities allocated by the central Gossnab in 1988 led to a flood of reports of acute supply shortages in the provinces.[35] Some of these breakdowns were blamed on transport problems, but others were attributed to a widening sense of 'group egoism', with firms and regional authorities looking after their own first.[36] The most desperate complaints often came with respect to food and fodder supplies.[37] Despite the launch of many regional self-management plans, these projects could not be realized until decisive steps were taken towards economic reform at the national level.[38]

Most disappointing of all, there was little evidence of serious reform of the farm sector. Despite heavy promotion from the centre, most regional party authorities either ignored farmers wishing to lease land or repeatedly altered the terms of the lease, all the while keeping supplies of machinery and fertilizer out of the hands of private farmers.[39] By 1989 16 per cent of farm workers were working on leased fields, although there was much false reporting by local party officials wanting to give the appearance of embracing Moscow's reforms.[40] For example, despite reports in 1988 that there were 1,500 leaseholds in Voronezh oblast, it turned out that only two were actually in operation.[41]

Thus the impact of perestroika was to disrupt the operation of the central planning system, without replacing it with a functioning market mechanism. The glacial pace at which the system made progress towards the rule of law (*pravovoe gosudarstvo*) meant that the legal status of enterprises and local soviets remained vague on paper and unrealizable in practice.[42] In five years of perestroika, there was no sign that the legislatures or the legal system had taken any steps in the direction of defining the party's role in the economy.

Party interventions in the economy

Despite Gorbachev's appeals to the party to stop interfering in economic management, in practice perestroika did *not* bring about a systematic diminution in the party's role in the economy. On the contrary, judging by the voluminous press coverage of routine party interventions, it seems very much to have been business as usual.

It was true that in response to CC CPSU directives the full-time staff of obkomy and raikomy were cut by up to 40 per cent, and economic departments were merged and renamed.[43] However, these bureaucratic reshufflings did not signify a change in the way party officials perceived their rights and responsibilities. A survey of party members in Kiev found 55 per cent considered their party organization to be incapable of changing its own style of work.[44] After describing how they had abolished the economic departments, the first secretary if Iskitim gorkom added 'Regretably, we must still take over (*podmeniat*) economic bodies, at least for now.'[45] The prevailing attitude was summed up by the party secretary in a Volgograd shipyard, who said 'We do not have the right to walk away from the resolution of production decisions.'[46] The economic disruption unleased by perestroika was interpreted by party officials as requiring still more intervention in economic management.[47]

Party leaders continued to be held accountable by higher organs for the economic performance of their region. For example, Ul'ianovsk obkom gave party reprimands to officials they deemed responsible for interruptions in the supply of kvas (a type of root beer).[48] Even the Baikal Amur Railway, the biggest white elephant of the Brezhnev years, continued to be the subject of Komsomol recruitment drives.[49] There were very few press accounts where regional party officials, in the spirit of perestroika, reported that they were refusing to get involved in details of economic management.[50] The main themes of party activity in the economy after 1985, judging by the local press, were:

1 running the anti-alcohol campaign;
2 a struggle to adjust to the democratization of procedures for the selection of managers;
3 trying to stave off the crisis in agriculture;
4 improving the supply of consumer goods and services;
5 supervising the expansion of cooperatives.

1 The anti-alcohol campaign

The anti-alcohol campaign was launched with great fanfare in March 1985, and bore all the characteristics of a classic Brezhnevite campaign: irrational, arbitrary decisions; reliance on coercive methods to tackle economic problems (there were 2.7 million arrests); and the spawning of a massive new bureaucracy (the Sobriety Society, with 6,500 full-time officials).[51]

Moreover, its impact was counterproductive. Drinking continued to be a severe social problem, since moonshine production expanded to meet demand. Alcohol-related worktime losses may actually have increased because of the lengthening queues at alcohol stores, and the 40 per cent cut-back in state alcohol sales led to a 36 billion rouble fall in budget revenues.[52] By 1988 the alcohol campaign was being quietly abandoned, with even the police recognizing that it had been a complete failure.[53]

2 Moves towards the democratization of industrial management

Despite the absence of full-blooded economic reform, there were nevertheless some signs of an erosion of party prerogatives in the factories – for example, where measures to promote the democratization of management had taken hold. Raikom officials in Donetsk, for example, protested that the party was being 'driven out' of the cadre selection process.[54] Party officials complained that managers made lavish promises to their workers to get themselves elected, and then tolerated slack work discipline in their plants.[55] In a small number of cases the elective works councils took advantage of their formal legal powers and began to exercise real influence over decision-making. This tended to undermine party control, since local party officials relied on their close personal relationship with the director to get their way (including, where necessary, threats to use party discipline).[56]

However, in practice most managerial elections were carefully orchestrated by party and management cadres, with a pre-selected candidate steered into office.[57] Even where a combatative new manager was elected, he often faced a 'closed circle' of hostile economic and political agencies that left innovators with little room for manoeuvre.[58] Amid growing complaints that the elective system was triggering wage inflation and undermining labour discipline, in June 1990 revisions were introduced to the 1983 Law on the State

Enterprise restoring the right of the 'owner' (in most cases, the ministry) to appoint managers.[59]

Some of the fiercest disputes came where workers and managers tried to carve out economic autonomy for themselves by leasing their plant. For example, the Naro-Fominsk gorkom launched an all-out campaign to undermine a successful car parts manufacturing plant which had gone on leasehold.[60] The PPO in a Kazan oil refinery blocked plans by the works council to go over to leasehold, and had to call in security guards from the ministry to enforce their decision.[61]

3 Party work in agriculture

Despite promises to lessen state purchases and allow farms to seek their own customers, in most areas local party officials continued to closely monitor farm activities, and procurement targets were still imposed 'to the last cucumber'.[62] In Riazan, for example, the obkom gave specific targets to each farm for the sowing season, and each cow was instructed to give 2 kg additional milk in May.[63] Despite the fact that the staff of the agricultural department of Krasnodar kraikom was cut by one-third in 1989, their responsibilities stayed the same. When meat deliveries began to fall they were accused of having slackened their supervision of the 'livestock front'.[64] And when launching an ambitious social welfare programme for isolated villages, the Belgorod obkom first secretary concluded that 'Party organizations are the main guarantor that the proposals will be implemented.'[65]

The most feverish efforts of party leaders came in the annual drive to squeeze manpower out of local industry to help with the harvest.[66] This continued unabated through 1988 and 1989, despite the fact that it was widely regarded as a wasteful and inefficient way to allocate resources.

There were admittedly some signs of change, with regional officials showing increasing reluctance to send manpower to the assistance of neighbouring provinces. In Kiev, for example, in 1988 student brigades were diverted from harvest work to construction projects inside the city.[67] In 1987 Iaroslavl obkom pioneered moves to put harvest assistance on a contract basis, with farms paying factories for the services they received.[68] Given the existing price and subsidy structure, many farms were near-bankrupt, and were unable to pay for such help. The slippage in party supervision of farming contributed to the 1990 harvest crisis. According to the head of the State Procurements Commission, V. Nikitin, the number of urban workers sent out to the farms was only one-fifth what it had been in previous years.[69] The same story was repeated in 1991 – when the shortfall in grain deliveries was still more acute.

4 Maintaining supplies of food and consumer goods

Party organs were ill-prepared to cope with the breakdown in consumer supplies that accelerated after 1988.[70] Obkom activities ranged from drumming up spare parts for the food processing industry to swapping goods with neighbouring regions.[71] Party officials complained that they were progressively losing control over food production, but were still being held responsible by the general public for food distribution.[72]

Local leaders struggled to create new institutional structures to make up for the breakdown in the old centralized system, with party officials working in tandem with the new democratic leaders who had swept into the soviets in fifty of the eighty major cities of the USSR in March 1990. The soviet in the Siberian mining region of Kemerovo, for example, set up its own territorial supplies agency to trade in food, medicines, etc., and lobbied for the right to issue 'territorial *goszakazy'* which would be binding on local firms.[73] These self-preservation strategies were of course even more pronounced in the non-Russian republics. Mostly, however, the new city managers found themselves without significant revenue sources and lacking influence over enterprises located on their territory.[74]

In some regions it was ministry officials and enterprises who took over the leading role in scavenging for supplies, since the soviets and even the obkomy themselves were paralysed by political feuding.[75] Reports revealed a new source of tension between party officials and local enterprises. Directors began ignoring party pleas to deliver to local firms, and instead swapped industrial materials outside the province in return for food and consumer goods for their own workers.[76]

Thus regional coordination was one of the party's functions most severely damaged by the political turmoil and high rate of turnover among the party apparatus under perestroika.[77]

5 The spread of cooperatives

The spread of cooperatives was one of the most visible and controversial achievements of perestroika.[78] The way the regional party apparatus responded to this reform bears close examination, as it can be regarded as a touchstone of their unwillingness to go along with radical economic reform.

The provincial press (which continued to be under the close control of regional party officials right up to 1991) mostly promulgated the official Gorbachev line that cooperatives were to be encouraged, within limits.[79] However, local newspapers also printed a flood of readers' letters protesting about poor service and high prices.[80] The coops were widely perceived as mere shelters for black marketeers seeking to launder their ill-gotten gains.[81] Surveys showed that while 14 per cent of the population used coops regularly (and another 37 per cent occasionally), only 38 per cent thought that they were a good idea.[82] Industrial leaseholders also came under attack, since they were seen as taking unfair advantage of slack budget rules.[83]

In many regions local authorities strove to restrict coop activity. In four Ukrainian oblasti there was not a single cooperative registered in 1988.[84] In Sverdlovsk 20 coops were disbanded, and in Kiev 171 out of 868.[85] There were the 'tomato wars' against private greenhouses in Volgograd; and a survey showed 88 out of 100 coops in Novosibirsk were being harrassed by the authorities.[86]

There were widespread fears that nomenklatura officials were 'diversifying' into coops to protect their privileges.[87] The leaders of one coop in Krasnodar, whose monthly salary was 6,000 roubles, 25 times the average wage, included relatives of the chairman of the district soviet and the regional prosecutor. The kraikom used this and similar cases as an excuse to close down 165 coops in 1987 and 1988.[88] However, by 1989 the Krasnodar paper had come around to the Moscow line, printing complimentary stories about coops producing medical equipment and operating roadside cafes.[89]

To avoid legal problems, and to secure access to supplies, coops often preferred to work under the sponsorship (*pod kryshoi*, literally 'under the roof') of state factories or public organizations such as the Komsomol. In fact, more than 75 per cent of coop turnover in 1989 was generated by selling materials to state firms.[90] To prevent such manoeuvres Iaroslavl gorkom banned state enterprises from doing business with coops, for which they were strongly criticized by a local crusading journalist.[91] Many local Komsomol committees were active sponsors of coops, ranging from fashion designers and computer consultants to the very successful MZhK (youth coops who build apartments on a 'sweat equity' basis).[92]

Summary

The Gorbachev years saw tremendous turbulence in the Soviet economic and political system. Perestroika was a top-down process which disrupted the centre's control over the levers of power but failed to generate the upsurge of independent activity by managers and regional party officials that Gorbachev anticipated.

Notwithstanding Gorbachev's reform efforts, close party tutelage over management proved to be an intrinsic, structural feature of the Soviet economic mechanism. The 1985–91 period showed that the more protracted the process of economic reform, and the deeper the crisis into which the economy sank, the more excuses there were for party officials to keep up their interventionist ways.

Under perestroika the party made some attempts to promote reform and to step back from interfering in economic management. The most positive example was their quest to promote the new cooperatives (although, as noted above, this drive went very slowly in many areas). Less satisfactory was the ill-conceived programme to promote the 'democratization' of industrial management. Unfortunately, most of the programmes the party ran during the 1985–91 period were straight out of the armoury of the 1960s and 1970s – mobilizing resources to help with the harvest, scrambling to secure supplies of consumer goods, and the like. In the chaotic conditions of the late 1980s, these campaigns were even less successful than they had been in earlier decades.

Conclusion: party and economy in the USSR: from stagnation to collapse

This book set out to explore the role of the CPSU in the Soviet economic system, and to try to identify whether party interventions helped or hindered Soviet economic progress.

Our conclusion, based on an exhaustive reading of the relevant national newspapers and journals from the period 1975 to 1985, is that the economic stagnation which crept over the USSR during the Brezhnev era was in no small part due to the close monitoring of economic life exercised by the CPSU. The latticework of vertical and horizontal bureaucratic controls was so firmly established that managers were left with little room for manoeuvre. Efforts to expand the scope for market-like forces, even on a modest scale, came to naught. This was not simply because of political opposition from conservative elements. It was more a case of the whole body politic rejecting the foreign cells of marketization, however modest, which local experiments or central reforms sought to inject.

There was a clear contradiction between the principles underlying party activities in the economy and the work of industrialists and farmers. The former had their own rules of the game, defined by the political logic of the CPSU – campaigns, slogans, orders, reports, reprimands, praise, initiatives, victories. The managers in turn had their own rules to follow, laid down by their ministry in Moscow. Their life involved petitioning for more resources, chasing down supplies, keeping their workers happy, and all with the goal of meeting output plan targets.

This contradiction between the logic of the party and the logic of the command economy rarely surfaced as a direct clash between managers and party functionaries. On the contrary, there was a surprising degree of symbiosis between managers and party officials: surprising because one would have expected the managers to be more assertive in defending their interests.

There are several possible explanations for the apparent political quiescence of the economic elite. One is the legacy of the Stalin era, when managers were taught in no uncertain terms not to challenge the authority of the party. A second is the argument that by the 1970s the economic system had been in place for decades, and it was hard to shed acquired habits and ways of thinking. Managers found it difficult to imagine a Soviet economy in which the CPSU did *not* intervene, and it was idle for them to speculate over whether the CPSU was a help or a hindrance to economic efficiency. Innovators and would-be entrepreneurs who did challenge the status quo were very quickly shown the door.

A third possible explanation would be that managers were more or less content with the status quo. Behind the scenes, so the argument goes, they enjoyed considerable autonomy in the allocation of economic resources, and did not object to paying lip-service to the party's domination of the public political arena.

It does seem true that over the course of time the respective groups of political and economic functionaries had managed to establish a *modus vivendi*. Each group tried to cooperate with the other to their own mutual advantage, while recognizing their respective spheres of influence.

In most of Soviet industry, routine decision-making was in the hands of the plant director, while strategic decisions over investment allocation rested with the central ministry in Moscow. By and large, this chain of command tended to shut out party officials from decision-making. At plant level, the leaders of the Primary Party Organization typically accepted the director's 'right to manage', and saw their fate as tied to the director's ability to meet his plan targets. Regional party officials similarly saw the virtues of cooperation with local economic elites, acknowledging that the ministry-factory relationship was something over which their influence was limited.

On occasion, however, the relationship between politicians and managers could turn antagonistic – for example, where a local plant was subordinate to an enterprise headquartered in another province. Party–industry relations were the most strained in newly developing regions such as Tiumen in Siberia, where ministries were preoccupied with bringing their production projects on stream, and ignored the pressing need to develop the social and economic infrastructure (for these cases, see chapter 4). In such regions the political and economic elites were struggling to find their feet and had not yet forged the informal, inter-personal bonds which were so crucial to the functioning of the Soviet system.

The tension between party and economic officials was more acute in the rural sphere than in industry. Farm chairmen were subordinate to the local raikom, which exercised a far more direct managerial role over agriculture than was the case in industry (on this point, see chapter 8). In the West, the CPSU has been regarded first and foremost as a party rooted in the urban, industrial economy, one that to a degree articulated the interests of the managerial and working classes.

This was indeed true – but was only half the story. Our investigation of regional officials' career patterns showed that roughly one in four of the regional party elite worked their way up through assignments overseeing the rural economy (see tables 10.4 and 10.7 in chapter 10). A content analysis of the party press confirmed that a sizeable proportion of the party's time and effort was devoted to work in the farm sector (see Appendix A.2 for details). The party's predominant role in agriculture spilled over into their work in industry, from the annual campaign to mobilize help for the harvest, through to assisting factory managers to develop and run their own farms.

The material presented in chapter 11 suggests that perestroika did not bring any major structural changes in the party's role in economic management, although the progressive paralysis of the central leadership made their job even more difficult. Gorbachev's avowed intent to free managers from 'petty tutelage' by party officials was contradicted by his reliance on the party to push through his reform programme, and to deal with the mounting crises which gripped the country in the late 1980s. Multiple economic, political and national crises led to the attempted coup of August 1991, in the wake of which the CPSU was banned, and its monopoly of political and economic power dismantled.

The second half of the conclusion will discuss the changing character of the Soviet political system during its last five years, and the reasons for its demise.

The collapse of the Brezhnevite consensus

The crucial factor which triggered the collapse of the Soviet system was the multinational character of the state.

In 1988 nationalist groups in the Baltic republics and Armenia, sensing the paralysis of the Moscow leadership, seized the opportunity to mount a challenge to the status quo. Nationalist separatism then became the battering ram which loosened the stones of the Soviet state, and the multinational structure of the USSR meant that when the collapse came in the wake of the August coup, the country broke up into its fifteen (and more) constituent republics.

The ethnic heterogeneity of the Soviet state no doubt meant that sooner or later the USSR was doomed to go the way of all empires. However, by constructing a viable ruling coalition, the CPSU under Brezhnev was able to postpone the day of reckoning for several decades. Under Gorbachev this ruling coalition lost its nerve, and lacked the will to use force on the scale needed to keep nationalist separatism in check. (The only occasion during this period when the Soviet leadership showed itself capable of using ruthless force to suppress national dissent was the military occupation of Baku in January 1990.)

Thus nationalism provides both an immediate cause and a long-run explanation for the collapse of the USSR. However, a crucial *intermediate* causal factor was the breakdown in solidarity and coherence of the ruling CPSU elite. The introductory chapter suggested that six values were shared by the communist elite during the Brezhnev era: the right of the elite to rule; cognitive control; the validity of generational divisions; the separation of public and private domains; the superpower status of the USSR; and the viability of the command economy. After 1985, every one of these agreed values broke down. It is worth examining each of the six pillars of the Brezhnevite consensus in turn, to show how they crumbled after 1985.

1 Elite rule

The arrival of competitive elections rapidly undermined the legitimacy of the established ruling elite. Ironically, Gorbachev appears to have expected that it would have had the opposite effect. He was taken by surprise by the drubbing party officials received in the March 1989 elections, and never really regained the political initiative from that point on.

The 'ideological' wing of the CPSU elite in particular lost their credibility, and their views became an object of open public ridicule under glasnost. Fragments of the CPSU elite experimented unsuccessfully with Russian nationalism in a bid to maintain some influence. However, their desire to hold on to a multi-national union, and their inability or unwillingness to distance themselves from the Soviet past, stymied their capacity to adopt the rhetoric of Russian nationalism. It was the democratic opposition, rallying behind Boris Eltsin, that was able to play the nationalist card in Russia, and they used it against

Gorbachev. Unlike their Russian brethren, communist elites in Central Asia and Azerbaijan were able to make the switch from Marxism–Leninism to nationalism, and managed to cling to power.

In contrast to the ideological wing of the elite, the economic managers showed more staying power, and were still a coherent force in 1991. Like the ideological elite, they had a hard time winning elections, but they started to express themselves through a series of new organizations which sprang up in 1989–91. For example, the Scientific-Industrial Union united more than 2,000 leading factories, and began organizing commodity exchanges and barter agreements to fill the vacuum caused by the collapse of central planning.

In 1990 and 1991 many directors abandoned the sinking ship of the CPSU and shifted their allegiance to the Eltsin camp. It was symptomatic that Eltsin's choice as RSFSR Prime Minister in 1990 was Ivan Silaev, who had spent his entire career as a manager of a defence factory. An alliance seemed to be forming between some of the new democratic political leaders, and the old guard of industrial directors. This process was well advanced even before the coup occurred in such bastions of the military-industrial complex as Leningrad.[1]

The rural-based elements in the party also became politically assertive, and provided the backbone of the opposition to market-oriented reform. After 1989, in the newly elected local and republican soviets they formed powerful blocs of deputies, calling themselves 'Agrarians' (*Agrarniki*). A similar pattern has revealed itself in much of Eastern Europe. In free elections from Bulgaria to Czechoslovakia support for the former communist parties has been concentrated in rural areas, where there are fears that subsidies to loss-making state farms will be slashed.

2 Cognitive control

With the glasnost genie out of the bottle, cognitive control proved impossible to maintain. Journals such as *Moscow News* and *Ogonek*, read mainly by the intelligentsia, started to express independent views in 1987, and were shortly followed by mass circulation papers such as *Argumenty i fakty* (which shot up to 34 million subscribers).

In late 1989, and again after his 'turn to the right' in December 1990, Gorbachev made some efforts to regain control over the mass media, particularly Central Television, but these were largely ineffectual, and of course were abandoned after August 1991. Ironically, in republics such as Uzbekistan and Georgia censorship increased after the break-up of the Union, as local leaders struggled to consolidate their power.

3 Generational change

In the late 1980s the old generational pattern of elite politics was also in disarray. The aging, conservative generation was still an identifiable group, and was very slow to exit from the scene. The main problem was not the protracted nature of their departure, however, but the fact that there was no clearly defined successor generation to follow them. Gorbachev failed in his attempt to find and mobilize a cohort of like-minded, pro-perestroika officials within the CPSU apparatus. The bland machine politics of the Brezhnev era failed to generate a new, assertive, self-conscious generation of political leaders. In one editorial, the journal *Kommunist* explicitly discussed the situation in these terms, arguing that some of the younger generation were gripped by 'the mentality of social apathy and cynicism of "not sticking out" and "doublethink", ... an inheritance from which they must be encouraged to escape'.[2]

Gorbachev's allies within the party appartus, such as they were, were mostly fellow members of the 1950s generation which had been stunned by Khrushchev's secret speech. Their opponents in the democratic movement were largely remnants of the dissident movement of the 1960s. After them, there was a politically apathetic 'lost generation', which did not throw up a clearly identified political elite.

4 The separation of the public and private spheres

Glasnost and democratization also caused the public/private split to evaporate. After 1985 the empty shell of official politics cracked open, and the subterranean private sphere flooded in. In 1989, conversations which ten years previously could only be heard around a kitchen table were being broadcast nightly on TV from one of several parliaments. The private sphere invaded the public sphere, and national politics became dominated by personality clashes and accusations of corruption and betrayal.

5 The USSR as a superpower

The superpower status of the USSR took a beating after 1989. The withdrawal of Soviet forces from Afghanistan and the abandonment of the East European regimes to democratic revolutions signified the demise of the USSR as a military and political rival to the USA.

This retreat demoralized the Soviet elite in general and the armed forces in particular, and was taken by the public and the democratic opposition as a sign that they had lost their nerve. In a sense Gorbachev continued to play the superpower card, by trying to parlay his international prestige into domestic authority. This tactic was effective in shoring up Gorbachev's personal power over an increasingly hostile Communist Party elite, but did not arrest the decline in his public prestige.

By the end, this tactic of Gorbachev degenerated into a crude plea for Western economic aid to stave off the economic collapse. The implicit message to the Soviet public was that only Gorbachev could persuade the West to provide aid. This was an extremely shaky foundation upon which to make a bid for popular support, and alienated Gorbachev from the remnants of the ruling elite. Marshall D. Iazov cited Gorbachev's cap-in-hand appeals to the West as a major reason for launching the August coup. In any event, aid in the sort of quantities required was not forthcoming from the West. (And one may doubt whether *any* quantity would have been enough to halt the collapse.)

6 The viability of the command economy

By 1990 few economists or political leaders were prepared to argue that the 'administrative-command' system inherited from the Brezhnev era was capable of leading the USSR into the twenty-first century. Critics of market reform rested their case for the maintenance of central planning only on the grounds that temporary, emergency measures were needed to ward off economic chaos. They no longer disputed the virtues of the market, but argued that in the given conditions an attempt to introduce a market economy in the USSR would be disastrous.

This idea of the need for a 'crisis programme', slender though it was, could possibly have served as a rallying point for fragments of the old political elite. This argument was particularly appealing, of course, to the economic managers of the military-industrial complex, and perhaps to their workers. However, the other factors mentioned above had so eroded their authority and self-confidence that when such a programme was launched, by Prime Minister V. Pavlov in July 1991, it was dead on arrival.

The chances of forming an elite consensus around the preservation of elements of central planning were shattered, above all, by the economic confusion which accompanied the break-up of the Union. After the August coup almost all the major political players recognized that some sort of market relations, and not a return to central planning, offered the best chance to bond together the new 'economic space' which was emerging on the territory of the former USSR.

With the collapse of elite faith in the viability of central planning, the last plank of the Brezhnevite consensus was sundered, and a political vacuum opened up at the centre of the former Soviet system.

After the August 1991 coup, the rules of the old political and economic game in the USSR were torn up. The country was convulsed by the painful and protracted process of giving birth to a new system. The Communist Party was dramatically ejected from its central role in the political system, although in some outlying regions and in the Central Asian republics it may be able to cling to power under a new name.

The old economic elites, however, have shown no sign of wishing to yield their ground. Unlike the landed aristocracies of an earlier age, society cannot afford to drive them out of office, nor does it particularly want to. Yet this economic elite was created and sustained by the very same command economy which upheld the Communist Party. Thus it is not impossible that elements of the command economy will outlive the political organization which created and maintained it. If this occurs, it will be intriguing to see what sort of political institutions emerge to fill the void opened up by the exit of the Communist Party.

Appendix 1 A note on working with obkom and oblast data

The purpose of this appendix is to explain how the career data discussed in chapter 10 were arrived at, and to discuss the procedures used to rank oblasti by agricultural and industrial importance.

Career biographies of party officials were mainly drawn from the yearbooks of the Great Soviet Encyclopedia, since each time a new CC CPSU was selected this source published short biographies of all its members.[1] Biographies were also published of all officials elected to the USSR Supreme Soviet.[2] In addition, *Radio Liberty Research Bulletins, Foreign Broadcast Information Service – USSR Reports* and the *Current Digest of the Soviet Press* were used to track down sundry other items of information about obkom first secretaries which appeared in the Soviet press.

The data available are extremely sparse. Almost all the biographical data depend upon sources such as the following entry from the 1981 yearbook:

> BANNIKOV, NIKOLAI VASIL'EVICH: born 1914, member CC CPSU, elected at the 26th Congress of the CPSU in 1981. CPSU member since 1940. Completed the Kuibyshev Industrial Institute in 1937. From 1937–45 worked in a factory (mechanic, shop head, chief mechanic, deputy director, *partorg* CC CPSU). From 1945 – on party work. From 1955–59 – first secretary of Kuibyshev gorkom. From 1959–63 – second secretary, and from 1963–68 – first secretary of the Karaganda obkom of the Kazakh CP. (1963–65 – first secretary of the Karaganda industrial obkom.) Since 1968 – first secretary of the Irkutsk obkom. Candidate member of the CC CPSU 1966–68, full member since 1968. Deputy to the Supreme Soviet of the USSR for the seventh to tenth convocations.

Bannikov's biography as a Supreme deputy adds that between 1945 and 1955 he was an obkom secretary, a raikom first secretary and a department head in the Kuibyshev gorkom. Occasionally, newspaper biographies may contain a few additional morsels of information, such as place of birth and 'social origin'.

For this study it was decided to exclude from the sample those obkomy which did not have direct representation at all-union CPSU congresses. The excluded group comprises the obkomy of the ten autonomous oblasti, and various obkomy in the ten smallest republics, which lack a complete obkom structure. Of the latter group, it was decided to include Leninabad (Tadzhikistan) and Osh (Kirgizia) in the sample, because they are large in size, and their first secretaries consistently enjoyed CC CPSU membership. Of the city parties (gorkomy) Moscow and Kiev are included, since they were granted direct representation at party congresses. The sample thus consisted of 138 obkomy (including Navoi, which was created in Uzbekistan in 1980).

There are various ways of ranking the obkomy to estimate their importance. One can look at the formal status of its first secretary in the Central Committee CPSU: full member; candidate member (without voting rights); or merely a member of its Central Auditing Commission (a purely formal body, bestowing a status one step below Candidate member). The proportion of obkomy whose first secretaries were full members of the CC CPSU in 1981 ranged from 80 per cent in the RSFSR and 50 per cent in Ukraine, to less than 30 per cent in the other republics. As McAuley's study showed in the early 1970s, granting full membership in the CC CPSU was a reflection of the status of the obkom, rather than the personal prestige of the individual occupying the post of first secretary.[3]

Data were also available on the number of party members in each oblast, since this determines the number of delegates they are allotted at party congresses. At the 26th Congress in 1981 there was one delegate for every 3,500 members.[4] Moscow city was the largest party organization, with 1.1 million communists, representing 13 per cent of the population. Party density was highest in the old Russian industrial cities (7–9 per cent), and lowest in rural areas and in Central Asia (where it was in the 3–5 per cent region). Demographics are a major factor in explaining the differences, since these population data include children.

The career analysis conducted in chapter 10 required the compilation of a list of the top twenty-five agricultural and industrial oblasti. McAuley and Hough's studies used urban population as a rough and ready measure of industrial importance. Direct data on the volume of production for each oblast are not available, so the author constructed a crude proxy using data which are in the republican statistical

Table A.1.1. *Ranking of USSR oblasti by industrial importance*

(1) Ranking according to capital investments and highly trained labour, 1975	(2) By size of urban population, 1981	(3) McAuley's ranking for 1970, RSFSR only
1 Moscow city	(1)	–
2 Moscow oblast	(3)	(11)
3 Leningrad	(2)	(1)
4 Sverdlovsk	(5)	(2)
5 Donetsk (Uk)	(4)	–
6 Tatar ASSR	(18)	(17)
7 Krasnodar krai	(11)	(20)
8 Dnepropetrovsk (Uk)	(6)	–
9 Krasnoiarsk krai	(15)	(10)
10 Rostov	(8)	(16)
11 Kuibyshev	(12)	(4)
12 Gor'kii	(9)	(6)
13 Cheliabinsk	(7)	(3)
14 Bashkir ASSR	(17)	(5)
15 Tiumen	(32)	(46)
16 Irkutsk	(20)	(9)
17 Sarataov	(22)	(14)
18 Kemerovo	(10)	(8)
19 Khar'kov (Uk)	(14)	–
20 Perm	(19)	(7)
21 Novosibirsk	(21)	(13)
22 Kiev city (Uk)	(16)	–
23 Vologograd	(23)	(12)
24 Voroshilovgrad (Uk)	(13)	–
25 Odessa (Uk)	(25)	–

Source: see text. Uk = Ukraine

handbooks – level of capital investment and number of workers with higher or specialized secondary education. (Unfortunately, both these data sets include the rural sector, and the data series were discontinued after 1975.)[5] Table A.1.1 shows the ranking arrived at, and compares it with the measures utilized by Hough and McAuley. The only region which would not make it into the top 25 on the basis of urban population, but which makes it on our scale, is Tiumen – thanks to its massive investments (R12 billion between 1971 and 1975 alone).

Some direct data on agricultural output were available by oblasti.[6]

Table A.1.2. *Ranking of USSR oblasti by agricultural importance*

The top 25 oblasti,[a]
in descending order:

RSFSR	Non-RSFSR
Altai krai	Vinnitsa (Uk)
Orenburg	Chernigov (Uk)
Stavropol krai	Poltava (Uk)
Omsk	Khmel'nitski (Uk)
Voronezh	Minsk (Bel)
Kurgan	Kiev oblast (Uk)
Kursk	Crimea (Uk)
Tambov	Cherkassy (Uk)
Penza	Kirovograd (Uk)
Ulianovsk	Zaporozhe (Uk)
Lipetsk	
Belogorod	
Riazan	
Orel	
Tula	

Ranking based on gross output of agricultural sector 1971–5, for purposes of inter-republic comparison and ranking within the non-RSFSR republics; and on basis of grain purchases for the purpose of ranking the RSFSR oblasti.
[a] The list excludes regions already included in our list of the top 25 industrial oblasti (Table A.1.1). No less than 14 of the regions on that list would have ranked in the top 25 agricultural regions, had they been considered. They are: Krasnodar krai, Rostov, Saratov, Vologograd, Bashkir ASSR, Krasnoiarsk krai, Novosibirsk, Kuibyshev, Tatar ASSR, Cheliabinsk, Odessa (Uk), Dnepropetrovsk (Uk), Kharkov (Uk), Donetsk (Uk).
Source: see text.

For RSFSR oblasti only data for 'state purchases of grain' were available, and not gross output (*valovaia produktsiia*). Thus the RSFSR ranking underestimates areas specializing in potatoes, flax, beet and vegetables. Outside the RSFSR, the republic handbooks did provide gross output data for agriculture. The resulting ranking is shown in Table A.1.2.

Republic level gross output data allow one to calculate that the ranking should include nineteen oblasti from the RSFSR, none from Ukraine and Minsk from Belorussia, since Russia provided 49 per cent of value output, Ukraine 23 per cent, Kazakhstan 7 per cent, Belorussia 5 per cent and Uzbekistan 4 per cent. Given the crazy-quilt of Soviet agricultural pricing policy, these calculations are nothing more than a rough approximation of a region's level of importance and visibility.

Appendix 2 Ekonomicheskaia gazeta as a source on policy-making, 1976–1985

Ekonomicheskaia gazeta (The Economic Gazette) was a 24-page weekly journal affairs published by the CC CPSU and devoted to the party's economic policy. Although its coverage was limited and its journalists conservative, some of its writers (such as V. Varavka) did manage to produce consistently insightful reporting. Other journals exhaustively read for this study included the party's theoretical bimonthlies, *Kommunist* and *Voprosy istorii KPSS* (Questions of CPSU History), and the rather dull journal for party officials, *Partiinaia zhizn* (Party Life). These sources contained a few interesting items, but by and large they were highly politicized, and several notches further removed from reality than *Ekonomicheskaia gazeta*.

Academic and technical journals, such as *Voprosy ekonomiki (Economic Issues)* or *Planovoe khoziatsvo* (The Planned Economy), and even the iconoclastic Novosibirsk-based *EKO* (short for Economics and Organization of Industry) seemed to be forbidden from making any reference to the party's role in the economy. Thus *Ekonomicheskaia gazeta* was the principal source of information on the CPSU's routine economic policy during the Brezhnev years. In January 1990 the journal was renamed *Ekonomika i zhizn* (Economics and Life), and it has subsequently lost its hegemony to independent newspapers such as *Kommersant*.

Most *Ekonomicheskaia gazeta* articles dealt with aspects of economic management in a fairly technical fashion, and tended to avoid discussion of party interventions in decision-making, beyond ritual invocations of the party's wisdom in opening and closing paragraphs. In articles written by party officials themselves, the authors were obviously freer to refer to party activities – although the information provided was of dubious veracity.

Apart from feature articles, certain sections of the paper were devoted to items of a publicistic or hortatory nature – short reports on economic achievements, articles on the 'economic education' page, and so forth. This material could be 'read' in a Kremlinological (or deconstructionist) sense, as a way of gleaning information on shifts in party policy. One can assume that the newspapers' editors were closely following signals emanating from the CC CPSU secretaries responsible for economic policy. In interviews with the economics editors of *Partiinaia zhizn* in November 1988, it was the author's impression that they did *not* receive direct instructions from the CC CPSU on a daily basis – although this could merely have been a sign of the erosion in effectiveness of the CC CPSU apparatus after 1985.

The tables which follow are a modest effort at quantifying some of the patterns in economic reporting in *Ekonomicheskaia gazetta* over the years 1976–85. Despite the limitations, some interesting patterns emerged, most notably the prominent role of agriculture in the party's economic policy, and the shockingly small amount of attention devoted to consumer goods and services. One hopes that future Sovietologists will not have to rely on such sources to gather insights into the functioning of the Soviet system.

Table A.2.1. *Major articles authored by party officials published in* Ekonomicheskaia gazeta, *1976–1985*

	industry	economic education	general economic	Principal subject matter agro.	socialist competition	science/ technol.	consumer goods	cadres	
1976	38	21	9	14	27	4	2	1	
1977	29	16	12	17	6	1	6	2	
1978	34	16	10	17	13	2	3	2	
1979	15	12	6	17	13	3	1	2	
1980	24	14	22	7	2	4	1	1	
1981	18	6	19	7	4	2	1	/	
1982	22	12	13	15	1	2	3	/	
1983	27	7	18	13	7	3	1	6	
1984	16	16	10	4	7	1	2	4	
1985	13	7	6	4	1	6	1	3	
Totals	236	127	125	115	81	28	24	21	= 757

Note: 'Industry' includes transport and wood processing.
'General economy' includes regional planning, and articles with an even mix of say agriculture and industry.
'Socialist competition' includes a small number of articles on the labour collective. No article was double counted, although the categories are difficult to define with any degree of precision.
Articles or letters less than 8 column inches in length were excluded.

Table A.2.2. *Main subject matter of replies from party officials to criticism published in* Ekonomicheskaia gazeta, *1976–1986*

	Agriculture	Industry	Economic education	Industry construction	Agro. construction	Energy conservation	Transport
1976	2	7	2	2	7	–	–
1977	13	11	2	3	–	–	1
1978	5	31	5	7	2	1	–
1979	9	14	11	3	2	2	–
1980	4	8	1	2	8	–	–
1981	5	6	–	2	1	2	–
1982	29	13	7	5	5	–	–
1983	19	13	7	2	1	–	4
1984	20	10	11	7	1	1	2
1985	34	9	6	5	1	32	3
1986[a]	4	1	–	2	1	1	1
Totals	144	123	52	40	29	39	11

= 438

Note: [a] – 1986 includes issues 1–31 only. 'Industry' includes housing, services, etc. Categorization of replies was easier than was the case with articles as they were usually specific to a single problem. Although 'socialist competition' was mentioned in several of the replies, it was in no case the primary issue.

Table A.2.3. *Status of party officials replying to criticism published in* Ekonomicheskaia gazeta, *1976–1986*

Status of respondent:	agriculture	industry	economic education	industr. constr.	agro. constr.	energy conservation	transport	*total*
Republic CC secretary	–	–	–	1	–	12	3	16
Obkom secretary	128	10	6	13	26	18	5	206
Raikom or gorkom secretary	15	15	14	15	1	1	2	63
PPO partkom secretary	–	56	23	7	1	5	–	91
Partkom secretary and plant director	1	42	9	5	1	3	1	62
Total	144	123	52	40	29	39	11	= 438

Note: In a few cases the replies were signed by the chief engineers rather than the plant director, and sometimes they were also signed by the plant trade union secretary.

Table A.2.4. *Subject matter of regional conferences convened jointly by obkomy and* Ekonomicheskaia gazeta, *1976–1985*

	economic education	industry	agriculture	general economy	socialist competition	consumer goods	energy cons.	role of soviets
1976	5	5	2	–	–	–	–	–
1977	7	3	4	1	1	–	–	–
1978	7	3	3	–	3	–	–	1
1979	4	–	2	–	5	–	1	–
1980	4	4	3	4	1	–	–	–
1981	–	1	1	1	–	1	1	–
1982	2	2	1	1	–	1	–	–
1983	1	2	3	2	–	–	–	–
1984	6	2	1	1	–	–	–	–
1985	2	2	–	–	–	2	–	–
Totals	39	26	20	10	10	4	2	1 . = 112

Note: In this table construction is subsumed under the category 'general economy', as it tended to be treated as part of regional planning, urban development, etc. in these conferences.

Table A.2.5. *Special series of articles run by Ekonomicheskaia gazeta, 1976–1985*

	1976	1977	1978	1979	1980	1981	1982	1983	1984	1985
Environmental protection	X	X	X	X						X
Territorial complexes			X	X	X	X	X			X
Agricultural brigades								X	X	X
Industrial brigades							X	X	X	X
Quality control							X	X	X	X
People's control						X	X	X	X	X
Transport				X	X	X	X	X	X	X
Livestock				X	X	X	X	X	X	X
Role of the soviets								X	X	X
Conservation						X	X	X	X	X
Trade unions							X			
Discipline								X		

Note: The livestock series began in 1975, and the quality control series (sometimes titled 'effectiveness and quality') began in 1974. There was a series on counter plans in 1974 only. In 1973 the series entitled 'economic reform' ended. Each series had a special logo and was listed in the annual index printed in no. 52 each year.

Notes

Preface

1 This argument is presented in P. Rutland, *The Myth of the Plan: Lessons of Soviet Planning Experience* (London, Hutchinson, 1985).
2 J. F. Hough, *The Soviet Prefects: The Local Party Organs in Industrial Decision Making* (Cambridge, Mass., Harvard University Press, 1969).
3 P. Gregory, *Restructuring the Soviet Economic Bureaucracy* (Cambridge University Press, 1990).
4 G. Lowell Field and J. Higley, *Elitism* (London, Routledge, 1980).

Introduction: the party in the post-totalitarian system

1 Z. Brzezinski, *The Grand Failure* (New York, Scribners, 1989).
2 K. Jowitt, 'Inclusion and mobilization in Leninist regimes', *World Politics*, 28, 1 (1975), 69–96; S. P. Huntington, *Authoritarian Politics in Modern Society* (New York, Basic Books, 1970), ch. 2; R. Lowenthal, 'Development versus utopia in communist policy', in C. Johnson (ed.), *Change in Communist Systems* (Stanford, Stanford University Press, 1970), pp. 33–116.
3 S. G. Solomon (ed.), *Pluralism in the Soviet Union* (London, Macmillan, 1983); H. G. Skilling and F. Griffiths (eds.), *Interest Groups in Soviet Politics* (Princeton, NJ, Princeton University Press, 1971); H. W. Morton, 'Who gets what, when and how? Housing in the Soviet Union', *Soviet Studies*, 32, 2 (1980), 235–59.
4 Cited in B. Ruble, *The Applicability of Corporatists Models to the Study of Soviet Politics* (Pittsburgh, University of Pittsburgh, Carl Beck Paper no. 33, 1983), p. 1. Bialer considers the Soviet system under Brezhnev to be authoritarian, not totalitarian – S. Bialer, *Stalin's Successors*, (Cambridge, Cambridge University Press, 1980), p. 145. Similarly, J. Hough has argued that: 'It becomes painfully clear that at no time during the Stalin period did the Soviet Union actually correspond to the Totalitarian model.' J. F. Hough, 'The Cultural Revolution and Western understanding of the Soviet system', in S. Fitzpatrick (ed.), *Cultural Revolution in Russia* (Bloomington, Indiana University Press, 1978), pp. 251–3, p. 248.
5 H. Arendt, *The Origins of Totalitarianism* (New York, Harcourt Brace Jovanovich, 1968). Her work, of course, focussed on Nazi Germany.

237

6 Z. K. Brzezinski and C. Friedrich (eds.), *Totalitarian Dictatorship and Autocracy* (Cambridge, Mass., Harvard University Press, 1956); C. Friedrich, *Totalitarianism* (Cambridge, Mass., Harvard University Press, 1954).

7 The first five points were listed by Friedrich in his 1954 work, *Totalitarianism*. The sixth point, on the economy, was added by Brzezinski in the first edition of their jointly published work, in 1956.

8 M. Weber, 'Politics as a vocation', in H. H. Gerth and C. W. Mills (eds.), *From Max Weber: Essays in Sociology* (Oxford, Oxford University Press, 1973).

9 For example, J. A. Getty, *Origins of the Great Purges* (Cambridge, Cambridge University Press, 1985); Fitzpatrick, *Cultural Revolution*.

10 For example, M. Broszat (ed.), *The Hitler State* (New York, Longman, 1984).

11 J. F. Hough and M. Fainsod, *How the Soviet Union is Governed* (Cambridge, Mass., Harvard University Press, 1979), p. 520.

12 Arendt, *Origins*; A. Zinoviev, *The Reality of Communism* (London, Gollancz, 1984).

13 Z. K. Brzezinski, *The Permanent Purge* (Cambridge, Mass., Harvard University Press, 1956).

14 M. Fainsod, *Smolensk Under Soviet Rule* (Cambridge, Mass., Harvard University Press, 1958), pp. 449, 85.

15 K. Deutsch, 'The limited capacity of centralized decision making', in Friedrich (ed.), *Totalitarianism*, pp. 308–32, p. 312.

16 J. T. Gross, 'A note on the nature of Soviet totalitarianism', *Soviet Studies*, 34, 3 (1982), 367–76.

17 See S. Hekman, *Weber, the Ideal Type and Contemporary Social Theory* (Notre Dame, University of Notre Dame, 1983).

18 *Websters Collegiate Dictionary*, 9th edn (Springfield, Mass., Mirriam-Webster, 1985).

19 J. L. Linz, 'Totalitarian and authoritarian regimes', in N. Polsby and F. Greenstein (eds.), *Handbook of Political Science* (New York, Addison-Wesley, 1975), ch. 3.

20 M. Heller, *Cogs in the Wheel* (New York, Knopf, 1988), p. 80, citing Soviet dictionaries.

21 G. O'Donnell and P. Schmitter, *Transitions from Authoritarian Rule* (Baltimore, Johns Hopkins, 1986); Z. Arat, 'Democracy and economic development', *Comparative Politics*, 21, 1 (1988), 21–36.

22 A. Zdravomyslov et al., *Politicheskoe soznanie trudiashchikhsia i problema ego konsolidatsii* (Moscow, Akademiia Obshchestvennykh Nauk, 1990), table 4.

23 Iu. Davydov, 'Totalitarizm i totalitarnaia biurokratiia', *Nauka i zhizn*, 8 (1989), 44–51. Davydov offers a Weberian analysis, in which a mobilized bureaucracy collapses into a particularized bureaucracy after 1953.

24 G. W. Breslauer, *Khrushchev and Brezhnev as Leaders: Building Authority in Soviet Politics* (London, Allen and Unwin, 1982).

25 T. F. Remington, *The Truth of Authority: Ideology and Communication in the Soviet Union* (Pittsburgh, University of Pittsburgh, 1988). For an intriguing insight into the degree of control over detail which censors sought to exercise, see the translation of the smuggled Polish censor's book – A. Niczow, *Black Book of Polish Censorship* (South Bend, Indiana, And Books, 1982).

26 D. Bahry and B. Silver, 'Intimidation and the symbolic uses of terror in the USSR', *American Political Science Review*, 81, 1 (1987), 1065–98; and *The Intimidation Factor in Soviet Politics* (Urbana, Il., Soviet Interview Project, working paper no. 31, February 1987), pp. 12, 25.

27 'Glasnost i demokratiia', *Izvestiia TsK KPSS*, 4 (1989), 105–8.

28 S. F. Cohen, 'The Stalin question since Stalin', in *Rethinking the Soviet Experience: Politics and History Since 1917* (Oxford, Oxford University Press, 1985), ch. 4.

29 Cf. A. Kassof, 'Totalitarianism without terror', *World Politics*, 26, 4 (1964), 558–75. Barrington Moore argues that 'Stalinist Russia was a totalitarian state, most of whose features remain standing today', in his *Authority and Inequality Under Capitalism and Socialism* (Oxford, Clarendon Press, 1987), p. 36.

30 Although it is by now standard practice to divide Soviet history up into the 'regimes' of successive individual leaders, this may lead one to exaggerate the impact of individual General Secretaries. Given the continuities in institutions and personnel over the post-1953 period, it is arguably more appropriate to treat the era as a single whole.

31 S. F. Starr, 'The changing nature of change in the USSR', in S. Bialer and M. Mandelbaum (eds.), *Gorbachev's Russia and American Foreign Policy* (Boulder, Col., Westview Press, 1988), pp. 3–36.

32 K. Marx, 'The German ideology', in *Selected Works* (Moscow, Progress, 1969), 3 vols., vol. 1, pp. 16–80, p. 47.

33 This division corresponds roughly to the distinction Gregory draws between the *khoziastvenniki* and *apparatchiki* – P. Gregory, *Restructuring the Soviet Economic Bureaucracy* (Cambridge, Cambridge University Press, 1990), p. 54.

34 As in his disappointing speech commemorating the seventieth anniversary of the 1917 revolution, entitled 'October and perestroika: the revolution continues' – reprinted in M. S. Gorbachev, *Izbrannye rechi i stat'i* (Moscow, Politizdat, 1987–90), 7 vols., vol. 5, pp. 386–436.

35 *Kommunist*, 7 (1988), 11.

36 V. Zaslavsky, *The Neostalinist State: Class Ethnicity and Consensus in Soviet Society* (Armonk, New York, M. E. Sharpe, 1982); V. Shlapentokh, *Public and Private Life in the Soviet Union: Changing Values in Post-Stalin Russia* (New York: Oxford University Press, 1989).

37 P. Hauslohner, 'Gorbachev's social contract,' *Soviet Economy*, 3, 1 (1987), 54–89.

38 P. Frank and R. Hill, *The Soviet Communist Party* (London: Allen and Unwin, 1981).

39 M. Djilas, *The New Class* (London, Allen and Unwin, 1966; K. Simis, *USSR: Secrets of a Corrupt Society* (London, Dent, 1982); I. Zemtsov, *La Corruption en Union Soviétique* (Paris, Hachette, 1976); M. Voslensky, *Nomenklatura* (New York, Doubleday, 1984); Skilling and Griffiths, *Interest Groups*; S. P. Huntington, *Political Order in Changing Societies* (New Haven, Yale University Press, 1968); G. W. Breslauer, 'On the adaptibility of Soviet welfare-state authoritarianism,' in K. W. Ryavec (ed.), *Soviet Society and the Communist*

Party (Amherst, Mass., University of Massachusetts, 1978), pp. 3–26; Hauslohner, 'Gorbachev'; Lowenthal, 'Development'.

40 A. Nove, *The Soviet Economic System* (London: Allen and Unwin, 1977); M. Kaser, *Soviet Economics* (London: Weidenfeld and Nicholson, 1970); J. Berliner, *Factory and Manager in the USSR* (Cambridge, Mass., Harvard University Press, 1957).

41 S. Fortescue, 'The regional party apparatus in the "sectional society"', *Studies in Comparative Communism*, 21, 1 (1988), 11–24.

42 This point is made in M. Mikhailov, 'Po povodu vedomstvennosti', *Kommunist*, 8 (1981), 104–15.

43 *Izvestiia*, 2 January 1984, p. 2; E. I. Kapustin, *Organizatsiia sorevnovaniia i sovershenstvovanie khoziaistvennogo mekhanizma* (Moscow: Politizdat, 1982), p. 178.

44 On housing, see *Pravda*, 4 March 1980, p. 3; on streetcars – *Kommunist*, 2 (1979), 53; for a farm – *Ekonomicheskaia gazeta*, 4 (1982), 4. See also G. Popov, 'Razvitie otraslevogo upravleniia promyshlennost'iu', *Kommunist*, 18 (1982), 48–59.

45 Hough, *The Soviet Prefects*.

46 B. Moore, Jnr., *Terror and Progress: USSR* (Cambridge, Mass., Harvard University Press, 1954).

47 Hough, *Prefects*, p. 303.

48 For example, G. Grossman, 'The party as manager and entrepreneur', in G. Guroff and F. V. Carstensen (eds.), *Entrepreneurship in Imperial Russia and the Soviet Union* (Princeton, New Jersey: Princeton University Press, 1983); T. Gustafson, *Reform in Soviet Politics: Lessons of Recent Policies on Land and Water* (Cambridge, Cambridge University Press, 1981).

49 For a general argument on the innate economic limitations of the command economy, see Rutland, *The Myth of the Plan*.

1 The party and the economy: structures and principles

1 *Fundamental Law of the Socialist State of the Whole People* (Moscow, Social Sciences, 1978), p. 70.

2 As stated in the party program – 'Programma KPSS', in *Materialy 27 s"ezda KPSS* (Moscow, Politizdat, 1986), p. 139.

3 'Ustav KPSS' (Party Rules), in *Materialy*, pp. 188–206, p. 204. See also *Partiinaia zhizn*, 24 (1982), 22.

4 S. I. Surnichenko, *Leninskie printsipy partiinogo rukovodstva khoziaistvennym stroitel'stvom* (Moscow, Politizdat, 1979); L. A. Openkin, 'Partiinoe rukovodstvo uskoreniem nauchno-tekhnicheskogo progressa v sovremennykh usloviiakh', *Voprosy istorii KPSS*, 2 (1985), 135–43.

5 L. I. Brezhnev, *Leninskim kursom* (Moscow, Politizdat, 1976), p. 9.

6 *Kommunist*, 10 (1981), 23.

7 *Kommunist*, 17 (1985), 15.

8 *Materialy*, p. 1898.

9 *Kommunist*, 6 (1978), 32.

10 Surnichenko, *Leninskie*, p. 20; *Povyshenie roli pervichnykh partiinykh organizat-sii* (Moscow, Politizdat, 1983), pp. 54, 174.

11 *KPSS v rezoliutsiiakh i resheniiakh*, 8th edn (Moscow, Politizdat, 1973–84), vols. 9–13; 387 pages of decrees surveyed. The 50 per cent on economic themes broke down into 14 per cent on agriculture, 6 per cent on construction, and the rest general topics.

12 *Spravochnik partiinogo rabotnika* (Moscow, Politizdat, 1973–82), vols. 8–23; 495 pages of decrees surveyed.

13 *Argumenty i fakty*, 28 (1988), p. 2. This pattern is confirmed by the ministry officials, both current and *émigré*, interviewed by Gregory – Gregory, *Restructuring*, ch. 7.

14 For the best general survey, see Frank and Hill, *The Soviet Communist Party*.

15 See article 52 of the Party Statutes, in *Materialy*, p. 22. These residential organs were reported to be very weak – for example, in *Kommunist*, 18 (1985), 6; 17 (1985), 82.

16 The source for data in the following sections is 'KPSS v tsifrakh', *Partiinaia zhizn*, 15 (1983), 14–33.

17 For a complete breakdown of the regional and administrative structure of the USSR, see *Administrativno-territorial'noe delenie soiuznykh respublikh* (Moscow, Izvestiia, 1983).

18 For examples of critical CC CPSU decrees on the work of obkomy, see those on Samarkand and Krasnodar in *Partiinaia zhizn*, 22 (1981), 10; and *Ekonomicheskaia gazeta*, 10 (1977), 4.

19 These two examples are from Kaliningrad and Zaporozhe. *Ekonomicheskaia gazeta*, 36 (1984), 5; 7 (1984), 10.

20 Thus, for example, the Nikolaevo obkom was taken to task for allowing 50 of its enterprises to lower their plan targets; Dzhambul obkom was blamed for a 9.1 per cent rise in industrial production 1977–79 against a planned rise of 17.4 per cent; and Vitebsk obkom first secretary reported that 54 of their 136 industrial plants missed their output targets in the first half of 1985. *Partiinaia zhizn*, 1 (1979), 61, 32; *Ekonomicheskaia gazeta*, 10 (1985), 5.

21 *Partiinaia zhizn*, 6 (1980), 39; *Kommunist*, 11 (1978), 39.

22 Examples being CC CPSU decrees on the party organizations of Estonia, Armenia and Kazakhstan. See *Kommunist*, 12 (1984), 3; *Partiinaia zhizn*, 2 (1984), 18; 5 (1986) 17.

23 'Pervyi sekretar', *Pravda*, 22 July 1986, p. 2.

24 Reprinted in *Kommunist*, 5 (1982), 101–13.

25 For Pskov, see *Partiinaia zhizn*, 18 (1984), 3; for Khorezm, see Table 1.1.

26 *Kommunist*, 4 (1988), 86–89. The size of the staff had risen by 50 per cent since 1965.

27 *Partiinaia zhizn*, 11 (1980), 30; and C. Ross, *Local Government in the Soviet Union* (New York, St Martins, 1987), p. 21.

28 We found no full accounts of the work of an obkom orgotdel. For an account of the work of Dnepropetrovsk gorkom orgotdel, see *Voprosy istorii KPSS*, 3 (1982), 39–51.

29 *Kommunist*, 4 (1983), 145.
30 A. V. Cherniak, *Tovarishch instruktor* (Moscow, Politizdat, 1984), p. 216.
31 For reviews of their work in Latvia and Donetsk, see *Partiinaia zhizn*, 8 (1982), 47–52; 8 (1985), 48–51.
32 For a typical report on the appeals taken to the national KPK, see *Izvestiia TsK KPSS* 7 (1989), 59–64. Between 1934 and 1952, and again between 1962 and 1965, the Committee of Party Control was itself known as the Party Control Commission.
33 On the work of the *revkomy*, see *Partinaia zhizn*, 18 (1982), 21–7; 14 (1983), 28–33; G. Sizov, *Nekotorye voprosy revizionny raboty v partiinykh organizatsiiakh* (Moscow, Politizdat, 1984); and 'Ob itogakh raboty TsRK v 1988', *Izvestiia TsK KPSS*, 4 (1989), 24–30.
34 See the report of the TsRK head, G. Sizov, to the 27th Party Congress, in *Materialy*, pp. 207–15; and *Voprosy istorii KPSS*, 3 (1982), 44.
35 *Partiinaia zhizn*, 5 (1979), 40–7.
36 *Partiinaia zhizn*, 18 (1982), 21–7.
37 *Kommunist*, 17 (1986), 36.
38 N. E. Rosenfeldt, *Knowledge and Power: the Role of Stalin's Secret Chancellery in the Soviet System of Government* (Copenhagen, Rosekilde and Bagger, 1978).
39 *Raionnyi komitet partii* (Moscow, Politizdat, 1974), p. 235.
40 *Partiinaia zhizn*, 9 (1981), 37, reports that the Andizhan obkom put seventy-five decisions under its supervision each year.
41 *Partiinaia zhizn*, 17 (1980), 27.
42 *Raionnyi*, p. 129.
43 Ibid., p. 152. See also *Partiinaia zhizn*, 6 (1977), 37–45; and 27 (1983), 42.
44 As specified in a 1960 CC CPSU decree, reprinted in *KPSS v rezoliutsiiakh*, vol. 8, p. 121. Some did use full-time officials – for example, Leningrad obkom after 1972 had one full-time official in each raikom handling commission work – *Partiinaia zhizn*, 5 (1979), 42.
45 *Raionnyi*, pp. 199–234; *Partiinaia zhizn*, 2 (1977), 25–32; 2 (1979), 45. Since May 1982 agricultural departments have been compulsory for raikomy (as they were before 1965) – *Voprosy istorii KPSS*, 6 (1983), p. 3.
46 Hough, *Prefects*, p. 23; M. Voslensky, *Nomenklatura* (New York, Doubleday, 1984), p. 94.
47 For example, Kuntsev raikom in Moscow had 34 staff workers (to handle a membership totalling 23,000); while rural raikomy in Ul'ianovsk and Omsk were reported as having only 14 staff workers – *Partiinaia zhizn*, 14 (1981), 52; 5 (1979), 49; 3 (1978), 67.
48 J. V. Stalin, 'Address to the graduates of the Red Army Academy', in *Collected Works* (New York, Red Star Press, 1978), vol. 14, p. 75.
49 Cited in *Ekonomicheskaia gazeta*, 14 (1984), 3.
50 Cited in *Kommunist*, 1 (1982), 34.
51 See Voslensky, *Nomenklatura*; and Hough, *Prefects*, pp. 150–5.
52 *Partiinaia zhizn*, 15 (1981), 16.
53 The lists include both party and non-party personnel: for example, at the Magnitka metal combine half of the cadre reserve were not party members. *Partiinaia zhizn*, 4 (1981), 25.

54 *Partiinaia zhizn*, 6 (1979), 41.
55 Cherniak, pp. 45, 108.
56 V. G. Chufarov (ed.), *Deiatel'nost partiinykh organizatsii Urala* (Sverdlovsk, Ural'skii gosudarstvennyi universitet, 1976), p. 91.
57 Hough, *Prefects*, p. 194.
58 Examples include Vinnitsa obkom choosing to restore collective and state farm chairmen to their nomenklatura in 1977; the Zhitomir obkom expanding the number of engineering personnel it appoints; Voronezh obkom deciding to put farm brigade leaders on the raikomy nomenklatura; and Bryansk obkom moving the heads of agro-mechanization teams onto its own lists. Sources: *Voprosy istorii KPSS*, 1 (1979) 14; *Partiinaia zhizn*, 4 (1986) 38; 7 (1979) 45; and *Ekonomicheskaia gazeta*, 38 (1985) 5.
59 Voslensky, *Nomenklatura*, p. 94.
60 *Partiinaia zhizn*, 4 (1980), 19.
61 For example, in the face of lagging fish catches a Rostov obkom secretary reported that 'It was decided together with the RSFSR Ministry for the Fish Industry to strengthen the leadership of the trust.' *Ekonomicheskaia gazeta*, 10 (1984), 4.
62 For example, selection of plant directors in Azerbaijdan seemed to be the remit of the large Baku-based industrial trusts – *Kommunist*, 12 (1981) 52.
63 For example, Klaipeda gorkom selected the directors of the postal service and a tobacco factory, because the administrations could not find candidates of their own. *Ekonomicheskaia gazeta*, 22 (1977), 5.
64 For example, in Vladimir the obkom second secretary personally supervised the appointment of farm chairmen. *Ekonomicheskaia gazeta*, 46 (1982), 18.
65 Examples range from Alma Ata to Khabarovsk – *Ekonomicheskaia gazeta*, 25 (1985), 5; and 35 (1981), 6.
66 For example, Neryungri gorkom got the heads of a coal trust and a hydro-electric station removed in this way. *Ekonomicheskaia gazeta*, 25 (1985), 3.
67 A point made by A. Pel'she, head of the People's Control Committee, in *Kommunist*, 11 (1981), 6.
68 *Partiinaia zhizn*, 11 (1986), 73.
69 *Ekonomicheskaia gazeta*, 31 (1979), 14.
70 *Partiinaia zhizn*, 15 (1983), 52.
71 Cherniak, *Tovarishch*, pp. 113, 192.
72 Ibid., p. 190.
73 J. F. Hough, *The Role of Local Party Organs in Industrial Decision Making* (Cambridge, Mass., Harvard University Ph. D. thesis, 1961), pp. 25, 28.
74 Cherniak, *Tovarishch*, p. 219.
75 *Partiinaia zhizn*, 10 (1983), 50; Cherniak, *Tovarishch*, p. 197.
76 *Kommunist*, 8 (1985), 43.
77 *Partiinaia zhizn*, 5 (1986), 11.
78 *Partiinaia zhizn*, 18 (1984), 36; Cherniak, p. 7. Similar turnover rates are reported in Hough and Fainsod, *How the Soviet Union is Governed*, p. 496.
79 Cherniak, *Tovarishch*, p. 7.

80 For example, the Kirgizh CC issued 676 resolutions in two years; Dagestan obkom 160 in 1985; and Samarkand obkom 248 in 1985. Over half of Kiev raikom decrees were non-operational. *Partiinaia zhizn*, 1 (1986), 48; 3 (1986), 43; 3 (1986), 45; *Pravda*, 17 January 1980, p. 2.

81 For example, Leninabad gorkom required a 28-part report from each of its 236 PPOs every week, and Dzerzhinsk raikom in Moscow collected a 455-part form from its PPOs each month. *Partiinaia zhizn*, 17 (1981), 44; 10 (1981), 59.

82 *Partiinaia zhizn*, 18 (1981), 42. One factory PPO secretary complained that after being summoned to the gorkom sixteen times in one month, he was again called in – to explain why he was not spending much time on the factory floor. *Ekonomicheskaia gazeta*, 44 (1978), 5.

83 The CC CPSU complained, for example, that party reporting practices 'overburden enterprise employees' – *Ekonomicheskaia gazeta*, 24 (1986), 2.

84 *Partiinaia zhizn*, 21 (1983), 16–21.

85 *Partiinaia zhizn*, 1 (1981), 72.

86 *Partiinaia zhizn*, 19 (1976), 16.

87 *Partiinaia zhizn*, 20 (1980), 37; *Raionnyi*, p. 16.

88 Cherniak, *Tovarishch*, p. 34.

89 *Partiinaia zhizn*, 5 (1986), 15.

90 *Kommunist*, 6 (1978), 37; *Partiinaia zhizn*, 14 (1980), 13.

91 *Ekonomicheskaia gazeta*, 17 (1985), 5.

92 *Partiinaia zhizn*, 5 (1986), 10.

93 In Lipetsk, for example, the gorkom had to annul 30 per cent of PPO decrees on these grounds – *Kommunist*, 12 (1986), 36.

94 *Partiinaia zhizn*, 6 (1985), 35.

95 *Partiinaia zhizn*, 7 (1983), 55.

96 *Partiinaia zhizn*, 4 (1984), 13; *Ekonomicheskaia gazeta*, 4 (1981), 5.

97 Ross, *Local*, p. 27.

98 These quotes are from the article by Iu. Bondar, 'O politicheskom kharaktere partiinogo rukovodstva', *Voprosy istorii KPSS*, 2 (1984), 31–45, 41, 43.

99 *Partiinaia zhizn*, 2 (1982), 25; *Raionnyi*, p. 73.

100 A Murmansk obkom instructor complained: 'Even after many years, I have not been able to find a clear answer to the question of how to influence without being guilty of podmena.' *Partiinaia zhizn*, 5 (1982), 49.

101 For example, a Voronezh raikom official argued for and against the sending of plenipotentiaries into the countryside in succeeding sentences. *Kommunist*, 5 (1986), 54.

102 *Kommunist*, 18 (1981), 14.

103 'Ustav', in *Materialy*, p. 204, articles 60–2; *Kommunist*, 18 (1985), 64.

104 *Kommunist*, 15 (1985), 13. See for example A. Zhdanov's 1946 decree, in *KPSS v rezoliutsiiakh*, vol. 6, pp. 186–9.

105 *Materialy*, p. 192.

106 *Partiinaia zhizn*, 18 (1983), 13.

107 *Partiinaia zhizn*, 10 (1980), 6–11.

108 *Kommunist*, 8 (1985), 42; *Partiinaia zhizn*, 11 (1981), 50; 20 (1982), 21.

109 Hough, *Prefects*, 94; citing *Partiinaia zhizn*, 23 (1965), 34.

110 *Partiinaia zhizn*, 17 (1977), 61.
111 *Kommunist*, 11 (1981), 16.
112 'Ustav', in *Materialy*, p. 204. PPOs in housing and communal service establishments did not have the right of supervision. For a review of the history of this activity, see N. A. Petrovichev, *Vazhnyi faktor vozrastaniia rukovodiashchei roli KPSS* (Moscow, Politizdat, 1979), pp. 49, 97.
113 S. F. Fortescue, *Soviet Science and the Communist Party* (London, Macmillan, 1968), p. 133.
114 Iu. Bondar, 'Kontrol i proverki ispolneniia', *Voprosy istorii KPSS*, 7 (1985), 17–29, 21; *Partiinaia zhizn*, 11 (1981), 25.
115 Surnichenko, *Leninskie*, pp. 50–2.
116 *Ekonomicheskaia gazeta*, 1 (1976), 6.
117 These three were all highlighted in a Voronezh gorkom report – *Ekonomicheskaia gazeta*, 24 (1976), 6.
118 For example, A. Pel'she, head of the People's Control Committee, underscored 'the personal accountability of those responsible for carrying out decisions', in his article 'O trebovatel'nosti i ditsipline', *Kommunist*, 2 (1980), 21.
119 *KPSS v rezoliutsiiakh*, vol. 14, pp. 441–8; *Partiinaia zhizn*, 20 (1981), 24.
120 *KPSS v rezoliutsiiakh*, vol. 8, pp. 11–7. Workshop units do not have the right of supervision, even those with full powers of a PPO for recruitment procedures. Party commissions are not allowed to issue party instructions, nor to demand reports from officials. *Partiinaia zhizn*, 21 (1978), 56; 4 (1982), 46.
121 Based on the Sverdlovsk case – *Kommunist*, 11 (1983), 58.
122 *Partiinaia zhizn*, 10 (1980), 12–8; 2 (1981), 64. The Voronezh gorkom first secretary remarked that PPOs often 'do not want to bother' with supervision – *Voprosy istorii KPSS*, 8 (1983), 70.
123 *Partiinaia zhizn*, 21 (1982), 8.
124 *Pravda*, 3 March 1985, p. 2.
125 *Partiinaia zhizn*, 1 (1986), 70; 2 (1986), 53; 20 (1982), 25; 5 (1982), 33; 8 (1981), 57.
126 *Partiinaia zhizn*, 3 (1982), 64.
127 See the proceedings of an all-union conference on the subject, held in Tbilisi in April 1983 – *Povyshennye*; and the results of a survey of 1,140 party activists in Moscow, reported in V. Shostakovskii, 'V zerkale sotsiologii', *Kommunist*, 9 (1988), 31–5.
128 For example, the critical CC CPSU report on the PPOs of Voronezh region, in *Partiinaia zhizn*, 18 (1981), 3–6. The CC CPSU itself directly hears reports from three to four PPOs each year – *Kommunist*, 15 (1979), 44.
129 Examples ranges from a Leninsk coal mine to a tractor station in Uman – *Partiinaia zhizn*, 22 (1980), 54; 15 (1981), 19.
130 *Partiinaia zhizn*, 15 (1983), 30–1.
131 Of the 345 directors whose short biographies were printed in *Ekonomicheskaia gazeta* between 1976 and 1985, 39 had served as partkom secretary at some point in their career, 27 of them in the same plant which they subsequently headed.

132 *Izvestiia TsK KPSS*, 4 (1989), 87.
133 *Partiinaia zhizn*, 16 (1982), 43; *Ekonomicheskaia gazeta* 30 (1986), 19.
134 *Partiinaia zhizn*, 20 (1982), 22.
135 *Kommunist*, 3 (1980), 30.
136 *Pravda*, 28 December 1980, p. 6.
137 The Russian phrase is 'pocket secretary' (*karmannyi sekretar*) – *Kommunist*, 12 (1986), 47. For example, a Baku oil refinery director engineered the appointment of a PPO secretary who was allegedly 'excessively tolerant of dirty deeds'. *Kommunist*, 2 (1986), 88.
138 *Kommunist*, 15 (1984), 31, 35.
139 *Partiinaia zhizn*, 11 (1981), 86.
140 This is reported to be the case for almost half of the punishments issued by raikomy and gorkomy in the Kiev oblast. *Partiinaia zhizn*, 5 (1985), 19. A new clause was inserted into article 9 of the Party Statutes adoped in 1986, requiring for the first time that a higher party organ must inform the PPO if it imposes a disciplinary penalty on one of its members – 'Ustav', in *Materialy*, p. 192.
141 *Kommunist*, 2 (1985), 36.
142 Fortescue, *Soviet Science*, pp. 138–48.
143 Examples include PPOs in a garage in Kishinev and a hospital in Altai who got their directors dismissed – *Partiinaia zhizn*, 4 (1978), 36; 12 (1982), 72.
144 *Ekonomicheskaia gazeta*, 12 (1979), 16.
145 For example, from an Omsk building trust and a Latvian textile mill, see *Partiinaia zhizn*, 1 (1981), 73; 12 (1981), 68.
146 This impression of collusion rather than conflict being the Soviet bureaucratic style is confirmed by Gregory, *Restructuring*, ch.4.

2 Party interventions in industry

1 *Kommunist*, 9 (1985), 8.
2 K. Ryavec, *The Implementation of Soviet Economic Reforms* (New York, Praeger, 1975).
3 P. Hanson, 'Success indicators revisited: the July 1979 decree on planning and management', *Soviet Studies* 35, 1 (1983), 1–13.
4 *Ekonomicheskaia gazeta*, 32 (1985), 11–14.
5 *Voprosy ekonomiki*, 5 (1986), 68.
6 *Pravda*, 17 March 1983, p. 2.
7 For example, the CC CPSU reported that Tula oblast failed to meet its aggregate output targets for two years out of five, 1978–83; and a CC CCSU decree censured Khar'kov party organizations in 1985 for failing to keep the region's industries on course – *Pravda*, 6 July 1983, p. 2; *Partiinaia zhizn*, 14 (1985), 6–8.
8 For example, eight oblasti were criticized for failing to meet their industrial output targets in an editorial in *Kommunist*, 5 (1978), 7.
9 *Ekonomicheskaia gazeta*, 5 (1984), 5; 1 (1976), 14; 7 (1984), 10; 20 (1984), 5; 3 (1976), 6. The fact that all our examples come from the reports published in 1976 and 1984 suggests that some sort of political/editorial decision making

was taken in *Ekonomicheskaia gazeta* to print those cases in those particular years. Surely some regions missed targets in other years – but we failed to find any reports on them.

10 *Pravda*, 27 January 1984, p. 2.
11 *Partiinaia zhizn*, 23 (1983), 52–5.
12 *Ekonomicheskaia gazeta*, 52 (1983), 6.
13 Examples include *Ekonomicheskaia gazeta*, 9 (1976), 18, and 48 (1977), 5.
14 *Ekonomicheskaia gazeta*, 36 (1979), 7.
15 *Partiinaia zhizn*, 16 (1976), 46; *Kommunist*, 3 (1986), 39.
16 Examples from Chaikov gorkom and Penza obkom – *Ekonomicheskaia gazeta*, 7 (1980), 5; 15 (1978), 11.
17 *Ekonomicheskaia gazeta*, 2 (1980), 16; *Partiinaia zhizn*, 3 (1981), 70.
18 *Ekonomicheskaia gazeta*, 31 (1981), 12.
19 *Partiinaia zhizn*, 10 (1985), 44.
20 M. Beissinger, 'Economic performance and career prospects in the party apparatus' paper delivered to the American Association for the advancement of Slavic Studies, New Orleans, 11 November 1986.
21 P. Rutland, 'The search for stability: ideology, discipline and the cohesion of the Soviet elite', *Studies in Comparative Communism*, 24, 1, 1991.
22 Egor Ligachev apparently likes to take credit for Akademgorodok, since he was a secretary of Novosibirsk obkom in the late 1950s, when the project was being developed. (Interviews in the Institute of Economics, Siberian Branch of the Academy of Sciences, July 1988.)
23 Fortescue, *Soviet Science*.
24 R. F. Miller, 'The role of the Communist Party in Soviet research and development', *Soviet Studies*, 37, 1 (1987), 31–59.
25 Ibid. pp. 54, 57.
26 *Ekonomicheskaia gazeta*, 16 (1983), 6.
27 J. S. Berliner, *The Innovation Decision in Soviet Industry* (Cambridge, Mass., MIT Press, 1976).
28 R. Amann and J. Cooper (eds.), *Technical Progress and Soviet Economic Development* (Oxford, Blackwell, 1986), ch. 1).
29 Fortescue, *Soviet Science*, p. 97.
30 A. G. Osipov, 'Partiinye organizatsii i nachuno-tekhnicheskii progress', *Voprosy istorii KPSS*, 8 (1984), 22–34, 24.
31 *Partiinaia zhizn*, 8 (1977), 39.
32 See for example the approving CC CPSU decree on Leningrad's work in this sphere – *Partiinaia zhizn*, 16 (1984), 5–6.
33 *Ekonomicheskaia gazeta*, 43 (1978), 12.
34 Osipov, 'Partiinye', p. 24.
35 *Voprosy ekonomiki*, 6 (1986), 113–17.
36 Osipov, 'Partiinye', p. 29.
37 This section picks up the story from Hough, *Prefects*, chs. 8 and 9.
38 *Ekonomicheskaia gazeta*, 2 (1979), 7. On the delays in introducing this technique, see *Pravda*, 12 July 1982, p. 7.
39 *Kommunist*, 16 (1985), 90.
40 *Ekonomicheskaia gazeta*, 14 (1986), 9.

41 *Ekonomicheskaia gazeta*, 7 (1982), 5.
42 *Ekonomicheskaia gazeta*, 26 (1986), 8.
43 Storming examples include *Ekonomicheskaia gazeta*, 45 (1978), 5; and *Partiinaia zhizn*, 21 (1985), 128.
44 *Ekonomicheskaia gazeta*, 30 (1976), 8.
45 *Ekonomicheskaia gazeta*, 21 (1981), 5.
46 E.g. the manager of an asphalt plant in Andizhan – *Ekonomicheskaia gazeta*, 50, (1977), 5.
47 For example, communists were barred from quitting a Vilnius radio plant when it ran into production problems – *Partiinaia zhizn*, 21 (1980), 49.
48 For example, Mari obkom set up Turkmenistan's first irrigation vocational school (PTU) in 1978 – *Partiinaia zhizn*, 9 (1978), 5. A history of party activity in Sverdlovsk devoted no less than eleven of its chapters to questions of training and cadre selection. (Chufarov, *Deiatel'nost*.)
49 *Partiinaia zhizn*, 2 (1981), 46; 22 (1981), 30.
50 *Voprosy ekonomiki*, 6 (1986), 43–51.
51 For example, in the Crimea – *Ekonomicheskaia gazeta*, 9 (1979), 5.
52 See a CC CPSU/Council of Ministers resolution on this subject, in *Ekonomicheskaia gazeta*, 37 (1982), 3.
53 Successful examples would include Ivanovo obkom's reconstruction of the region's textile plants, or Liuberets gorkom's rebuilding of an agricultural machinery plant – *Ekonomicheskaia gazeta*, 26 (1981), 6; and 32 (1982), 15.
54 *Partiinaia zhizn*, 15 (1976), 29.
55 *Partiinaia zhizn*, 23 (1983), 52–5.
56 D. Slider, 'Reforming the workplace: the 1983 Soviet Law on Labour Collectives', *Soviet Studies*, 37, 2 (1985), 173–83.
57 *Pravda*, 2 August 1987, p. 1.
58 *Ekonomika i zhizn*, 25 (1990), 19–21.
59 *Direktor N. A. Ligachev i vospominaniia sovremennikov* (Moscow, Moskovskii rabochii, 1971).
60 *Partiinaia zhizn*, 15 (1980), 53.
61 Examples can be found in *Izvestiia*, 3 February 1984, p. 3; and in *Ekonomicheskaia gazeta*, 21 (1983), 5; and 3 (1984), 5.
62 *Ekonomicheskaia gazeta*, 28 (1985), 16.
63 *Kommunist*, 2 (1985), 122.
64 *Partiinaia zhizn*, 15 (1985), 47.
65 For a trenchant analysis of the costs of autarchy, see G. Popov, 'Razvitie otraslevogo upravleniia promyshlennost'iu', *Kommunist*, 18 (1982), 48–59.
66 The average truck was only on the road for three hours a day. *Ekonomicheskaia gazeta*, 34 (1976), 3; also *Kommunist*, 16 (1986), 51.
67 *Ekonomicheskaia gazeta*, 5 (1983), 5.
68 *Kommunist*, 9 (1986), 62.
69 An example would be Kuibyshev obkom mobilizing a team from the Volzhski car plant to assist a local ailing cement plant – *Ekonomicheskaia gazeta*, 32 (1981), 8.
70 *Izvestiia*, 16 October 1980, p. 2; and 16 April 1981, p. 2; *Pravda*, 24 December 1981, p. 3.

71 Ministries did closely monitor their press image. For example, an iron and steel ministry official noted that 'More than half of all published references to the ministry are positive'. *Ekonomicheskaia gazeta*, 14 (1983), 9.

72 Typically, annual plans are changed eight to twelve times in the course of the year. For examples, see *Ekonomicheskaia gazeta*, 18 (1978), 7; *Partiinaia zhizn* 5 (1985), 21.

73 Plan reductions were criticized for example at a Tula obkom conference, or in an article by a Moscow gorkom official criticizing the agriculture ministry – *Ekonomicheskaia gazeta*, 4 (1981), 5; 33 (1978), 7. The Gor'kii obkom first secretary accused ministries of deliberately leaving plants with a 'safety valve' (*otdushina*), not penalizing them for underfulfilment – *Ekonomicheskaia gazeta*, 12 (1984), 5.

74 For example, the Cheliabinsk obkom first secretary reproached a manager who cut his plan with the 'silent approval' of his PPO – *Ekonomicheskaia gazeta*, 24 (1985), 7.

75 *Pravda*, 13 March 1983, p. 2.

76 *Ekonomicheskaia gazeta*, 44 (1984), 4.

77 For example, a Rostov obkom official complained that only one in five local plants succeeded in getting counter plans accepted by their branch superiors – *Ekonomicheskaia gazeta*, 45 (1978), 8.

78 *Ekonomicheskaia gazeta*, 32 (1978), 8; 39 (1978), 5.

79 Other cases range from an oil refinery in Volgograd to a Tomsk polypropylene plant operating at 25 per cent capacity – *Izvestiia*, 5 January 1984, p. 2; *Pravda* 28 November 1980, p. 2.

80 For a typical Brezhnev speech, see *Ekonomicheskaia gazeta*, 16 (1978), 4. Gorbachev's collected works has a special entry on *mestnichestvo* and *vedomstvennost* in the index – *Izbrannye rechi i stat'i*.

81 Quoted in *Detente*, 7 (1986), 3.

82 *Kommunist*, 16 (1986), 42.

83 *Kommunist*, 1 (1980), 83.

84 For example, the Ministries of Transport and Procurements could not agree on who should pay for grain lost during rail shipment – *Ekonomicheskaia gazeta*, 35 (1985), 10.

85 *EKO*, 12 (1984), 73.

86 This can be seen in letters replying to criticism in *Ekonomicheskaia gazeta* from obkom secretaries in Novosibirsk and Irkutsk, or in Volgoda where the poor record of the important Cherepovets steel plant came up for discussion – *Ekonomicheskaia gazeta*, 30 (1986) 2; 4 (1980) 2; 5 (1976) 6.

87 *Ekonomicheskaia gazeta*, 34 (1980), 4; 22 (1980), 5.

88 *Ekonomicheskaia gazeta*, 5 (1977), 18; 7 (1977), 17.

89 S. F. Fortescue, 'The primary party organizations of branch ministries', paper presented to the Third World Congress for Soviet and East European Studies, Washington DC, 30 October 1985.

90 *KPSS v rezoliutsiiakh*, vol. 8, pp. 463–6.

91 *Partiinaia zhizn*, 10 (1978), 53; 22 (1978), 44–50; 17 (1980), 49–53.

92 *Ekonomicheskaia gazeta*, 43 (1983), 4.

93 For example, criticism of the partkom in Ministry Machine Tools and

Instruments in *Ekonomicheskaia gazeta*, 7 (1986), 3–4. The paper refused to accept a letter in reply from the ministry, claiming that it was nothing but a catalogue of 'alleged successes' – *Ekonomicheskaia gazeta*, 15 (1986), 2.

94 *Ekonomicheskaia gazeta*, 27 (1986), 3.

95 D. Slider, *Social Experiments and Soviet Policy Making* (New Haven, Yale University, Ph. D, 1981).

96 On this, see P. Rutland, 'The role of the Communist Party on the Soviet shopfloor', *Studies in Comparative Communism*, 21, 1 (1988), 25–44.

97 P. Rutland, 'The Shchekino method and the struggle to raise labour productivity in Soviet industry', *Soviet Studies*, 36, 3 (1984), 345–65.

98 Slider, *Social*, ch. 3.

99 This happened to the 'goal programmes' for labour supply, quality control and environmental protection which the Latvian republic introduced in 1971. *Kommunist*, 15 (1981), 33.

100 A. Prigozhin, 'Upravlencheskie novovedeniia i khoziaistvennye eksperimenty', *Kommunist*, 7 (1984), 57–67.

101 See for example, the first secretary of Vologda obkom, quoting the saying 'an initiative is worth more than money', in *Kommunist*, 15 (1985), 60. For an article by Gorbachev on this theme when he was first secretary of Stavropol kraikom, see 'Peredovoi opyt – vazhnyi rezerv', *Kommunist*, 14 (1978), 72–8.

102 *Kommunist*, 14 (1977), 62–71; *Partiinaia zhizn*, 21 (1978), 21–36.

103 *Kommunist*, 15 (1985), 61, 65.

104 Quoted in *Partiinaia zhizn*, 17 (1982), 13.

105 *Kommunist*, 13 (1981), 30.

106 This received recognition in the form of a CC CPSU commendation, a book, a special supplement in *Ekonomicheskaia gazeta*, and numerous conferences. *Ekonomicheskaia gazeta*, 38 (1977), 19; 9 (1978), 11–14; 13 (1978), 18; 8 (1979), 33; *Ipatovo metod – v zhizn* (Moscow, Pravda, 1978).

107 On this, see C. Schmidt-Hauer, *Gorbachev: the Path to Power* (London, Tauris, 1986), pp. 61–2.

108 For example, similar techniques were being used in Ukraine – *Ekonomicheskaia gazeta*, 33 (1977) 19.

109 Rutland, 'Shchekino'.

110 'Sovershenstvuia rukovodstvo ekonomikoi', *Voprosy istorii KPSS*, 4 (1984), 68–107. The original five ministries were the USSR Heavy/Transport Machinery and Electrotechnical Ministries, the Ukrainian Food Ministry, the Belorussian Light Industry Ministry and the Lithuanian Local Industry Ministry.

111 *Ekonomicheskaia gazeta*, 32 (1985), 11–14; 47 (1986), 17.

112 *Pravda*, 22 March 1983, p. 1; *Kommunist*, 2 (1986), 28; also based on interviews conducted by the author in the Togliatti Engineering-Economics Institute in Leningrad in October 1984.

113 Engineers' pay fell from 215 per cent of workers' pay in 1940 to 151 in the mid-1960s and 110 by 1981 – *Kommunist*, 12 (1986), 20. On this issue, see Hauslohner, 'Gorbachev', 54–89.

114 'Sovershenstvuia', p. 74. Similar reports came from Belorussia, Leningrad, Khar'kov, Cheboksary and Volgograd – *Partiinaia zhizn*, 19 (1985), 24; *Ekonomicheskaia gazeta*, 30 (1984), 8; 36 (1984), 8; 43 (1984), 7; 12 (1984), 7.

115 A point made in Prigozhin, 'Upravlencheskie', p. 54.

116 For example, in 'Sovershenstvuia', p. 93; and in a CC CPSU decree in *Partiinaia zhizn*, 24 (1985), 17–20.

117 *Partiinaia zhizn*, 16 (1984), 50; *Ekonomicheskaia gazeta*, 51 (1983), 3.

118 *Ekonomicheskaia gazeta*, 32 (1985), 11–14, clause 26.

119 *Ekonomicheskaia gazeta*, 7 (1986), 3.

120 See the complaints of a Moscow textile mill director, in *Ekonomicheskaia gazeta*, 16 (1985), 4.

121 See for example G. Schroeder, 'The Soviet economy on a treadmill of "reforms"', *Soviet Economy in a Time of Change* (Washington, DC, US Congress Joint Economic Committee, 1979), vol. 1, 312–40.

3 Interventions in industry: case studies

1 Hough, *Prefects*, ch. 10, p. 224.

2 N. Zhalalov, *Sovershenstvovanie material'no-teknichestkoe snabzheniia* (Tashkent, Uzbekistan, 1979), pp. 80ff.

3 *Voprosy istorii KPSS*, 10 (1985), 6.

4 Zhalalov, *Sovershenstvovanie*, p. 91; A. S. Nurseitov, *Snabzhenie kapital'nogo stroitel'stva v planovom khoziaistve* (Alma Ata, Kazakhstan, 1981).

5 For example, as of 1965 in Uzbekistan there were twelve different supply organizations working under the republican Gosplan (Zhalalov, *Sovershenstvovanie*, p. 88). While Gossnab distributed 13,200 types of product in the late 1970s, ministry-controlled supply agencies handled another 25,000, and republican organs not under Gossnab handled 15,000 more (Nurseitov, *Snabzhenie*, p. 96).

6 L. E. Kumel'ski, *Povyshenie stimuliruiushchei roli zarabotnoi platy* (Moscow, Ekonomika, 1975), p. 43.

7 *Kommunist*, 8 (1986), 43. See also B. Kolodykh, 'Kak vliiaet ritmichnost proizvodstva na distiplinu truda?', *Sotsiologicheskie issledovaniia*, 2 (1984), 42–51, 46.

8 *Ekonomicheskaia gazeta*, 7 (1976), 15; W. J. Conyngham, *The Modernization of Soviet Industrial Management* (Cambridge, Cambridge University Press, 1982), p. 32.

9 *Ekonomicheskaia gazeta*, 35 (1982), 8; *Pravda*, 1 September 1983, p. 1; *Partiinaia zhizn*, 12 (1978), 29; 22 (1983) 47; 15 (1981), 39. In Kazakhstan, for example, one cement plant received 2,800 appeals in 1980, and 22 different ministries were driven to set up their own cement works. *Ekonomicheskaia gazeta*, 4 (1982), 9.

10 *Ekonomicheskaia gazeta*, 6 (1979), 9.

11 *Kommunist*, 12 (1981), 106–8; *Partiinaia zhizn*, 4 (1982), 23–24; *Ekonomicheskaia zhizn*, 15 (1983), 18; 10 (1982), 18.

12 *Ekonomicheskaia gazeta*, 14 (1979), 20; *Izvestiia*, 8 January 1983, p. 3.

13 *Ekonomicheskaia gazeta*, 13 (1986), 5.

14 An Omsk plastics plant was idle for most of its first year because of supply problems. *Pravda*, 1 November 1983, p. 3.
15 N. A. Safronov, *Novye formy upravleniia proizvodtsvom* (Moscow, NII Truda, 1977), p. 1.
16 Iu. V. Todorski, *Rukovodstvo mestnykh sovetov razvitiem sotsialisticheskoi promyshlennosti* (Moscow, Nauka, 1982), p. 92; Kapustin, *Organizatsiia*, p. 178.
17 Examples are legion, from the all-union Ministry of Power to the Bashkir forestry ministry. *Ekonomicheskaia gazeta*, 5 (1978), 14; *Kommunist*, 1 (1985), 68.
18 *Pravda*, 8 December 1982, p. 2; *Izvestiia*, 18 November 1983, p. 2.
19 G. Schroeder, 'The Soviet economy on a "treadmill" of reforms', in *Soviet Economy in a Time of Change* (Washington, DC, US Congress JEC, pp. 312–40, p. 336.
20 *Kommunist*, 1 (1980), 74; *Ekonomicheskaia gazeta*, 45 (1985), 19. A Sverdlovsk obkom secretary argued that factories should be given more resources for their machine tool shops, while conceding that 'Of course, it would be logical to arrange for central supplies, but it is unrealistic to rely fully on this source.' *Ekonomicheskaia gazeta*, 48 (1984), 11.
21 *Ekonomicheskaia gazeta*, 15 (1983), 16. For other examples from Latvia and Kazakhstan, see *Ekonomicheskaia gazeta*, 24 (1983), 22; 21 (1985), 7.
22 *Ekonomicheskaia gazeta*, 39 (1977), 7; 1 (1986), 15. Excessive stocking was actually encouraged by regional Gossnab agencies, whose performance was measured by the gross value of supplies that they carried each year. *Pravda*, 18 May 1981, p. 2.
23 *Ekonomicheskaia gazeta*, 4 (1985), 7; 40 (1983), 9.
24 Examples are legion, such as the Karaganda steel mill that was visited by thirty *tolkachi* a week. *Partiinaia zhizn*, 15 (1981), 39.
25 *Pravda*, 6 January 1983, p. 2.
26 *Ekonomicheskaia gazeta*, 28 (1981), 22.
27 *Ekonomicheskaia gazeta*, 7 (1982), 2.
28 V. I. Zorkaltsev, 'Anatomiia defitsita', *EKO*, 2 (1982), 84–94, 89.
29 *Ekonomicheskaia gazeta*, 7 (1980), 5; *Sovetskaia Rossiia*, 28 January 1984, p. 1.
30 For example, in 1981 a gorkom first secretary pointed to the absurdity of surplus machinery being scrapped when it could have usefully been transferred to a neighbouring plant. *Partiinaia zhizn*, 2 (1981), 43.
31 *Ekonomicheskaia gazeta*, 24 (1983), 5.
32 *Pravda*, 28 November 1980, p. 2.
33 *Kommunist*, 3 (1980), 34.
34 *Kommunist*, 13 (1984), 59.
35 *Partiinaia zhizn*, 7 (1981), 30. The average Ukrainian obkom received 2–3,000 telegrams a year. *Partiinaia zhizn*, 20 (1981), 24.
36 *Ekonomicheskaia gazeta*, 35 (1976), 5.
37 *Pravda*, 24 April 1980, p. 2.
38 *Partiinaia zhizn*, 24 (1983) 25.
39 *Ekonomicheskaia gazeta*, 32 (1976), 5; *Partiinaia zhizn*, 4 (1984), 21.
40 *Ekonomicheskaia gazeta*, 26 (1986, 4. For quotes on this theme from Andropov and Chernenko, see *Voprosy istorii KPSS*, 2 (1984), 44.

41 *Ekonomicheskaia gazeta*, 33 (1981), 5.
42 Iu. Belik, 'Partiinoe rukovodtsvo khoziaistvom', in *Ekonomicheskaia gazeta*, 6 (1980), 9–10.
43 This very point was made in a forthright article by a factory economist, who confessed to be confused by the competing priority claims emanating from party organs – A. Dobralevskii, 'Kak voznikaet defitsit', *Ekonomicheskaia gazeta*, 35 (1982), 8.
44 For examples from such powerful obkomy as Cheliabinsk, Tula and Gor'kii, see *Ekonomicheskaia gazeta*, 22 (1978), 9; 4 (1981), 5; and 12 (1984), 5.
45 *Ekonomicheskaia gazeta*, 11 (1977), 8.
46 *Partiinaia zhizn*, 10 (1978), 33.
47 *Kommunist*, 1 (1985), 58.
48 For example, in 1985 only 12 per cent of enterprises had a 100 per cent contract fulfilment record. *Kommunist*, 13 (1985), 46.
49 The relevant 1981 regulations even assumed 2–3 per cent under-fulfilment of contracts – *Kommunist*, 1 (1985), 59.
50 A point recognised by Gorbachev himself, *Partiinaia zhizn*, 18 (1985), 14.
51 *Ekonomicheskaia gazeta*, 17 (1983), 5. Five out of the twenty-three paragraphs in the decree addressed the duties of party organs – a high proportion, compared to other joint economics decrees.
52 On tea, *Pravda*, 20 February 1984, p. 7; on cement, *Kommunist*, 3 (1978), 71; on milk, F. I. Kushnirsky, 'Inflation Soviet-style', *Problems of Communism*, 33, 1 (1984), 48–53.
53 In 1977, 10 per cent of consumer goods were rejected, according to GOST, although the Odessa obkom first secretary thought it ran as high as 25 per cent. Schroeder, 'Soviet', p. 337; *Ekonomicheskaia gazeta*, 36 (1976), 5; 8 per cent of tractors, and 15 per cent of furniture, were returned by purchasers as unusable (after passing quality control!). *Ekonomicheskaia gazeta*, 30 (1985), 6; *Planovoe khoziaistvo*, 5 (1981), 93–98.
54 One account graphically described refrigerators being unloaded from railway wagons in Gor'kii by being pushed down onto a truck: one in ten did not survive the fall. *Pravda*, 24 November 1980, p. 3. On the shortage of packing products for milk, fish and other goods, see *Ekonomicheskaia gazeta*, 13 (1977), 15; *Izvestiia*, 24 August 1980, p. 2; and 30 March 1983, p. 2.
55 *Ekonomicheskaia gazeta*, 28 (1986), 14.
56 *Ekonomicheskaia gazeta*, 21 (1984), 9.
57 See M. Hill and R. McKay, 'Soviet product quality', in R. Amann and J. Cooper (eds.), *Technical Progress and Soviet Economic Development* (Oxford, Blackwell, 1986), ch. 5.
58 *Kommunist*, 5 (1985), 110–13.
59 *Ekonomicheskaia gazeta*, 3 (1976), 5; 18 (1976), 9.
60 *Kommunist*, 16 (1979), 25.
61 For an example of fines being levied, see *Ekonomicheskaia gazeta*, 42 (1980), 3.
62 Examples are legion: *Ekonomicheskaia gazeta*, 6 (1977), 15; 41 (1977), 15; 43 (1978), 15.
63 *Partiinaia zhizn*, 5 (1980), 52.

64 *Ekonomicheskaia gazeta,* 7 (1982), 9.
65 *Ekonomicheskaia gazeta,* 32 (1976), 15.
66 *Ekonomicheskaia gazeta,* 51 (1977), 15; on ministry sloth see *Partiinaia zhizn,* 18 (1980), 6; *Ekonomicheskaia gazeta,* 16 (1976), 5.
67 For articles on the scheme, see *Ekonomicheskaia gazeta,* 6 (1976), 8; 21 (1981), 5; and *Voprosy istorii KPSS,* 3 (1976), 16–28. The supplement was in *Ekonomicheskaia gazeta,* 7 (1976), 11–14.
68 *Ekonomicheskaia gazeta,* 31 (1976), 3.
69 *Ekonomicheskaia gazeta,* 29 (1976), 11–12; 12 (1978), 7; 17 (1978), 15; 37 (1978), 6.
70 *Ekonomicheskaia gazeta,* 6 (1980), 5; 28 (1981), 6; *Kommunist,* 7 (1983), 48; *Partiinaia zhizn,* 10 (1981), 33; *Voprosy istorii KPSS,* 3 (1984), 68.
71 *Kommunist,* 5 (1985), 110–13; *Ekonomicheskaia gazeta,* 38 (1977), 12; *Voprosy istorii KPSS,* 3 (1976), 20.
72 For example, the Lv'ov norms for vacuum cleaners allowed for a 10 per cent defect rate. *Kommunist,* 5 (1985), 110–13.
73 *Ekonomicheskaia gazeta,* 41 (1978), 7.
74 For a complaint to this effect by Novocherkassk gorkom first secretary. *Ekonomicheskaia gazeta,* 45 (1978), 8.
75 *Ekonomicheskaia gazeta,* 25 (1977), 5.
76 *Ekonomicheskaia gazeta,* 35 (1984), 1–2.
77 The number covered doubled 1974–84, to reach 2,300 – *Kommunist,* 11 (1984), 57.
78 *Ekonomicheskaia gazeta,* 32 (1985), 11–14. On this approach, see V. Cherniavskii, 'Orientatsiia na kachestvo', *Kommunist,* 11 (1984), 38–48.
79 *Ekonomicheskaia gazeta,* 22 (1986); *Kommunist,* 11 (1984), 57.
80 *Kommunist,* 11 (1983), 124.
81 *Ekonomicheskaia gazeta,* 22 (1986), 19; G. Schroeder, 'Gorbachev – "radically" implementing Brezhnev's reforms', in *Soviet Economy,* 2, 4 (1986), 289–301.
82 *Izvestiia,* 4 December 1986, p. 2. The 15 per cent estimate is from the CIA, cited in *Soviet Economy,* 3, 1 (1987), 35.
83 *Ekonomicheskaia gazeta,* 22 (1986), 19. Output subsequently rose to 500 per day.
84 *Partiinaia zhizn,* 17 (1980), 54. Similar stories were told about bridge builders and pipe layers – *Pravda,* 15 May 1981, p. 2; 16 June 1984, p. 3.
85 *Kommunist,* 11 (1981), 46.
86 *Kommunist,* 10 (1977), 47. An example of the issue's growing significance was the creation of a new State Committee on Materials Conservation in 1978.
87 *Ekonomicheskaia gazeta,* 30 (1976), 5; 22 (1978), 9; 42 (1980), 22; 12 (1981), 5; *Partiinaia zhizn,* 23 (1977), 45–52; *Kommunist,* 4 (1984), 114–17.
88 *KPSS v rezoliutsiiakh,* vol. 11, pp. 326–31; vol. 13, pp. 593–97; *Kommunist,* 11 (1981), 30.
89 *Kommunist,* 10 (1981), 8.
90 *Ekonomicheskaia gazeta,* 28 (1981), 3; 50 (1981), 3; 24 (1984), 3; 51 (1984), 3; 2 (1985), 4; 28 (1985), 2.
91 *Partiinaia zhizn,* 20 (1982), 25.
92 *Ekonomicheskaia gazeta,* 15 (1980), 6; 27 (1980), 5; 2 (1982), 5; 28 (1983), 9.

93 *Ekonomicheskaia gazeta,* 1 (1984), 4–10.
94 *Partiinaia zhizn,* 11 (1984), 13.
95 *Partiinaia zhizn,* 3 (1985), 25.
96 Examples from Kiev and Tambov, see *Ekonomicheskaia zhizn,* 28 (1985), 11; and 11 (1985), 20.
97 *Ekonomicheskaia gazeta,* 3 (1984), 19; 35 (1978), 6.
98 *Ekonomicheskaia gazeta,* 45 (1984), 7. Such complaints were duplicated by party officials from Magnitogorsk to Grodno – *Partiinaia zhizn,* 10 (1979), 48–51; *Ekonomicheskaia gazeta,* 19 (1981), 7.
99 *Ekonomicheskaia gazeta,* 27 (1985), 12; 3 (1984), 19. This point was acknowledged in a CC CPSU decree of December 1984 – *Ekonomicheskaia gazeta,* 51 (1984), 3.
100 *Ekonomicheskaia gazeta,* 23 (1986), 19.
101 For example, a new rolling mill in Zaporozhstal, or new power generators designed by Elektrosila – *Ekonomicheskaia gazeta,* 41 (1982), 13. On new plastics technology, see *Ekonomicheskaia gazeta,* 48 (1977), 8.
102 *Ekonomicheskaia gazeta,* 23 (1984), 10.
103 *Kommunist,* 11 (1986), 15. A similar result came in a metals conservation drive in a Gor'kii diesel plant. *Ekonomicheskaia gazeta,* 36 (1982), 10.
104 E. Hewett, *Energy, Economics and Foreign Policy in the Soviet Union* (Washington, Brookings Institution, 1984), p. 105.
105 See the CC CPSU decree praising the work of Kemerovo obkom in *KPSS v rezoliutsiiakh,* vol. 13, pp. 46–50; also *Voprosy istorii KPSS,* 2 (1984), 3–17.
106 See the CC CPSU decree in *Ekonomicheskaia gazeta,* 26 (1979), 5.
107 *KPSS v rezoliutsiiakh,* vol. 14, pp. 382–4 and 414–28.
108 *Ekonomicheskaia gazeta,* 16 (1983), 3.
109 *Ekonomicheskaia gazeta,* 40 (1984), 22; 44 (1984), 12.
110 *Partiinaia zhizn,* 4 (1985), 9.
111 Running from *Ekonomicheskaia gazeta,* 12 (1985), 3, through to 45 (1985), 4.
112 *Ekonomicheskaia gazeta,* 38 (1985), 3; 26 (1985), 3; followed up in *Partiinaia zhizn,* 14 (1985), 22.
113 *Ekonomicheskaia gazeta,* 20 (1978), 8; 14 (1985), 4.
114 *Partiinaia zhizn,* 6 (1982), 51.
115 *Pravda,* 21 January 1983, p. 2.
116 *Pravda,* 10 October 1982, p. 2.
117 Calculated from data kindly provided by Thane Gustafson.
118 *Kommunist,* 13 (1981), 111–14.
119 *Ekonomicheskaia gazeta,* 7 (1983), 4; 50 (1983), 10; 19 (1984), 11.
120 *Ekonomicheskaia gazeta,* 16 (1978), 15.
121 *Ekonomicheskaia gazeta,* 38 (1982), 5; 10 (1983), 5; 20 (1976), 15; *Partiinaia zhizn,* 21 (1980), 46; *Kommunist,* 16 (1986), 124.
122 *Pravda,* 31 August 1981, p. 3.
123 *Ekonomicheskaia gazeta,* 25 (1983), 8.
124 *Ekonomicheskaia gazeta,* 35 (1985), 4.
125 Hewett, *Energy,* pp. 114–16.
126 *Narodnoe khoziastvo v SSSR v 1985* (Moscow, Finansy i statistika, 1986), p. 71.

4 The party as regional coordinator

1 Hough, *Prefects*, p. 213.
2 By 'governor' we have in mind those found in Tsarist Russia or imperial Spain, and *not* US governors, who are highly autonomous, independently elected figures who act as representatives of their states before the federal authorities.
3 T. M. Shtamba, *KPSS i organy okhrany pravo-poriadka* (Moscow, Mysl, 1979); A. N. Vitruchenko, *Rukovodstvo KPSS ukrepleniem sotsialisticheskoi zakonnosti* (Kiev, Vyshcha shkola, 1983). On the *druzhina*, see *Izvestiia*, 2 March 1984, p. 3; on police recruitment, see *Pravda*, 29 May 1985, p. 5.
4 V. Treml, 'Gorbachev's anti-drinking campaign', *Radio Liberty Supplement*, 2 (1987).
5 *Partiinaia zhizn*, 2 (1982), 28.
6 *Ekonomicheskaia gazeta*, 30 (1984), 17; *Kommunist*, 13 (1981), 26.
7 *Ekonomicheskaia gazeta*, 23 (1986), 10–11; R. Mould, *Chernobyl: the Real Story* (New York, Pergammon, 1988).
8 *Izvestiia*, 5 January 1984, p. 1. The landslide was caused by an illegally built group of shacks on a hillside near the city centre.
9 Fortescue, 'The regional party apparatus', 11–24; J. A. Dellenbrant, *The Soviet Regional Dilemma* (New York, M. E. Sharpe, 1986); D. B. Shaw, 'Regional planning in the USSR', *Soviet Geography*, 27, 7 (1986), 469–84.
10 For the rejection of bourgeois planning, see A. Lavrishchev, 'O predmete ekonomicheskoi geografii SSSR', *Kommunist*, 15 (1979), 91–9. For critical views, see A. N. Alisov, 'Predpriiatie i oblastnoi narodnokhoziaistvennyi kompleks', in *Trudovoi kollektiv v sisteme upravleniia proizvodstvom* (Moscow, AON, 1980), ch. 5; and L. Zlomanov, 'Sovety i territorial'nye rezervy uskoreniia', *Kommunist*, 8 (1986), 18–27.
11 *Kommunist*, 7 (1984), 61. The complaint is echoed in *Pravda*, 28 November 1982, p. 2.
12 *Argumenty i fakty*, 30 (1989), 1.
13 Dellebrant, *Soviet Regional*, p. 45.
14 In his speech 'Uskorenie i obnovlenie', *Kommunist*, 15 (1986), 8–23, 10.
15 M. Fainsod, *How Russia is Ruled* (Cambridge, Mass., Harvard University Press, 1963), pp. 222–42.
16 Khrushchev even devised a plan to pay party leaders bonuses tied to their region's plan performance. W. J. Conyngham, *Industrial Management in the Soviet Union* (Stanford, Hoover Institution, 1973), p. 79.
17 Fainsod, *Russia*, p. 203; B. A. Chotiner, *Khrushchev's Party Reform: Coalition Building and Institutional Innovation* (London, Greenwood Press, 1984).
18 J. R. Azrael, *Managerial Power and Soviet Politics* (Cambridge, Mass., Harvard University Press, 1966), p. 146.
19 For example, an Altai kraikom secretary commented that 'in the absence of sufficiently authoritative coordination organs, these functions are performed by the kraikom and raikomy.' *Ekonomicheskaia gazeta*, 28 (1979), 9.
20 In 1978, for example, Brezhnev commented that (e.g. in the new Astrakhan gas field 'Departmentalism definitely fears the party.' *Kommunist*, 8 (1981), 104.

21 *Pravda*, 28 January 1987, p. 5.
22 *Ekonomicheskaia gazeta*, 36 (1985), 5; 24 (1983), 11.
23 *Ekonomicheskaia gazeta*, 4 (1982), 5.
24 For a history, see *Voprosy istorii KPSS*, 3 (1979), 43–54.
25 As of 1981, there were thirteen: Kursk, Bratsk, Ekibastuz, West Siberia, South Iakutiia, BAM, Mangyshlak, Timano-Pechorsk, Dzhambul, Saiansk, Kansk-Achinsk, South Tadzhikistan and Orenburg. *Ekonomicheskaia gazeta*, 30 (1981), 6. On their role in Siberia, see *Territorial'no-proizvodstvennye kompleksy* (Novosibirsk, Nauka, 1984); and D. E. Pinsky, *Industrial Development of Siberia and the Far East* (Santa Monica, Rand, 1984), pp. 37–41.
26 *Ekonomicheskaia gazeta*, 21 (1984), 5. This complaint comes from Kansk-Achinsk – which was one of the few TPKs to have its own inter-branch management agency, *Pravda*, 27 April, 1983, p. 2.
27 N. Zenchenko, 'Istoricheskii opyt i zadachi narodnokhoziastvennogo planirovaniia', *Kommunist*, 16 (1977), 55–66, 64.
28 *Ekonomicheskaia gazeta*, 21 (1983), 10.
29 *Ekonomicheskaia gazeta*, 3 (1982), 15.
30 T. Gustafson, 'Soviet energy policy: from big coal to big gas', in S. Bialer and T. Gustafson (eds.), *Russia at the Crossroads: the 26th Congress of the CPSU* (London, Allen and Unwin, 1982), ch. 6, p. 124. The Tiumen case is discussed in some detail in chapter 6.
31 *Ekonomicheskaia gazeta*, 4 (1981), 41.
32 Iu. Iakovets, *Povyshenie urovnia planovoi raboty* (Moscow, Ekonomika, 1982), p. 7; *Pravda*, 1 June 1979, p. 2–3. Forty-one of them were for projects in Siberia – *Ekonomicheskaia gazeta*, 39 (1984), 16.
33 *Ekonomicheskaia gazeta*, 43 (1985), 10; 28 (1984), 10.
34 *Kommunist*, 2 (1979), 57.
35 *EKO*, 2 (1982), 62–71. Such clubs received official approval in *Pravda*, 15 April 1982, p. 1.
36 *EKO*, 2 (1982), 67; *Praktika sotsialisticheskogo khoziaistvovaniia: opyt Leningradskikh predpriiatii* (Leningrad, Lenizdat, 1981), p. 60.
37 'We invited the obkomy and *oblispolkomy* to send permanent representatives ... all four obkomy responded.' *EKO*, 2 (1982), 65. However, in Melitpol it was reported that a directors' club was formed at the initiative of the party gorkom – *EKO* 10 (1981), 3–14.
38 On this, see L. Holmes, *The Policy Process in Communist States* (London, Sage, 1981).
39 *Narodnoe khoziaistvo SSSR 1922–82* (Moscow, Finansy i statistika, 1982), p. 149.
40 Todorski, *Rukovodstvo*, p. 88.
41 *Partiinaia zhizn*, 15 (1981), 33.
42 *Kommunist*, 3 (1981), 31; 13 (1977), 54.
43 *Kommunist*, 13 (1977), 54; *Ekonomicheskaia gazeta*, 18 (1982), 8.
44 See for example the article by the director of the Kemerovo coal trust in *Pravda*, 11 June 1983, p. 2.
45 *Ekonomicheskaia gazeta*, 34 (1982), 5.
46 *Ekonomicheskaia gazeta*, 15 (1976), 2.

47 *Ekonomicheskaia gazeta,* 40 (1976), 9.

48 *Kommunist,* 13 (1982), 67.

49 *Kommunist,* 1 (1978), 117; Todorskii, *Rukovodstvo,* p. 90.

50 *Pravda,* 17 April 1982, p. 2.

51 *Kommunist,* 16 (1985), 89.

52 T. Dunmore, 'Local party organizations in industrial decision making: the case of the *ob'edinenie* reform', *Soviet Studies,* 23, 2 (1980), 195–217; P. A. Rodinov (ed.) *Partiinaia rabota v usloviiakh proizvodstvennykh ob'edinenii* (Moscow, Politizdat, 1984); V. P. Sergeiko, *Partiinyi kontrol deiatel'nostiu administratsii* (Krasnodar, Krasnodarskoe knizhnoe izdatel'stvo, 1979), p. 93.

53 *Kommunist,* 1 (1978), 116.

54 *Partiinaia zhizn,* 6 (1981), 52–6; 17 (1976), 3–6; 9 (1977), 22–37; 12 (1978), 37–42.

55 *Kommunist,* 1 (1978), 117.

56 *Voprosy istorii KPSS,* 2 (1979), 68.

57 On the role of soviets, see Ross, *Local Government; Sovety . . . Spravochnik;* and *Sovety narodnykh deputatov: status, kompetentsiia, organizatsiia, deiatel'nost* (Moscow, Iuridicheskaia literatura, 1980)

58 See Ross, *Local Government,* e.g. p. 79 on differences in budget structures.

59 M. Vitiutskii, 'S dobrotoi i chutkost'iu k liudiam', *Kommunist,* 3 (1984), 32–9.

60 *Kommunist,* 3 (1984), 36.

61 *Sovety . . . Spravochnik,* p. 276.

62 *Sovety . . . Spravochnik,* p. 37; *Kommunist,* 8 (1981), 104–13; *Ekonomicheskaia gazeta,* 16 (1984), 5; N. N. Demochkin, *Partiinoe rukovodstvo sovetam narodnykh deputatov* (Moscow, Znanie, 1980), p. 49.

63 *Izvestiia,* 29 March 1981, p. 1; progress reviewed in *Ekonomicheskaia gazeta* 41 (1982), 10.

64 *Ekonomicheskaia gazeta,* 30 (1984), 3.

65 *Ekonomicheskaia gazeta,* 27 (1986), 8.

66 *Kommunist,* 4 (1984), 55.

67 *Kommunist,* 1 (1984), 19.

68 The phrase is used, for example, in *Kommunist,* 2 (1979), 53; and 4 (1984), 53.

69 *Kommunist,* 7 (1986), 29.

70 *Ekonomicheskaia gazeta,* 1 (1981), 16; 21 (1983), 5.

71 The quote is from the first secretary of Astrakhan obkom, in *Ekonomicheskaia gazeta,* 33 (1985), 13. In 1986, for example, the Latvian Light Industry Ministry banned the export of shoes from the republic – *Kommunist,* 16 (1986), 45.

72 *Ekonomicheskaia gazeta,* 20 (1984), 6; *Partiinaia zhizn,* 5 (1980), 37–42.

73 *Ekonomicheskaia gazeta,* 30 (1976), 7.

74 Ross, *Local Government,* p. 125. Several dozen data sets are required, beyond raw plan targets – *Ekonomicheskaia gazeta,* 41 (1982), 10.

75 *Ekonomicheskaia gazeta,* 35 (1976), 4.

76 *Ekonomicheskaia gazeta,* 36 (1978), 17.

77 *Ekonomicheskaia gazeta,* 8 (1976), 9.

78 *Kommunist,* 9 (1978), 16.

79 Examples include a dispute over a Leningrad pram factory, and abandoned plans for a new port in Kolyma and a power line in Kurgan – *Ekonomicheskaia gazeta*, 6 (1983), 17; 2 (1976), 8; *Pravda*, 23 January 1981, p. 2.

80 *Kommunist*, 12 (1977), 8.

81 *Pravda*, 1 August 1981, p. 2.

82 *Ekonomicheskaia gazeta*, 14 (1978), 3; 32 (1980), 10; *Kommunist*, 4 (1984), 3.

83 *Ekonomicheskaia gazeta*, 44 (1978), 5.

84 This particularly applied to the session which approved the next year's plan. In the 1983 sessions pleas covered such issues as the inadequacy of off-shore oil exploration in Sakhalin; the need to move Khar'kov airport; and the desirability of more local control over hard currency earnings (Georgia) – *Izvestiia*, 30 December 1983, p. 6; 31 December 1983, pp. 2–3.

85 Ross, *Local Government*, ch. 5.

86 Ibid., pp. 155, 169.

87 Witness the director of Novolipetsk steel mill, complaining that he must give 450 out of the 1,000 apartments they build each year to the local soviet. *Kommunist*, 11 (1986), 28.

88 Examples from Uzbekistan and Primor'e: *Ekonomicheskaia gazeta*, 49 (1985), 7; *Izvestiia*, 26 March 1983, p. 2.

89 Ross, *Local Government*, p. 163.

90 Ibid., p. 63.

91 Iu Bocharov, 'Gorod – tselostnyi sotsial'no-ekonomicheskii kompleks', *Kommunist*, 2 (1979), 53.

92 V. I. Oleinikov claimed that the party had mastered the 'new science' of conquering these harsh new regions – 'O partiinom rukovodstve promyshlennym osvoeniem novykh raionov', *Voprosy istorii KPSS*, 11 (1981), 19–32. See also the remarks of the Krasnoiarsk kraikom first secretary, L. G. Sizov, explaining why podmena was sometimes necessary, in his article 'Ob izuchenii opyta partiinogo rukovostsva kompleksnym razvitiem proizvodstvennykh sil krupnogo regiona', *Voprosy istorii KPSS*, 7 (1983), 110.

93 Han Ku Chung, *Interest Representation in Soviet Policy Making: A Case Study of a West Siberian Energy Coalition* (Boulder, Col., Westview, 1987).

94 *Voprosy istorii KPSS*, 7 (1981), 18–29; *Pravda*, 20 August 1980, p. 2.

95 *Ekonomicheskaia gazeta*, 14 (1981), 14; *Pravda*, 17 August 1981, p. 2. The gorkom and obkom were also attacked for 'unacceptable inertness', in *Sovetskaia Rossiia*, 9 August 1985, p. 2; and 31 January 1986, p. 3.

96 Dellebrandt, *Soviet Regional*, ch. 5.

97 *Kommunist*, 2 (1979), 54.

98 *Kommunist*, 7 (1986), 20.

99 The complaint comes from a Poti gorkom secretary, interviewed in *Ekonomicheskaia gazeta*, 6 (1982), 16. On the Poti experiment, see *Ekonomicheskaia gazeta*, 21 (1982), 7.

100 *Ekonomicheskaia gazeta*, 5 (1983), 5. After 1979 ministries were obliged to write labour limits into their annual plans – *Ekonomicheskaia gazeta*, 43 (1980), 7.

101 *Ekonomicheskaia gazeta*, 38 (1982), 5.

102 *Ekonomicheskaia gazeta*, 3 (1983), 6. Other examples from Latvia and Brest can be found in *Partiinaia zh.zn*, 10 (1981), 34; and *Kommunist*, 5 (1985), 33.

103 E.g. the Uzbek CC got enterprises to set up 290 subsidiaries in the labour rich countryside. *Ekonomicheskaia gazeta*, 46 (1981), 5.

104 On this topic, see T. Gustafson, *Reform in Soviet Politics: Lessons of Recent Policies on Land and Water* (Cambridge, Cambridge University Press, 1981), chs. 4, 8; J. DeBardeleben, *Marxism–Leninism and the Environment* (Boulder, Col., Westview, 1985), chs. 5–8.

105 *Kommunist*, 5 (1978), 101–16; *Ekonomicheskaia gazeta*, 46 (1978), 19.

106 *Ekonomicheskaia gazeta*, 3 (1979), 3.

107 *Partiinaia zhizn*, 2 (1981), 55; *Kommunist*, 14 (1982), 34.

108 *Kommunist*, 14 (1982), 34.

109 *Ekonomicheskaia gazeta*, 5 (1984), 3.

110 *Ekonomicheskaia gazeta*, 27 (1977), 17; *Kommunist*, 4 (1984), 52.

111 *Izvestiia*, 22 February 1984, p. 3.

112 *Pravda*, 5 January 1984, p. 3; *Izvestiia*, 27 October 1983, p. 6.

113 *Kommunist*, 18 (1982), 55.

114 *Kommunist*, 14 (1982), 32.

115 Zlomanov, 'Sovety', 18–27, 19.

116 P. Rutland, 'The dynamics of the Soviet economic mechanism: insights from reform debates 1977–87', in D. Bahry and J. C. Moses (eds.), *Political Implications of Economic Reform in Communist Systems* (New York, New York University Press, 1989), pp. 70–108.

117 In the words of one author, in taking over coordination functions from the soviets, 'The party tried to correct one distortion by adopting another.' A. Degtiarev, 'Pervoosnova partiinoi zhizni', *Kommunist*, 6 (1988), 7–17, p. 11.

5 Regional coordination: case studies

1 *Narodnoe khoziaistvo*, pp. 149, 400. For an analysis of the construction industry, see D. Dyker, *The Future of the Soviet Economy* (New York, M. E. Sharpe, 1985), pp. 111–24.

2 The author's understanding of this sector was greatly aided by a month spent in 1977 working in the 'Georgi Dimitrov' youth brigade in the Devnia port construction project in Bulgaria.

3 *Ekonomicheskaia gazeta*, 45 (1978), 4.

4 *Narodnoe khoziaistvo*, p. 37; *Pravda*, 26 July 1979, p. 2.

5 *Kommunist*, 4 (1984), 43.

6 *Ekonomicheskaia gazeta*, 4 (1985), 15.

7 *Ekonomicheskaia gazeta*, 49 (1983), 5.

8 *Pravda*, 12 December 1981, p. 2.

9 For example, a new Tula metals plant was built by twenty different construction trusts – *Partiinaia zhizn*, 19 (1979), 49.

10 *Ekonomicheskaia gazeta*, 23 (1984), 6.

11 L. Volodarskii, 'Nazrevshie zadachi gosudarstvennoi statistiki', *Kommunist*, 17 (1977), 90–100; also *Kommunist*, 11 (1980), 125.

12 For example, at the November 1976 and November 1978 CC CPSU plena – *Kommunist*, 18 (1976), 12; 17 (1978), 11. The journal *Partiinaia zhizn* called for 'concrete involvement' of party committees in construction problems, and said that 'Local party organs and ministry partkomy cannot stand aside from resolution of these important questions.' *Partiinaia zhizn*, 8 (1985), 12; 17 (1983), 24.

13 *Ekonomicheskaia gazeta*, 1 (1979), 11; *Partiinaia zhizn*, 17 (1983), 25.

14 *Ekonomicheskaia gazeta*, 24 (1984), 5; 34 (1978), 4; *Pravda*, 31 May 1981, p. 2. The Volgograd obkom was able to push through a new cattle farm despite a cost overrun of 1300 per cent and the efforts of Gosbank to close it down.

15 *Kommunist*, 12 (1981), 49. On reconstruction, see the articles by J. Dmitriev, head of the CC CPSU Construction Department, in *Ekonomicheskaia gazeta*, 45 (1976), 5 and *Partiinaia zhizn*, 10 (1983), 29–37.

16 *Ekonomicheskaia gazeta*, 10 (1985), 5.

17 Editorials in *Partiinaia zhizn* criticized eight obkomy for poor supervision of construction policy, in 1980 and 1984 – 17 (1980), 5–8; 7 (1984), 9–12. Brezhnev criticized four construction ministers by name at the November 1981 CC plenum *Kommunist*, 17 (1981), 8. For examples of CC CPSU decrees, see *Partiinaia zhizn* 12 (1980), 6–8; 14 (1980), 24.

18 A. Pel'she, 'O trebovatel'nosti i ditsipline', *Kommunist*, 2 (1980), 18–32, 22, 27.

19 Examples range from a new building for the Volgograd tractor plant, and a polyclinic in Chita, to a chicken farm in Primorsk: *Ekonomicheskaia gazeta*, 28 (1986), 5; 11 (1979), 9; 31 (1981), 5.

20 *Kommunist*, 12 (1981), 44.

21 *Partiinaia zhizn*, 5 (1986), 15.

22 *Partiinaia zhizn*, 9 (1977), 21. Other examples of obkom secretaries leading teams come from Leningrad, Orenburg and elsewhere – *Kommunist*, 3 (1982), *Partiinaia zhizn*, 16 (1978), 24.

23 The words are from an article by the first secretary of Odessa obkom – *Ekonomicheskaia gazeta*, 14 (1981), 5.

24 *Kommunist* 2 (1981), 84.

25 E.g. the construction of a Ternopol sugar plant that dragged on for four years, despite direct supervision by a deputy minister of the Ukraine. *Ekonomicheskaia gazeta*, 27 (1984), 7.

26 Example of Lipetsk obkom complaining about this – *Partiinaia zhizn*, 1 (1980), 42.

27 *Partiinaia zhizn*, 20 (1982), 32.

28 *Kommunist*, 16, *Partiinaia zhizn*, 61.

29 *Ekonomicheskaia gazeta*, 6 (1979), 9; 10 (1981), 18.

30 *Ekonomicheskaia gazeta*, 29 (1978), 8 (1977), 5.

31 *Ekonomicheskaia gazeta*, 17 (1982), 9; *Partiinaia zhizn*, 24 (1976), 37. The Orel model was copied by obkomy from L'vov to Iakutiia – *Kommunist*, 7 (1983), 59; *Partiinaia zhizn*, 10 (1985) 41.

32 R. K. Beliaev, 'Iz opyta raboty Naberezhno-Chelinskogo gorkoma KPSS', *Voprosy istortii KPSS*, 11 (1980), 31–42. The construction site employed no less than 35,000 workers.

33 Examples of Sumy, Nizhnekamsk and Donetsk – *Ekonomicheskaia gazeta*, 2 (1986), 13; *Partiinaia zhizn* 1 (1981), 38; 14 (1980), 33.
34 *Ekonomicheskaia gazeta*, 20 (1982), 15.
35 In 1977, 740,000, in 1982, 800,000 – *Ekonomicheskaia gazeta*, 2 (1978), 16; 20 (1982), 15.
36 *Ekonomicheskaia gazeta*, 21 (1982), 2.
37 *Ekonomicheskaia gazeta*, 15 (1983), 6; *Komsomol'skaia pravda*, 29 May 1982, p.3.
38 *Ekonomicheskaia gazeta*, 20 (1982), 15.
39 *Ekonomicheskaia gazeta*, 7 (1985), 5.
40 *Kommunist*, 12 (1983), 53.
41 *Ekonomicheskaia gazeta*, 21 (1980), 5; *Partiinaia zhizn*, 5 (1979), 61; and an article by the head of the Commission: I. Novikov, 'Okruzhaiushchei srede – sotsialisticheskie otnoshenie', *Kommunist*, 14 (1982), 43–53.
42 *Sovetskaia Rossiia*, 21 January 1984, p. 2.
43 *Kommunist*, 11 (1984), 54.
44 *Sovety narodnykh deputatov: Spravochnik* (Moscow, Politizdat, 1984), p. 278.
45 Schroeder, 'Soviet economy', p. 336; *Pravda*, 10 December 1982, p. 2.
46 *Kommunist*, 4 (1982), 106.
47 *Ekonomicheskaia gazeta*, 6 (1977), 10; 32 (1982), 7.
48 *Ekonomicheskaia gazeta*, 2 (1985), 7.
49 J. Cooper, 'The civilian production of the defence industry', in Amann and Cooper, *Technical Progress*, ch. 2, pp. 34, 41.
50 *Ekonomicheskaia gazeta*, 14 (1983), 16; Ia. Orlov, 'promyshlennost i torgovliia', *Kommunist*, 11 (1984), 49–59, 50.
51 The phrase was used by an author in *Kommunist*, 5 (1985), 37.
52 *Partiinaia zhizn*, 13 (1984), 52.
53 *Ekonomicheskaia gazeta*, 20 (1979), 17.
54 *Pravda*, 27 February 1984, p. 7.
55 *Partiinaia zhizn*, 13 (1984), 54; *Kommunist*, 1 (1984), 19.
56 *Ekonomicheskaia gazeta*, 16 (1983), 17. Forty of the oblasti also lacked food inspection laboratories – *Sovetskaia Rossiia*, 16 November 1980, p. 3.
57 *Sovety*, p. 237.
58 *Ekonomicheskaia gazeta*, 29 (1985), 2. For examples from Brezhnev and Andropov, see *Ekonomicheskaia gazeta*, 49 (1979), 15; and 48 (1982), 3.
59 *Ekonomicheskaia gazeta*, 47 (1979), 3; 15 (1983), 6; 20 (1983), 3; 26 (1981), 4; 7 (1977), 3; 41 (1985), 3–7.
60 *Ekonomicheskaia gazeta*, 41 (1985), 3–7. Five out of twenty-five paragraphs in the May 1983 decree addressed the role of party organs (unusually high for this type of joint decree) – *Ekonomicheskaia gazeta*, 20 (1983), 3.
61 *Ekonomicheskaia gazeta*, 48 (1983), 3.
62 *Ekonomicheskaia gazeta*, 31 (1985), 4.
63 *Ekonomicheskaia gazeta*, 42 (1981), 5; 32 (1983), 5; 43 (1985), 19.
64 *Ekonomicheskaia gazeta*, 48 (1977), 4. In Soviet parlance this is known as *shefstvo*, or 'patronage'.
65 *Ekonomicheskaia gazeta*, 39 (1983), 6.
66 For examples from Latvia, Cheliabinsk and Tambov, see *Voprosy istorii KPSS*, 5 (1985), 24; *Ekonomicheskaia gazeta*, 4 (1979), 4; and 11 (1985), 20.

67 *Ekonomicheskaia gazeta*, 32 (1983), 5; 30 (1984), 18; 26 (1985), 22.
68 *Kommunist*, 2 (1983), 110–15.
69 For example of local parties responding to food shortages, see *Partiinaia zhizn*, 18 (1977), 22; *Voprosy istorii KPSS*, 8 (1983), 52; *Ekonomicheskaia gazeta*, 4 (1976), 8.
70 *Zaria Vostoka*, 25 January 1981, p. 1.
71 *Kommunist*, 8 (1977), 94–103. Such experiments go back to 1964.
72 *Partiinaia zhizn*, 7 (1983), 48–52.
73 *Ekonomicheskaia gazeta*, 29 (1979), 7.
74 *Ekonomicheskaia gazeta*, 32 (1982), 7; 33 (1984), 16; 32 (1981), 5; *Kommunist*, 13 (1979), 43.
75 *Ekonomicheskaia gazeta*, 32 (1980), 10; 29 (1982), 3.
76 *Partiinaia zhizn*, 22 (1983), 14–18.
77 *Ekonomicheskaia gazeta*, 28 (1983), 18.
78 *Ekonomicheskaia gazeta*, 39 (1984), 5.
79 This according to B. El'tsin, writing in *Ekonomicheskaia gazeta*, 32 (1981), 5.
80 *Partiinaia zhizn*, 14 (1983), 51.
81 *Partiinaia zhizn*, 6 (1979, 44; *Narodnoe khoziaistvo*, pp. 400, 483. This amounted to less than 5 per cent of the 9.7 million workforce in the sector.
82 *Ekonomicheskaia gazeta*, 4 (1985), 19.
83 *Ekonomicheskaia gazeta*, 33 (1984), 16.
84 *Pravda*, 11 February 1982, p. 3.
85 *Pravda*, 22 January 1982, p. 3.
86 *Ekonomicheskaia gazeta*, 18 (1985), 18.

6 The party as fireman: party interventions in the transport and energy sectors

1 G. Schroeder, 'The slowdown in Soviet industry', *Soviet Economy* 1, 1 (1985), 42–74.
2 *Izvestiia*, 19 October 1981, p. 3.
3 *Izvestiia*, 10 October 1981, p. 3.
4 *Ekonomicheskaia gazeta*, 16 (1982), 22.
5 *Planovoe khoziastvo*, 1 (1981), 106.
6 Personal communication, 1984.
7 J. Ambler, D. Shaw and L. Symons (eds.), *Soviet and East European Transport Problems* (London, Croom Helm, 1985), especially ch. 2, 'Soviet railways', p. 24.
8 *Ekonomicheskaia gazeta*, 3 (1982), 8; *Pravda*, 12 December 1980, p. 3.
9 *Ekonomicheskaia gazeta*, 48 (1976), 14; 3 (1982), 8.
10 *Izvestiia*, 23 July 1981, p. 3. This problem should have been ameliorated by the shift in 1982 'tonne-kilometers' to 'tonnes loaded'. In practice, nothing seems to have charged – Ambler, *Soviet ... Transport*, p. 73.
11 *Pravda*, 18 January 1981, p. 3.
12 For example, at Kaliningrad in 1981 – *Sovetskaia Rossiia*, 27 December 1981, p. 1.
13 *Ekonomicheskaia gazeta*, 14 (1979), 3. In January 1977 the CC CPSU had

passed a resolution urging party committees to step up their monitoring of the railways – *KPSS v rezoliutziiakh*, vo. 12, pp. 403–7.

14 *Kommunist*, 17 (1979), 9.

15 *Kommunist*, 5 (1980), 14–17; *KPSS v rezoliutsiiakh*, vol. 14, pp. 401–3; 487–92.

16 See *Ekonomicheskaia gazeta*, 48 (1982), 3, for the Andropov speech; and *Ekonomicheskaia gazeta*, 51 (1982), 4, for a new CC CPSU decree on the transport sector; and *Moskovskaia pravda* 17 November 1982, p. 1, for the Moscow party's response.

17 *Partiinaia zhizn*, 11 (1980), 5–11; 14 (1978), 64–9; 7 (1981), 49–52; 17 (1981), 40–3.

18 *Ekonomicheskaia gazeta*, 38 (1980), 5.

19 *Ekonomicheskaia gazeta*, 20 (1978), 33; 28 (1980), 4; 22 (1978), 3.

20 *Ekonomicheskaia gazeta*, 35 (1983), 15.

21 *Ekonomicheskaia gazeta*, 24 (1978), 6.

22 *Ekonomicheskaia gazeta*, 25 (1978), 3.

23 *Partiinaia zhizn*, 2 (1983), 5.

24 *Partiinaia zhizn*, 16 (1980), 46.

25 *Ekonomicheskaia gazeta*, 9 (1983), 3; 18 (1983), 7.

26 While in the seven years 1976–83 only 1 party official replied to criticism in *Ekonomicheskaia gazeta* over transport policy, in 1983–5 9 such replies were published, 4 of them from obkom first secretaries. The latter was highly unusual: only 12 out of 438 such replies in 1976–85 came from first secretaries.

27 A strongly critical resolution on the work of the ministry partkom was passed by the CC CPSU in March 1983 – *Pravda*, 14 October 1983, p. 2.

28 *Ekonomicheskaia gazeta*, 29 (1984), 22. The deputy minister of railways himself, V. Morozov, was reprimanded for fiddling the statistics on track repair – *Pravda*, 10 October 1983, p. 3.

29 *Kommunist*, 2 (1984), *Partiinaia zhizn*, 6 (1982), 30.

30 *Ekonomicheskaia gazeta*, 9 (1984), 9.

31 *Partiinaia zhizn*, 15 (1980), 36.

32 *Voprosy istorii KPSS*, 7 (1984), 41.

33 *Voprosy istorii KPSS*, 7 (1984), 41; *Kommunist*, 15 (1985), 34.

34 *Pravda*, 12 December 1981, p. 2.

35 For example, the obkomy of Kemerovo, Stavropol and Gor'kii – *Ekonomicheskaia gazeta*, 30 (1978), 13; 39 (1976), 2; 39 (1978), 2.

36 *Voprosy istorii KPSS*, 7 (1984), 41; *Partiinaia zhizn*, 13 (1981), 53.

37 *Ekonomicheskaia gazeta*, 25 (1977), 9.

38 *Ekonomicheskaia gazeta*, 48 (1980), 19; *Partiinaia zhizn*, 5 (1981), 70.

39 *Ekonomicheskaia gazeta*, 50 (1985), 5.

40 *Ekonomicheskaia gazeta*, 46 (1978), 2; 27 (1986), 7; *Kommunist*, 7 (1977), 53.

41 *Kommunist*, 7 (1977), 55; *Ekonomicheskaia gazeta*, 26 (1978), 2.

42 *Pravda*, 3 January 1980, p. 3.

43 *Ekonomicheskaia gazeta*, 22 (1983), 5.

44 *Ekonomicheskaia gazeta*, 14 (1984), 2.

45 *Ekonomicheskaia gazeta*, 15 (1984), 3; 29 (1984), 3.

46 *Partiinaia zhizn*, 20 (1984), 31–4.

47 *Kommunist*, 15 (1985), *Pravda*, 4 May 1987, p. 2; *Ekonomicheskaia gazeta*, 28 (1986), 8.

48 T. Gustafson, *The Soviet Gas Campaign* (Santa Monica, Ca., Rand, 1983); and his *Crisis Amid Plenty: The Politics of Soviet Energy under Brezhnev and Gorbachev* (Princeton, NJ, Princeton University Press, 1989); Chung, *Interest Representation*.
49 Gustafson, *Crisis*, pp. 30–5.
50 Gustafson, *Soviet Gas*, p. 11.
51 *Ekonomicheskaia gazeta*, 15 (1976), 24; Gustafson, *Soviet Gas*, p. 92.
52 *Ekonomicheskaia gazeta*, 4 (1980), 9.
53 *Ekonomicheskaia gazeta*, 47 (1981), 3. On this aspect of the campaign, see Gustafson, *Crisis*, ch. 6.
54 *Partiinaia zhizn*, 19 (1982), 51; Gustafson, *Crisis*, p. 206.
55 *Kommunist*, 11 (1983), 9; *Ekonomicheskaia gazeta*, 13 (1982), 9.
56 Gustafson, *Soviet Gas*, pp. 96–8; also D. Wilson, *Soviet Energy to 2000* (London, *Economist* Special Report no. 231, 1986), p. 136.
57 *Ekonomicheskaia gazeta*, 4 (1983), 4.
58 Chung, *Interest Representation*, p. 47.
59 *Ekonomicheskaia gazeta*, 35 (1982), 8.
60 *Pravda*, 5 January 1984, p. 2.
61 *Kommunist*, 11 (1983), 4.
62 *Ekonomicheskaia gazeta*, 37 (1985), 3.
63 *Ekonomicheskaia gazeta*, 31 (1983), 16.
64 First Deputy Minister Iu. Batalin became chairman of the State Committee on Labour and Social Problems in 1983; and Minister B. Shcherbina became a deputy chairman of the USSR Council of Ministers in 1984.
65 *Ekonomicheskaia gazeta*, 4 (1982), 15.
66 V. Petrov, 'Effekt initsiativy', *Kommunist*, 16 (1983), 35–46.
67 Petrov, 'Effekt', p. 39.
68 *Ekonomicheskaia gazeta*, 40 (1983), 4.
69 V. Alekseev, 'Partiinoe rubkovodstvo sozdaniem i razvitiem neftegazovogo kompleksa zapadnoi Sibiri', *Voprosy istorii KPSS*, 6 (1983), 55–67, 55.
70 *Ekonomicheskaia gazeta*, 40 (1983), 4.
71 *Ekonomicheskaia gazeta*, 41 (1983), 19; Gustafson, *Soviet Gas*, p. 78.
72 Wilson, *Soviet Energy*, p. 60
73 H. Hunter, P. Dunn, V. Kontorovich and J. Szyrmer, 'Soviet transport trends', *Soviet Economy*, 1, 3 (1985), 195–227, 213.
74 Alekseev, 'Partiinoe', p. 65.
75 For example, *Pravda* commented that 'The Tiumen obkom is not paying proper attention to the development of trade facilities. In the past four years, the obkom has not once discussed the situation regarding retailing and public catering in the oil and gas workers' cities', *Pravda*, 31 September 1979, p. 2.
76 Gustafson, *Soviet Gas*, pp. 54, 57.
77 *Ekonomicheskaia gazeta*, 8 (1978), 39.
78 *Ekonomicheskaia gazeta*, 9 (1986), 6.
79 *Ekonomicheskaia gazeta*, 46 (1983), 9.
80 Gustafson, *Soviet Gas*, pp. 63–8.
81 *Ekonomicheskaia gazeta*, 8 (1980), 5. Ligachev, of course, went on to be a

Politburo member and one of the founders of the Russian Communist Party. Gustafson does not see the 'outpost method' as an item of major controversy, arguing that it was a reasonable short-term solution to the manpower problem – *Crisis*, p. 178.

82 *Ekonomicheskaia gazeta*, 15 (1980), 15; 21 (1982), 16.
83 *Ekonomicheskaia gazeta*, 36 (1984), 9.
84 Alekseev, 'Partiinoe', p. 59.
85 *Ekonomicheskaia gazeta*, 34 (1981), 3; 16 (1980), 3; 40.
86 *Ekonomicheskaia gazeta*, 38 (1980), 9.
87 *Partiinaia zhizn*, 18 (1985), 13.
88 *Ekonomicheskaia gazeta*, 12 (1983), 18.
89 *Kommunist*, 12 (1986), 72.
90 T. Shabad, 'News notes', *Soviet Geography*, 27, 4 (1986), 248–79, 250; J. Thornton, 'Soviet electric power after Chernobyl', *Soviet Economy*, 2, 2 (1986), 131–79, 139.
91 *Ekonomicheskaia gazeta*, 12 (1977), 9; 4 (1978), 9.
92 See the speech by Politburo member A. Kirilenko at Atommash, in *Partiinaia zhizn*, 18 (1978), 17–24.
93 *Ekonomicheskaia gazeta*, 9 (1978), 11.
94 *Ekonomicheskaia gazeta*, 30 (1981), 4.
95 Contrast his article in *Ekonomicheskaia gazeta*, 37 (1980), 5, with other reports in the same newspaper, such as in no. 45 (1980), 10; or 4 (1982), 9.
96 *Ekonomicheskaia gazeta*, 7 (1982), 3.
97 *Ekonomicheskaia gazeta*, 46 (1982), 14.
98 *Pravda*, 26 July 1984, p. 2. On corruption in Rostov, see *Pravda*, 30 January 1986, p. 2.
99 For example, in Rovno, Murmansk and Khmel'nitskii – *Pravda*, 9 August 1983, p. 2; *Ekonomicheskaia gazeta*, 25 (1982), 5; *Partiinaia zhizn*, 4 (1980), 41.
100 Shabad, 'News Notes', p. 250.
101 Gustafson, 'Soviet energy', ch. 6.
102 Shabad, 'News Notes', p. 265.
103 D. Warner and L. Kaiser, 'Development of the USSR's Eastern coal basins', in *Gorbachev's Economic Plans* (Washington, DC, US Congress Joint Economic Committee, 1987), vol. 1, pp. 533–44.
104 *Ekonomicheskaia gazeta*, 20 (1976), 24.
105 *Ekonomicheskaia gazeta*, 17 (1978), 9; A. Korkin, 'Razvitie Pavlodar-Ekibatuzskogo kompleksa', *Partiinaia zhizn*, 3 (1979), 36–42.
106 *Ekonomicheskaia gazeta*, 32 (1978), 5.
107 *Ekonomicheskaia gazeta*, 47 (1980), 5.
108 Isaev came out with the familiar refrain of frustrated regional officials – 'Not all problems can be solved here.' *Ekonomicheskaia gazeta*, 44 (1980), 5.
109 *Partiinaia zhizn*, 2 (1980), 17.
110 *Izsvestiia*, 16 August 1983, p. 2.
111 For one of the few examples, see *Ekonomicheskaia gazeta*, 19 (1981), 12.
112 *Ekonomicheskaia gazeta*, 7 (1985), 4.
113 Shabad, 'News Notes', p. 268.
114 Wilson, *Soviet Energy*, p. 198.

115 V. I. Chalov, 'Nekotorie problemy partiinogo rukovodtsva sozdaniem TPK', *Voprosy istorii KPSS*, 3 (1979), 43–54, 48.
116 *Ekonomicheskaia gazeta*, 23 (1976), 5.
117 *Kommunist*, 6 (1978), 17.
118 *Ekonomicheskaia gazeta*, 34 (1982), 18; *Izvestiia*, 26 June 1983, p. 2.
119 *Ekonomicheskaia gazeta*, 24 (1986), 15.
120 *Ekonomicheskaia gazeta*, 12 (1983), 15.
121 *Ekonomicheskaia gazeta*, 42 (1983), 15; 4 (1986), 14.
122 *Ekonomicheskaia gazeta*, 21 (1984), 5.
123 *Kommunist*, 10 (1978), 34–43; 4 (1983), 40–50; *Voprosy istorii KPSS*, 1 (1983), 3–8; 3 (1985), 14–27.
124 L. G. Sizov, 'Ob izucheniia opyta partiinogo rukovodtsva', *Voprosy istorii KPSS*, 7 (1983), 102–13.
125 *Pravda*, 14 October 1983, p. 2.
126 *Ekonomicheskaia gazeta*, 19 (1979), 11; 39 (1979), 2.
127 *Ekonomicheskaia gazeta*, 18 (1979), 11.
128 *Partiinaia zhizn*, 4 (1980), 59, 61.
129 *Kommunist*, 11 (1981), 10.
130 *Ekonomicheskaia gazeta*, 42 (1978), 5.
131 Gustafson, *Crisis*, p. 59.

7 The role of the party in agriculture

1 Hough, *Prefects*, p. 201; and J. F. Hough, 'The party *apparatchiki*', in H. G. Skilling and F. Griffiths (eds.), *Interest Groups in Soviet Politics* (Princeton, Princeton University Press, 1971), ch. 3, p. 62.
2 Fainsod, *Russia*, chs. 7, 12–15; C. S. Kaplan, *The Party and Agricultural Crisis Management in the USSR* (Ithaca, Cornell University Press, 1987); and her article 'The CPSU and local policy implementation', *Journal of Politics*, 45 (1983), 2–27.
3 For example, in Kirov oblast 25 per cent of farms lacked paved roads, and 50 per cent of district centres lacked a paved road to the regional capital of Kirov – *Izvestiia*, 20 February 1984, p. 2.
4 Gustafson, *Reform in Soviet Politics*, ch. 2.
5 *Kommunist*, 1 (1984), 52.
6 A. Yanov, *The Drama of the Soviet 1960s: A Lost Reform* (Berkeley, Institute of International Studies, 1984). Stories of farm officials persecuted in the 1960s for introducing the link system continue to surface e.g. from Dagestan – *Pravda* 1 September 1988, p. 6.
7 The Food Programme was printed as a supplement to *Partiinaia zhizn*, 12 (1982).
8 *Narodnoe khoziaistvo SSSR 1922–82* (Moscow, Finansy i statistika, 1982), pp. 361, 397.
9 By 1988 meat was rationed in twenty-three of the seventy Russian oblasti, butter in thirty-two and sugar in fifty-three – *Pravda*, 1 September 1988, p. 3. By 1990 such rationing had spread to hitherto protected areas such as Moscow and Leningrad.

10 *Voprosy istorii KPSS*, 12 (1983), 62.

11 *Partiinaia zhizn*, 18 (1983), 12.

12 S. Hedlund, *Crisis in Soviet Agriculture* (Lund, Lund Economic Studies, 1973), pp. 155–66. For a literary account of a battle between a West Siberian kolkhoz chair and a raikom secretary in the late 1960s, see A. Strelianyi, 'Deputatskii zapros', *Novyi mir*, 2 (1986), 24–76.

13 *Partiinaia zhizn*, 19 (1978), 44. Kaplan shows that RSFSR kolkhoz directors with higher education rose from 22 per cent in 1965 to 57 per cent in 1977 ('CPSU', p. 17).

14 For example, 77 per cent over five years in Yaroslavl – *Pravda*, 11 June 1981, p. 2.

15 Chotiner, *Khrushchev's Party Reform*.

16 Cherniak, *Tovarishch*, p. 44.

17 Fainsod, *Russia*, p. 565.

18 K. A. Bondrenkov, *Bor'ba partiinykh organizatsii RSFSR za pod"em kolkhoznogo proizvodstva 1965–70* (Kursk, Pedagogicheskii Institut, 1975), pp. 73, 296.

19 *Ekonomicheskaia gazeta*, 4 (1982), 2.

20 Bondrenkov, *Bor'ba*, p. 57.

21 *Vestnik Moskovskogo Universiteta: Seriia Ekonomika*, 5 (1983), 61–75.

22 *Partiinaia zhizn*, 22 (1981), 40.

23 *Izvestiia*, 25 September 1981, p. 3.

24 *Kommunist*, 15 (1985), 117.

25 Farms could not even hire their own electricians, because pay and conditions were better in the trusts. *Ekonomicheskaia gazeta*, 6 (1976), 17.

26 *Partiinaia zhizn*, 22 (1981), 39.

27 R. F. Miller, 'The politics of policy implementation in the USSR: Soviet policies on agricultural integration', *Soviet Studies*, 32, 2 (1980), 171–94, pp. 173, 191.

28 *Ekonomicheskaia gazeta*, 48 (1980), 20.

29 *Ekonomicheskaia gazeta*, 43 (1980), 16.

30 *Ekonomicheskaia gazeta*, 23 (1976), 3–5.

31 *Ekonomicheskaia gazeta*, 28 (1978), 8; *Voprosy istorii KPSS*, 7 (1979), 46.

32 *Kommunist*, 17 (1982), 81.

33 Gorbachev, quoted in *Pravda*, 27 March 1984, p. 1.

34 See for example *Ekonomicheskaia gazeta*, 27 (1983), 3.

35 *Voprosy istorii KPSS*, 9 (1982), 125.

36 *Ekonomicheskaia gazeta*, 27 (1983), 3; 48 (1985), 17.

37 *Kommunist*, 5 (1982), 37; *Ekonomicheskaia gazeta*, 24 (1982), 6.

38 *Ekonomicheskaia gazeta*, 19 (1986), 14.

39 *Kommunist*, 13 (1985), 115–20.

40 *Partiinaia zhizn*, 7 (1981), 33; *Ekonomicheskaia gazeta*, 40 (1982), 6.

41 *Ekonomicheskaia gazeta*, 16 (1985), 4.

42 D. Van Atta, 'Further reshuffling of agricultural management', *Radio Liberty Research Bulletin*, 38 (1989), 9–11.

43 *Kommunist*, 17 (1981), 5; *Partiinaia zhizn*, 3 (1981), 15.

44 *Ekonomicheskaia gazeta*, 14 (1983), 3; 20 (1984), 2.

45 *Ekonomicheskaia gazeta*, 16 (1985), 2.

46 *Ekonomicheskaia gazeta*, 2 (1976), 18; 37 (1976), 3.

47 *Ekonomicheskaia gazeta*, 14 (1984), 4.

48 *Partiinaia zhizn*, 18 (1985), 8.

49 For example, no less than sixteen obkomy and three republic party committees were criticized in *Ekonomicheskaia gazeta*, 14 (1984), 4.

50 *Ekonomicheskaia gazeta*, 31 (1982), 7.

51 *Ekonomicheskaia gazeta*, 7 (1976), 9.

52 *Ekonomicheskaia gazeta*, 38 (1977), 19; 43 (1981), 3.

53 *Voprosy istorii KPSS*, 3 (1982), 27.

54 *Ekonomicheskaia gazeta*, 38 (1981), 5; 7 (1981), 18; 34 (1976), 7.

55 *Partiinaia zhizn*, 11 (1981), 5–10.

56 For example, *Ekonomicheskaia gazeta*, 3 (1979), 5; 35 (1980), 19.

57 *Kommunist*, 13 (1981), 30.

58 For examples, see *Ekonomicheskaia gazeta*, 6 (1979), 7; 37 (1985), 16; 3 (1979), 7; 33 (1979), 6.

59 *Voprosy istorii KPSS*, 7 (1981), 12.

60 *Ekonomicheskaia gazeta*, 21 (1981), 19.

61 *Kommunist*, 1 (1984), 59.

62 *Partiinaia zhizn*, 16 (1981), 40; 5 (1970), 53.

63 Kalinin obkom vetoed such a plan in 1981, for example – *Izvestiia*, 18 September 1982, p. 3.

64 For example, those reported in *Ekonomicheskaia gazeta*, 7 (1981), 19; 19 (1986), 14.

65 *Kommunist*, 4 (1982), 109.

66 *Ekonomicheskaia gazeta*, 37 (1983), 5; *Partiinaia zhizn*, 22 (1982), 19.

67 *Partiinaia zhizn*, 22 (1980), 51.

68 *Pravda*, 22 February 1983, p. 2.

69 *Izvestiia*, 27 September 1981, p. 2; 7 November 1981, p. 3.

70 *Izvestiia*, 26 May 1985, p. 2.

71 *Kommunist*, 7 (1986), 52.

72 K. Pankova, 'Obiazatel'noe slagaemoe uspekha', *Kommunist*, 14 (1981), 36–47, p. 36.

73 A. Salutskii, 'Slabye i sil'nye', *Nash sovremennik*, 9 (1987), 100–19.

74 *Izvestiia*, 20 January 1982, p. 2; *Ekonomicheskaia gazeta*, 3 (1981), 19.

75 *Partiinaia zhizn*, 18 (1985), 5.

76 *Kommunist*, 13 (1986), 71. V. Treml came up with an estimate of R60 billion – *Soviet Economy*, 3, 1 (1987), 46.

77 *Narodnoe khoziastvo 1985*, p. 559.

78 The title of an article by V. Golikov in *Partiinaia zhizn*, 17 (1977), 8–17.

79 V. P. Gagnon, 'Gorbachev and the collective contract brigade', *Soviet Studies*, 34, 1 (1987), 1–23.

80 *Ekonomicheskaia gazeta*, 13 (1983), 3; 31 (1983), 18; 11 (1985), 16. For sceptical views on the significance of these reforms, see K. R. Gray, 'Reform and resource allocation in Soviet agriculture', in *Gorbachev's Economic Plans* (Washington, DC, US Congress Joint Economic Committee, 1987), pp. 9–25; and K. M. Brooks, 'Soviet agriculture's halting reform', *Problems of Communism*, 40, 2 (1990), 29–41.

81 *Ekonomicheskaia gazeta*, 10 (1985), 6.
82 Yanov, *Drama*.
83 For a history of the legal status of private plots, see Vitrichenko, pp. 86–93.
84 *Narodnoe khoziastvo 1985*, p. 185.
85 *Ekonomicheskaia gazeta*, 41 (1980), 19; 50 (1980), 18; 25 (1981), 9.
86 *Voprosy istorii KPSS*, 6 (1983), 14.
87 *Ekonomicheskaia gazeta*, 25 (1986), 10.
88 *Kommunist*, 15 (1986), 92.
89 *Ekonomicheskaia gazeta*, 23 (1986), 4.
90 R. and Zh. Medvedev, *Khrushchev: the Years in Power* (Oxford, Oxford University Press, 1977), ch. 9.
91 D. Gale Johnson and K. McConnell Brooks, *Prospects for Soviet Agriculture in the 1980s* (Bloomington, Indiana University Press, 1983), pp. 13, 17, 60; D. Jones and J. Smogorzewska, 'Dairy farming in the USSR', *Soviet Studies*, 34, 2 (1982), 254–69; B. Severin, 'Solving the livestock feed dilemma', in *Gorbachev's Economic Plans* (Washington, DC, US Congress Joint Economic Committee, 1987), 533–44.
92 Severin, 'Solving the livestock feed dilemma'.
93 *Kommunist*, 1 (1985), 107.
94 *Kommunist*, 8 (1986), 32; *Partiinaia zhizn*, 22 (1977), 56.
95 See the CC CPSU/Council of Ministers joint resolution on the subject in *Ekonomicheskaia gazeta*, 28 (1978), 18. On the annual campaigns, see *Ekonomicheskaia gazeta*, 51 (1979), 2; 35 (1985), 2.
96 For example, with regard to Krasnodar and Karakalpakiia – *Kommunist*, 9 (1978), 43; *Ekonomicheskaia gazeta*, 14 (1983), 5.
97 *Partiinaia zhizn*, 4 (1985), 18.
98 *Ekonomicheskaia gazeta*, 27 (1981), 5; 38 (1983), 5.
99 *Partiinaia zhizn*, 24 (1985), 32.
100 *Pravda*, 19 July 1982, p. 3; *Izvestiia*, 12 January 1984, p. 3.
101 A problem serious enough to merit banning by a CC CPSU decree – *Ekonomicheskaia gazeta*, 15 (1985), 16.
102 *Ekonomicheskaia gazeta*, 37 (1981), 7. Typically, the report added that the man had been protected by his local patrons, and was subsequently appointed to head a local supermarket.
103 Johnson and Brooks, *Prospects*, p. 66. These prices were raised further in 1980, and in 1986 bonuses for above-plan deliveries were doubled – *Ekonomicheskaia gazeta*, 52 (1980), 5; *Pravda*, 29 March 1986, p. 1.
104 *Narodnoe khoziastvo 1982*, p. 275.
105 *Ekonomicheskaia gazeta*, 13 (1978), 19.
106 *Kommunist*, 10 (1981), 76; *Partiinaia zhizn*, 12 (1979), 28; 3 (1981), 16.
107 *Ekonomicheskaia gazeta*, 8 (1979), 5.
108 For example, in Irkutsk – *Ekonomicheskaia gazeta*, 2 (1980), 16.
109 *Partiinaia zhizn*, 3 (1981), 18.
110 *Kommunist*, 10 (1981), 76.
111 *Ekonomicheskaia gazeta*, 13 (1978), 19.
112 *Ekonomicheskaia gazeta*, 38 (1976), 1; 4 (1978), 1.
113 *Ekonomicheskaia gazeta*, 36 (1980), 19.

114 *Ekonomicheskaia gazeta*, 36 (1978), 1.
115 *Ekonomicheskaia gazeta*, 42 (1978), 2; 23 (1978), 18; 26 (1976), 19.
116 *Ekonomicheskaia gazeta*, 32 (1976), 6. There were nine published replies from obkom secretaries during the 1976–78 elevator campaign – for example, in *Ekonomicheskaia gazeta*, 3 (1977), 8.
117 For example, in Orenburg – *Ekonomicheskaia gazeta*, 4 (1980), 18; 24 (1977), 18.
118 *Ekonomicheskaia gazeta*, 11 (1977), 18.
119 *Ekonomicheskaia gazeta*, 31 (1977), 19; 29 (1978), 20.
120 *Ekonomicheskaia gazeta*, 14 (1979), 7.
121 *Ekonomicheskaia gazeta*, 34 (1985), 14.
122 *Ekonomicheskaia gazeta*, 23 (1978), 16; 17 (1976), 8. In some cases construction resources were diverted into the building of hotels and dachas – *Pravda*, 16 May 1981, p. 3.
123 *Ekonomicheskaia gazeta*, 9 (1981), 23.
124 *Ekonomicheskaia gazeta*, 26 (1980), 17.
125 *Ekonomicheskaia gazeta*, 16 (1982), 22. Unfortunately, data for elevator construction in subsequent years either was not published at all in annual plan reports, or switched to reports in cubic metres (e.g. *Pravda*, 26 January 1986, p. 2). No data on the overall impact of the party's campaign is therefore available.
126 *Kommunist*, 1 (1984), 53.
127 *Voprosy ekonomiki*, 9 (1981), 55–66. Iu. Rytov came up with an estimate of 75 million individuals, for an average of only 2.6 days apiece – totalling 197 million man-days. *Izvestiia*, 21 May 1988, p. 2.
128 *Izvestiia*, 2 March 1983, p. 2; *Partiinaia zhizn*, 7 (1982), 33–6.
129 *Ekonomicheskaia gazeta*, 16 (1979), 3.
130 *Ekonomicheskaia gazeta*, 12 (1978), 24. The non-black earth zone covers twenty-nine oblasti of central Russia.
131 *Ekonomicheskaia gazeta*, 45 (1983), 17.
132 *Kommunist*, 7 (1986), 29.
133 For examples of director complaints, see *Ekonomicheskaia gazeta*, 24 (1986), 13; *Pravda* 26 December 1980, p. 3.
134 *Voprosy ekonomiki*, 9 (1981), 60.
135 *Ekonomicheskaia gazeta*, 15 (1985), 16.
136 *Kommunist*, 17 (1979), 16.
137 *Izvestiia*, 23 October 1983, p. 6; *Pravda*, 11 November 1982, p. 3.
138 An estimated 9 million children were involved in 1977 – *Kommunist*, 8 (1977), 104. Frunze raikom in Kirghizia issued a decree restricting the use of children to pick cotton for months on end – *Pravda*, 4 August 1982, p. 3.
139 A CC CPSU decree of December 1978 commended their role, and they received favourable mentions in speeches by Brezhnev and Andropov. See *KPSS v rezoliutsiiakh*, vol. 13, pp. 298–301; *Kommunist*, 17 (1978), 11; 17 (1982), 17.
140 *Ekonomicheskaia gazeta*, 25 (1978), 17.
141 *Partiinaia zhizn*, 24 (1983), 21; *Kommunist*, 6 (1986), 32.
142 *Ekonomicheskaia gazeta*, 5 (1983), 18; 13 (1979), 17.

143 *Partiinaia zhizn*, 24 (1983), 24.
144 *Kommunist*, 18 (1981), 40.
145 *Partiinaia zhizn*, 18 (1981), 33–7; 4 (1982), 58.
146 For example, in wage payments of farms in Leningrad and Tomsk – *Partiinaia zhizn*, 9 (1982), 54; 24 (1983), 24.
147 *Ekonomicheskaia gazeta*, 4 (1982), 18.
148 *Kommunist*, 18 (1981), 39.
149 *Ekonomicheskaia gazeta*, 9 (1983), 12. Other examples of obkomy helping auxiliary farms come from Gomel and Syrdaria – *Ekonomicheskaia gazeta*, 34 (1983), 10.
150 *Ekonomicheskaia gazeta*, 21 (1982), 18.
151 *Partiinaia zhizn*, 18 (1977), 22; *Izvestiia*, 8 August 1983, p. 2.
152 A. Salutskii, 'Smychka', *Nash sovremennik*, 12 (1987), 133–53.
153 A. Meledin, 'Agrarnyi tsekh Timano-Pechorskii kompleksa', *Partiinaia zhizn*, 18 (1981), 33–7.
154 *Ekonomicheskaia gazeta*, 19 (1983), 18; *Raionnyi*, pp. 232–5.
155 *Ekonomicheskaia gazeta*, 42 (1985), 3.
156 *Ekonomicheskaia gazeta*, 23 (1985), 16.

8 Non-party control organs

1 *Pravda*, 28 January 1987, p. 3.
2 *Kommunist*, 15 (1982), 102.
3 On this history of the control organs, see M. S. Smiriukov, *Sovetskii gosudarstvennyi apparat upravleniia* (Moscow, Politizdat, 1982), pp. 196–210; and J. S. Adams, *Citizen Inspectors in the Soviet Union* (New York, Praeger, 1977).
4 The law is reprinted in *V pomoshch predsedateliu gruppy narodnogo kontrolia* (Moscow, Ekonomika, 1984), pp. 4–24.
5 *Kommunist*, 10 (1979), 104.
6 *V pomoshch*, p. 109.
7 *V pomoshch*, p. 20.
8 One of his last public appearances was a televised speech to a KNK conference – *Partiinaia zhizn*, 20 (1984), 15–21.
9 *Voprosy istorii KPSS*, 12 (1981), 31.
10 For example, in Ashkhabad in 1984 forty raids were conducted, resulting in ninety-two managers reprimanded and three sacked. In Sakhalin seventy-seven managers were criticized in 1984, and three sacked (all for abuse of company cars) – *Partiinaia zhizn*, 7 (1985), 37; *Ekonomicheskaia gazeta*, 7 (1984), 22.
11 *Ekonomicheskaia gazeta*, 23 (1984), 22; 38 (1983), 22.
12 As in the firings of a Pushkin garage manager, and a Khabarovsk repair trust accountant. *Ekonomicheskaia gazeta*, 8 (1983), 22; 41 (1983), 22.
13 *Partiinaia zhizn*, 17 (1982), 59.
14 *Partiinaia zhizn*, 18 (1982), 22; *Ekonomicheskaia gazeta*, 2 (1981), 22.
15 *Ekonomicheskaia gazeta*, 30 (1980), 22.
16 *Ekonomicheskaia gazeta*, 27 (1978), 11.
17 *Partiinaia zhizn*, 2 (1979), 57.
18 *Ekonomicheskaia gazeta*, 28 (1980), 22.

19 For example, in the Chebakul metals plant the partkom secretary was criticized for ignoring a KNK report on metal conservation – *Ekonomicheskaia gazeta*, 48 (1980), 22.

20 *Partiinaia zhizn*, 13 (1976), 52.

21 For example, KNK water protection measures were ignored by firms in Novokuznetsk, while a Kirov building materials plant treated KNK controllers as hostile (*chuzhoi*) representatives – *Ekonomicheskaia gazeta*, 20 (1980), 22; 11 (1984), 22.

22 *Ekonomicheskaia gazeta*, 20 (1980), 22.

23 *Pravda*, 31 October 1978, p. 2.

24 *Partiinaia zhizn*, 5 (1985), 15; 17 (1981), 46; *Voprosy istorii KPSS* 12 (1981), 31.

25 *Voprosy istorii KPSS*, 12 (1981), 31.

26 For example, in 1982 a Novgorod building site ran out of money and found deliveries stopped because 'Who will deliver supplies knowing full well that they will not be paid for?' – *Ekonomicheskaia gazeta*, 17 (1982), 9.

27 *Ekonomicheskaia gazeta*, 7 (1984), 16.

28 *Ekonomicheskaia gazeta*, 15 (1982), 5; 9 (1977), 19; *Pravda*, 26 April 1982, p. 2.

29 *Ekonomicheskaia gazeta*, 22 (1985), 7.

30 *Kommunist*, 11 (1983), 56.

31 *Ekonomicheskaia gazeta*, 35 (1984), 11; *Kommunist*, 2 (1986), 124.

32 On this, see N. Lampert, 'Law and order in the USSR', *Soviet Studies*, 36, 3 (1984), 366–85; and Shtamba, *KPSS*.

33 *Ekonomicheskaia gazeta*, 29 (1986), 8.

34 A quote from the new director of Amurenergo, replacing a man who was sacked for making illegal wage payments – in *Pravda*, 28 December 1982, p. 6.

35 On this, see P. Solomon, *Soviet Politicians and Criminal Prosecutions: The Logic of Party Intervention* (Urbana, Il., University of Illinois Soviet Interview Project, paper no. 33, 1987).

36 See for example Remington, *The Truth of Authority*; E. P. Mickiewicz, *The Media and the Russian Public* (New York, Praeger, 1981).

37 For example, the Tadzhik Ministry of Construction Materials had its reply rejected in *Ekonomicheskaia gazeta*, 1 (1979), 15.

38 *Partiinaia zhizn*, 11 (1986), 61.

39 For example, from the Bashkir agricultural machinery plant, or the Ekistabuz coal complex *Ekonomicheskaia gazeta*, 49 (1984), 49; 16 (1976), 9.

40 *Ekonomicheskaia gazeta*, 41 (1978), 6; 8 (1984), 20.

41 *Partiinaia zhizn*, 19 (1982), 3–6.

42 *Kommunist*, 11 (1979), 60.

43 *Kommunist*, 3 (1986), 71.

44 *Partiinaia zhizn*, 4 (1980), 43–5; R. Solchanyk, Radio Liberty Research Bulletin, 174, (1987).

45 D. R. Kelley, 'Environmental problems as a new policy issue', in Ryavec, *Soviet Society*, pp. 88–108; Gustafson, *Reform in Soviet Politics*, pp. 40–46.

46 *Vestnik Leningradskogo universiteta*, 6, 1 (1986), 112–16.

47 *Ekonomicheskaia gazeta*, 41 (1978), 6.

48 *Kommunist*, 9 (1984), 59.

49 *Partiinaia zhizn*, 9 (1981), 68.

50 Chufarov (ed.), *Deiatel'nost*, pp. 52–58.
51 *Ekonomicheskaia gazeta*, 8 (1982), 15.
52 *Partiinaia zhizn*, 4 (1979), 71.
53 S. White, 'Political communications in the USSR', *Soviet Studies*, 31, 1 (1983), 43–60.
54 *Partiinaia zhizn*, 13 (1982), 77; *Kommunist*, 15 (1982), 101.
55 *Voprosy istorii KPSS*, 2 (1981), 57.
56 *Partiinaia zhizn*, 2 (1981), 48.
57 According to surveys in Ivanovo oblast and the Latvian republic, reported in *Partiinaia zhizn*, 6 (1979), 41–3; and *Kommunist*, 11 (1980), 50–61.
58 C. C. Hood, *The Limits of Administration* (London, Wileu, 1976).
59 T. J. Colton, *Commissars, Commanders and Civilian Authority: The Structure of Soviet Military Politics* (Cambridge, Mass., Harvard University Press, 1979).
60 *Ekonomicheskaia gazeta*, 30 (1976), 7.
61 *Ekonomicheskaia gazeta*, 11 (1984), 5. This comment reportedly caused 'stirrings in the hall' amongst his listeners – a rare sign of enthusiasm for a speech by Mr Chernenko.
62 A. Prigozhin, in *Kommunist*, 7 (1984), 65. In August 1990, President Gorbachev really did set up a commission to review the reports of the commissions studying economic reform.
63 *Kommunist*, 6 (1985), 87. This source may not be entirely neutral, however, since his enterprise was subsequently condemned for ineptitude – *Kommunist*, 9 (1986), 66.
64 *EKO*, 9 (1984), 76.
65 *Trud*, 12 May 1983, p. 2; *Kommunist*, 10 (1983), 21; *Ekonomicheskaia gazeta*, 23 (1983), 22.
66 *Ekonomicheskaia gazeta*, 34 (1981), 3.
67 By 1984 125 such councils had been set up at oblast level – *Voprosy istorii KPSS*, 11 (1984), 26.
68 *Voprosy istorii KPSS*, 11 (1984), 26.
69 *Ekonomicheskaia gazeta*, 31 (1984), 22.
70 *Ekonomicheskaia gazeta*, 40 (1983), 22.
71 Azrael, *Managerial Power*, p. 117.
72 *Ekonomicheskaia gazeta*, 21 (1986), 21.
73 *Kommunist*, 17 (1986), 36.
74 *Ekonomicheskaia gazeta*, 42 (1983), 22.
75 The first case is from an article by the General Procurator of the USSR, A. Rekunkov 'Na strakhe pravoporiadka i sotsial'noi spravedlivosti', *Kommunist* 1 (1986), 41–51; the second is from *Partiinaia zhizn* 10 (1981), 67.

9 The principles underlying the party's work with cadres

1 Thus for example the editor of *Planovoe khoziaistvo*, P. Ignatovski, writing in *Kommunist* in 1983: 'What is needed is not so much new principles of economic management, as people able to apply them in new conditions, with greater vigour.' 'O politicheskom podkhode k ekonomike', *Kommunist*, 12 (1983), 60–72, p. 67.

2 For example, in Rodinov, *Partiinaia*, ch. 15.

3 For example, *Ekonomicheskaia gazeta*, 44 (1980), 8; 1 (1981), 9.

4 On party cadres policy, see the round table discussion in *Voprosy istorii KPSS*, 9 (1982), 30–54.

5 Reviewed in *Literaturnaia gazeta*, 8 December 1982, p. 8. The oblasti of Iakutia and Krasnoiarsk are indeed four times as big as France, although their population is only around 2 million. On the production genre, see N. Lampert, 'Social criticism in Soviet drama: the plays of A. Gel'man', *Soviet Studies*, 39, 1 (1987), 101–15.

6 V. I. Lenin, *Polnoe sobranie sochetanii* (Moscow, various years), vol. 53, p. 97. One should not dwell too deeply on the profundity of these lines: they come from a very short note written by Lenin concerning the appointment of a fish industry specialist.

7 Quoted in N. I. Kurochkin and N. A. Maksimov, *Rukovoditel i kollektiv* (Moscow, Ekonomika, 1979), p. 63.

8 F. Petrenko, *Sekrety rukovodstva* (Moscow, Moskovskii Rabochii, 1968), p. 99.

9 A. Yanowitch, *Social and Economic Inequality in the Soviet Union* (London, Martin Robertson, 1977), pp. 135–64; M. E. Urban, *The Ideology of Administration: Soviet and American Cases* (New York, SUNY Press, 1982), p. 45.

10 J. Klugman, *The New Soviet Elite: How They Think and What They Want* (New York, Praeger, 1989).

11 A. A. Godunov, *Sotsial'no-ekonomicheskie problemy upravleniia sotsialisticheskim proizvodstvom* (Moscow, Ekonomika, 1975), p. 100.

12 Cited in A. G. Kovalev, *Kollektiv i sotsial'no-psikhologicheskie problemy rukovodtsva* (Moscow, Politizdat, 1975), pp. 248ff. The original studies were carried out in Liepzig by H. Hibsch and M. Vorberg.

13 It found the democratic/collegial style to predominate in one plant, while the authoritarian style prevailed in the other. A. L. Zhuravlev (ed.), *Individual'nyi stil rukovodstva proizvodstvennym kollektivom* (Moscow, Institut Marodnogo Khoziaisvta, 1976), p. 59.

14 S. I. Shkurko, *Stimulirovanie kachestva i effektivnosti proizvodtsva* (Moscow, Mysl, 1977), p. 97.

15 *Ekonomicheskaia gazeta*, 51 (1980), 11.

16 For example, in an attestation drive at the Vladimir instrument plant in 1985 less than 1 per cent of specialists were rejected – *Partiinaia zhizn*, 13 (1985), 18. On the other hand, when G. Kolbin took over Ul'ianovsk obkom he used attestations to effect a clean-out of the regions's managers – *Kommunist*, 2 (1985), 49.

17 *Partiinaia zhizn*, 13 (1989), 47.

18 *Kommunist*, 18 (1986), 11.

19 P. C. Emshin and A. A. Godunov, *Metodika otsenki delovykh i moral'no-politicheskikh kachestv rukovoditelei i spetsialistov sotsialisticheskogo proizvodstva* (Leningrad, Leningradskii Gosudarstvennyi Universitet, 1971), pp. 22–5.

20 According to party theorists, *partiinost* did not simply mean loyalty to the CPSU. Godunov defined it as 'putting the interest of society first' (*Metodika*, p. 50).

21 See for example the letter from an aviation ministry official, V. Selivanov, in *Pravda*, 2 May, 1988, p. 2.
22 *Kommunist*, 1 (1982), 43.
23 For an analysis of the wave of party purges in the early 1980s, see Rutland, 'The search for stability'.
24 *Kommunist*, 4 (1985), 33.
25 S. Khabeishvili, 'Polnee uchitivat mnenie kommunistov', *Partiinaia zhizn*, 21 (1980), 31–6.
26 *Pravda*, 5 August 1983, p. 1; *Partiinaia zhizn*, 5 (1985), 27–30.
27 *Pravda*, 28 January 1987, p. 3.
28 E. Teague, *Solidarity and the Soviet Worker: the impact of the Polish Events of 1980 on Soviet Internal Politics* (London, Croom Helm, 1988).
29 F. G. Krotov, *Shkola ideinoi zakalki: istoriia Marksistko-Leninski obrazovaniia v KPSS* (Moscow, Politizdat, 1978).
30 *Voprosy istorii KPSS*, 4 (1977), 68.
31 *KPSS v rezoliutsiiakh*, vol. 9, pp. 215–21; vol. 11, pp. 160–3; *Partiinaia zhizn*, 18 (1976), 12–19; 13 (1978), 3–5, 7 (1978), 3.
32 *Voprosy istorii KPSS*, 9 (1983), 20.
33 *Partiinaia zhizn*, 18 (1976), 12–19.
34 Ibid.
35 Krotov, *Shkola*; 'Deiatel'nost KPSS po ideino-teoreticheskoi podgotovke rukovodiashchikh kadrov', *Voprosy istorii KPSS*, 12 (1982), 98–106.
36 *Partiinaia zhizn*, 13 (1978), 3–5. Apart from the republic capitals, they were located in Gor'kii, Novosibirsk, Rostov, Saratov, Khabarovsk, Odessa and Sverdlovsk. The longer courses (4 years full-time, 5 years part-time), were for party officials under 35 who had missed out on higher education.
37 *Sovety narodnykh deputatov*, p. 40.
38 *Partiinaia zhizn*, 13 (1978), 3–5; V. Medvedev, 'Kachestvenno novoe partiinoe uchebnoe zavedenie', *Partiinaia zhizn*, 8 (1979), 27–32.
39 *Voprosy istorii KPSS*, 1 (1981), 71; 12 (1982), 100, *Partiinaia zhizn*, 13 (1978), 3.
40 A 1981 CC CPSU decree stated that the system 'still does not fully answer life's demands' – *Partiinaia zhizn*, 12 (1981), 9–11; and in 1986 the Politburo drew attention to the 'need for serious work to improve the party political education of leaders' – *Ekonomicheskaia gazeta*, 27 (1986), 3.
41 Quotes are from *Kommunist*, 6 (1986), 7.
42 Letter from teacher V. Fetisov in *Kommunist*, 14 (1983), 110–14; comments in conference reported in *Kommunist*, 18 (1983), 28.
43 *Partiinaia zhizn*, 6 (1983), 48; 4 (1985), 79.
44 *Narodnoe ... 1922–82*, p. 507; *Statistical Abstract of the US, 1982–3* (Washington, DC, US Census Bureau, 1983), p. 167.
45 These comments are based on the author's examination of curricula during a three-month visit to the Plekhanov Institute of National Economy, Moscow, in 1984. On the general weakness of the Soviet economics profession, see the CC CPSU decree on this subject in *Ekonomicheskaia gazeta*, 24 (1986), 4.
46 *Nedelia*, 6 (1987), 6.

47 For example, only 17 per cent of 'senior accountants' had higher education
   – *Voprosy istorii KPSS*, 11 (1984), 25. The accountancy profession was
   unregulated until 1984 *Ekonomicheskaia gazeta*, 29 (1985), 7.
48 For example, the director of an Alma Ata textile plant, who rose through
   the labour and wages office – *Ekonomicheskaia gazeta*, 37 (1976), 8.
49 For a devastating critique of the environmental impact of the lack of cost
   awareness in major building projects, see S. Zalygin, 'Proekt: Nauchnaia
   obosnovannost i otvetstvennost', *Kommunist*, 13 (1985), 63–73.
50 *Voprosy istorii KPSS*, 8 (1981), 9, for the 2 per cent figure. On this issue, see
   L. Shelley, *Lawyers in Soviet Work Life* (New Brunswick, NJ, Rutgers University Press, 1984).
51 Quote from S. V. Mitrosin, a secretary of Voronezh obkom, cited in *Voprosy
   istorii KPSS*, 4 (1976), 50.
52 V. N. Ptsitsyn, in *Voprosy istorii KPSS*, 1 (1977), 27.
53 See K. Bailes, *Technology and Society Under Lenin and Stalin* (New Jersey,
   Princeton University Press, 1978); and S. Fitzpatrick, *Education and Social
   Mobility in the USSR 1921–34* (Cambridge, Cambridge University Press,
   1979).
54 Hough, *Prefects*, p. 67.
55 J. F. Hough, *Soviet Leadership in Transition* (Washington DC, Brookings
   Institution, 1980), p. 20.
56 On this, see B. D. Silver, 'Political beliefs on the Soviet citizen', in J. R. Millar
   (ed.), *Politics, Work and Daily Life in the USSR* (Cambridge, Cambridge
   University Press, 1987), ch. 4.
57 *Voprosy istorii KPSS*, 9 (1985), 17; Hough, *Soviet Leadership*, p. 28.
58 *Partiinaia zhizn*, 15 (1983), 30.
59 *Kommunist*, 3 (1982), 114.
60 Hough, *Soviet Leadership*, p. 26.
61 Azrael, *Managerial Power*, p. 156.
62 Bahry and Silver, 'Intimidation', p. 1074.
63 The proportion fluctuated erratically, peaking at 68 per cent in 1981 and
   then dropping to a trough of 8 per cent in 1982 (for no apparent reason).
64 B. Harasymiw, *Political Elite Recruitment in the Soviet Union* (London, Macmillan, 1984), p. 189.
65 For an example from Gor'kii, see *Kommunist*, 2 (1986), 86.
66 *Kommunist*, 4 (1981), 58.
67 *Kommunist*, 1 (1982), 34.
68 I. Boldyrev, in *Kommunist*, 14 (1986), 44.

10 The obkom elite in the 1980s

1 For details on the methods and conventions used to gather the biographical
  data used in this chapter, see Appendix 1.
2 M. McAuley, 'The hunting of the hierarchy: RSFSR obkom first secretaries
  and the Central Committee', *Soviet Studies*, 26, 4 (1974), 473–501.
3 On collegiality in Soviet bureaucracies, see E. Jones, 'Committee decision
  making in the Soviet Union', *World Politics*, 36, 2 (1984), 165–88.

4 Hough and Fainsod, *How the Soviet Union*, pp. 497, 505.
5 Even in Western elite studies, there is a strong tendency to tailor the model to suit the data available – M. Czudnowski and H. Eulau (eds.), *Elite Recruitment in Democratic Polities* (New York, Sage, 1976), p. 40.
6 M. Beissinger, 'In search of generations in Soviet politics', *World Politics*, 38, 1 (1986), 288–314.
7 S. P. Huntington, 'Generations, cycles and their role in American development', in R. J. Samuels (ed.), *Political Generations and World Development* (Lexington, Mass., D. C. Heath, 1977), ch. 2, p. 13.
8 G. W. Breslauer, 'Provincial party leaders' demand articulation and the nature of centre-periphery relations in the USSR', *Slavic Review*, 45, 4 (1986), 650–72; 'Is there a generation gap?', *Soviet Studies*, 36, 1 (1984), 1–25. The quote is from G. W. Breslauer, 'Research note', *Soviet Studies*, 23, 3 (1981), 446–7.
9 Hough, *Soviet Leadership*, p. 58.
10 The 1981 data in the table closely parallels Rigby's study of the 1976 cohort, and Miller's study of all obkom secretaries holding office 1945–80. Rigby found 65 per cent coming from these two posts, and Miller 53 per cent. T. H. Rigby, 'The Soviet regional leadership: the Brezhnev generation', *Slavic Review*, 37, 1 (1978), 1–24, 13; J. Miller, 'Nomenklatura: check on localism?', in T. H. Rigby and B. Harasymiw (eds.), *Leadership Selection and Patron-Client Relations in the USSR and Yugoslavia* (London, Macmillan, 1983), ch. 2, p. 71.
11 The sample comprised the 111 members of the USSR Council of Ministers in 1981, plus 10 officials of equivalent rank, such as the head of Tass and the General Procurator.
12 Rigby, 'Soviet regional', 13; R. E. Blackwell, 'Cadres policy in the Brezhnev era', *Problems of Communism*, 28, 2 (1979), 29–42, 41.
13 G. Hodnett, *Leadership in the Soviet National Republics* (Ontario, Mosaic, 1978), p. 137.
14 Bialer reports only two of this group coming straight from Moscow, but the biographical data do not support this – S. Bialer, *Stalin's Successors* (Cambridge, Cambridge University Press, 1980), p. 218.
15 Rigby, 'Soviet regional', p. 13.
16 Blackwell, 'Cadres', p. 41.
17 For example, the deputy head of the CC CPSU organization and party work department, E. Z. Razumov; CC CPSU Secretary I. V. Kapitonov; and Donetsk obkom first secretary V. Mironov – *Kommunist*, 14 (1977), 55; *Partiinaia zhizn*, 14 (1980), 19; 11 (1984), 29.
18 Gorbachev comments from a speech reported in *Pravda*, 28 January 1987, p. 3. The Kazakh events were reported in *Izvestiia*, 16 December 1986, p. 2.
19 On this policy shift, see T. Gustafson and D. Mann, 'Gorbachev at the helm: building power and authority', *Problems of Communism*, 35, 3 (1986), 1–19.
20 Provisional data reported in a paper by W. Reissinger and P. Willerton, 'Obkom elite turnover', to the annual conference of the American Association for the Advancement of Slavic Studies, 20 October 1990, Washington DC.
21 E. E. Schattschneider, *Two Hundred Million Americans in Search of Government* (New York, Holt, Rinehart and Winston, 1969), p. 83.

22 Hough, *Soviet Leadership*.

23 Blackwell, 'Cadres', p. 13.

24 Fainsod, *How Russia*, pp. 200, 226.

25 Separate calculations were done for the groups of obkom first secretaries entering and leaving office: these are not shown in Table 10.3.

26 N. S. Patolichev, *Ispytanie na zrelost* (Moscow, Politizdat, 1982), p. 178.

27 Hough, *Soviet Prefects*, p. 63.

28 Ibid. The total number of oblasti fluctuated between 105 and 115.

29 Hough, *Soviet Leadership*, p. 142.

30 Hough and Fainsod, *How the Soviet Union*, p. 498.

31 The procedures followed for arriving at the oblast ranking are discussed in Appendix 1.

32 About half of the difference between Russians and non-Russians can be attributed to the fact that the latter were older – 3.5 years, on average, with seventeen being born before 1917, compared to only four from the non-Russian regions.

33 J. L. Moses, 'Functional career specialization in Soviet regional elite recruitment', in Rigby and Harasymiw, *Leadership*, ch. 1, pp. 48, 51.

34 Moses, 'Functional', p. 36.

11 Party and economy under perestroika

1 *Kommunist*, 5 (1988), 42–3.

2 On the Caucasus and Central Asia, see *Moscow News*, 37 (1988), 2. See the interviews with first secretaries from Grodno, Belorussia and Latvia in *Argumenty i fakty*, 20 (1988), 1; 27 (1988), 2; 37 (1988), 3; and reports from *Ul'ianovskaia pravda*, 6 August 1988, p. 2; *Vechernii Kiev*, 23 June 1988, p. 2; *Zvezda* (Perm), 13 February 1990, p. 2.

3 For example, Krasnodar kraikom cut its nomenkatura from 3,600 to 1,300 – *Sovetskaia Kuban*, 7 July 1989, p. 2.

4 On this, see Rutland, 'The search for stability'.

5 V. I. Kudashkin, 'O razvitii vnutripartiinoi demokratii na etape perestroiki', *Nauchnyi kommunizm*, 6 (1988), 11–18.

6 An official of the Rubtsov gorkom, quoted in *Altaiskaia pravda*, 28 July 1989, p. 1.

7 V. Brovkin, 'First party secretaries: an endangered species?', *Problems of Communism*, 39, 1 (1990), 15–27. I. D'iakov, Astrakhan obkom first secretary, is one of the few to fit Gorbachev's ideal. See his profile in V. Alekseev, 'Bez prava na monopoliu vlast', *Dialog*, 5 (1990), 29–37.

8 A survey of delegates to an obkom conference in Moscow found less than one in five considered the PPOs to be 'active fighters for perestroika' – *Argumenty i fakty*, 40 (1989), 2.

9 P. Rutland 'Democratic Platform prepares for CPSU Congress', *Report on the USSR*, 29 June 1990, pp. 1–3.

10 V. Rukavishnikov, 'Sotsial'naia napriazhennost', *Dialog*, 8 (1990), 6–11.

11 Zdravomyslov et al., *Politicheskoe soznanie*, p. 26. Among the non-party members surveyed, the percentages were 3, 4 and 41.

12 *Argumenty i fakty*, 38 (1988), 7; 'Perestroika otraslevykh shtabov', *Pravda*, 27 September 1987, p. 2.

13 *Izvestiia TsK KPSS*, 4 (1989), 24. This source also reported that 7,000 jobs were cut in the entire CPSU apparatus – 8 per cent, by our calculation.

14 The general arguments in this paragraph, and in the chapter as a whole, come from interviews with the editors of *Partiinaia zhizn* in December 1988, and with editors and journalists at *Argumenty i fakty* between 1988 and 1990. Complaints about lack of CC CPSU direction were prominent during the Russian Communist Party's founding conference – for example, in the speech of the Iakut obkom first secretary (Moscow TV, 20 June 1990).

15 Gorbachev, *Izbrannye*, vol. 5, p. 131.

16 Ibid., p. 357.

17 'Brezhnev i krushenie ottepeli', *Literaturnaia gazeta*, 14 September 1988, 13–14; referring to 'Gosudarstvo vsego naroda', *Pravda*, 6 December 1964, p. 1.

18 Thus he calls for 'transforming activism' rather than transforming goals, the position being summarized in the title of his October 20, 1987 speech 'Be in the vanguard: work in a new way' – *Izbrannye*, vol. 5, pp. 379, 461.

19 Gorbachev, *Izbrannye*, vol. 5, p. 364, in a speech to the Leningrad party organisation on 13 October 1987.

20 M. S. Gorbachev, 'Perestroika raboty partii', *Partiinaia zhizn*, 15 (1989), 5–16.

21 *Pravda*, 12 March 1990, p. 1.

22 For example, with regard to farming in Briansk and social planning in Astrakhan – *Izbrannye*, vol. 5, p. 379; *Pravda*, 28 January 1987, p. 5. On the CC CPSU, see *Izbrannye*, vol. 5, p. 139.

23 Gorbachev, *Izbrannye*, vol. 5, p. 375; *Ekonomicheskaia gazeta*, 29 (1985), 2.

24 *Ekonomicheskaia gazeta*, 12 (1985) 4; and then weekly until 45 (1985), 4. It seems reasonable to assume this was Gorbachev's idea.

25 See for example his speech to the workers of the Ramen agricultural district on 5 August 1987, when the closest he came was warning against the danger of turning the leaseholding drive into a formal campaign – Gorbachev, *Izbrannye*, vol. 5, p. 253.

26 *Ekonomicheskaia gazeta*, 14 (1984), 4; also on the virtues of fallow land in a speech reported in *Partiinaia zhizn*, 18 (1985), 8.

27 The most comprehensive survey of the state of the Soviet economy at the end of 1990 is *A Study of the Soviet Economy* (Washington, DC, OECD, 1991), 3 vols.

28 I. Klimenko, 'Vzgliad iz kabineta ministra', *Sotsialisticheskai industriia*, 21 February 1990, p. 2.

29 *Kaliniskaia pravda*, 31 May 1988, p. 2; *Vostochno-Sibirskaia pravda* (Irkutsk), 7 June 1988, p. 1; *Sovetskaia Bashkiria*, 11 May 1988, p. 2.

30 For a collection of the relevant decrees, see *O korennoi perestroike upravlenie ekonomikoi* (Moscow, Politizdat, 1988).

31 *Zvezda* (Perm), 19 May 1988, p. 3; *Vostochno-Sibirskaia pravda*, 26 January 1988, p. 2; *Vechernii Kiev*, 17 June 1988, p. 1.

32 Eighty per cent of directors saw no slackening of plan controls by 1988 – L. Shcherbakova, 'Anketa direktorov', *EKO*, 3 (1988), 59–75. For individual

examples see *Vechernii Kiev*, 22 September 1988, p. 2; *Sotsialisticheskii Donbass*, 11 June 1988, p. 2; *Vostochno-Sibirskaia pravda*, 17 May 1988, p. 2; *Priokskaia pravda* (Riazan), 7 April 1988, p. 3.

33 Iu. Maliukov, head of Gosplan, in *Pravda*, 28 October 1988, p. 2. For example, a Riazan shoe factory went bankrupt because state orders forced them to switch from producing high-priced women's boots to unprofitable children's shoes. *Priokskaia pravda*, 14 April 1988, p. 2.

34 *Vostochno-Sibirskaia pravda*, 4 May 1988, p. 2, quoting a manager at the Angarsk chemicals plant.

35 Gossnab chief L. Voronin claimed that the central agency was down to 15 per cent of the volume it had handled two years earlier – *Pravitel'stvennyi vestnik*, 14 (1989), 2. See also G. Bazhutin, 'Rytsar bez doslekhov', *Sotsialisti-cheskaia industriia*, 30 June 1989, p. 2, who describes the new system as 'a bombshell for enterprises'.

36 Phrase used by trade union official in *Krasnoe znamia* (Komi), 20 October 1990, p. 2.

37 *Sovetskaia Kuban* (Krasnodar), 11 July 1989, p. 2; *Sovetskaia Sibir*, 9 August 1989, p. 3.

38 For regional *khozraschet* plans, see *Krasnoe znamia* (Komi), 6 October 1990, p. 2; *Volgogradskaia pravda*, 13 February 1990, p. 1; *Krasnoe znamiia* (Primorsk), 18 February 1990, p. 3; *Sovetskii Sakhalin*, 16 February 1990, p. 2.

39 *Ul'ianovskaia pravda*, 24 May 1988, p. 2; *Sovetskaia Sibir*, 31 May 1988, p. 1; 8 August 1989, p. 2; 21 May 1988, p. 2; *Sovetskaia Bashkiria*, 2 February 1989, p. 2.

40 *Argumenty i fakty*, 30, 1989, 4.

41 *Moscow News*, 36 (1988), 10.

42 Iu. Tikhomirov, 'Na puti k pravovoi ekonomike', *Pravitel'stvennyi vestnik*, 12 (1989), 7.

43 *Partiinaia zhizn*, 19 (1989), •7; V. Lomako, 'Kakim byt ekonomicheskomy otdely?', *Ekonomicheskaia gazeta*, 43 (1988), 2; *Kommunist*, 9 (1988), 39–41.

44 *Partiinaia zhizn*, 16 (1989), 36.

45 *Moscow News*, 26 (1988), 8.

46 *Volgorgadskaia pravda*, 29 May 1988, p. 2.

47 In the words of A. Gordeev, second secretary of Sakhalin obkom: 'Economic laws are almost ceasing to function, so it would be wrong to weaken the party's attention to the economy' – *Sovetskii Sakhalin*, 11 February 1990, p. 2.

48 *Ul'ianovskaia pravda*, 26 June 1988, p. 1.

49 *Sovetskaia sibir*, 29 April 1988, p. 1.

50 One such report is provided by a Moscow obkom secretary, V. Novikov, refusing to get involved in the allocation of scarce construction materials. 'Ovladevat politicheskim metodami' – *Partiinaia zhizn*, 16 (1989), 26–31, p. 27.

51 For a withering critique of this campaign, see M. Miroshnichenko, 'Vo chto obkhoditsia – trezvost', *Ogonek*, 39 (1988), 20–23.

52 Equal to 7 per cent of the total budget. *Pravda*, 28 October 1988, p. 4.

53 *Zvezda*, 18 May 1988, p. 4.

54 *Sotsialisticheskii Donbass*, 11 February 1990, p. 2.
55 *Vostochno-Sibirskaia pravda*, 29 January 1988, p. 2; *Sovetskaia bashkiria*, 31 May 1988, p. 2, with reference to the Ufa instrument plant.
56 *Volgogradskaia pravda*, 25 May 1988, p. 2, specifically with regard to managers refusing to respect wage limits.
57 A survey of workers in eight plants where managers had been elected found only 23 per cent thought the process was democratic. N. Andreenkova, *Perekhod predpriiatii na novye usloviia khoziastvovaniia* (Moscow, Institut Sotsiologii, 1989), p. 31.
58 *Vechernii Kiev*, 21 June 1988, p. 1; 24 June 1988, p. 2.
59 *Ekonomika i zhizn*, 25 (1990), 11–21, article 14. Ministries were given the discretion to run manager elections if they wished. For complaints, see A. Krylov, 'Teni sovetskoi ekonomiki', *Ekonomicheskie nauki*, 5 (1990), 103–8, p. 105; or Gosplan chair Iu. Masliukov in *Pravda*, 30 June 1990, p. 2.
60 *Izvestiia TsK KPSS*, 3 (1989), 93–9. A similar thing happened to a transport firm in Urengoi – *Tiumen'skaia pravda*, 11 April 1990, p. 2.
61 *Ekonomika i zhizn*, 9 (1990), 12.
62 N. Shmelov, 'Novye trevogi', *Novyi mir*, 4 (1988), 160–75, 162. See *Pravda*, 11 September 1988, p. 3, for examples of joint party/soviet decrees in Orel ordering enterprises to help farms. For counter-examples, of raikomy losing their grip, see *Volgogradskaia pravda*, 25 January 1990, p. 3.
63 *Priokskaia pravda*, 5 April 1988, p. 1. Similarly, Rezh gorkom was held responsible for poor vegetable production – *Ural'skii rabochii* (Sverdlovsk), 20 May 1988, p. 2.
64 *Sovetskaia Kuban*, 7 July 1989), p. 1. Other examples of obkomy heavily involved in livestock farms include *Kommuna* (Voronezh), 24 January 1990, p. 1; and *Sovetskii Krym*, 3 June 1990, p. 1.
65 *Politicheskoe obrazovanie*, 16 (1989), 34.
66 In Kalinin, factories had to release 12,000 drivers to help with the harvest, while in Karelia newspaper staff themselves had to go out to pick carrots – *Kaliniskaia pravda*, 7 June 1988, p. 2; *Leninskaia pravda*, 15 July 1989. Such examples can be multiplied from all around the country – *Ural'skii rabochii*, 16 June 1988, p. 1; *Ul'ianovskaia pravda*, 10 July 1988, p. 3.
67 *Vechernii Kiev*, 17 June 1988, p. 2.
68 *Severnyi rabochii* (Iaroslavl), 14 April 1988, p. 2. This was also the approach taken by Poltava obkom – *Partiinaia zhizn*, 19 (1989), 32.
69 Interviewed on Moscow TV, 2 August 1990.
70 *Zvezda*, 14 May 1988, p. 1.
71 *Sovetskaia bashkiria*, 13 July 1989, p. 2; *Ul'ianovskaia pravda*, 6 August 1988, p. 1.
72 For example, a point made by a Latvian raikom first secretary in *Pravda*, 28 August 1988, p. 2.
73 A. Gekov, 'Lekarstvo dlia Kuzbassa', *Ekonomika i zhizn*, 10 (1990), 8. Cheliabinsk oblast soviet was awarded the right to issue such *goszakazy* – *Cheliabinskii rabochii*, 12 January 1990, p. 1. On the situation in Kemerovo, see P. Rutland, 'Labour unrest and movements in 1989 and 1990', *Soviet Economy*, 6, 4 (1990), 345–84.

74 See the cry for help from the chair of Moscow city ispolkom, V. Saikin, 'Proryv vedomstvennoi blokady', *Ekonimika i zhizn*, 8 (1990), 13. Also, from Novosibirsk, see A. Granberg, 'Sibir na ukhabakh reformy', *Sovetskaia Sibir*, 17 February 1990, p. 1.
75 This was most apparent in Tiumen – *Tiumen'skaia pravda*, 4 May 1990, p. 1; also similar reports in *Sotsialisticheskii Donbass*, 10 March 1990, p. 1.
76 For example, in Gor'kii – *Partiinaia zhizn*, 13 (1989), 23.
77 CC CPSU instructor M. Sokolov argued that a 'vacuum' had opened up in the management of regional economies, in his article 'Kakim byt partiinomy apparaty', *Partiinaia zhizn*, 19 (1989), 20–25, p. 23.
78 See A. Jones and W. Moskoff, *Koops: the Rebirth of Entrepreneurship in the Soviet Union* (Bloomington: Indiana University Press, 1991); and A. A. Glushetskii, *Kooperatsiia: rol v sovremennoi ekonomike* (Moscow, Profizdat, 1991).
79 *Severnyi rabochii*, 24 April 1988, p. 2; *Kaliniskaia pravda*, 5 June 1987, p. 3; *Ul'ianovskaia pravda*, 22 May 1988, p. 2.
80 *Sovetskii Krym*, 24 Febvruary 1988, p. 2; 24 May 1988, p. 3.
81 P. Zharikhin, 'Kto zakazyvaet muzyku?', *Krasnoe znamia*, 18 November 1989, p. 2.
82 L. Babaeva, 'Ostrov rynok v okeane raspredeleniia', *Dialog*, 6 (1990), 46–49.
83 *Altaiskaia pravda*, 27 July 1989, p. 2, with reference to the Altai tractor factory.
84 *Kommunist Ukrainy*, 7 (1988), 49.
85 *Ural'skii rabochii* 31 May 1988, p. 3; Iu. Kachaturov, 'Tseli i sredstva kooperativnoi politiki', *Ekonomicheskie nauki*, 4 (1990), 40–48, 44.
86 *Volgogradskaia pravda*, 18 January 1990, p. 3; *Sovetskaia Sibir*, 11 April 1988, p. 2.
87 *Ekonomika i zhizn*, 10 (1990), p. 10.
88 *Sovetskaia Kuban*, 11 July 1989, p. 2.
89 *Sovetskaia Kuban*, 2 July 1989, p. 3.
90 *Politicheskoe obrazovanie*, 16 (1989), 39.
91 *Severnyi rabochii*, 10 April 1988, po. 2.
92 *Vostochno-Sibirskaia pravda*, 10 June 1988, p. 2; *Vechernii Kiev*, 8 September 1988, p. 3.

Conclusion: Party and economy in the USSR: from stagnation to collapse

1 On this, see P. Rutland, 'From perestroika to paralysis: the stalemate in Leningrad', *Report on the USSR*, 22 March 1991, pp. 12–17.
2 *Kommunist*, 5 (1988), 6.

Notes to appendices

1 *Ezhegodnik bolshoi sovetskoi entsiklopedii* (Moscow, Sovetskaia entsiklopediia, various years).
2 For example, *Deputaty verkhovnogo soveta SSSR, desiatyi sozyv* (Moscow, Izdanie prezidiuma V. S. S. S.S.R., 1979).
3 McAuley, 'Hunting'.

4 Regional party memberships were calculated from *26 s"ezd KPSS. Stenografi-cheskii otchet* (Moscow, Politizcat, 1981), p.473–501.

5 *Narodnoe khzoziastvo SSSR 1975* (Moscow, Finansy i statistika, 1976), pp. 512, 536, 554; *Nar. khoz. RSFSR 1975*, pp.362, 328; *Nar. khoz. SSSR 1922–82*, p.15–20; *Nar. khoz. Uk.SSR 1983*, pp.268, 234.

6 *Nar. khoz. SSSR 1975*, p.374; *Nar. khoz. RSFSR 1975*, p.225, *1980*, p.379; *Nar. khoz. UkSSR 1975*, p.168; *Nar. khoz. KazSSR 1981*, pp.56, 80; *Nar. khoz. UzSSR 1979*, p.70.

Select bibliography

Books and articles in English

Adams, J. S. *Citizen Inspectors in the Soviet Union*, New York, Praeger, 1977.

Amann, R. and Cooper J. (eds.) *Technical Progress and Soviet Economic Development*, Oxford, Blackwell, 1986.

Ambler, J. et al. (eds.) *Soviet and East European Transport Problems*, London, Croom Helm, 1985.

Arat, Z. 'Democracy and economic development', *Comparative Politics*, 21, 1 (1988), 21–36.

Arendt, H. *The Origins of Totalitarianism*, New York, Harcourt Brace Jovanovich, 1968.

Aslund, A. *Gorbachev's Struggle for Economic Reform*, Ithaca, Cornell University Press, 1989.

Azrael, J. R. *Managerial Power and Soviet Politics*, Cambridge, Mass., Harvard University Press, 1966.

Bahry, D. and Silver, B. 'Intimidation and the symbolic uses of terror in the USSR', *American Political Science Review*, 81, 4 (1987), 1065–98.

Bailes, K. *Technology and Society Under Lenin and Stalin*, Princeton, New Jersey, Princeton University Press, 1978.

Beissinger, M. 'In search of generations in Soviet politics', *World Politics*, 38, 1 (1986), 288–314.

Berliner, J. S. *Factory and Manager in the USSR*, Cambridge, Mass., Harvard University Press, 1957.

  The Innovation Decision in Soviet Industry, Cambridge, Mass., MIT Press, 1976.

Bialer, S. *Stalin's Successors*, Cambridge, Cambridge University Press, 1980.

Blackwell, R. E. 'Cadres policy in the Brezhnev era', *Problems of Communism*, 28, 2 (1979), 29–42.

Breslauer, G. W. 'Is there a generation gap?', *Soviet Studies*, 36, 1 (1984), 1–25.

  Khrushchev and Brezhnev as Leaders: Building Authority in Soviet Politics, London, Allen and Unwin, 1982.

  'On the adaptability of Soviet welfare-state authoritarianism', in Ryavec (ed.), *Soviet Society* (1978), pp. 3–26.

  'Provincial party leaders' demand articulation and the nature of centre-periphery relations in the USSR', *Slavic Review*, 45, 4 (1986), 650–72.

Brooks, K. M. 'Soviet agriculture's halting reform', *Problems of Communism*, 40, 2 (1990), 29–41.

Broszat, M. (ed.) *The Hitler State*, New York, Longman, 1984.

Brovkin, V. 'First party secretaries: an endangered species?', *Problems of Communism*, 39, 1 (1990), 15–27.

Brzezinski, Z. K. and Friedrich, Cd. (eds.) *Totalitarian Dictatorship and Autocracy*, Cambridge, Mass., Harvard University Press, 1956.

Chotiner, B. A. *Khrushchev's Party Reform: Coalition Building and Institutional Innovation*, London, Greenwood Press, 1984.

Chung, Han Ku. *Interest Representation in Soviet Policy Making: A Case Study of a West Siberian Energy Coalition*, Boulder, Col., Westview, 1987.

Cohen, S. F. *Rethinking the Soviet Experience: Politics and History Since 1917*, Oxford, Oxford University Press, 1985.

Colton, T. J. *Commissars, Commanders and Civilian Authority: The Structure of Soviet Military Politics*, Cambridge, Mass., Harvard University Press, 1979.

Conyngham, W. J. *Industrial Management in the Soviet Union*, Stanford, Hoover Institution, 1973.

The Modernization of Soviet Industrial Management, Cambridge, Cambridge University Press, 1982.

Cooper, J. 'The civilian production of the defence industry', in Amann and Cooper, *Technical Progress*, ch. 2.

Czudnowski, M. and Eulau, H. (eds.) *Elite Recruitment in Democratic Polities*, New York, Sage, 1976.

DeBardeleben, J. *Marxism–Leninism and the Environment*, Boulder, Col., Westview, 1985.

Dellenbrant, J. A. *The Soviet Regional Dilemma*, New York, M. E. Sharpe, 1986.

Deutsch, K. 'The limited capacity of centralized decision making', in Friedrich (ed.), *Totalitarianism*, pp. 308–32.

Djilas, M. *The New Class*, London, Allen and Unwin, 1966.

Dunmore, T. 'Local party organizations in industrial decision making: the case of the *ob''edinenie* reform', *Soviet Studies*, 23, 2 (1980), 195–217.

Dyker, D. *The Future of the Soviet Economy*, New York, M. E. Sharpe, 1985.

Fainsod, M. *How Russia is Ruled*, Cambridge, Mass., Harvard University Press, 1963.

Smolensk Under Soviet Rule, Cambridge, Mass., Harvard University Press, 1958.

Fitzpatrick, S. *Education and Social Mobility in the USSR 1921–34*, Cambridge, Cambridge University Press, 1979.

Fortescue, S. 'The regional party apparatus in the "sectional society"', *Studies in Comparative Communism*, 21, 1 (1988), 11–24.

Fortescue, S. F. *Soviet Science and the Communist Party*, London, Macmillan, 1986.

Frank, P. and Hill, R. *The Soviet Communist Party*, London, Allen and Unwin, 1981.

Friedrich, C. (ed.) *Totalitarianism*, Cambridge, Mass., Harvard University Press, 1954.

Gagnon, V. P. 'Gorbachev and the collective contract brigade', *Soviet Studies*, 34, 1 (1987), 1–23.

Gorbachev's Economic Plans, Washington, DC, US Congress Joint Economic Committee, 1987.

Gray, K. R. 'Reform and resource allocation in Soviet agriculture', in *Gorbachev's Economic Plans*, vol. 2, pp. 9–25.

Gregory, P. *Restructuring the Soviet Economic Bureaucracy*, Cambridge, Cambridge University Press, 1990.

Gross, J. T. 'A note on the nature of Soviet totalitarianism', *Soviet Studies*, 34, 3 (1982), 367–76.

Grossman, G. 'The party as manager and entrepreneur', in G. Guroff, and F. V. Carstensen (eds.), *Entrepreneurship in Imperial Russia and the Soviet Union*, Princeton, NJ, Princeton University Press, 1983.

Gustafson, T. *Crisis Amid Plenty: The Politics of Soviet Energy Under Brezhnev and Gorbachev*, Princeton, New Jersey, Princeton University Press, 1989.

Reform in Soviet Politics: Lessons of Recent Policies on Land and Water, Cambridge, Cambridge University Press, 1981.

'Soviet energy policy from big coal to big gas', in S. Bialer and T. Gustafson (eds.), *Russia at the Crossroads: The 26th Congress of the CPSU*, London, Allen and Unwin, 1982, ch. 6.

The Soviet Gas Campaign, Santa Monica, Ca., Rand, 1983.

Gustafson, T. and Mann, D. 'Gorbachev at the helm: Building power and authority', *Problems of Communism*, 35, 3 (1986), 1–19.

Hanson, P. 'Success indicators revisited: the July 1979 decree on planning and management', *Soviet Studies*, 35, 1 (1983), 1–13.

Harasymiw, B. *Political Elite Recruitment in the Soviet Union*, London, Macmillan, 1984.

Hauslohner, P. 'Gorbachev's social contract', *Soviet Economy*, 3, 1 (1987), 54–89.

Hedlund, S. *Crisis in Soviet Agriculture*, Lund, Lund Economic Studies, 1973.

Hekman, S. *Weber, the Ideal Type and Contemporary Social Theory*, Notre Dame, University of Notre Dame, 1983.

Helf, G. *A Biographical Directory of Soviet Regional Party Leaders*, Munich, Radio Liberty Research, 2nd edn, August 1988.

Heller, M. *Cogs in the Wheel*, New York, Knopf, 1988.

Hewett, E. *Energy, Economics and Foreign Policy in the Soviet Union*, Washington, Brookings Institution, 1984.

Hill, M. and McKay, R. 'Soviet product quality', in Amann and Cooper, *Technical Progress* (1986), ch. 5.

Hodnett, G. *Leadership in the Soviet National Republics*, Ontario, Mosaic, 1978.

Holmes, L. *The Policy Process in Communist States*, London, Sage, 1981.

Hood, C. C. *The Limits of Administration*, London, Wiley, 1976.

Hough, J. F. 'The Cultural Revolution and Western understanding of the Soviet system', in S. Fitzpatrick (ed.), *Cultural Revolution in Russia*, Bloomington, Indiana University Press, 1978, pp. 251–53.

'The party apparatchiki', in Skilling and Griffiths, *Interest Groups* (1971), ch. 3.

The Role of Local Party Organs in Industrial Decision Making, Cambridge, Mass., Harvard University Ph. D. thesis, 1961.

Soviet Leadership in Transition, Washington, DC, Brookings Institution, 1980.

The Soviet Prefects: the Local Party Organs in Industrial Decision Making, Cambridge, Mass., Harvard University Press, 1969.

Hough, J. F. and Fainsod, M. *How the Soviet Union is Governed*, Cambridge, Mass., Harvard University Press, 1979.

Huntington, S. P. *Authoritarian Politics in Modern Society*, New York, Basic Books, 1970.

'Generations, cycles and their role in American development', in R. J. Samuels (ed.), *Political Generations and World Development*, Lexington, Mass., D. C. Heath, 1977, ch. 2.

Political Order in Changing Societies, New Haven, Yale University Press, 1968.

Johnson, D. Gale and McConnell Brooks, K. *Prospects for Soviet Agriculture in the 1980s*, Bloomington, Indiana University Press, 1983.

Jones, A. and Moskoff, W. 'The new cooperatives in the USSR', *Problems of Communism*, 38, 6 (1989), 27–39.

Jones, D. and Smogorzewska, J. 'Dairy farming in the USSR', *Soviet Studies*, 34, 2 (1982), 254–69.

Jones, E. 'Committee decision making in the Soviet Union', *World Politics*, 36, 2 (1984), 165–88.

Jowitt, K. 'Inclusion and mobilization in Leninist regimes', *World Politics*, 28, 1 (1975), 69–96.

Kaplan, C. S. 'The CPSU and local policy implementation', *Journal of Politics*, 45 (1983), 2–27.

The Party and Agricultural Crisis Management in the USSR, Ithaca, Cornell University Press, 1987.

Kaser, M. *Soviet Economics*, London: Weidenfeld and Nicholson, 1970.

Kassof, A. 'Totalitarianism without terror', *World Politics*, 26, 4 (1964), 558–75.

Kelley, D. R. 'Environmental problems as a new policy issue', in Ryavec, *Soviet Society* (1978), pp. 88–108.

Klugman, J. *The New Soviet Elite: How They Think and What They Want*, New York, Praeger, 1989.

Kushnirsky, F. I. 'Inflation Soviet-style', *Problems of Communism*, 33, 1 (1984), 48–53.

Lampert, N. 'Law and order in the USSR', *Soviet Studies*, 36, 3 (1984), 366–85.

'Social criticism in Soviet drama: the plays of A. Gel'man', *Soviet Studies*, 39, 1 (1987), 101–15.

Linz, J. L. 'Totalitarian and authoritarian regimes', in N. Polsby and F. Greenstein (eds.), *Handbook of Political Science*, New York, Addison-Wesley, 1975, ch. 3.

Lowenthal, R. 'Development versus utopia in communist policy', in C. Johnson (ed.), *Change in Communist Systems*, Stanford, Stanford University Press, 1970, pp. 33–116.

McAuley, M. 'The hunting of the hierarchy: RSFSR obkom first secretaries and the Central Committee', *Soviet Studies*, 26, 4 (1974), 473–501.

Medvedev, R. and Zh. *Khrushchev: the Years in Power*, Oxford, Oxford University Press, 1977.

Mickiewicz, E. P. *The Media and the Russian Public*, New York, Praeger, 1981.

Miller, M. 'Nomenklatura: check on localism?', in T. H. Rigby and B. Harasymiw (eds.), *Leadership Selection and Patron-Client Relations in the USSR and Yugoslavia*, London, Macmillan, 1983, ch. 2.

Miller, R. F. 'The politics of policy implementation in the USSR: Soviet policies on agricultural integration', *Soviet Studies*, 32, 2 (1980), 171–94.

'The role of the Communist Party in Soviet research and development', *Soviet Studies* 37, 1, 1987, 31–59.

Moore, Barrington. *Authority and Inequality Under Capitalism and Socialism*, Oxford, Clarendon Press, 1987.

Morton, H. W. 'Who gets what, when and how? Housing in the Soviet Union', *Soviet Studies*, 32, 2 (1980), 235–59.

Moses, J. L. 'Functional career specialization in Soviet regional elite recruitment', in T. H. Rigby and B. Harasymiw (eds.), *Leadership Selection and Patron-Client Relations in the USSR and Yugoslavia*, London, Macmillan, 1988, ch. 1.

Niczow, A. *Black Book of Polish Censorship*, South Bend, Indiana, And Books, 1982.

Nove, A. *The Soviet Economic System*, London, Allen and Unwin, 1977.

O'Donnell, G. and Schmitter, P. *Transitions from Authoritarian Rule*, Baltimore, Johns Hopkins, 1986.

Pinsky, D. E. *Industrial Development of Siberia and the Far East*, Santa Monica, Rand, 1984.

Remington, T. F. *The Truth of Authority: Ideology and Communication in the Soviet Union*, Pittsburgh, University of Pittsburgh, 1988.

Rigby, T. H. 'The Soviet regional leadership: the Brezhnev generation', *Slavic Review*, 37, 1 (1978), 1–24.

Rosenfeldt, N. E. *Knowledge and Power: the Role of Stalin's Secret Chancellery in the Soviet System of Government*, Copenhagen, Rosekilde and Bagger, 1978.

Ross, C. *Local Government in the Soviet Union*, New York, St Martins, 1987.

Ruble, B. *The Applicability of Corporatists Models to the Study of Soviet Politics*, Pittsburgh, University of Pittsburgh, Carl Beck Paper no. 33, 1983.

Rumer, B. and Vatkin, Y. 'Metal-saving as a fundamental precondition for industrial modernization', in *Gorbachev's Economic Plans*, vol. 1, pp. 293–304.

Rutland, P. 'The dynamics of the Soviet economic mechanism: insights from reform debates 1977–87', in D. Bahry and J. C. Moses (eds.), *Political Implications of Economic Reform in Communist Systems*, New York, New York University Press, 1989, pp. 70–108.

'Labor unrest and movements in 1989 and 1990', *Soviet Economy*, 6, 4 (1990), 345–84.

The Myth of the Plan: Lessons of Soviet Planning Experience, London, Hutchinson, 1985.

'The role of the Communist Party on the Soviet shopfloor', *Studies in Comparative Communism*, 21, 1 (1988), 25–44.

'The search for stability: ideology, discipline and the cohesion of the Soviet elite', *Studies in Comparative Communism*, 24, 1 (1991), 24–57.

'The Shchekino method and the struggle to raise labour productivity in Soviet industry', *Soviet Studies*, 36, 3 (1984), 345–65.

Ryavec, K. W. *The Implementation of Soviet Economic Reforms*, New York, Praeger, 1975.

Ryavec. K. W. (ed.) *Soviet Society and the Communist Party*, Amherst, Mass., University of Massach, 1978.

Schroeder, G. 'The slowdown in Soviet industry', *Soviet Economy*, 1, 1 (1985), 42–74.

'The Soviet economy on a "treadmill" of reforms', in *Soviet Economy in a Time of Change*, Washington, DC, US Congress JEC, pp. 312–40.

Severin, B. 'Solving the livestock feed dilemma', in *Gorbachev's Economic Plans*, vol. 2, pp. 533–44.

Shaw, D. B. 'Regional planning in the USSR', *Soviet Geography*, 27, 7 (1986), 469–84.

Shelley, L. *Lawyers in Soviet Work Life*, New Brunswick, New Jersey, Rutgers University Press, 1984.

Shlapentokh, V. *Public and Private Life in the Soviet Union: Changing Values in Post-Stalin Russia*, New York, Oxford University Press, 1989.

Silver, B. D. 'Political beliefs of the Soviet citizen', in J. R. Millar (ed.), *Politics, Work and Daily Life in the USSR*, Cambridge, Cambridge University Press, 1987, ch. 4.

Simis, K. *USSR: Secrets of a Corrupt Society*, London, Dent 1982.

Skilling, H. G. and Griffiths, F. (eds.) *Interest Groups in Soviet Politics*, Princeton, New Jersey, Princeton University Press, 1971.

Slider, D. 'Reforming the workplace: the 1983 Soviet law on labour collectives', *Soviet Studies*, 37, 2 (1985), 173–83.

Social Experiments and Soviet Policy Making, New Haven, Yale University, Ph.D., 1981.

Solomon, P. *Soviet Politicians and Criminal Prosecutions: The Logic of Party Intervention*, Urbana, Il., University of Illinois Soviet Interview Project, paper no. 33, 1987.

Solomon, S. G. (ed.) *Pluralism in the Soviet Union*, London, Macmillan, 1983.

Starr, S. F. 'The changing nature of change in the USSR', in S. Bialer and M. Mandelbaum (eds.), *Gorbachev's Russia and American Foreign Policy*, Boulder, Col., Westview Press, 1988, pp. 3–36.

A Study of the Soviet Economy, Washington, DC, OECD, 1991, 3 vols.

Teague, E. *Solidarity and the Soviet Worker: The Impact of the Polish Events of 1980 on Soviet Internal Politics*, London, Croom Helm, 1988.

Thornton, J. 'Soviet electric power after Chernobyl', *Soviet Economy*, 2, 2 (1986), 131–79.

Urban, M. E. *The Ideology of Administration: Soviet and American Cases*, New York, SUNY Press, 1982.

Voslensky, M. *Nomenklatura*, New York, Doubleday, 1984.

Warner, D. and Kaiser, L. 'Development of the USSR's eastern coal basins', in *Gorbachev's Economic Plans*, vol. 1, pp. 533–44.

Weber, M. 'Politics as a vocation', in H. H. Gerth and C. W. Mills (eds.), *From Max Weber: Essays in Sociology*, Oxford, Oxford University Press, 1973.

White, S. 'Political communications in the USSR', *Soviet Studies*, 31, 1 (1983), 43–60.

Yanowitch, A. *Social and Economic Inequality in the Soviet Union*, London, Martin Robertson, 1977.
Zaslavsky, V. *The Neostalinist State: Class, Ethnicity and Consensus in Soviet Society*, Armonk, New York M. E. Sharpe, 1982.
Zinoviev, A. *The Reality of Communism*, London, Gollancz, 1984.

Books and articles in Russian

Administrativno-territorial'noe delenie soiuznykh respublikh, Moscow, Izvestiia, 1983.
Alekseev, V. 'Bez prava na monopoliu vlast', *Dialog*, 5 (1990), 29–37.
'Partiinoe rukovodstvo sozdaniem i razvitiem neftegazovogo kompleksa zapadnoi Sibiri', *Voprosy istorii KPSS*, 6 (1983), 55–67.
Alisov, A. N. 'Predpriiatie i oblastnoi narodnokhoziaistvennyi kompleks', in *Trudovoi kollektiv v sisteme upravleniia proizvodstvom*, Moscow, AON, 1980, ch. 5.
Andreenkova, N. *Perekhod predpriiatii na novye usloviia khoziastvovaniia*, Moscow, Institut Sotsiologii, 1989.
Babaeva, L. 'Ostrov rynok v okeane raspredeleniia', *Dialog*, 6 (1990), 46–49.
Bazhutin, G. 'Rytsar bez doslekhov', *Sotsialisticheskaia industriia*, 30 June 1989, p. 2.
Bondar, Iu. 'Kontrol i proverki ispolneniia', *Voprosy istorii KPSS*, 7 (1985), 17–29.
'O politicheskom kharaktere partiinogo rukovodstva', *Voprosy istorii KPSS*, 2 (1984), 31–45.
Brezhnev, L. I. *Leninskim kursom*, Moscow, Politizdat, 1976.
Burlatski, F. 'Brezhnev i krushenie ottepeli', *Literaturnaia gazeta*, 14 September 1988, pp. 13–14.
Chalov, V. I. 'Nekotorie problemy partiinogo rukovodtsva sozdaniem TPK', *Voprosy istorii KPSS*, 3 (1979), 43–54.
Cherniak, A. V. *Tovarishch instruktor*, Moscow, Politizdat, 1984.
Cherniavskii, V. 'Orientatsiia na kachestvo', *Kommunist*, 11 (1984), 38–48.
Chufarov, V. G. (ed.), *Deiatel'nost partiinykh organizatsii Urala*, Sverdlovsk, Ural'skii gosudarstvennyi universitet, 1976.
Davydov, Iu. 'Totalitarizm i totalitarnaia biurokratiia', *Nauka i zhizn*, 8 (1989), 44–51.
Degtiarev, A. 'Pervoosnova partiinoi zhizni', *Kommunist*, 6 (1988), 7–17, p. 11.
'Deiatel'nost KPSS po ideino-teoreticheskoi podgotovke rukovodiashchikh kadrov', *Voprosy istorii KPSS*, 12 (1982), 98–106.
Demochkin, N. N. *Partiinoe rukovodstvo sovetam narodnykh deputatov*, Moscow, Znaie, 1980.
Deputaty verkhovnoqo soveta SSSR, desiatyi sozyv, Moscow, Izdanie presidiuma V.S. SSSR, 1979.
Direktor N. A. Ligachev i vospominaniia sovremennikov, Moscow, Moskovskii rabochii, 1971.
Dobralevskii, A. 'Kak voznikaet defitsit', *Ekonomicheskaia qazeta*, 35 (1982), 8.
Emshin, P. C. and Godunov, A. A. *Metodika otsenki delovykh i moral'no-politicheskikh kachestv rukovoditelei i spetsialistov sotsialisticheskogo proizvodstva*, Leningrad, Lenigradskii Gosudarstvennyi Universitet, 1971.

Gekov, A. 'Lekarstvo dlia Kuzbassa', *Ekonomika i zhizn*, 10 (1990), 8.

'Glasnost i demokratiia', *Izvestiia TsK KPSS*, 4 (1989), 105–8.

Godunov, A. A. *Sotsial'no-ekonomicheskie problemy upravlenii sotsialisticheskim proizvodstvom*, Moscow, Ekonomika, 1975.

Gorbachev, M. A. 'Perestroika raboty partii', *Partiinaia zhizn*, 15 (1989), 5–16.

Gorbachev, M. S. *Izbrannye rechi i stat'i*, Moscow, Politizdat, 1987–90, 7 vols.

Granberg, A. 'Sibir na ukhabakh reformy', *Sovetskaia Sibir*, 17 February 1990, p. 1.

Gubanov, G. 'Nomenklatura', *Don*, 5 (1989), 3–85.

Iakovets, Iu. *Povyshenie urovnia planovoi raboty*, Moscow, Ekonomika, 1982.

Ignatovskii, P. 'O politicheskom podkhode k ekonomike', *Kommunist*, 12 (1983), 60–72.

Kachaturov, Iu. 'Tseli i sredstva kooperativnoi politiki', *Ekonomicheskie nauki*, 4 (1990), 40–48.

Kapustin, E. I. *Organizatsiia sorevnovaniia i sovershenstvovanie khoziaistvennogo mekhanizma*, Moscow, Profizdat, 1982.

Klimenko, I. 'Vzgliad iz kabineta ministra', *Sotsialisticheskaia industriia*, 21 February 1990, p. 2.

Kolodykh, B. 'Kak vliiaet ritmichnost proizvodstva na distiplinu truda?', *Sotsiologicheskie issledovaniia*, 2 (1984), 42–51.

Korkin, A. 'Razvitie Pavlodar-Ekibatuzskogo kompleksa', *Partiinaia zhizn*, 3 (1979), 36–42.

Kovalev, A. G. *Kollektiv i sotsial'no-psikhologicheskie problemy rukovodtsva*, Moscow, Politizdat, 1975.

KPSS v rezoliutsiiakh i resheniiakh, 8th edn Moscow, Politizdat, 1973–84, vols. 9–13.

Krotov, F. G. *Shkola ideinoi zakalki: istoriia Marksistko-Leninsko obrazovaniia v KPSS*, Moscow, Politizdat, 1978.

Krylov, A. 'Teni sovetskoi ekonomiki', *Ekonomicheskie nauki*, 5 (1990), 103–8.

Kudashkin, V. I. 'O razvitii vnutripartiinoi demokratii na etape perestroiki', *Nauchnyi kommunizm*, 6 (1988), 11–18.

Kumel'skii, L. I. *Povyshenie stimuliruiushchei roli zarabotnoi platy*, Moscow, Ekonomika, 1975.

Kurochkin, N. I. and Maksimov, N. A. *Rukovoditel i kollektiv*, Moscow, Ekonomika, 1979.

Kuz'menko, E. 'Tsena proscheta', *Ekonomika i zhizn*, 10 (1990), 11.

Lavrishchev, A. 'O predmete ekonomicheskoi geografii SSSR', *Kommunist*, 15 (1979), 91–99.

Lomako, V. 'Kakim byt ekonomicheskomy otdely?', *Ekonomicheskaia gazeta*, 43 (1988), 2.

Materialy 27 s"ezda KPSS, Moscow, Politizdat, 1986.

Medvedev, V. 'Kachestvenno novoe partiinoe uchebnoe zavedenie', *Partiinaia zhizn*, 8 (1979), 27–32.

Meledin, A. 'Agrarnyi tsekh Timano-Pechorskii kompleksa', *Partiinaia zhizn*, 18 (1981), 33–7.

Mihailov, M. 'Po povodu vedomosti', *Kommunist*, 8 (1981), 104–13.

Miroshnichenko, M. 'Vo chto obkhoditsia – trezvost', *Ogonek*, 39 (1988), 20–23.

Molokonov, I. 'Partiinyi rabotnik', *Partiinaia zhizn*, 11 (1989), 34–39.

Narodnoe khoziaistvo SSSR 1922–82, Moscow, Finansy i statistika, 1982.

Novikov, V. 'Ovladevat politicheskim metodami', *Partiinaia zhizn*, 16 (1989), 26–31.

Nurseitov, A. S. *Snabzhenie kapital'nogo stroitel'stva v planovom khoziaistve*, Alma Ata, Kazakhstan, 1981.

O korennoi perestroike upravlenie ekonomikoi, Moscow, Politizdat, 1988.

Openkin, A. 'Partiinoe rukovodstvo uskoreniem nauchno-tekhnicheskogo progressa v sovremennykh usloviiakh', *Voprosy istorii KPSS*, 2 (1985), 135–43.

Orlova, T. V. *Kritika burzhuaznykh falsifikatsii partiinogo stroitel'stva KPSS*, Kiev, Vyshcha shkola, 1987.

Pankova, K. 'Obiazatel'noe slagaemoe uspekha', *Kommunist*, 14 (1981), 36–47.

Patolichev, N. S. *Ispytanie na zrelost*, Moscow, Politizdat, 1982.

Pel'she, a. 'O trebovatel'nosti i ditsipline', *Kommunist*, 2 (1980), 21.

Petrenko, F. *Sekrety rukovodstva*, Moscow, Moskovskii Rabochii, 1968.

Petrov, V. 'Effekt initsiativy', *Kommunist*, 16 (1983), 35–46.

Petrovichev, N. A. *Vazhnyi faktor vozrastaniia rukovodiashchei roli KPSS*, Moscow, Politizdat, 1979.

Popov, G. 'Razvitie otraslevogo upravleniia promyshlennost'iu', *Kommunist*, 18 (1982), 48–59.

Povyshenie roli pervichnykh partiinykh organizatsii, Moscow, Politizdat, 1983.

Praktika sotsialisticheskogo khoziaistvovaniia: Opyt Leningradskikh predpriiatii, Leningrad, Lenizdat, 1981.

Prigozhin, A. 'Upravlencheskie novovedeniia i khoziaistvennye eksperimenty', *Kommunist*, 7 (1984), 57–67.

Raionnyi komitet partii, Moscow, Politizdat, 1974.

Rekundov, A. 'Na strakhe pravoporiadka i sotsial'noi spravedlivosti', *Kommunist*, 1 (1986), 41–51.

Rodinov, P. A. (ed.) *Partiinaia rabota v usloviiakh proizvodstvennykh ob"edinenii*, Moscow, Politizdat, 1984.

Rukavishnikov, V. 'Sotsial'naia napriazhennost', *Dialog*, 8 (1990), 6–11, p. 9.

Safronov, N. A. *Novye formy upravleniia proizvodtsvom*, Moscow, NII Truda, 1977.

Saikin, V. 'Proryv vedomstvennoi blokady', *Ekonomika i zhizn*, 8 (1990), 13.

Salutskii, A. 'Slabye i sil'nye', *Nash sovremennik*, 9 (1987), 100–19.

'Smychka', *Nash sovremennik*, 12 (1987), 133–53.

Sergeiko, V. P. *Partiinyi kontrol deiatel'nostiu administratsii*, Krasnodar, Krasnodarskoe knizhnoe izdatel'stvo, 1979.

Shcherbakova, L. 'Anketa direktorov', *EKO*, 3 (1988), 59–75.

Shkurko, S. I. *Stimulirovanie kachestva i effektivnosti proizvodtsva*, Moscow, Mysl, 1977.

Shmelov, N. 'Novye trevogi', *Novyi mir*, 4 (1988), 160–75.

Shostakovskii, V. 'V zerkale sotsiologii', *Kommunist*, 9 (1988), 31–5.

Shtamba, T. M. *KPSS i organy okhrany pravo-podriaka*, Moscow, Mysl, 1979.

Sizov, G. *Nekotorye voprosy revizionny raboty v partiinykh organizatsiiakh*, Moscow, Politizdat, 1984.

Smiriukov, S. M. *Sovetskii gosudarstvennyi apparat upravleniia*, Moscow, Politizdat, 1982.

Sokolov, M. 'Kakim byt partiinomy apparaty', *Partiinaia zhizn*, 19, (1989), 20–25.

'Sovershenstvuia rukovodstvo ekonomikoi', *Voprosy istorii KPSS*, 4 (1984), 68–107.

Sovety narodynkh deputatov: Spravochnik, Moscow, Politizdat, 1984.

Sovety narodnykh deputatov: status, kompetentsiia, organizatsiia, deiatel'nost, Moscow, Iuridicheskaia literatura, 1980.

Spravochnik partiinogo rabotnika, Moscow, Politizdat, various years, vols. 12–23.

Strelianyi, A. 'Deputatskii zapros', *Novyi mir*, 2 (1986), 24–76.

Surnichenko, S. I. *Leninskie printsipy partiinogo rukovodstva khoziaistvennym stroitel'stvom*, Moscow, Politizdat, 1979.

Territorial'no-proizvodstvennye kompleksy, Novosibirsk, Nauka, 1984.

Tikhomirov, Iu. 'Na puti k pravovoi ekonomike', *Pravitel'stvennyi vestnik*, 12 (1989), 7.

Todorski, Iu. V. *Rukovodstvo mestnykh sovetov razvitiem sotsialisticheskoi promyshlennosti*, Moscow, Nauka, 1982.

V pomoshch predsedateliu gruppy narodnogo kontrolia, Moscow, Ekonomika, 1984.

Vitruchenko, A. N. *Rukovodstvo KPSS ukrepleniem sotsialisticheskoi zakonnosti*, Kiev, Vyshcha shkola, 1983.

Zalygin, S. 'Proekt: Nauchnaia obosnovannost i otvetstvennost', *Kommunist*, 13 (1985), 63–73.

Zdravomyslov, A. et al., *Politicheskoe soznanie trudiashchikhsia i problema ego konsolidatsii*, Moscow, Akademiia Obshchestvennykh Nauk, 1990.

Zenchenko, N. 'Istoricheskii opyt i zadachi narodnokhoziastvennogo planirovaniia', *Kommunist*, 16 (1977), 55–66.

Zhalalov, N. *Sovershenstvovanie material'no-tekhnicheskoe snabzheniia*, Tashkent, Uzbekistan, 1979.

Zhuravlev, A. L. (ed.) *Individual'nyi stil rukovodstva proizvodstvennym kollektivom*, Moscow, Institut Narodnogo Khoziaisvta, 1976.

Zlomanov, L. 'Sovety i territorial'nye rezervy uskoreniia', *Kommunist*, 8 (1986), 18–27.

Zorkaltsev, V. I. 'Anatomiia defitsita', *EKO*, 2 (1982), 84–94.

26 s'ezd KPSS. Stenograficheskii otchet, Moscow, Politizdat, 1981.

Index

Soviet and East European Studies

Soviet and East European Studies

Soviet and East European Studies